The Absolute Weapon
Revisited

THE ABSOLUTE WEAPON REVISITED

Nuclear Arms and the Emerging International Order

Edited by
T. V. PAUL,
RICHARD J. HARKNETT,
and
JAMES J. WIRTZ

Ann Arbor
THE UNIVERSITY OF MICHIGAN PRESS

First paperback edition 2000
Copyright © by the University of Michigan 1998
All rights reserved
Published in the United States of America by
The University of Michigan Press
Manufactured in the United States of America
∞ Printed on acid-free paper

2003   2002   2001   2000   6   5   4   3

No part of this publication may be reproduced, stored in a retrieval system, or transmitted in any form or by any means, electronic, mechanical, or otherwise, without the written permission of the publisher.

A CIP catalog record for this book is available from the British Library.

Library of Congress Cataloging-in-Publication Data

The absolute weapon revisited : nuclear arms and the emerging
    international order / edited by T.V. Paul, Richard J. Harknett,
and James J. Wirtz.
    p. cm.
    Revised papers originally presented at a conference held at McGill
University in Montreal in Nov. 1995.
    Includes bibliographical references and index.
    ISBN 0-472-10863-8 (cloth : acid-free paper)
    1. Nuclear weapons—Congresses.   2. Deterrence (Strategy)—
Congresses.   3. World politics—1989-   —Congresses.   I. Paul, T.V.
II. Harknett, Richard J., 1963-   .   III. Wirtz, James J., 1958-   .
U264.A27   1997
327.1'747—dc21   97-33943
                                                                                       CIP

ISBN 0-472-08700-2 (pbk. : alk. paper)

Acknowledgments

This volume benefited from the efforts of many individuals and financial support of several institutions and agencies. The initial impetus for the book came from an International Studies Association (ISA) convention panel organized by Richard Harknett and T. V. Paul on "Nuclear Weapons in a Transformed World," at Chicago in February 1995. Subsequently, a two-day conference was held at McGill University in Montreal in November 1995, where all the chapters were presented and underwent thorough revisions. We thank the participants at that conference for a lively exchange of ideas, especially the panel chairs and discussants: Michael Altfeld, Mark Brawley, Michael Brecher, Michel Fortmann, Peter Lavoy, Jacques Lévesque, Pierre Martin, Baldev Raj Nayar, and Blema Steinberg. We especially appreciated the comments of Michael Brecher, who found interesting similarities between our endeavor and the original Brodie effort of 1945, which he witnessed as a graduate student at Yale University.

Financial assistance was provided by the Canadian Departments of Foreign Affairs and National Defense, the latter under its Security and Defense Forum (SDF), the Charles Phelps Taft Memorial Fund, the Navy International Program Office (IPO), and the U.S. Airforce Institute of National Security Studies (INSS). Small conference grants were also provided by McGill University, the Chair of Strategic Studies at University of Montreal, and the Center for Foreign Policy and Security Studies at University of Quebec at Montreal. We thank the officials and faculty in charge of these programs, especially Earnest Gilman of the SDF Program, Anthony Melone and Patrick Wittman of the Department of Foreign Affairs, Thomas Skrobala at Navy IPO and Jeffrey Larsen and Peter Hays at INSS, Michel Fortmann of the University of Montreal, and Jacques Lévesque of the University of Quebec. We also acknowledge R. Daniel McMichael for his backing of our efforts. Research and editorial assistance was provided by Marc Lanteigne, Kirsten Rafferty, Saira Khan, and Michelle Day-Curtis.

Last but not least are our family members who saw us through the conferences and revisions of this volume. T. V. Paul thanks his wife, Rachel Tara, and daughters, Kavya and Leah. Richard Harknett thanks Kathryn and Margot Elizabeth for their sacrifices. James Wirtz thanks his wife Janet for her support and his son Daniel for many entertaining distractions.

We believe that nuclear weapons form an important issue area at the end of the Cold War and that new approaches based on creative thinking are essential to avert "the unthinkable," that is, a future nuclear war. This book represents a renewed effort at understanding the complexities that face us as the second phase of the nuclear era dawns.

Contents

Introduction: Understanding Nuclear Weapons in a
   Transforming World   1
   *Richard J. Harknett, James J. Wirtz,
   and T. V. Paul*

Part 1. The Revolutionary Weapon: A Debate

Power, Influence, and Nuclear Weapons:
   A Reassessment   19
   T. V. Paul

State Preferences, Systemic Constraints, and the
   Absolute Weapon   47
   Richard J. Harknett

The Escalating Irrelevance of Nuclear Weapons   73
   John Mueller

Nuclear Weapons and the Revolution in
   Military Affairs   99
   Colin S. Gray

Part 2. Deterrence: Fifty Years Later

Beyond Bipolarity: Prospects for Nuclear Stability
   after the Cold War   137
   James J. Wirtz

The Continuing Debate on Minimal Deterrence   167
   George H. Quester

U.S. Nuclear Policy and the End of the Cold War   189
   Eric Mlyn

Deterrence and Alternative Images of
   Nuclear Possession   213
   William C. Martel

Part 3. Controlling the Absolute Weapon

New Nuclear States and the International
   Nuclear Order   237
   Ashok Kapur

Nonproliferation and Denuclearization 263
Robert A. Manning and Zachary S. Davis

Contributors 299

Index 301

Introduction: Understanding Nuclear Weapons in a Transforming World

RICHARD J. HARKNETT, JAMES J. WIRTZ,
AND T. V. PAUL

The immediate aftermath of great power war represents both an end and a beginning. As combat comes to a close, a transition begins toward a new pattern of global power distribution. Such transitionary periods and the subsequent "world orders" that emerge are defined by the victors of the just-completed war.[1] Military victory and its international political consequences thus reflect the superior power of the victorious state or coalition. The source of this superiority varies but often rests on some technical, tactical, or strategic innovation that allows a state or coalition to dominate its opponents.

International politics in the 1990s share many similarities with previous transitionary periods produced by the end of great power conflict.[2] The Soviet Union suffered the political collapse, economic disruption, societal upheaval, and environmental degradation that historians would expect to find in the wake of great power war. As the international transition away from the Cold War began in the early 1990s, diplomacy also mirrored past periods when defeated great powers and their lesser allies were reintegrated into the victorious side's new international order.[3] What distinguishes 1992 from the end of other modern great power conflicts in 1815, 1919, and 1945 is that the Cold War was not punctuated by direct hostilities or by battlefield employment of the central military asset that defined great power status.[4] A great military superpower collapsed without even a hint that it would employ its military capability to save itself. The fact that the denouement of the Cold War followed the pattern of nuclear nonuse from 1946 to 1992 might explain why so little scholarly attention has been paid to examining the role of nuclear weapons in the twenty-first century.

In contrast, the explosive conclusion of the Second World War drew immediate attention to the importance of the nuclear era. In the aftermath of Hiroshima, international relations scholars quickly began thinking about how the new and awesome destructive force of the atomic bomb would affect the emerging systemic order. Attention turned to assessing the bomb's impact on the preparations for and conduct of war, world politics, great power foreign policy, the United Nations, and the prospects for devising some mechanism for the international control of the new weapon.[5]

In the spring of 1946, a collection of essays written by Frederick Dunn, Bernard Brodie, Arnold Wolfers, Percy Corbett, and William Fox presented a set of first principles for understanding the nuclear age. Entitled *The Absolute Weapon: Atomic Power and World Order,* the volume assessed the likely impact atomic weapons would have on international politics and how they would affect the establishment of a new postwar international order.

Shortly thereafter, however, a more narrowly defined question came to dominate scholarship: what role would atomic weapons play in superpower relations? As the world descended into the Cold War, the dynamics of the bipolar competition and nuclear weapons issues became inextricably linked in the minds of policymakers and security analysts.[6] The emergence of a mutual condition of strategic vulnerability to nuclear attack raised the stakes of conflict profoundly. The superpower nuclear relationship set the context for both the study and conduct of world politics. Most of the scholarship produced over the next fifty years concerning nuclear weapons was premised on the specific bipolar distribution of power between the United States and the Soviet Union. The conceptual impact of the Cold War may have been as profound as its influence on policy. The logic of strategic stability, which became embedded in arms control negotiations and treaties, for example, focused attention on numerical parity. The link established in scholarship and policy between parity and stability made sense in a bilateral context in which the competing states were similar in geographic size and population dispersion. But what if history had ordained China and Japan as the first two nuclear superpowers? It is unlikely that the academic study of arms control and the actual treaties that were produced would have considered parity a stabilizing condition. What China would have required to assure the destruction of Japan would have been a fraction of what Japan would have needed to assure China's destruction. The disappearance of the particular American-Soviet nuclear competition thus not only opens the door to a new world politics, but requires a rethinking of those politics as well.

The end of the Cold War presents today's scholars with a systemic shift in the distribution of power similar to that which confronted the authors of *The Absolute Weapon* in 1946. Brodie and his colleagues analyzed the potential impact of atomic weapons at a time when only one country possessed but a handful of the devices. In 1996, the transition to a new international order proceeds in a strategic environment in which a sizable number of states possess the technical knowledge and industrial capacity to manufacture a weapon capable of global destruction; we now live in a world in which there exist tens of thousands of these devices. Given this reality, it seems appropriate to pose fundamental questions about the role and impact of nuclear weapons on international politics. It is time for scholars, freed from the conceptual filter of the Cold War, to examine first principles once again. This new volume, *The Absolute Weapon Revisited: Nuclear Arms and the Emerging International Order*, sets out to reappraise the atomic bomb as an instrument of contemporary international politics.[7]

Competing Views of the Nuclear Future: First Principles Reexamined

The analysis presented in Brodie et al. extrapolated from a very limited basis of experience and knowledge. The historical example of Hiroshima was supplemented with an understanding of the technical properties behind atomic weapons. What is remarkable about the volume, however, is the relative consensus that it presents. In general, Brodie and his colleagues viewed atomic weapons as revolutionary military devices, judged retaliation in kind to be the guiding strategic principle of the nuclear age, and concluded that international control of atomic weapons would be exceedingly difficult to achieve.

By contrast, the contributors to *The Absolute Weapon Revisited* diverge widely in their analysis of nuclear weapons and emerging twenty-first-century international politics. The experience of five decades of living with nuclear weapons has fostered conflicting perspectives on the significance of these weapons for state relations. While our authors draw on this history, each was asked to reevaluate fundamentally the role of nuclear military capability in contemporary international politics. The following chapters adopt the premise that the Cold War competition itself may have biased much of our thinking. Each author begins (explicitly in some cases) by questioning the relevancy of these past five decades, rather than merely accepting history as a guide to the future. Our authors question whether the study of a bipolar arms race can assist in uncovering anything about how these weapons may be constricted or spread in multipolar or unipolar worlds. Is an arms control history, based on concepts like force structure parity and assured destruction, relevant for emerging nuclear weapons states of unequal strength and territorial size?[8] How helpful is scholarship that emphasizes clear communication of credible deterrence commitments and capabilities when emerging states have adopted opaque forms of nuclear possession?[9] How important are concepts like extended nuclear deterrence, strategic defense, and hard-kill counterforce in an international system devoid of a global balancing dynamic?[10] Is the history of nuclear nonuse a product of bipolarity or the weapons themselves? What supports the perpetuation of a taboo against nuclear use?[11]

The first fifty years of the nuclear era are highly ambiguous history. Therefore, the orientation of this volume is to press forward theoretically, rather than to confirm existing notions through in-depth case studies or broad statistical analysis of the Cold War period. The choice to emphasize deductive heuristic theorizing over empiricism by all of the contributors highlights concerns over reliance on such a limited data set. Since the Second World War, the number of nuclear wars remains zero, while immediate nuclear deterrence situations either directly or indirectly involving the superpowers remain few, raising problems of selection bias.

Much of the empirical work on nuclear issues that was completed during the Cold War extrapolated from conventional war and deterrence cases to avoid some of these methodological difficulties. The use of conventional military cases to inform analysis of nuclear weapons, however, creates its own problems.[12] If nuclear weapons do indeed create unique dynamics, as Brodie et al. contends, then analysis drawn from conventional cases may be, by definition, inappropriate data for nuclear theory construction. The contributors to this volume draw on previous scholarship and history but focus most of their attention on highlighting fundamental theoretical issues and frameworks that might support future empirical examination. This volume is not focused on general international relations theory (although a number of chapters deal with contemporary debates), but rather on the pursuit of specific conceptualizations that will help to clarify our understanding of nuclear weapons. In this manner, this volume parallels the approach taken in *The Absolute Weapon*.

Brodie's work was premised on the simple observation that "everything about the atomic bomb is overshadowed by the twin facts that it exists and that its destructive power is fantastically great."[13] The main dilemma facing policymakers in the nuclear era who wish to avoid all-out nuclear warfare, according to *The Absolute Weapon,* is that a true international solution to the nuclear threat rests on the voluntary agreement of sovereign territorial states, whose willingness and ability to act collectively always will be open to suspicion. The most apparent strategy for avoiding nuclear warfare becomes, paradoxically, reliance on the independent ability of sovereign states to retaliate in kind (or have a benefactor willing to do so) against any state initiating an attack.

The dilemma remains for contemporary policymakers concerned about advancing national interests, while managing international politics to avoid any pressures to employ nuclear weapons. The contributors to this volume offer distinct views of this dilemma and how it may be affected by the transitioning between international orders. A debate over the very nature of nuclear weapons runs through much of the arguments that follow. Whether nuclear weapons represent a revolutionary increase in military capability is challenged by John Mueller and T. V. Paul and defended by Richard Harknett and Colin Gray. The Brodie conceptualization of deterrence based on rational assumptions is reexamined by William Martel, how it has been translated into policy is highlighted by Eric Mlyn, and how it will function in different strategic environments is explored by James Wirtz and George Quester. Ashok Kapur, Robert Manning, and Zachary Davis are divided on the issue of international control, and they offer perspectives that validate and challenge Brodie's skepticism about a negotiated solution to the nuclear threat. *The Absolute Weapon* argued that the revolutionary nature of nuclear destruction created an imperative of deterrence, which, when recognized, could serve as a national basis for international control. Our approach to thinking about nuclear weapons reexamines the three themes that Brodie explored in his volume: the revolutionary nature of nuclear weapons, deterrence, and international control of nuclear arsenals.

The Revolutionary Weapon: A Debate

The contributors to Brodie's volume agreed on one basic assertion: that nuclear weapons represented a revolutionary development that required a fundamental rethinking of how military and political affairs should be conducted. As Frederick Dunn put it, atomic power represented a "different kind of difference."[14] Brodie et al. considered nuclear weapons revolutionary because they alter the very nature of warfare by reducing the efficacy of defenses and the benefits provided by quantitative and qualitative superiority on the battlefield. In the preatomic era, victory in war generally limited potential damage to the home front. Battlefield success offered protection against further depredations from the losing side. However, in the nuclear era, battlefield advances might have little consequence. The stronger military state still could be mortally wounded by a defeated nuclear adversary. Dunn insisted that "it was becoming very hard to see how a tolerable war could be fought any more."[15] The revolutionary nature of the bomb highlighted an inescapably high degree of societal vulnerability to attack.[16]

Brodie and his colleagues argued that the military and political consequences of nuclear weapons followed from the exponential leap in scope and speed of destruction possible in nuclear warfare. Richard

Harknett renews a focus on the nature of the weapons as the basis for explaining the robustness of nuclear stability. Harknett employs the logic of the relative-absolute gains debate in contemporary international relations theory to reveal the significance of treating these devices as the "absolute" weapon. Harknett builds upon Brodie by suggesting that cooperation in war avoidance is an absolute gain in that all sides benefit by avoiding nuclear holocaust. Such cooperation does not produce a relative advantage that can threaten directly the territorial integrity of nuclear states. In Colin Gray's view, the distinctiveness of nuclear devastation continues to overshadow contemporary developments in conventional precision guidance and information technology's "systems of systems," which have been touted as the post–Cold War Revolution in Military Affairs. Although Gray does not fully accept the Brodie-Harknett view of nuclear weapons, he still regards the weapons as the most significant military innovation of the century.

By contrast, John Mueller and T. V. Paul question the very notion that nuclear weapons have had a revolutionary impact on war or international politics. Mueller concedes that nuclear weapons added a new element of terror to the superpower standoff but sees little in the way of a revolutionary shift in politics produced by their existence. If there has been a shift in the view of international security and warfare, Mueller argues, it emanates from the fear of massive conventional war produced by the lessons of the First and Second World Wars. The link between superpower bipolarity and nuclear weapons leads Mueller to conclude that as the former is no longer important, the latter will increasingly become less relevant. Paul notes that nuclear weapons, as with any other military capability that presents an opponent with the threat of destruction, can add to deterrent power. Unlike conventional military forces, however, nuclear weapons have not been translated into significant compellent power despite their support of a unique status in international politics. Paul, similarly to Mueller, connects the significance of nuclear weapons to the peculiarities of the American-Soviet bipolar competition and thus asserts a vision of waning importance in the twenty-first century.

The four authors in part 1 raise some intriguing avenues for future study. Paul and Harknett pose interesting questions about competing understandings of power and influence in international politics. They essentially agree that nuclear weapons enhance deterrent power but split on the significance of such power. Paul sees power as contextual and relational. Divorced from the high-stakes zero-sum context of the Cold War, in which deterrent power was relevant, the significance of deterrent power deriving from nuclear weapons possession is, in his view, waning. Harknett counters that deterrent power based on incontestable costs alters the security interactions between states. Since security remains scarce in anarchy, the limits nuclear possession places on force projection mark the potential for a fundamental shift in the conduct of world politics.

The contrast between Gray and Mueller is also intriguing. While Gray might grant Mueller that there are few true revolutions in military affairs, he suggests that more robust conventional forces still do not attain the distinctiveness that can be ascribed to nuclear weapons. Debate over the destructive potential of modern conventional weapons will increasingly become important as the leading military power at the end of the twentieth century—the United States—begins to expand upon its perceived technological advantages in conventional weaponry.

Deterrence: Fifty Years Later

Brodie himself asserted that military planners have always had to assume that a future situation might arise in which "war looked less dangerous or less undesirable than the prevailing conditions of peace." Such calculation, however, has required there be some prospect of winning; that victory could be claimed. For Brodie, this is the logic nuclear weapons challenged; they necessitated a shift in military planning, structure, and objectives. He argued that an imperative had been created for states to "hold themselves in readiness at all times for instant retaliation on the fullest possible scale."[17] A key observation offered by Brodie is that the battlefield benefits of using the bomb only outweigh the risks when one state possesses nuclear weapons. Once several states acquire nuclear capabilities, the advantages of nuclear first use are negated by the destruction wrought in retaliation. The central implication for military policy in the nuclear age, according to Brodie, is that states must guarantee for themselves the ability to retaliate in kind. Although Brodie did not coin the phrase, he advocated possession of what came to be known as a second-strike assured destruction capability as the principal objective of military planning.[18] Brodie concluded that the chief purpose of military establishments in the nuclear age is to deter, not win, war.

The logic of Brodie's argument about the centrality of deterrence is impressive. He ties both the preparation for war and the actual conduct of hostilities to the idea of retaliation in kind. The connection is important, because it is mutually reinforcing. For Brodie, thinking about combat leads to plans and force structures that ensure retaliation, since the vulnerability of cities makes traditional notions of battlefield victory obsolete. With war plans and force structures focused on guaranteeing retaliation, prewar policy and thinking become heavily focused on deterrence, that is, war avoidance.[19] As Brodie's colleague Frederick Dunn notes, "thus we come to the final paradox that while the best way to avoid atomic warfare is to get rid of war itself, the strongest present ally in the effort to get rid of war is the capacity to resort to atomic warfare at a moment's notice."[20]

Underlying the consensus presented in the original volume was the assumption that all states would share a similar view of nuclear devastation and thus a common interest in avoiding a major nuclear exchange. In stark contrast, William Martel questions the universality of deterrence as both a concept and strategy. For Martel, different states with different ideological and political persuasions may not hold similar conceptions about deterrence or the utility of nuclear weapons as an instrument of statecraft. Leaders or regimes may hold a millenarian image of conflict that differs sharply from rational instrumental calculations of benefit and cost tied to the goal of societal preservation. In Martel's view, the interaction between groups or regimes that hold millenarian and Brodie images of rationality would create highly unstable deterrence environments, especially following a millenarian state's acquisition of nuclear weapons.

Eric Mlyn also identifies another conception of deterrence that is different from Brodie's logic, which essentially anticipated and accepted the prospect of mutual assured destruction (MAD). Mlyn examines American Cold War and post–Cold War nuclear weapons policy and finds a disjunction between rhetoric and military planning. While the notion that nuclear weapons were revolutionary required military planning to prioritize deterrence, Mlyn argues that the American military has never come to terms with MAD and continues to think about nuclear weapons largely in conventional terms. He shows that this view has persisted after the Cold War, accounting for the lack of a shift in nuclear deterrence strategy following the demise of the Soviet Union.

The contributors to *The Absolute Weapon* assumed that the United States would not maintain sole possession of the atomic bomb indefinitely. They assumed that unilateral possession by the United States would spur others (particularly the Soviet Union) to acquire the bomb. Deterrence, if it were to remain stable in a world of multiple nuclear states, would require an "equality in deterring power."[21] The examination of how deterrence dynamics might evolve as nuclear weapons proliferated focused primarily on the question of arms races. Wolfers and Brodie argued that the creation of nuclear weapons would not invariably produce a massive arms race. If there were a rapid buildup of nuclear arsenals, it would result from the appearance not "of new and powerful weapons but of a deterioration of relations between nations."[22] If anything, they went on to argue, the unique nature of the atomic bomb might encourage a natural limit to the size of nuclear arsenals that is not present in conventional arms races. Citing the law of diminishing returns, Brodie and Wolfers noted that after a certain number of nuclear weapons are deployed, additional capacity to retaliate becomes unnecessary. The very inability to avoid the enormous destruction in nuclear war might serve to limit the size of nuclear arsenals: resources spent on "making rubble bounce" could be spent better elsewhere.

Exactly how the principle of "equality in deterring power" might be put into practice is examined in the two chapters offered by George Quester and James Wirtz. A relatively benign international political environment might find stability in a rough equality of nuclear capabilities at relatively low force levels compared to those of the Cold War. Quester evaluates the traditional arguments for minimal deterrence in light of the new security environment confronting the international community. For Quester, issues of crisis stability will raise significant impediments for states that wish to maintain only the minimal level of nuclear armaments. Wirtz focuses attention on how different political dynamics might animate future strategic relationships. He identifies the kinds of force structures that would foster arms-race and crisis stability under different political conditions. While Quester and Wirtz agree with Brodie that stability can be found in a dispersed equality of deterring power, both challenge the contemporary focus on drastically reducing the size of nuclear arsenals. To them, equality in deterring power will be more stable at high force levels.

While Wirtz, Quester, Martel, and Mlyn endorse Brodie's notion that nuclear deterrence should rest on secure retaliatory forces, each highlights impediments to achieving a future balance of assured destruction capabilities. Martel and Mlyn, for example, suggest that nuclear doctrines, bureaucratic inertia, ideological blinders, and utopian dreams can support dangerous ideas about the political and military utility of nuclear weapons. Both warn against the belief that benign nuclear weapons policies automatically accompany the acquisition of nuclear arsenals. Similarly, Quester and Wirtz suggest that the number of nuclear powers and the size of their nuclear arsenals might undermine the balance of retaliatory capabilities. Quester argues that technical problems or tactical innovations can make nuclear balances unstable at minimal force levels. Wirtz worries that shifting alliances or acute international tensions might make small arsenals appear inadequate for deterrence in times of crisis. All four contributors strike less optimistic tones than Brodie about the prospect that nuclear possession will invariably produce stable balances of retaliatory forces.

Controlling the Absolute Weapon

The destruction of Hiroshima and Nagasaki sparked an immediate debate over the need to control these new weapons of mass destruction. Many argued for some supranational solution to the potential problem of nuclear proliferation.[23] William Fox, Bernard Brodie, and others thought that such reasoning lacked a sophisticated understanding of international politics. The arguments presented in *The Absolute Weapon* concerning international control of atomic capabilities posited that any plan for control had to reflect the rudimentary nature of international society and the absence of a global sense of equity. Fox asserted that one could not "create a machinery of central control before one created a machinery of central justice."[24] Since no global set of values existed, Brodie's volume concluded that any international arrangement must ultimately rely on and therefore reflect the systemic distribution of power.[25] True international control requires not only the agreement of disinterested states or those who support control, but also a solution for the hard cases: those states that find a world absent any controls over the possession of nuclear weapons to be in their own interest. The contributors to Brodie's volume also emphasized that advocates of an international regime had to acknowledge that control invariably meant convincing great powers and rising states to abstain from a perceived great power asset.[26]

In assessing the prospects for international control of atomic weapons, Brodie and his colleagues were pessimistic. They predicted that the nuclear weapons control issue would ultimately become caught up in a balance of power dynamic with states likely grouping themselves around the "neighbor who combines the greatest capacity to launch atomic attack with the greatest capacity to survive it."[27] This was a fairly prescient observation. They also noted that even if an international regime could be established divorced from the balance of power dynamic, a system of safeguards and inspection would be necessary. Since no inspection regime could ever be developed that would eliminate the possibility of secret conversion from civilian nuclear energy production to military weaponization, prudence would dictate suspicion. Suspicion, they argued, would ultimately undermine confidence in any regime. In a world made "bombless by treaty," the first to build an arsenal clandestinely would have a tremendous advantage. Brodie and his colleagues concluded, paradoxically, that disarmament might make nuclear use more likely.[28] International control would be enhanced by some level of national nuclear capability and the concomitant promise of retaliation.

Despite pessimism expressed in Brodie's volume, only a few entrants have made it into the nuclear club. After fifty years, the count remains at five declared, three undeclared, and a handful of aspiring nuclear powers. The international efforts at nuclear nonproliferation, especially through the establishment of the Non-proliferation Treaty (NPT) and the safeguards system under the International Atomic Energy Agency (IAEA), have helped to arrest the spread of nuclear weapons. About 185 nations are signatories to the NPT, despite its discriminatory nature. National choices in this regard reflected a lack of technical ability, lack of interest in converting benign security environments to malign ones, and a belief in the nonutility of a nuclear weapon capability. The prediction of a nuclear-armed crowd of twenty-five to thirty nations has yet to come to pass. However, the continuation of this trend in the twenty-first century is debated by the authors of this volume. Outstanding questions remain about whether the security guarantees afforded by the superpower nuclear umbrellas suppressed proliferation and whether the closing of those umbrellas might spur new interest in developing nuclear arsenals.

Ashok Kapur updates the reasoning found in Brodie's text in a chapter informed by the perspectives of the opaque nuclear states: India, Israel, and Pakistan. Kapur argues that acceptance of the Brodie perspective on nuclear control would lead to a stable and less contentious relationship between the declared nuclear states and these three undeclared countries. Kapur notes that the problems that Brodie's volume anticipated about the pursuit of a universal approach to controlling nuclear capabilities have arisen. Examining how these three states have approached nuclear weapons, Kapur raises the interesting notion, again in line with Brodie, that these states might possess nuclear arsenals to link themselves to the arsenals, and thus protection, of larger nuclear powers in times of crisis. For Kapur, India, Israel, and Pakistan have viewed control of nuclear capabilities in very Brodie-like terms.

In contrast, Robert Manning and Zachary Davis challenge Brodie's assertion that denuclearization is a fundamentally unstable method of controlling nuclear forces. In contrast to Kapur and Brodie, they argue that nonproliferation objectives can be achieved through reliance on a universal regime. Manning and Davis demonstrate how a reassessment of the Acheson-Lilienthal Report and the Baruch Plan—the international approaches found lacking by Brodie—can serve as a basis for limiting the role of nuclear weapons in twenty-first-century international politics. Manning and Davis believe that the end of the Cold War provides an opportunity to reduce reliance on nuclear weapons and to address the regional security concerns that increase the attractiveness of nuclear weapons for some states. The declared nuclear powers should honor their part of the nonproliferation bargain and work to eliminate their nuclear arsenals and infrastructures.

The Second Stage of the Nuclear Era: The Way Ahead

Writing at the dawn of the nuclear era, Brodie and his contributors concluded that a mutual ability to guarantee retaliation would eliminate the incentive for all states to use these weapons first. The authors recognized that reliance on the "primitive and drastic safeguard of retaliation" alone would create a "world of half-peace at best." They believed that international efforts at control combined with an overall focus on conciliatory diplomacy through reliance on such institutions as the United Nations would be the best approach. Ultimately, however, it was the national possession of these weapons that would serve as the foundation for peace in the nuclear age.

The five decades that encompassed the first phase of the nuclear age—the Cold War—were influenced by an odd mixture of acceptance and rejection of these first principles offered in *The Absolute Weapon*. In the case of the United States, military targeting, planning, and acquisition of capability seemed to reject the shift, advocated by Brodie, away from conventional thinking. Yet simultaneously in rhetoric and crisis behavior, American political and military leaders tended to treat nuclear weapons as something unique and not at all like conventional weapons.

This new volume highlights competing visions of the nuclear era. The contributors, freed from the constraints of Cold War logic, find themselves in a similar conceptual context to 1946. In our examination of nuclear weapons at the beginning of the second stage of the nuclear era, the broad themes found in *The Absolute Weapon* serve as a touchstone for debate. There is little of the consensus, however, that marked that earlier analysis. Our authors both challenge and support the view that because of nuclear weapons' revolutionary character, systemic stability as well as the international control of nuclear weaponry must rest on assured destruction capabilities. While each chapter offers a unique contribution to thinking about nuclear weapons, the distinctive message of this volume is in its diversity. Fifty years of experience has led to a range of intellectual views about the significance of this terribly destructive force. This contrast of views was not wholly unanticipated. As Frederick Dunn wrote in the introduction to the first volume, "the profound significance of atomic energy as a physical force called for political thinking on a commensurate scale. Initial probings with the ordinary tools of political analysis brought disappointingly small results. . . . No clue could be found to a simple formula . . . in fact there was reason to believe that nothing of the sort ever would be found and that the job was one of arduous and patient examination of a whole mosaic of related problems extending indefinitely into the future."[29]

The competing arguments presented in this volume capture an expansive range of theoretical suppositions about the future of state security relations in a system in which the knowledge, if not the capability, exists to threaten catastrophic destruction. The chapters represent a fresh start in thinking about the nuclear predicament that was so eloquently described by William Fox in *The Absolute Weapon:* "Absolute freedom from the fear of the absolute weapon may not be for our time; but let us, with intelligence, determination, persistence and good will, get on with the task of meeting this new threat."[30]

It is in that spirit we offer the following observations for the second phase of the nuclear era.

NOTES

1. See Robert Gilpin, *War and Change in International Politics* (New York: Cambridge University Press, 1981); William Thompson, *On Global War: Historical-Structural Approaches to World Politics* (Columbia: University of South Carolina Press, 1988); William Domke, *War and the Changing Global System* (New Haven, Conn.: Yale University Press, 1988); Greg Cashman, *What Causes War? An Introduction to Theories of International Conflict* (New York: Lexington, 1993); and C. J. Bartlett, *The Global Conflict: The International Rivalry of Great Powers, 1880–1990* (London: Longman, 1994).

2. President George Bush's invocation of a "New World Order" harkened back to previous twentieth-century efforts undertaken by American leaders like Woodrow Wilson and Franklin D. Roosevelt. For an astonishingly Wilsonian approach, see *National Security Strategy of the United States,* January 1993 (Washington, D.C.: GPO, 1993). The document received little coverage since it was published as Bush left the presidency. On Wilson, see Thomas Knock, *To End All Wars: Woodrow Wilson and the Quest for a New World Order* (New York: Oxford University Press, 1992); and Warren Kimball, *The Juggler: Franklin Roosevelt as Wartime Statesman* (Princeton, N.J.: Princeton University Press, 1991).

3. The parallel between the reintegration of post-Napoleonic France and post-Soviet Russia into the great power system is intriguing. Despite its economic collapse, Russia was invited to G-7 economic meetings and continued to be a visible sponsor of Middle East peace negotiations, even though its diplomatic leverage was nonexistent. Discussions of future NATO expansion consistently have been linked to the establishment of a special relationship with Russia. For example, see William J. Clinton, "Remarks by the president to the people of Detroit," 22 October 1996, <http://www.whitehouse.gov>.

4. For an overview of the post-Napoleonic settlement, see Henry Kissinger, *A World Restored: Metternich, Castlereagh, and the Problems of Peace, 1812–22* (Boston: Houghton Mifflin, 1973).

5. Only weeks after Hiroshima, a conference was held at the University of Chicago to discuss how this new technology might be controlled. The conference was attended by many of the scientists, scholars, and policymakers who would later influence early thinking about the bomb. The participants included David Lilienthal, Leo Szilard, Edward Mead Earle, Harold Lasswell, and Jacob Viner. See Fred Kaplan, *The Wizards of Armageddon* (Stanford, Calif.: Stanford University Press, 1983), 24–28.

6. Some of the classics with this focus include Albert Wohlstetter, "The Delicate Balance of Terror," *Foreign Affairs* 37 (January 1959): 211–34; Henry Kissinger, *Nuclear Weapons and Foreign Policy* (New York: Council on Foreign Relations, 1957); William W. Kaufmann, ed., *Military Policy and National Security* (Princeton, N.J.: Princeton University Press, 1956); Bernard Brodie, *Strategy in a Missile Age* (Princeton, N.J.: Princeton University Press, 1959); and Herman Kahn, *On Thermonuclear War* (Princeton, N.J.: Princeton University Press, 1960).

7. Bernard Brodie, "The Atomic Bomb as Policy-maker," *Foreign Affairs* (October 1948): 24.

8. For an overview of arms control theory and practice in the Cold War, see Thomas C. Schelling and Morton Halperin, *Strategy and Arms Control* (New York: Twentieth Century Fund, 1961); J. David Singer, *Deterrence, Arms Control, and Disarmament* (Columbus: Ohio State University Press, 1962); and Scientific American, *Progress in Arms Control*, 9th ed. (San Francisco: W. H. Freeman, 1979).

9. The importance of signaling—communication in establishing credible commitments—is discussed in such classics as William W. Kaufmann, *The Requirements of Deterrence* (Princeton, N.J.: Center for International Studies, 1954); Glenn Snyder, *Deterrence and Defense: Toward a Theory of National Security* (Princeton, N.J.: Princeton University Press, 1961); Thomas Schelling, *The Strategy of Conflict* (New York: Oxford University Press, 1963); Schelling, *Arms and Influence* (New Haven, Conn.: Yale University Press, 1966); and Oran Young, *The Politics of Force: Bargaining during International Crises* (Princeton, N.J.: Princeton University Press, 1968). On the concept of opaque deterrence, see Ben Frankel, *Opaque Proliferation* (London: Frank Cass, 1990); and Zachary Davis and Ben Frankel, *The Proliferation Puzzle: Why Nuclear Weapons Spread and What Results* (London: Frank Cass, 1994).

10. For the classics on these concepts, see McGeorge Bundy et al., "Nuclear Weapons and the Atlantic Alliance," *Foreign Affairs* 60 (Spring 1982): 753–68; Karl Kaiser et al., "Nuclear Weapons and the Preservation of Peace," *Foreign Affairs* 60 (Summer 1982): 1157–70; Hedley Bull, "European Self-Reliance and the Reform of NATO," *Foreign Affairs* 61 (Spring 1983): 874–92; Earl Ravenal, "Counter-force and the Alliance: The Ultimate Connection," *International Security* 6 (Spring 1982): 26–43; and Colin Gray and Keith Payne, "Victory Is Possible," *Foreign Policy* 39 (Summer 1980): 14–27.

11. T. V. Paul, "Nuclear Taboo and War Initiation in Regional Conflicts," *Journal of Conflict Resolution* 39 (December 1995): 696–717.

12. This is detailed in Richard J. Harknett, "Nuclear Prominence: Reconsidering Conventional Deterrence in the Nuclear Era," unpublished manuscript.

13. Bernard Brodie, ed., *The Absolute Weapon: Atomic Power and World Order* (New York: Harcourt, Brace, 1946), 52.

14. Frederick Dunn, "The Common Problem," in Brodie, *The Absolute Weapon*, 4.

15. Dunn, "The Common Problem," 5.

16. John Herz picked up on this theme of vulnerability in his analysis of territo-

rial states. See John H. Herz, *International Politics in the Atomic Age* (New York: Columbia University Press, 1959). For a reexamination of Herz, see Richard J. Harknett, "Territoriality in the Nuclear Era," in Eleonore Kofman and Gillian Youngs, eds., *Globalization: Theory and Practice* (London: Pinter, 1996), 138–49.

17. Bernard Brodie, "War in the Atomic Age," in Brodie, *The Absolute Weapon*, 22.

18. The debate over whether mutual assured destruction is stable was extensive. Some classics include Wolfgang Panofsky, "The Mutual Hostage Relationship between America and Russia," *Foreign Affairs* 52 (October 1973): 109–18; Herbert Scoville, "Flexible MADness," *Foreign Policy* 14 (Spring 1974): 164–77; George Rathjens, "Flexible Response Options," *Orbis* 18 (Fall 1974): 667–88; Paul Nitze, "Deterring Our Deterrent," *Foreign Policy* 25 (Winter 1976–77): 195–210; Robert Jervis, "Why Nuclear Superiority Doesn't Matter," *Political Science Quarterly* 94 (Winter 1979–80): 617–33; and Spurgeon Keeny and Wolfgang Panofsky, "MAD vs. NUTS," *Foreign Affairs* 60 (Winter 1981–82): 287–304.

19. The classic critiques of deterrence theory include Robert Jervis et al., *Psychology and Deterrence* (Baltimore: Johns Hopkins University Press, 1985); Richard Ned Lebow, *Between Peace and War* (Baltimore: Johns Hopkins University Press, 1981); and Lebow and Janice Gross Stein, "Rational Deterrence Theory: I Think, Therefore I Deter, " *World Politics* 41 (January 1989): 208–24. For empirical studies in support of deterrence theory, see Paul Huth and Bruce Russett, "What Makes Deterrence Work? Cases from 1900–1980," *World Politics* 36 (July 1984): 496–526; and Huth and Russett, "Testing Deterrence Theory," *World Politics* 42 (April 1990): 466–501.

20. Dunn, "The Common Problem," 17.

21. Arnold Wolfers, "The Atomic Bomb in Soviet-American Relations," in Brodie, *The Absolute Weapon*, 135.

22. Wolfers, "Soviet-American Relations," 130.

23. The link between dealing with the nuclear threat and moving toward a world government was made almost immediately. See Norman Cousins, "Modern Man Is Obsolete," *Saturday Review of Literature* (19 August 1945).

24. William T. R. Fox, "International Control of Atomic Weapons," in Brodie, *The Absolute Weapon*, 174.

25. This argument is quite compatible with modern realist theory. See Kenneth Waltz, *Theory of International Politics* (New York: Random House, 1979); and David Baldwin, *Neorealism and Neoliberalism* (New York: Columbia University Press, 1993).

26. Dunn, "The Common Problem," 9; Fox, "International Control," 191.

27. Percy Corbett, "Effect on International Organization," in Brodie, *The Absolute Weapon*, 164.

28. Dunn, "The Common Problem," 15.

29. Dunn, "The Common Problem," 5–6.

30. Fox, "International Control," 203.

PART 1

The Revolutionary Weapon: A Debate

Power, Influence, and Nuclear Weapons: A Reassessment

T. V. PAUL

Realist theory and foreign policies based on realpolitik assume that nations acquire both conventional and nuclear arms with the intention of increasing their power capabilities. A preponderant conventional and/or nuclear capability is deemed to allow a state freedom of action vis-à-vis other actors who will be deterred from undertaking militarily provocative behavior. The notion of "peace through strength" suggests that nuclear capability is an essential ingredient for the survival of great powers in an international system composed of self-seeking actors who might otherwise be tempted to exploit military opportunities for their political, economic, and territorial advancement. These motivations have been evident in the acquisition of nuclear weapons by the five declared nuclear weapon states. Some regional actors also seem to believe that nuclear weapons serve not only as weapons of deterrence, but also as instruments of power in the international system and in their respective regional subsystems.[1]

This chapter asks the following questions: Under what conditions are nuclear weapons the most salient power resource? What is the significance of system change for the utility of weapons of mass destruction as a source of power? Do nuclear weapons provide the same amount of power and influence during the absence of systemwide high conflict as they do during the ongoing phase of such a conflict, for example the Cold War? Do policymakers in nuclear states give the same value to nuclear weapons as instruments of power and influence as they did during the Cold War? Do theoretical analyses and empirical research during the fifty years of the nuclear era provide sufficient evidence for corroborating, or refuting, beliefs about the utility of nuclear weapons as instruments of power and influence? Answers to these questions are important, given that nuclear weapons are still maintained and modernized by the five declared nuclear weapons states and some undeclared ones, while they are coveted by several threshold states even when the Cold War has come to an end.

In this chapter, I look at three significant dimensions of power that have relevance to nuclear weapons: *structural, deterrent, and compellent.*

On these dimensions, nuclear weapons are ascribed the role of an independent causal factor in the power relationship between two or more nation-states.[2] The significance of the structural conflict in the maintenance of this power resource and the changing dimensions of that conflict form the key discussion points. I argue that only under restricted conditions can a nuclear weapon state transform its destructive capability into power, largely because of the political, normative, and environmental considerations that constrain the effective use of nuclear weapons. The chapter then addresses the question of the role of nuclear weapons in the post–Cold War era and concludes that when the zero-sum conflict disappeared, the chief military instrument of its conduct, nuclear weapons, also depreciated in its utility. The general theoretical conclusion is that power is a relational and contextual phenomenon and therefore the translation of power resources into influence outcomes varies in different historical and systemic contexts. Moreover, the possession of different power resources is necessary to maintain major power status in the changed circumstances in which nuclear deterrent power alone would not guarantee top position in the international system. By contrast, this analysis suggests that integrative power is essential for the assumption and maintenance of a systemic or subsystemic leadership role.

Nuclear Weapons as a Source of Power

The structural, deterrent, and compellent power attributes of nuclear weapons are based on the assumption that nuclear weapons are the ultimate source of coercion in the international system. Coercion is deemed to be successful when an actor adopts a particular behavior "in compliance with, or in anticipation of another actor's demands, wishes or proposals," largely due to fear of sanctions or threat of force.[3] Deterrence is presumed to be the most significant outcome of the coercive quality of nuclear weapons. To some theorists, nuclear weapons also provide the holder "an infrangible guarantee of its independence and physical integrity."[4]

Of the three power attributes of nuclear weapons, the structural variety is most significant. Nuclear weapons are believed to bestow on the possessor structural power, which is the highest form of military and diplomatic power in the international system. Structural power, as defined by Susan Strange, involves four dimensions and is available to those states that have the capacity to threaten, defend, deny, or increase the security of other states from violence. Such states are able to control the system of goods and services, determine the structure of finance, and exert the highest influence over the acquisition and dissemination of knowledge.[5] Structural power, in the military and economic sense, would be the power to choose and shape the structures of global security and political economy within which other states have to operate.[6] Accordingly, the superpowers possessed structural power during the Cold War (especially in their respective spheres of influence), largely due to their overwhelming possession of military and economic capabilities, particularly nuclear weapons.[7]

The structural power accorded to the two leading actors in international politics, owing to their possession of preponderant military, economic, and political capabilities, made possible the creation and maintenance of a bipolar international system. The asymmetries in resources vis-à-vis other actors enabled the superpowers to affect the other states' policies by depriving them of or providing them with the desired exchanged goods.[8] These goods included, among others, extended deterrence, security assistance, arms, market access, and other forms of economic and military assistance. During the Cold War, this type of power was largely a product of the systemwide superpower conflict and the fact that a number of smaller actors were allies or were under the nuclear umbrellas of these dominant states.

Since the allies depended on the superpowers for security, the latter could develop patron-client relationships with the former. The Western allies, for instance, heavily depended on the United States' capability for their protection against the Soviet Union during the Cold War, and this dependence provided the United States with structural power over the security policies of these allies.[9] During this period of intense superpower conflict, several smaller states joined the leading actors because this brought them side-payments and security free rides.

A second dimension of structural power derived from nuclear weapons possession during the Cold War (and still persisting to a certain extent) is the general expectation that they are a currency of great power status.[10] To Robert Gilpin, the possession of nuclear weapons largely determines a nation's "rank in the hierarchy of international prestige," and they confer an enhanced status that has been coveted by a number of other states.[11] To John Gaddis, nuclear capability provided a power gradient to the United States and the Soviet Union that distinguished them from the rest of the world.[12] A related dimension of structural power was the capacity of the superpowers to engage in crisis bargaining without provoking a war. Although the danger of war existed, and war avoidance was a key goal of the superpowers, nuclear deterrence allowed them to engage in coercive threats and military/diplomatic maneuvers without risking war.[13] The superpowers thus could intervene in conflict regions of the developing world, engage in crisis bargaining, and contain their conflict, without resorting to a general war.

Nuclear weapons guaranteed the vital interests of the superpowers and other great powers. These interests have been: preventing a systemwide conflict; intervening in smaller state conflicts, crises, and wars; and acting as systemic leaders. Nuclear monopoly also presumably allowed the great powers to intervene in regional conflicts with the assurance that their adversaries would not attack their home territories or their closest allies. Thus, structural power reflected putative power to the extent that potential challengers understood the limits of challenging the superpowers. This was said to have reduced the environmental uncertainty with respect to the limits up to which a challenger to the great powers could proceed in international affairs in advancing its particular agendas. In addition, at the structural level, nuclear weapons also have been viewed as "proof of national excellence and industrial depth" of the great power. The size and quality of these weapons "implants the general estimation of the possessor in the eyes of other capitals and societies."[14]

The five nuclear states, especially the United States and the Soviet Union, attempted to make the nuclear club exclusive so that the aura of nuclear status would be confined to great powers. The nuclear nonproliferation regime, especially its chief component, the Non-proliferation Treaty (NPT), was aimed at arresting the spread of nuclear weapons beyond the established five nuclear powers. They fear that the proliferation of nuclear weapons would undercut the structural dominance of the great powers. Weaker states, armed with nuclear weapons and missiles, could prevent great power interventions in conflicts around the world. Smaller nuclear states could also use their potential or existing nuclear capability as bargaining chips, thereby eliciting concessions from the great powers. In addition, non–great power nuclear states could move away from the control or influence of great powers as they reduced their dependence on the protection offered by the latter.

A second important source of power that nuclear weapons provide their possessors is *deterrent power* vis-à-vis their adversaries. Bernard Brodie's suggestion that the main purpose of the U.S. military in the past was to win wars, while in the atomic age it would be to deter wars has been accepted largely by the other nuclear weapon states in their strategic policies.[15] The possession of a nuclear retaliatory capability by the deterring state and its willingness to use such a capability could deter potential adversaries who might be contemplating an attack. The costs of attack are so high that there would be little incentive on the part of the challenging state to engage in military aggrandizement. The U.S.-Soviet mutual assured destruction relationship was based on the expectation that nuclear weapons created deterrence through the superpowers' possession of a second-strike capability and their ability to inflict damage on each other's cities and military installations.[16] Nuclear weapons have especially been viewed as instruments for deterrence by punishment.[17]

Nuclear deterrent relationships are most pertinent among enduring rivals, states that are involved in a long-standing conflict relationship over fundamental issues or core values.[18] The probability of war is high in conflict relationships marked by enduring rivalries, and a defining characteristic of such a rivalry is high military readiness. Crises are endemic in such a relationship, and parties could engage in interstate violence if an opportunity arose. Nuclear weapons are presumed to reduce the opportunity and willingness of enduring rivals to initiate war, as the cost of attack is higher than any perceived benefits gained through battle.

Besides deterrence, a third important dimension of power attributed to nuclear weapons is compellence. Unlike deterrence, which is intended to prevent an adversary from doing something harmful, compellence involves a threat made to another state to do something or to cease doing some action or policy. It thus embodies initiating an action or an irrevocable commitment to an action that will cease only when the opponent complies with the compellent threat.[19] The American success in the Cuban missile crisis in forcing the Soviets to withdraw nuclear weapons from Cuba is often cited as an example of the compellent power of nuclear weapons, even though it involved painstaking diplomacy and quid pro quos.[20]

The Limitations of Nuclear Weapons as a Source of Power

Having discussed the multifaceted power that nuclear weapons have provided their possessors during the Cold War, it is worth asking whether these considerations are permanent or transient. Does the effectiveness of nuclear weapons as a power resource derive from the intensity of the Cold War conflict? If so, does this effectiveness remain when the Cold War ends? What role do they have in a nation's power capability in the post–Cold War era? This section addresses these questions by discussing each of the power attributes of nuclear weapons and their limitations in the post–Cold War era.

Structural Power

In terms of structural power, a weapon of mass destruction is most useful as a power resource during a period of intense structural conflict between enduring major power rivals. A power resource in this context is relational. The value of a good in terms of power is relational because it derives its social and political meaning from the context in which it is located. In addition, the value of a good stems from unequal distribution of it among groups or states in a given context.[21] The argument in the nuclear realm is that these weapons mattered most during an intense structural conflict but diminished in value as a structural power asset when that conflict ended.

During a systemwide conflict era such as the Cold War, the weapon of mutual deterrence served a number of purposes in great power relationships. First, it deterred antagonistic great powers from resorting to warfare. Second, by facilitating extended deterrence to those states that did not have the capacity to resist aggression unilaterally, it allowed the provider structural power over its allies. Third, it enabled enduring rivals to engage in crisis bargaining without resorting to war. On all these counts, the end of the Cold War has helped to depreciate the power resource that the nuclear states possessed. The argument is not that nuclear weapons are completely obsolete, but that with the end of the Cold War they have become less salient as a power asset at the structural level in international relations.

A number of reasons can be stated to support the notion of nuclear depreciation. First, allies need extended deterrence during an acute phase of a structural conflict. Extended deterrence has less salience if allies are not afraid of a military attack or if allies know that they can deter potential opponents through conventional capability or other political means. Second, with respect to crisis bargaining, it is difficult to brandish a nuclear threat between states that have ended a structural conflict, because such a threat could resurrect that conflict.[22] Bargaining will become more subtle and political when erstwhile enemies handle crisis situations during a period of rapprochement. Russian and American crisis bargaining behavior in Bosnia in 1995 attests to this argument. The American willingness to heed some Russian demands was produced not by Russia's nuclear capability, but by Moscow's capacity to veto U.S.-sponsored UN resolutions and potential to supply conventional military aid to the Bosnian Serbs.

Third, when a high systemic conflict ends, other sources of power become more salient to maintaining structural power. The factors keeping America's predominant position at the structural level in the post–Cold War era are largely its economic power and, at the military level, conventional capability, which was manifested during the 1991 Gulf War. The stable international order also provides public goods to the allies who regard U.S. leadership as being essential for their continued security and prosperity. This shows that enduring structural power is based not on coercive force alone, but on legitimate authority, created through an institutionalized normative order that defines different situations for lower-ranking states in the system.[23] This is because power without authority, and the required normative base, is neither respected nor fully acknowledged by lower-ranking actors. Integrative power, or the ability to integrate and co-opt different states, becomes more important when no major conflict exists. As Kenneth Boulding states, "neither threat power nor economic power is really very effective without integrative power."[24] This is evident in the reduced structural influence of Russia in Eastern Europe and China in East Asia. For neither state does its possession of conventional and nuclear weapons capability translate into integrative power.

With respect to major power status, history illustrates that different sources of weapons held prominence during different eras. During the eighteenth, nineteenth, and early twentieth centuries, naval power and overseas bases were supreme in determining great power status and successful outcomes in war. Land powers such as Germany could not win wars during this era partly because of their perpetual weakness in naval capacity. Battleships held sway in determining great power status as the struggle for tonnage prior to the First World War attested. Robert Osgood and Robert Tucker contend: "The development of the battleship altered the distribution of power, stimulated far-reaching rivalries and shaped new political alignments. More than ever before, a single weapon became the pre-dominant test and symbol of national greatness."[25] With the arrival of long-range aircraft and intercontinental ballistic missiles (ICBMs), naval power declined as the dominant gauge of major power status. The end of the colonial era also heralded the decline of gunboat diplomacy and the naval power attached to it. The norms of international conduct, especially those relating to sovereignty, helped to preserve small states that otherwise could easily be occupied by larger powers with predatory ambitions.

In the Cold War era, nuclear weapons replaced earlier instruments of great power status such as battleships. In the post–Cold War era, it is yet to be determined what form of capability would hold sway in determining military superiority. If the Gulf War and the Bosnian conflicts are any indication, nuclear weapons are unlikely to be the weapons that determine the ability of a major power to intervene in or win regional conflicts. Instead, it is likely to be precision-guided munitions and satellite technology that will allow pinpointed accurate attacks on the military facilities of smaller challengers. In an era of instant global communication, war is also fought to gain support from world public opinion. Great powers in the previous eras did not have to worry much about this factor, and civilian casualties were high as a result. A nuclear attack by a great power would inevitably result in massive collateral damage and the generation of adverse global public opinion. Moreover, during the early years of the nuclear age, nuclear capability was also viewed as a sign of national technical excellence. This was true when only a few states could possess the technical capacity to build a nuclear weapon. But when the capacity spread to economically less developed countries, the halo surrounding these weapons also faded.[26]

In sum, nuclear weapons were a major source of structural power during the Cold War. The superpowers enjoyed structural power from their ability to provide extended deterrence to their allies with their preponderant nuclear capability. During the Cold War, nuclear deterrence, arms control, and crisis management also dominated the international security agenda. The end of the Cold War has removed these items from the top position, which in turn has helped to depreciate the structural power deriving from nuclear possession. In the altered system, the remaining superpower, the United States, derives its structural power largely from its integrative power and conventional military and economic capabilities.

Deterrent Power

The second source of power produced by nuclear possession, deterrent power, is most relevant when adversaries hold intense hostility toward each other and when a military window of opportunity may be converted by the challenging state if no deterrence exists. Nuclear weapons provide this deterrent to even weak nuclear opponents because the cost of a limited retaliatory strike can be unbearable for large nuclear states. When the long-term rivalry ends, the threat of massive destruction for deterrent purposes, however, becomes less salient, unless the enduring rivalry resurfaces again. When the structural conflict ends, containment of potential challengers is possible through means other than nuclear deterrence.

The end of the Cold War decreased the value of nuclear weapons as a powerful deterrent asset because for deterrence to work effectively, the retaliatory threat has to be clearly communicated, sufficient capability should be present to carry out the threat, and it should be a credible threat for the target state. The deterrer also should have the commitment to carry out the threat. On all of these counts, change is evident. Deterrent threats are no longer easy to communicate as security challenges have become diffused. The Soviet menace to Western Europe is no longer the identifiable security concern. New kinds of threats on security agendas include ethnic conflicts, environmental challenges, and global drug trafficking, as well as subnational group activities. Nuclear threats are least credible in deterring these types of challenges. Communication of deterrent threats is equally difficult because these new targets are not easily identifiable, nor are the deterrent threats credible to the targets.[27]

At the systemic level, when non-nuclear states are unlikely to use force against the core interests of nuclear weapon states, the threat of devastation becomes less relevant. A general problem associated with coercive power that has been identified by David Baldwin is relevant in this respect. "B's estimates of A's capabilities do not suffice to explain the coercion of B. If B has no intention of committing murder, he will not feel coerced by his government's threat of hanging murderers. To explain the coerciveness of a threat, one must look not only at B's estimates of A's capabilities and intentions but also at B's estimates of his own capabilities and intentions."[28] This is indeed a major reason why more and more countries are joining the NPT and renouncing their right to build nuclear weapons. They seem to be no longer afraid of the nuclear weapons of major powers as tools of coercion because they do not envisage themselves engaging in the type of military conflicts with the nuclear weapon states that would produce a nuclear response. A large number of states have given up their right to build nuclear weapons as they have realized the difficulty in using such weapons as a source of power.

Unambiguous threats are described as the basis for a credible deterrent policy, and the end of the Cold War has made threats of this nature less relevant. Subtle economic and political threats are more appropriate in the changed circumstances. Weapons that are meant for mutual deterrence tend to decrease their role as the nature of mutual threats changes. In fact, in a less adversarial relationship, the costs of making and implementing a military threat increase. Thomas Schelling has argued that whereas some threats are inherently credible, others have to be made credible and some others are bound to be incredible bluffs.[29] Kenneth Boulding adds: "Little threats that are fairly sure to be carried out are much more effective in deterring adverse human behavior than large threats that are unlikely to be carried out."[30]

During the Cold War, when the conflict was based on an intense great power rivalry, the presence of nuclear weapons contributed greatly to preventing wars. Post–Cold War era conflicts are of a less serious nature, and by using or threatening to use nuclear weapons, conflicts could get worse, nullifying the intent of the threat itself. Nuclear threats are also not credible to deter minor challengers. Deterrent power, under such circumstances, need not come from the holding of weapons of mass retaliation, but from the possession of a capability to make other forms of credible threats to potential challengers.

Compellent Power

With respect to the third source of power deriving from nuclear possession, compellent power, nuclear weapons have offered little effective power even during the Cold War. These constraints have increased with the end of the Cold War. Attempts to compel using nuclear threats were less successful than efforts to deter. Nuclear weapons are ineffective as weapons for persuasion or compellence chiefly because of the credibility problem. Compellence against non-nuclear states is also fraught with complications as leaders of these states tend to understand that nuclear weapons are unlikely to be used. The "nuclear taboo," or the tradition of nonuse, has increased the credibility problem of using nuclear weapons. Nuclear punishment has also become less salient in the expectations of the nuclear weapon states themselves, as is evident in their new defense strategies.

The end of the Cold War has further weakened the limited compellent power associated with nuclear weapons. Not only are nuclear weapon states unlikely to use compellent threats against each other because of fear of retaliation, but in the absence of a systemwide conflict, they are least apt to do so as such threats would encourage resurrection of hostile relationships. In the post–Cold War era, nuclear compellence against non–nuclear weapon states (NNWS) would hinder efforts at nonproliferation as well. If nuclear compellence is applied against NNWSs, they may attempt to acquire nuclear weapons and thereby accelerate the proliferation process.

Constraints on Exercising Nuclear Threats

Although nuclear weapons served a number of functions in the Cold War era, the exercise of compellent power was problematic even during this period. With the end of the Cold War, these constraints have indeed multiplied. In this section, I trace the constraints during the Cold War to identify how they have increased at the end of the Cold War. Some such constraints were apparent to the authors of *The Absolute Weapon* at the early stage of the atomic age itself.[31] Other constraints have evolved during the nuclear age.

Theoretically, in terms of raw destructive power, nuclear weapons should increase the possessor's putative military capability: a nuclear-armed state can destroy an opponent's population and industry. But if influence is the goal of possessing power capability, the wanton destruction of an enemy need not result in realizing that objective. The behavior modification that may occur as a result of a devastating attack may not reflect the desired outcome for the attacker. In that sense, transforming the putative into actualized power seems a formidable task because the costs of attack for the attacker may be higher than the benefits he might derive from such an action. The costs could be human suffering, radioactive fallout to the environment, adverse impact on reputation, and international and domestic condemnation. Normative and moral questions also would emerge from using weapons of mass destruction that do not discriminate combatants from noncombatants, thereby violating two key principles of just war theory: proportionality and minimal civil damage.[32]

The arguments by the advocates of limited-nuclear-war options, to make nuclear weapons more usable, have also not been very convincing.[33] As Klaus Knorr contends, "the extent to which power will be employed clearly depends on the sensitivity of the power holder to the costs of its use," and asymmetries in putative power "affect international power only to the extent that there is the will, expressed in government action, to transform basic capabilities into forms" that would be directly "usable for the exercise of power, and eventually to use the transformed resources in actual power plays."[34] A major criticism of basic force models is that "they frequently fail to show how a given resource base is relevant for actually achieving compliance."[35] The costs of nuclear use are so high that the possessor is often constrained from actualizing the putative capability to influence the choices of another state. Thus, the compellent use of nuclear capability has been extremely limited because attempts to compel a nuclear-armed adversary could raise the possibility of a devastating response and therefore lack credibility. In addition, for a nuclear weapon state "to threaten (let alone actually use) nuclear weapons against a non-nuclear state would open it to enormous opprobrium from the international community and perhaps even from many of its own citizens."[36]

Not surprisingly, defenders and challengers rarely have found nuclear threats for limited objectives credible. During the early stages of the nuclear era, the United States and the Soviet Union attempted to use nuclear threats to elicit concessions from adversaries. During the Cold War era, twenty-one nuclear threats were made by the superpowers in their attempts to influence bargaining outcomes in crises. The outcomes, however, offered little evidence that the nuclear threats were the critical factors in the adversary's particular behavior.[37] The result of these attempts is described by McGeorge Bundy as the "unimpressive record of atomic diplomacy."[38]

The constraints on nuclear coercion were evident even during the period when the United States held nuclear superiority, that is, until 1949, when it could not translate this preponderance into power capable of changing Soviet policies.[39] In fact, from 1945 to 1949, according to Bundy, Soviet and Chinese power and influence expanded "at a rate not remotely equalled since then, and there is no evidence whatsoever that fears of the American bomb had any restraining effect on this enormous process."[40] During the Eisenhower administration there was agreement between the president and his secretary of state on the "value of readiness to threaten use" of nuclear weapons. They made attempts to threaten China during the Korean War, but U.S. actions ultimately did not match the threats that were made.[41] Similarly, the Soviets also refrained from the use of nuclear weapons even when they faced large political reverses in Yugoslavia, Egypt, and China. In 1989, the Soviets withdrew from Afghanistan after failing to crush the resistance by mujahideen guerrillas, while suffering countless casualties and political setbacks. The Soviet behavior during this conflict was as if nuclear weapons had never been invented.

More than anything else, for the Soviet Union, it was the inability to use its nuclear and conventional capability to prevent its collapse as a single unit that attests to the limitations of military power, especially nuclear capability. The downfall of communism and the disintegration of the Soviet empire occurred rather suddenly and nonviolently, a feat unparalleled in history for a dominant ideology or the position of a great power. The Soviet possession of enormous nuclear and conventional capability could not deter the breaking away of its republics or the declaration of independence by the erstwhile Eastern bloc states from Moscow's control. In the past, empires rarely dismantled themselves without violent struggles. It is not clear why even under conditions of self-destruction, force was not used to hold the state together.

In some respects, the possession of nuclear weapons decreased the Soviet leadership's ability to compel the seceding republics to stay together and prevent the collapse of the state. Any use of force would have led to an escalation of the conflict and intensified the hostility of the West, from which Gorbachev was attempting to gain support for his policies of perestroika and glasnost. In that sense, nuclear capability was a constraint rather than a facilitating factor in exercising national power. Additionally, the expensive arms race had helped to destroy the Soviet economy, forcing the Gorbachev regime to make some radical changes in foreign and domestic policies and thereby accelerating the collapse of the state.

The Normative Limits

The constraints in using nuclear weapons for achieving limited objectives have been largely based on two nuclear age norms—the "nuclear taboo" and the "no-first-use" pledge. The "nuclear taboo," or the tradition of nonuse, has slowly become entrenched in international politics since 1945. It involves a recognition based on a powerful tradition that nuclear weapons are unique and that they may not be used despite declarations of readiness or even when there are tactical advantages in using them.[42] Thomas Schelling argues that the convention of the nonuse of nuclear weapons grew over several decades and that the inhibition to use them has been based on a fear that nuclear weapons, once introduced into combat, could not be contained.[43] It suggests that like "poison gas they should not be used at all, or used only in cases of supreme national emergency." A nation that uses nuclear weapons for any other purposes is likely to receive the world's condemnation and could be stigmatized for breaking the taboo. In the words of Douglas Lackey, there is "a threshold that must be reached before a nuclear power will break the nuclear peace, and since 1945, no nation possessing nuclear weapons has reached that threshold."[44]

The no-first-use pledge has been a major political gesture by the nuclear weapon states to each other and to non–nuclear weapon states indicating that they would not be the first to initiate a nuclear attack. This was originally a pledge given by China but was adopted later by the Soviet Union and the United States, although the latter did so in an equivocal fashion.[45] During negotiations leading to the NPT renewal in 1995, the nuclear weapon states reiterated their commitment not to use nuclear weapons against NPT signatories not allied with nuclear-armed states.[46] These two norms have been reinforced by the limited international legal prohibitions against nuclear use. The 1961 UN General Assembly declaration prohibited the use of nuclear and thermonuclear weapons by contending that their use would cause unnecessary human suffering and was therefore contrary to the rule of international law and the laws of humanity. A 1981 General Assembly resolution also proclaimed that "states and statesmen that resorted first to the use of nuclear weapons would be committing the gravest crime against humanity and that there would [not] be any justification or pardon for statesmen who would take the decision to be the first to use nuclear weapons."[47] Although the United States voted against these two resolutions, Washington and Moscow had signed two Red Cross protocols that prohibited indiscriminate attacks against civilians and pledged that they would direct their military operations only against military targets.[48]

These normative factors have gradually helped to depreciate the coercive value of nuclear weapons, especially vis-à-vis non-nuclear states.[49] Non-nuclear states tend to be aware that they cannot "be easily coerced by nuclear threats from others, because both history and logic make it clear that no government will resort to nuclear weapons over a less than mortal question."[50] This explains to a great extent why non-nuclear states—pre-1964 China, Egypt, Argentina, and Iraq—went to war against nuclear-armed adversaries anticipating no nuclear retaliation.[51]

Thus in a compellent sense, nuclear weapons cannot be immediately translated into effective power. They cannot easily be transformed into instrumental forms that would allow the exercise of power and eventually influence. The putative aspect was strong during the acute conflict phase of the Cold War era, when the superpowers deterred each other with massive capabilities. But when that conflict was over, the logic of mutual assured destruction (MAD) and the power that derived from instruments of devastation declined, mainly because parties do not hold such an intense hostility anymore and because of the increased difficulties in making and implementing an effective threat or obtaining others' compliance due to that threat.

Finally, the growing interdependence in economic, ecological, and security spheres has decreased the usefulness of nuclear weapons as a power resource, especially given the risk of global radiation. As Joseph Nye argues, in an interdependent world, "power is less fungible, less coercive and less tangible. . . . Cooptive behavioral power—getting others to want what you want—and soft power resources—cultural attraction, ideology and international institutions"—become more important. In addition, the use of force for gaining economic objectives is too risky for modern-day great powers. "Even short of aggression, the translation of economic into military power resources may be very costly."[52] The worst-case assumptions that formed the basis for nuclear policies during the Cold War may be less relevant during the post–Cold War era. Baldwin identifies one of the problems in this respect: "the lack of fungibility of political power resources means that preparing to deal with the worst contingencies may hinder one's ability to deal with less severe ones." Policymakers who anticipate the worst and ignore the intentions of others may wind up "preparing for a very costly but unlikely contingency at the expense of a less devastating but more likely contingency."[53] Nuclear weapons are built around worst-case assumptions, but often threats seem to come from lower-level challenges, and nations appear to be less prepared to deal with them. In that sense, a transition from worst-case contingencies to most probable scenarios could radically alter the need for and perceived utility of nuclear weapons.

A strong argument could be made that the decline of nuclear weapons as a power asset could be reversed if structural conflict reappears in some form or other.[54] The possibility of a new systemwide conflict could indeed restore nuclear weapons as a key instrument of deterrence unless another, more effective deterrent is available through a new technological innovation or unless future ballistic missile defense (BMD) technologies make nuclear weapons ineffective. There is also a general belief among nuclear states in the danger of nuclear weapons in the hands of some developing states and that the continued nuclear possession by the five major powers may be essential to deter possible nuclear threats by these states against themselves and their regional allies.[55]

The Second-Tier Nuclear States

The second-tier states—Britain, France, and China—have been holding on to their nuclear weapons at the end of the Cold War, believing that the capability would preserve their great power status. Britain and France especially acquired nuclear weapons on the conviction that these capabilities would endow them with a major say in the security affairs of allies and adversaries alike. Although the declared purpose of nuclear capability was a mini-deterrent (for example, *force de frappe*) against the Soviet threat, the larger rationale for nuclear acquisition was political in character. They believed that by developing a nuclear capability, they would gain strategic independence from the United States and insurance in case Washington did not live up to its security promises. The British leaders believed that a nuclear capability would endow them with the role of a second decision-making center in times of crisis.[56] According to one analyst, nuclear weapons also provided a measure of distinction between the second-tier states that possessed them and the second- and third-tier non-nuclear states.[57]

For instance, the British decision to build nuclear weapons was not in response to an immediate military threat but was based on a belief that Britain as a great power must possess all major new weapons, and a "feeling that atomic weapons were a manifestation of the scientific and technological superiority on which Britain's strength, so deficient if measured in sheer numbers of men, must depend."[58] Similarly, the French decision to acquire nuclear weapons was primarily taken following the failure of the Anglo-French military adventure against Egypt in the 1956 Suez crisis. Although it was American economic pressure that led to the British decision to halt military operations, the French political leadership and strategists believed that "if France were to stand up for herself in such cases in the future, she must have the bomb."[59] French decision makers also believed that nuclear weapons would provide them with the ability to meet France's extra-European commitments.[60]

In assessing the status and power of nuclear weapons, policymakers in these states generally believed that it was nuclear possession that gave them major power status in international politics during the Cold War era. However, some others contend that nuclear weapons did not bestow on them any additional influence.[61] Some suggest that the British claim of strategic independence from the United States through nuclear possession did not materialize.[62] McGeorge Bundy argues that with the exception of nuclear arms control, nuclear weapons did not provide Britain and France admission to any top political table. He contends that Britain's diplomatic and political position saw a gradual decline as it accelerated its withdrawal from its erstwhile colonies in Africa and the Middle East. Similarly, France did not achieve a larger international role due to its possession of nuclear weapons. To Bundy, France's influence was not visibly greater in Moscow, or London, or Washington, or any of France's West European allies.[63]

Notwithstanding Bundy's pessimism, it is possible that the United States paid more attention to the British and French nuclear weaponry in the later years when the Cold War became intense. These capabilities were viewed as part of NATO's deterrent against the Soviet Union.[64] It can be argued that the political influence that Britain and France held in NATO and Europe was due not only to their possession of nuclear weapons, but also to the fact that they were nations with key economic and political attributes. Major power status came to these countries before they acquired nuclear weapons, as victors of the Second World War and as members of the UN Security Council with veto power; the latter was bestowed upon them much earlier than their nuclear acquisition. It is unlikely that they would have lost their Security Council seats had they not been nuclear weapon states. Second, their nuclear capability was not useful in the different crises and wars in which they have engaged since 1945. Both Britain and France backed out of the Suez crisis, allowing the weaker Egypt to win, although Britain had possessed nuclear weapons since 1952. France's retreat from Algeria occurred after it became a nuclear power, despite earlier expectations about the utility of nuclear capability in protecting France's extra-European commitments. Similarly, the British possession of nuclear weapons had no major effect on the Argentine decision to invade the Falkland Islands.[65]

Third, during the Cold War, non-nuclear Germany and Japan held equal or more weight than Britain and France in European and Asian alliance politics respectively. It is assumed that in the alliance relationship with the United States, nuclear weapons gave Britain a higher profile. However, a non-nuclear Britain probably would still have received attention from the United States, given the historical and cultural connections and the fact that Washington needed reliable European partners during the Cold War. Moreover, since the 1970s, in terms of economic power, Japan and Germany wielded greater influence in international politics than nuclear-armed France and Britain did.

If nuclear possession is so critical for major power status, why hasn't the acquisition of a nuclear weapons capability moved India, Israel, and Pakistan into the ranks of the second-tier states? The answer is that Britain and France possess other attributes such as economic power, technological superiority, conventional military capability, alliance with the status quo power, their major historical and current role in Europe, political cohesion, language and culture. The simple fact that they were significant players on the world scene until recently also provides them with a key ingredient of major power status. Most importantly, these states were the winners of the Second World War, and no new challengers have arisen since then with the ability to replace them. Nuclear weapon possession alone would not have provided them with power and influence, although it probably did influence their security relationship with their allies, especially the United States.

The end of the Cold War has further weakened the role of nuclear weapons for the second-tier states. Attempts to modernize their nuclear capability are receiving increasing international and domestic criticism. Behind the French rationale for the resumption of nuclear testing in 1995 was a belief that without a modernized nuclear force, France would not be treated as a great power. This unilateral French search for security and great power status has elicited major criticism among its European partners, especially Germany. This forced France to cut back the number of tests and to agree to sign the Comprehensive Test Ban Treaty (CTBT).[66] However, it is possible that continued nuclear possession could allow Paris to play a major role in a future security arrangement in Europe if such an arrangement is based on nuclear deterrence.

With the dawn of the twenty-first century approaching, past instruments of great power status may not be relevant in the future. A great army and navy with the capacity to intervene in regional and extraregional conflicts have been essential attributes of great power status during the previous eras. The changing power resources needed to sustain a dominant position in international politics are becoming more apparent.[67] In the post–Cold War period, therefore, the type of military resources that held supreme during the previous era may not be of much significance. The post–Cold War era has already witnessed the depreciation of nuclear weapons that have a battlefield application. The American and Russian decisions to remove and dismantle tactical nuclear weapons from Europe suggest that even for these states, the perceived utility of nuclear weapons is only at the strategic level and not at the tactical or battlefield level. Moreover, both Germany and Japan are maintaining their non-nuclear policies. In addition, a number of technologically capable states, notably South Africa, Brazil, Argentina, and Ukraine, have declared their intentions to become non-nuclear states. In their calculations, nuclear weapons do not add much to their power or influence in international politics, but impede economic development and obstruct regional cooperation.

In the changed climate of international politics, the British and French nuclear weapons are coming under scrutiny, as is evident in the unprecedented worldwide opposition to French nuclear testing during 1995–96. Britain and France must now determine, in terms of structural, deterrent, and compellent power, whether nuclear weapons are adding to their strength. Nuclear possession may still give them some form of influence with their allies. Yet the modest level of structural power these states wield is largely the result of their being status quo states with economic and conventional military capability. This economic capacity provides interaction opportunity and influence in the developing world, especially in those regions that were their colonies, the attractions of culture and language and history providing soft power resources. Nuclear weapons hardly figure in their association with the developing states, except at the NPT review conferences, held once every five years. The one way nuclear weapons could become salient in their relationships with the developing countries would be by their acquisition of miniweapons usable in the battlefield. Yet such a development, followed by a threat or actual use, could further undermine their favorable position vis-à-vis developing countries and could seriously jeopardize the nonproliferation regime.

Deterrent power has again become less relevant for these states since the Soviet threat in Eastern Europe has vanished and, in both a general and immediate deterrence sense, the enemy has become elusive.[68] It could be argued that Russia could revert to an aggressive posture, that the United States could withdraw from its commitment in Europe, and therefore the second-tier states should possess nuclear weapons. Under this contingency, nuclear weapons may bring them more deterrent and structural power in the European context.[69]

Among the second-tier states, China's nuclear capability seems to be a source of limited political power for a state that has the potential to become a challenger to the existing international order. Although a number of factors that depreciate the nuclear weapons of France and Britain also are applicable to China, Beijing's case for nuclear possession is somewhat different. Unlike Britain and France, who were under the U.S. nuclear umbrella, China developed nuclear weapons after a period of nuclear coercion by the United States during the Korean War and Offshore Island crises of 1954 and 1958.[70] In the post–Cold War era, China has emerged as a semichallenger to the international order and is yet to be fully integrated in the international economic and political system. Given the uncertainties in the security environment in the Asia-Pacific region,

China may find nuclear possession a source of insurance against potential enemies. During the Cold War, the Chinese leadership believed that nuclear possession was essential to remain independent of both the United States and the Soviet Union. In the post–Cold War era, they continue to believe in the effectiveness of these weapons for maintaining China's strategic independence.[71]

However, even for Beijing, nuclear possession is largely of symbolic value in the post–Cold War era, as nuclear weapons are unlikely to be effective against the internal security threats that China is likely to face in the twenty-first century. Nuclear weapons also are unlikely to be effective in a conflict with Taiwan except to deter U.S. intervention.[72] Moreover, nuclear threats against neighboring states could hamper China's efforts to integrate into Asian and international economic systems. China will not be able to achieve superpower status without integrative power and the ability to attract potential allies. The failure of communism further reduced China's limited ideological integrative power. If China makes nuclear threats against regional states, it is likely to antagonize its Asian neighbors whom it is courting for economic investment and market access.

The Third-Tier Nuclear States

Some regional states with enduring rivalries are continuing their quest to possess nuclear weapons for deterrence purposes even at the end of the Cold War. Regional states such as India, Pakistan, Israel, North Korea, Iran, and Iraq apparently believe that nuclear weapons can deter their regional adversaries and their great power opponents. They learned from the Cold War that war among enduring rivals could be prevented through nuclear deterrence. To a certain extent, the possession of nuclear weapons does provide them with deterrent power, especially for weaker states such as Pakistan vis-à-vis India and India vis-à-vis China, as long as their enduring rivalries persist as intense conflicts.

However, there are limitations to the power that regional states gain with nuclear weapons. Their nuclear capabilities could possibly prevent their adversaries' large-scale attacks, but they are of no use to deter limited, low-intensity operations. For instance, the Islamic fundamentalist groups, such as Hamas, that engage in terrorist attacks within Israel or the occupied territories are undeterred by nuclear or conventional threats. Similarly, the Pakistani training of militants in the Indian state of Kashmir is continuing even when these South Asian nations are reported to possess nuclear arms. What is interesting in these cases is that security challenges to the regional states now come from subnational groups that engage in guerrilla-type operations where the efficacy of conventional or nuclear military capability is low. Additionally, these states are not deterred from engaging in low-intensity warfare against each other even when they possess nuclear weapons. The risk, however, is that such low-intensity conflicts could escalate into nuclear confrontations if they are not carefully managed and controlled.[73]

Nuclear weapons also might provide the third-tier nuclear states with deterrent power against military intervention by major powers. However, this might be a factor only if the regional nuclear state has the ability to deliver nuclear weapons on large-scale concentrations of armed forces of great powers or the territories of their closest allies. The determination of nuclear weapon states to arrest proliferation and maintain their monopoly stems from this consideration.

Conclusions

The end of the Cold War has reduced the value of the central military instrument of its conduct, nuclear weapons. Nuclear deterrence was a product of the high-level zero-sum conflict that the superpowers had engaged in during the Cold War. The instrument fitted reasonably well into the high-stakes conflict in which adversaries were bent on pursuing their ideological and political agendas and in which maximization of relative gains mattered significantly. The Cold War system was based on "balance of power" and "balance of terror," and both were perceived to be essential for international stability. However, in an altered system, both factors become less significant. Specifically, when the nature of the conflict has changed, the instrument for waging the conflict also has changed. For instance, highly coercive military instruments have limited use in a relationship characterized by economic interdependence. In a dependent relationship of the North-South variety, coercion is still possible, but more feasible with conventional weapons or economic sanctions.

Moreover, in an asymmetric great power configuration, when the power of one of the erstwhile superpowers has declined considerably following the loss of large portions of its territory, nuclear weapons play a more limited role compared to the Cold War conditions of strategic parity. For the declining superpower, nuclear weapons could help to maintain a certain level of power status; it seems that power is only of short-run value and that it will be exposed if it does not gain more usable sources of power capability. For great powers in such an asymmetric relationship to rely on nuclear weapons assumes that the structural conflict could come back at the same level where it was during the Cold War. As Patrick Garrity has argued, during a period of transition, great powers would want to keep nuclear weapons "as a hedge in the event that international relations should deteriorate and as a means of keeping the major power competition at the political and economic and not the military level."[74] This argument indeed provides a strong reason for the continued existence of nuclear weapons. The coming of another round of systemic conflict could generate the impetus for the resurrection of nuclear weapons with structural and deterrent attributes.[75]

However, the dramatic changes in the international system in the 1990s suggest that the sources of power and influence in the future will be different from those in a bipolar system characterized by intense competition, as diffused challenges and threats emerge in the system. Nuclear weapons are instruments for conducting high-level conflicts without resorting to actual war, and therefore their utility as a power resource changes when the dimensions of conflict change. As a source of power and influence, they played a major role in international politics during the Cold War era, especially for the central Soviet-American deterrent relationship and alliance partnerships. The post–Cold War conflicts are mostly intrastate ethnic conflicts, and nuclear weapons have little role to play in containing or deterring such conflicts. The changing nature of power and the resources required for maintaining great power status are pointing toward a gradual depreciation of the importance of nuclear weapons in international politics.

NOTES

Portions of this chapter are drawn from the author's previous article "The Paradox of Power: Nuclear Weapons in a Changed World," *Alternatives* 20 (1995): 479–500. Copyright © 1995 by Lynne Rienner Publishers. Used with permission of the Publisher.

1. The authors in *The Absolute Weapon* assumed a number of these considerations in their pioneering work on the qualities, political consequences, and control of nuclear weapons. Bernard Brodie, ed., *The Absolute Weapon: Atomic Power and World Order* (New York: Harcourt, Brace, 1946). At this early stage of the atomic age, Brodie argued that the possession of the weapon would dramatically increase the offensive capacity of states and the ability to engage in surprise attack, especially if a nuclear state holds monopoly over it. Brodie, "War in the Atomic Age," in Brodie, *The Absolute Weapon,* 22.

2. There is somewhat general agreement that nuclear weapons are unsuited for defensive or offensive purposes because of the damage they can do to the attacker's own forces.

3. Klaus Knorr, *The Power of Nations: The Political Economy of International Relations* (New York: Basic Books, 1975), 4.

4. Ian Smart, "The Great Engines: The Rise and Decline of a Nuclear Age,"

International Affairs 51 (1975): 544–53; see also Richard Harknett, "The Logic of Conventional Deterrence and the End of the Cold War," *Security Studies* 4 (Autumn 1994): 86–114.

5. Susan Strange, "The Persistent Myth of Lost Hegemony," *International Organization* 41 (Autumn 1987): 565.

6. This definition modifies Strange's own definition in "Lost Hegemony," in which she confines it to economic structural power. I include military/security aspects also in defining structural power.

7. As Art states, the nuclear deterrent capability provided three potentially useful political advantages to superpowers: a wide margin of safety for diplomatic maneuvering, a capacity to trade nuclear protection for other things that the superpowers valued, and freeing up resources for other pursuits as security was efficiently provided by nuclear weapons. Robert J. Art, "To What Ends Military Power?" *International Security* 4 (Spring 1980): 3–35.

8. On structural power, see James A. Caporaso, "Dependence, Dependency, and Power in the Global System: A Structural and Behavioral Analysis," *International Organization* 32 (Winter 1978): 13–43.

9. Strange, "Lost Hegemony," 566.

10. Patrick J. Garrity, "The Depreciation of Nuclear Weapons in International Politics: Possibilities, Limits and Uncertainties," *Journal of Strategic Studies* 14 (December 1991): 463–514.

11. Robert Gilpin, *War and Change in World Politics* (Cambridge: Cambridge University Press, 1981), 215–16.

12. John Lewis Gaddis, "Nuclear Weapons, the End of the Cold War, and the Future of the International System," in Patrick J. Garrity and Steven A. Maaranen, eds., *Nuclear Weapons in the Changing World* (New York: Plenum Press, 1992), 24.

13. Glenn H. Snyder and Paul Diesing, *Conflict among Nations* (Princeton, N.J.: Princeton University Press, 1977), 451.

14. David C. Gompert, "Approaching the Nuclear Future," in Gompert et al., eds., *Nuclear Weapons and World Politics* (New York: McGraw-Hill, 1977), 3.

15. Bernard Brodie, "Implications for Military Policy," in Brodie, *The Absolute Weapon*, 76.

16. For a discussion on the deterrent value of nuclear weapons, see Robert E. Osgood, *The Nuclear Dilemma in American Strategic Thought* (Boulder, Colo.: Westview Press, 1988).

17. They are generally perceived to be not an effective instrument to provide deterrence by denial. Conventional weapons are more suited for denial purposes. Deterrence in the former is achieved by affecting the potential attacker's assessment of probable costs, in the latter by influencing his estimate of the probability of gaining his objectives. Glenn H. Snyder, *Deterrence and Defense: Toward a Theory of National Security* (Princeton, N.J.: Princeton University Press, 1961), 15.

18. For definitions of enduring rivalry, see Gary Goertz and Paul F. Diehl, "Enduring Rivalries: Theoretical Constructs and Empirical Patterns," *International Studies Quarterly* 37 (1993): 147–71; and Michael Brecher, *Crises in World Politics* (Oxford: Pergamon Press, 1993), 5.

19. Thomas C. Schelling, *The Strategy of Conflict,* 2d ed. (Cambridge: Harvard University Press, 1980), 195; Schelling, *Arms and Influence* (New Haven, Conn.: Yale University Press, 1966), 72.

20. The other key cases of compellent threats are the U.S. nuclear threats during the 1948 Berlin blockade, the 1950–53 Korean War, the 1958–59 Berlin deadline crisis, and the 1973 Middle East War. The Soviet Union's attempt at nuclear compellence occurred during the 1969 border skirmishes with China. For these cases, see Richard K. Betts, *Nuclear Blackmail and Nuclear Balance* (Washington, D.C.: Brookings Institution, 1987).

21. Robert Jackman, *Power without Force* (Ann Arbor: University of Michigan Press, 1993), 26. See also John A. Hall, *International Orders* (London: Polity Press, 1996), 35–36.

22. "Once the relevant weapons have been marginalized, however, it may not be possible to give them a revived role without aggravating a crisis. Bringing weapons out of store and putting others back on alert, coyness about deployment and targeting plans will appear provocative." Lawrence Freedman, "Great Powers, Vital Interests and Nuclear Weapons," *Survival* 36 (Winter 1994–95): 46.

23. On this type of power, see Talcott Parsons, "On the Concept of Political Power," *Proceedings of the American Philosophical Society* 107 (June 1963): 243; and Jackman, *Power without Force.*

24. Kenneth E. Boulding, "What Power Do Nuclear Weapons Give Their Possessors?" in Charles W. Kegley, Jr., and Kenneth L. Schwab, eds., *After the Cold War: Questioning the Morality of Nuclear Deterrence* (Boulder, Colo.: Westview Press, 1991), 108.

25. Robert E. Osgood and Robert W. Tucker, *Force, Order and Justice* (Baltimore: The Johns Hopkins Press, 1967), 50. For the importance of naval power, see A. T. Mahan, *The Influence of Seapower upon History* (London: Sampson, Low, Marston, 1890); and George Modelski and William R. Thompson, *Seapower in Global Politics, 1494–1993* (Seattle: University of Washington Press, 1988).

26. Additionally, there are questions about what constitutes a great power in the changed international politics. In the past, great power status depended on a state's record in war. William K. Domke, "Power, Political Capacity and Security in the Global System," in Richard J. Stoll and Michael D. Ward, eds., *Power in World Politics* (Boulder, Colo.: Lynne Rienner, 1989), 161. In the changed global context, war is likely to become less of a source for achieving great power status.

27. John M. Rothgeb, *Defining Power: Influence and Force in the Contemporary International System* (New York: St. Martin's Press, 1993), 156.

28. David A. Baldwin, *Paradoxes of Power* (New York: Basil Blackwell, 1989), 50.

29. Schelling, *Arms and Influence,* 36.

30. Boulding, "What Power?" 109.

31. For instance, Wolfers argued that the atomic weapon was not a suitable instrument for the United States to obtain concessions from the USSR with but was possibly an obstruction to U.S. diplomacy with the Russians. Arnold Wolfers, "The Atomic Bomb in the Soviet-American Relations," in Brodie, *The Absolute Weapon,* 114. Brodie himself argued that nuclear weapons served no other purpose except averting future wars. Brodie, "Atomic Age," 76.

32. These principles include just cause, exhaustion of peaceful alternatives, competent authority, effective means, proportionality, and minimal civil damage. For a discussion of these principles, see Michael Walzer, *Just and Unjust Wars* (New York: Basic Books, 1977). The moral cost of nuclear attack was well captured by a 1983 pastoral letter by U.S. Catholic bishops. According to them, "any use of nuclear weapons is bound to lead to such unconscionable destruction as to be beyond justification for any political purpose." National Conference of Catholic Bishops, *The Challenge to Peace: God's Promise and Our Response, A Pastoral Letter on War and Peace* (Washington, D.C.: National Conference of Catholic Bishops, 1983).

33. Robert S. McNamara, "The Military Role of Nuclear Weapons: Perceptions and Misperceptions," *Foreign Affairs* 62 (Fall 1983): 59–80.

34. Knorr, *Power of Nations,* 13, 18.

35. James A. Caporaso and Stephen Haggard, "Power in International Political Economy," in Stoll and Ward, *Power in World Politics,* 105.

36. Richard H. Ullman, "Denuclearizing International Politics," *Ethics* 95 (April 1985): 567–88.

37. Eric Herring, "The Decline of Nuclear Diplomacy," in Ken Booth, ed., *New Thinking about Strategy and International Security* (London: Harper Collins, 1991), 90–109. Betts concludes that the U.S. presidents, especially during the first twenty years of the nuclear age, when the United States held nuclear superiority, showed a proclivity toward making vague nuclear threats without thinking through whether they would be willing to use them credibly. Betts, *Nuclear Blackmail,* 213.

38. McGeorge Bundy, "The Unimpressive Record of Atomic Diplomacy," in Gwyn Prins, ed., *The Nuclear Crisis Reader* (New York: Vintage Books, 1984), 3–14.

39. John Lewis Gaddis, "NSC 68 and the Problem of Ends and Means," *International Security* 4 (Spring 1980): 164–70.

40. Bundy, "Unimpressive Record," 44.

41. McGeorge Bundy, *Danger and Survival* (New York: Random House, 1988), 587.

42. Schelling, *Strategy of Conflict,* 260.

43. Thomas C. Schelling, "The Conventional Status of Nuclear Weapons," The Center for International Relations, University of California, Los Angeles, *Working Paper* #5 (February 1994): 8.

44. Douglas P. Lackey, *Moral Principles and Nuclear Weapons* (Totowa, N.J.: Rowman and Allanheld, 1984), 75. See also T. V. Paul, "Nuclear Taboo and War Initiation in Regional Conflicts," *Journal of Conflict Resolution* 39 (December 1995): 696–717.

45. On these pledges, see Frank Blackaby, Jozef Goldblat, and Sverre Lodgaard, "No First Use of Nuclear Weapons," *Bulletin of Peace Proposals* 15, no. 4 (1984): 321–32. It should be noted that Russia in recent years has retracted its earlier no-first-use commitment due largely to domestic political considerations. On the Russian military change in this regard, see *New York Times* (4 November 1993),

A-8. On the no-first-use debate, see also David Gompert, Kenneth Watman, and Dean Wilkening, "Nuclear First Use Revisited," *Survival* 37 (Autumn 1995): 27–44.

46. *New York Times* (17 May 1995), A-11.

47. For a discussion of these two resolutions, see John Griffith, "Nuclear Weapons and International Law," in Prins, *Nuclear Crisis Reader*, 154–71.

48. Griffith, "Nuclear Weapons and International Law." In July 1996, the International Court of Justice at The Hague ruled that "the threat of nuclear weapons would generally be contrary to the rules of international law applicable in armed conflict," and in particular the principles and rules of humanitarian law. *New York Times* (9 July 1996), A-6.

49. The governments of non-nuclear states know that only enormous provocation could place them in deadly danger of a nuclear attack. Knorr, *Power of Nations*, 109. A former U.S. military commander in chief of the Pacific stated that he could not find, "in scrutinizing the whole of the Pacific command, any area where it would conceivably have made sense to explode nuclear weapons in order to carry out our military objectives." Noel Gayler, "A Commander-in-Chief's Perspective on Nuclear Weapons," in Prins, *Nuclear Crisis Reader*, 15–28.

50. Bundy, *Danger and Survival*, 588.

51. For a discussion on the calculations of these states, see T. V. Paul, *Asymmetric Conflicts: War Initiation by Weaker Powers* (Cambridge: Cambridge University Press, 1994), chaps. 5, 8.

52. Joseph S. Nye, *Bound to Lead: The Changing Nature of American Power* (New York: Basic Books, 1990), 188–89.

53. David A. Baldwin, "Power Analysis and World Politics: Some Trends versus Old Tendencies," *World Politics* 31 (January 1979): 161–94.

54. In this sense, Brodie's argument that nuclear weapons could "act as a powerful deterrent to direct aggression against the great powers" without allowing political crisis out of which wars generally develop is still relevant. Brodie, "Implications for Military Policy," 85.

55. It is my contention that the nuclear threat from the developing world is low, despite some commonly held assumptions about emerging threats. Barring a few, an overwhelming number of developing states have forsworn nuclear weapons. Analysts tend to mistake constraints on great powers to project power and pursue coercive diplomacy in the developing world as equivalent to direct threats to Western security. Only India and Israel have any hope of achieving ICBM capability in the next decade or two. Both these states are democracies and have few reasons to engage in military conflicts with the West. The other so-called minithreats can really be dealt with by conventional capability and diplomacy. On the exaggerated nature of these threats, see John Mueller, "The Catastrophe Quota: Trouble after the Cold War," *Journal of Conflict Resolution* 38 (September 1994): 355–75.

56. J. B. Poole, *Independence and Interdependence: A Reader on British Nuclear Weapons Policy* (London: Brassey's, 1990), 131.

57. Garrity, "Depreciation," 477.

58. Margaret Gowing, *Independence and Deterrence: Britain and Atomic Energy,*

1945–1952, vol. 1 (New York: St. Martin's Press, 1974), 184. It was also in response to perceived attempts by the United States to maintain atomic monopoly and to increase Britain's influence in Washington. Gowing, *Independence and Deterrence,* 185; see also Roger Ruston, *A Say in the End of the World* (Oxford: Clarendon Press, 1989).

59. Lawrence Scheinman, *Atomic Energy Policy in France under the Fourth Republic* (Princeton, N.J.: Princeton University Press, 1965), 171–74; Wilfrid Kohl, *French Nuclear Diplomacy* (Princeton, N.J.: Princeton University Press, 1971).

60. Scheinman, *Atomic Energy Policy in France,* 171.

61. To Scheinman, France experienced a substantial increase in its influence in international affairs in the 1960s owing partly to its nuclear acquisition. Scheinman, *Atomic Energy Policy in France,* xi. According to Kohl, however, the French efforts under Charles de Gaulle to form a closer European Union based on nuclear capability did not succeed as the European states were more interested in aligning with the United States and NATO. Nuclear capability did not elevate France's status in NATO, prompting France to withdraw in 1966. Kohl argues that the *force de frappe* had considerable "nuisance value," which allowed de Gaulle to challenge Anglo-American nuclear monopoly. Kohl, *French Nuclear Diplomacy,* 359–60.

62. Poole, *Independence and Interdependence,* 4.

63. As Bundy puts it, these weapons are not a replacement for the great fleets and armies that these countries had in earlier eras. The nuclear capability cannot undo the colonial losses they suffered during the postwar era. Bundy, *Danger and Survival,* 499–500. There is an argument that nuclear possession allowed France under de Gaulle to engage in more assertive policies vis-à-vis the United States and other West European states. These included getting closer to the USSR in the 1960s, vetoing British membership in the European common market, and siding with the Arab states in the 1967 Middle East War. But in subsequent years, some of these policies had to be changed by de Gaulle's successors. Frank Costigliola, *France and the United States: The Cold War Alliance since World War II* (New York: Twyne Publishers, 1992), 146.

64. Britain especially had deployed weapons in the NATO theater forces and played an important role in the alliance's nuclear planning group. Poole, *Independence and Interdependence,* 58. By the late 1980s, France had also increased cooperation with NATO even though Paris lost some independence in that process. Costigliola, *France and the United States,* 215.

65. On the Argentine expectation of no British military retaliation, see Nicanor Costa Mendez, "Beyond Deterrence: The Malvinas-Falklands Case," *Journal of Social Issues* 43 (1987): 119–22; and J. Busser and G. Enciso, interview by author, Buenos Aires, 26 May 1990.

66. On the French rationale for nuclear testing and criticisms by other states, see "Nuclear France—Argument," *Reuter News Analysis* (4 August 1995).

67. As Nye argues, during the five centuries of the modern state system, different power resources played critical roles in different periods. "The sources of power are never static and they continue to change in today's world." Nye, *Bound to Lead,* 33.

68. In general deterrent terms, adversaries keep forces to deter others who might attack if an opportunity arises. In immediate deterrence terms, when an adversary is planning an attack, the nuclear state mounts a retaliatory threat and the adversary backs off. On the distinction between these two types of deterrence, see Patrick Morgan, *Deterrence: A Conceptual Analysis* (Beverly Hills: Sage Publications, 1977), 30–32.

69. Although this is a distant possibility, the biggest deterrent would be a more institutionalized European security system in which Russia would be a partner for peace rather than a state that is looked upon with lingering suspicion. On the British and French post–Cold War nuclear programs, see Nicholas K. J. Witney, "British Nuclear Policy after the Cold War," *Survival* 36 (Winter 1994–95): 96–112; and David S. Yost, "Nuclear Debates in France," *Survival* 36 (Winter 1994–95): 113–39.

70. For the Chinese calculus on nuclear capability, see John Wilson Lewis and Xue Litai, *China Builds the Bomb* (Stanford, Calif.: Stanford University Press, 1988).

71. See Jonathan D. Pollack, "The Future of China's Nuclear Weapons Policy," in John C. Hopkins and Weixing Hu, eds., *Strategic Views from the Second Tier* (New Brunswick, N.J.: Transaction Publishers, 1995), 157–66.

72. A threat of nuclear attack on Taiwan is not credible because of the adverse impact it will have on the reunification efforts.

73. It could, however, be argued that the absence of large-scale war is due to the nuclear capability of Israel, India, and Pakistan. This needs to be analyzed more carefully, since a number of other factors—the decisive defeat of weaker adversaries in the 1971 India-Pakistan War and the 1973 Middle East War, the assuming of preponderance in conventional capability by the status quo states, India and Israel—might have contributed to the relative absence of war as well. In addition, in the Middle East, through the Camp David accords, Egypt, the main rival of Israel, defected from the Arab coalition that had waged war against the Jewish state in the past.

74. Garrity, "Depreciation," 465.

75. Another scenario could be the further institutionalization of nuclear weapons and doctrines in the current declared nuclear weapon states, which could prompt additional states to seek nuclear capability in the future. The research in miniaturization of nuclear weapons currently under way in the nuclear weapon states points toward a possible rethinking on the battlefield uses of a new generation of nuclear weapons. For a discussion of the different types of micronukes under research, see William M. Arkin, "Nuclear Junkies: Those Lovable Little Bombs," *The Bulletin of the Atomic Scientists* 49 (July/August 1993): 22–27.

State Preferences, Systemic Constraints, and the Absolute Weapon

RICHARD J. HARKNETT

When opposing states possess nuclear weapons at an assured destruction level, cooperation in avoiding major war becomes key to national security. In this security environment, the survival of each state depends upon the continued sanity of its opponent. This strategic position may be viewed as awkward and dangerous given that cooperative behavior over security between states has been difficult to achieve throughout history. Structural imperatives exist that encourage leaders to focus on relative calculations of power, raising an obstacle to cooperation. The relatively incontestable nature of nuclear weapons, however, supports the creation of a strategic military environment that moderates the self-help imperatives of anarchy. Mutual assured destruction (MAD) promises an absolute loss that creates a significant disincentive to cheat and overwhelms any expectations of exploitable relative gains. The "absolute weapon" makes cooperation in avoiding war an absolute gain for all states involved.

The end of the Cold War not only opened the door for new dynamics in international politics to emerge, but has created the opportunity for new thinking to take root. This chapter sets out to explore the logic concerning nuclear weapons that emerged immediately after the Second World War and to identify the implications of such logic for international politics in the aftermath of the Cold War.

On Competing Paradigms

While discovery can create the basis for revolution in thought, broad acceptance of such discovery "requires the reconstruction of prior theory and the re-evaluation of prior fact, an intrinsically revolutionary process that is seldom completed by a single man and never overnight."[1] Bernard Brodie recognized a few short months after the explosion of the first atomic bomb that "thus far the chief purpose of our military establishment has been to win wars. From now on its chief purpose must be to avert them."[2] Brodie noted a shift from the Clausewitzian notion of war as *a* political *option* to the notion of war avoidance as *the* political objective.[3]

The view of nuclear weapons contained in *The Absolute Weapon* necessitated a reconceptualization of national security. Prior to 1945, great powers could find security by using military force against each other. Brodie argued that great powers, once in possession of nuclear weapons, would find only devastation in their use. The implication of Brodie's famous dictum is that the approach needed to achieve security in the conventional realm is radically different than the approach required in a nuclear environment. In the conventional world, the struggle over power and the search for security occasionally require competition on the battlefield. According to Brodie's logic, that same struggle for power and security necessitates avoiding the battlefield when nuclear weapons are present. National security requires at least bilateral, if not multilateral, *cooperation.*

Thinking in conventional terms, the notion that success in the competition over security depends on cooperative strategies represents a paradox. If the distinctive nature of nuclear weapons is recognized and accepted widely, however, the paradox recedes. Despite Brodie's recognition that nuclear weapons required a rethinking about the role of military force, uncertainty over the effect of nuclear weapons on state security relations continues to run deep. Policymakers generally have professed rhetorical acceptance of Brodie's conceptualization, but it has not guided nuclear policy consistently.[4] Over the four decades that followed the writing of *The Absolute Weapon,* the two nuclear superpowers conducted their military relations, at times, as if governed by traditional conventions about the use of military force. And yet, when serious consideration of nuclear use was contemplated, war was considered to be an undesirable course of action. Nuclear weapons were viewed simultaneously by their main possessors as evolutionary and revolutionary devices.

The practices associated with conventional warfare are distinct from the laws, theories, and applications that should guide thinking about nuclear conflict. In essence, there are two definable paradigms[5] of military security: one in which the organizing construct rests on preparing to fight and win war, another in which war avoidance is the underlying goal of military preparations. What is intriguing about the first fifty years of the nuclear era is that both the nuclear and conventional paradigms on war coexisted simultaneously. Superpower relations were conditioned by the existence of assured destruction capabilities. These relations, however, were conducted in an international system in which conventional forces were prevalent and conventional notions of security were dominant. While superpower relations were captured by the logic of the nuclear paradigm, they were not immune from the applications and thinking dominant in the conventional paradigm.

The idea that there exists a realm of state security relations that does not fit the conventional paradigm does not mean that the traditional view of military force has been replaced.[6] Nuclear weapons alter state security relations when they are mutually possessed by opponents. In this realm of security relations, the practices and concepts natural to strategic environments dominated by conventional weapons may have little consequence. Yet since conventional war still dominates state security relations in most of the world, the theories and instrumentations as well as practitioners associated with conventional war remain highly relevant. The Cold War approach to nuclear weapons—attempting to fit them into conventional notions of war while treating them as revolutionary devices—had a Janus-like quality because two distinct conceptualizations of security simultaneously seemed relevant. Yet the nuclear and conventional paradigms rest on fundamentally different assumptions. The bipolar competition of the superpowers overshadowed that fact and sidetracked the debate over whether a fundamental change in international politics was initiated at Hiroshima (this is not to suggest that a debate never emerged, but rather that the debate was never divorced from the peculiarities of the Cold War).

General shifts between paradigms emerge through a period of competition between adherents of both old and new theories. In this sense, the first fifty years of the nuclear era represented a period of muted or distracted paradigmatic competition. The required Cold War focus on the interactions of the superpowers, which moderated in favor of conventional thinking about security, mixed uneasily with a notion of nuclear weapons as something unique. Now that the Cold War has ended, it is unclear whether the distinctiveness of the two paradigms will come to be seen more starkly. It is an open question as to whether the security calculations and preparations of states are to be dominated by concerns for fighting and winning wars (conventional paradigm) or for avoiding them (nuclear paradigm). Most fascinating is whether one paradigm will come to dominate the other, or will their uneasy coexistence continue?[7]

Answering such questions about future trends is always intriguing, but it remains a speculative art. This chapter is concerned with a much more fundamental objective. The case that there are two competing paradigms of state security relations assumes that a significant dividing line exists between state behavior in security environments dominated by these two different weapon types. Despite Brodie's presentation in 1946, this assumption is not universally accepted. Therefore, this chapter sets out to identify what is distinctive about conventional versus nuclear-dominated security relations.

This chapter suggests that to understand what drives state security calculations about peace and war, the specific strategic environment in which those relations are conducted must be identified. Traditional realists have focused on the state itself as agent. Modern realists have argued that the preferences of states are affected by the structural imperatives created by anarchy and the systemic distribution of power. A better explanation is found by focusing on the types of weapons relied upon to fight and to deter war because it is these tools of state power that structure the range of state interaction over security.

The key difference between nuclear and conventional weapons is in the strategic environments that each create. The security interactions found in a conventional environment are guided by practices and conceptualizations that are distinctive from those guiding relations in a nuclear environment. The strategic environment itself represents an intermediate structure between the state and system, which can constrain or promote certain state actions.

The chapter is divided into three sections. The first section examines the concept of contestability. The argument put forth is that the significance of nuclear weapons is found not in their high levels of potential destruction, nor in the speed at which such levels can be achieved, but in the limited range of interactions produced by being capable of achieving high levels of destruction quickly. The combination of rapidity and scope of damage means that the costs inflicted on an opponent by nuclear use cannot be effectively contested. This is the fundamental dividing line between conventional and nuclear warfare. The destruction associated with conventional weapons requires a degree of time and effort that ultimately allows for the possibility of adaptation on the part of an opponent. The opportunity to contest (or the belief one can contest) the costs threatened by the use of conventional forces is tied directly to the nature of the weapons themselves. Militaries and societies can adapt to the disruption and destruction possible with conventional weapons, even at severe levels. By contrast, nuclear weapons are capable of inflicting costs so quickly on such a vast scale, with lasting effect, that little adjustment can be made to blunt those costs to a significant degree. While conventional weapons allow for adaptation to costs, nuclear weapons permit little more than the absorption of punishment. Ultimately, the incontestable nature of nuclear weapons constrains the range of interaction between states in a military deterrence environment[8] and alters the range of options available to states contemplating the use of force.[9]

The second section of the chapter examines the concepts of contestability and distinct strategic environments within the context of the debate in international relations theory over relative versus absolute gains calculations. The logic of state preferences and structure is used to clarify the distinction between conventional and nuclear weapons. It is argued that the incontestable nature of nuclear weapons creates a set of constraints that heightens concern for absolute losses, thus making cooperation over war avoidance an acceptable absolute gain.[10] The final section offers an assessment of the possible alterations in state security relations that wider recognition of the incontestable nature of nuclear weapons may produce.

Contestability

The use of military force occurs when at least one state perceives that military action would produce a better state of affairs than if force was avoided.[11] Such a calculation may be made with the expectation of gaining some value or in the hope of avoiding the loss of some asset.[12] Regardless of whether the motivation is driven by a sense of opportunity or vulnerability, the underlying objective remains the same.

Most individuals trained in the art of war, however, recognize that it is an inherently unpredictable activity. Few initial military plans survive the vagaries of the battlefield.[13] The complexity of war springs from the fact that it is an interaction involving a multitude of variables. The outcome rests not simply on how well one's original plans are drawn, but on the reaction of one's opponent across technical, tactical, operational, and environmental (weather and topography) conditions. Decisions surrounding the use of force and the initiation of war certainly involve risk (that is, the decision involves the potential for multiple outcomes) and at times border on uncertainty, where the probability of those various outcomes cannot be determined.[14] Across the spectrum of policy options available to states, war is a sophisticated gamble. When taken, such a decision rests on a relative assessment of an enemy's competing capabilities and strategies. The risk and uncertainty underlying the gamble of war spring from the difficulty with making relative assessments of opposing militaries.

Weapons are at the core of such assessments. Military planning involves determining the tactical deployments and operational support necessary to achieve a weapon's full destructive potential. Military strategists recognize, however, that weapons cannot be divorced from the context in which they will be used. While the battle-ax is capable of producing great harm, if it is too heavy for the foot soldier to lift, its practical impact will be negligible. Deploying artillery with a range of 500 yards one mile from enemy lines can negate any potential such weaponry has for displacing enemy positions. Likewise, a tactical and operational innovation, such as using fighter aircraft in close ground support of swift-moving armor columns, can enhance each weapon's individual destructive potential and produce a smashing cumulative effect.

Both military planning and war are conducted in a dynamic environment. The impact of the relative capabilities of the opposing side combined with the anticipated vagaries produced by the friction and fog of war must be applied against the known technical capabilities of one's weapons to predict the likely consequence of combat.[15] Military history is a story of innovation and counteraction in the pursuit of maximizing or constraining the destructive potential of weaponry. Military history reveals that new innovation typically leads to advantage that in turn encourages a counteraction, which reverses or minimizes the original advantage.[16] The air war from 1940 to 1945 between British Bomber Command and Germany's air defense system is a good example of the dynamic nature of conventional warfare. In most every case, British innovations such as flying at night, electronic decoys, chaff, and improved radar were counteracted by the Germans. The counteraction was sufficient to blunt the effects of the Battle of Berlin. The British suffered a rate of loss in aircraft that was unsustainable.[17] Critical to this dynamic was the passage of time and a limit to the scope of damage produced by each innovation, which allowed for adaptation. In 1942, the British Bomber Command was averaging over 3,000 sorties a month and by August 1944 reached a monthly peak delivery of 20,149 tons of explosive. While these are impressive numbers, they depended on an extraordinary effort. In the end, the bombing did not disrupt overall German industrial war production in a significant manner.

The ability to contest, through countermeasure and adaptation, the destructive potential of conventional weapons is directly related to the effort and time it takes to reach that potential. This holds true for even modern bombing techniques, for example. During the Persian Gulf war, over 84,000 air sorties over forty-two days were required to deliver nearly 42,000 strikes on Iraqi strategic, ground force, and air-sea control targets.[18] Despite the coalition's total air supremacy, the cat-and-mouse game of conventional battle was played with great effect by Iraq, which was able to preserve its elite Republican Guard units and hide its Scud launchers.[19]

The strategic dynamic found in specific military competitions parallels the general patterns of behavior associated with the realist concept of the security dilemma.[20] The interplay of military strategy and war is directed by strategists' and generals' competing relative assessments. The necessity of assessing one's capabilities and tactics against those of one's opponents is driven by the probability of finding technical, tactical, and/or operational innovations that can greatly affect the actual force that will be brought to bear in combat. It is the expectation that the destructive potential of one's enemy can be contested that makes the gamble of war worth taking. While the outcome of war is rarely certain, the open promise that one has the potential to maximize the destructive effects of one's own weapons, while at the same time degrading the destructive effects of those of one's opponents, makes war a tempting roll of the dice. In this sense, it is not specifically the aggregate level of destruction that is critical, but whether that level can be avoided in its entirety or delayed at least long enough to gain some decisive advantage against one's enemies. From February to December 1916, France and Germany waged the battle of Verdun. Nine months of attack and counterattack resulted in 542,000 French and 434,000 German casualties, but little change in the territory held by each side.[21] Both sides remained committed to the attack based on the expectation that one more thrust might prove decisive. While the aggregate level of losses was appalling, both sides were able to adapt to each other's efforts and contemplate some tactical circumvention of defenses. The fact that such circumvention required huge expenditures of men and matériel and ultimately proved futile did little to alter this strategic reasoning. In fact, the French could classify the battle as a victory, despite the greater casualties, because Verdun was relatively more damaging to the German ability to continue the war. One might suspect that had the Crown Prince, who led the Fifth German Army in the offensive, been told prior to going on the attack that he would, *with certainty,* sustain 434,000 casualties without gaining any ground, he would not have proceeded. But since each additional increment of troops and each new day held the prospect of decisive breakthrough, he could continue to give orders to attack. The strategic logic behind America's incremental involvement in Vietnam was similar.[22]

What is clearly distinctive about conventional and nuclear weapons is how contestable the former is compared to the latter. Measured on a scale of contestability—the degree to which technical, tactical, or operational effects can impact the actual destruction to be borne in combat—the destructive potential of nuclear weapons tends to be highly resilient. At a low level of possession, nuclear weapons can maintain a relatively incontestable level of military force. Counterweapons, countertactics, and general friction can degrade nuclear destruction only on the margins. Adaptation during a nuclear attack would have little effect.[23] Without the ability to degrade or adapt in any significant manner, the ability to contest or believe that one can avoid significant nuclear destruction disappears. The incontestable nature of nuclear weapons creates an environment that affects state security relations in a manner distinguishable from prenuclear security dynamics.

The Absolute Weapon and Structural Constraints

The current debate between modern realist and neoliberal institutional theorists focuses on how cooperation can be achieved in an anarchical international system. Both sets of theorists agree that the lack of centralized authority above the level of the territorial state—anarchy—creates a set of structural imperatives that makes cooperation among states problematic. The complication this raises for the nuclear era is obvious. If national survival requires cooperative strategies and cooperation is exceedingly difficult to achieve and sustain, reliance on nuclear weapons for security ultimately may prove counterproductive. The deductively driven debate between modern realists and neoliberal institutionalists, when analyzed closely, indicates that this is not necessarily the case. These theoretical frameworks can be used to highlight the distinctive impact nuclear and conventional weapons can have on international security relations.[24] They provide a basis for determining how cooperation in the form of war avoidance can be promoted and how Brodie's dictum that militaries must prepare to avoid war can be sustained.

Deterrence policies attempt to induce calculations that in turn promote mutual incentives to avoid military combat. Thus, cooperation between opposing sides in a deterrence environment can be defined as mutual avoidance of war. Cooperating to avoid war does not necessitate a resolution of the conflict of interest that raised the specter of war in the first place, but it can serve as a solid foundation for the pursuit of such a resolution.[25] Defection or conflict can be defined as the outbreak of combat. When this occurs, the resolution of conflicting interests will be determined through encounter on the battlefield. Traditionally, deterrence theory has focused on the threat of retaliatory costs.[26] The focus has been on reaching a level of costs that will outweigh any expected gain. A focus on the level of costs is important, but it is not the most critical aspect in distinguishing deterrence outcomes. The type of strategic interaction created by deterrent threats can be viewed as a causal variable in military deterrence situations. The strategic dynamic of a deterrence environment can affect the type of actions states take. It can be hypothesized that when the strategic dynamic of a deterrence environment causes states to focus on absolute gains and losses rather than relative estimates, the prospect for war avoidance increases.

Neoliberal institutionalists argue that the primary stumbling block to achieving cooperation in an anarchical system is the ever-present opportunity to cheat on agreements.[27] There is no legitimate force in place to guarantee that cooperative agreements will be enforced or that the benefits of cooperating will be received. Not surprisingly, states are wary of making their ability to gain benefits dependent on the actions of others. Neoliberal institutional theorists, as the name implies, envision a possible solution to the systemic effects of anarchy. The probability of cooperation can be raised through the creation of formal international institutions and recognized regimes,[28] which can moderate the effects of anarchy with the creation of incentive structures that make defection less appealing. Much of this argument revolves around the game theoretic of prisoner's dilemma and the strategy of tit-for-tat.[29]

Implicit in the neoliberal institutionalist solution to cheating is the assumption that states tend to calculate interests based on a preference for absolute gains. States will cooperate if they gain from such cooperation and if they feel confident that the gain is forthcoming. Liberal, regime, and neoliberal institutional theories all assume that the prospect of cooperation will be enhanced as the assurance of benefits increases.[30] The reduction of uncertainty and the expectation of iteration are considered critical for cooperation under anarchy.[31]

Modern realists have argued that this neoliberal assumption about state preferences is incorrect. Modern realism holds that the structural imperative of self-help created by anarchy is a much more vexing problem than neoliberal thought allows.[32] Scholars like John Mearsheimer, Kenneth Waltz, and Robert Gilpin focus on how the distribution of power throughout the system, which reflects the relative positions of individual states, conditions state relations.[33] To ensure their basic objective of national security, states must be concerned with their relative position in the international system. Joseph Grieco has argued that states, therefore, are best described as "defensive positionalists." To remain secure and independent, states forever must be cognizant of where they stand relative to both potential opponents and allies.

This focus on relative position leads to a concern about the relative gains that may be produced by state interaction. Kenneth Waltz has argued that the relevant question traditionally asked by state policymakers is not whether their state will gain through a particular interaction with another state, but rather who will gain more. Waltz argues that "even the prospect of large absolute gains for both parties does not elicit their cooperation so long as each fears how the other will use its increased capabilities."[34] While two states may benefit from coordinating their actions, thus producing an absolute gain for both, the distribution of the gains is unlikely to be symmetrical. Therefore, while both states are better off in absolute terms than they were yesterday, one state may have gained more in comparison to the other state. There may appear a relative gap in the gains made by each state through their interaction. For example, I may decide to coordinate a garage sale with a neighbor. By combining our goods for sale, we can attract a larger crowd than if we had two separate sales on two separate days. In doing so, we both make money. I wind up with a $100 profit, my neighbor nets $150. We have both profited in absolute terms, but a $50 gap exists between our relative profits.

According to modern realists, the problem is that states in a self-help system have to be worried about how such a gap might affect their relative positioning in the system. Large relative gains made in comparison to another state may be used to the advantage of a state and, most importantly, to the disadvantage of other states. The key question for realists is whether my neighbor can use the $50 gap to his own advantage and to my detriment. Since such a "gap in gains" is unlikely to threaten the welfare of my family (we do not live in an anarchical system), the decision to cooperate will not be undermined. Internationally, however, such gaps can be exploited. The prospects for international cooperation therefore are more problematic, according to modern realists, than liberal theorists recognize because of the continued relevance of relative calculations. Gaps produced in gains intensify the salience of relative calculations of gains and diminish the probability for cooperation.

The pessimistic outlook of realist theory ultimately rests on the supposition that a focus on relative calculation tends to dominate across most issue areas of importance. Modern realists assume that states' preferences are guided primarily by whether they achieve relative gains compared to the states with whom they agree to cooperate. In a self-help system, states must not only ensure their own survival, but also guard their ability to act independently. If their autonomy is chiseled away by cooperative interaction with others, states ultimately may find themselves helpless to guarantee their survival unilaterally. The capacity for independent action is dependent on the relative power one possesses vis-à-vis the rest of the units that make up the international system. According to modern realists, therefore, the potential for stable cooperative behavior in a condition of anarchy is limited to cases in which states can confidently share in symmetrical benefits. In essence, cooperation becomes dependent on solving both the problems raised by the opportunity to cheat and the focus on relative gains calculations.[35] Such instances are rare. As a result, conflict in international politics remains a pervasive state of affairs.

When one examines the ideal condition for cooperation set out by modern realists, the issue of whether state preferences are guided by relative or absolute calculations becomes blurred. If one assumes near-symmetrical gain, thus making relative calculations moot, whether a state chooses cooperation over autonomous pursuit of gains will depend on which option leads to an overall better gain in absolute terms. That is, resolving the concern for relative gains leads the state back to a decision-making calculus driven by a concern for absolute gains. The more important contributor to cooperation, therefore, becomes not state preferences per se, but the influences on those preferences.

System constraints facing states can affect state concerns for relative versus absolute gains and thus the feasibility of cooperation. Robert Powell has argued similarly that the constraints that define the strategic environment in which states interact are critical to determining the prospects of cooperation.[36] While anarchy produces a general systemic effect on the possibility of cooperation, it is an insufficient explanatory variable when applied to specific cases of cooperation. Since both cooperation and conflict occur in a system organized around the principle of anarchy, the anarchical structure on its own cannot help explain when cooperation, rather than conflict, is more likely. The Waltzian focus on the distribution of power lends some greater clarity but is also insufficient.[37] While hegemonic theorists argue that predominance in power can create conditions for cooperation, balance of power theorists see general equilibrium as critical.[38] Structural effects—anarchy and the distribution of power—are important for explaining state security relations, but they can be enhanced significantly with a focus on particular strategic environments. These environments are structured around specific constraints that limit the range of state behavior.

Powell implies that particular realms of international activity can produce such significant constraints on state activity as to alter concerns over relative gaps in gains. He argues that a distinguishable strategic environment is one in which the use of force is at issue. The use of force is a latent concern in an anarchical system. It becomes a critical issue when the cost involved in using force is sufficiently low. Determining whether this is the case or not depends, according to Powell, on the nature of military technology: "If the nature of military technology is such that one state can turn a relative gain to its advantage and the disadvantage of others, then these constraints will induce a concern for relative gains, and this may impede cooperation."[39]

Powell emphasizes that even though one might assume that states are trying to maximize absolute gains (that is, that this is their preference utility), cooperative outcomes that offer unequal absolute gains cannot be sustained when the use of force is at issue. The prospects for cooperation become linked to whether unequal absolute gains can be militarily exploited to produce a significant relative gain in the future. This type of strategic environment constrains states' abilities to focus on absolute gains and forces a concern for relative calculations, thus reducing the likelihood of cooperative behavior. In Powell's model, maximizing absolute gains remains the consistent state preference. The particular environment that states must interact within, however, may require more or less consideration of relative gains. In this sense, the state is like the business firm that seeks to maximize profits but will change behavior depending on whether the market is competitive or defined by a monopoly. This focus on structural constraints rather than state attributes (utility preferences) to explain behavior also mirrors the distinction modern realists have drawn between themselves and traditional realists.[40]

Grieco has added to Powell's analysis by arguing that gaps in gains induce concern not only because of the specter of war, but also because of the persistence of uncertainty in international relations, the lack of a guarantee about the future costs of war, and the lack of a guarantee about other states' perceptions about the costs of war in the future. Grieco concludes that "this wider range of sources of concerns about gaps in gains causes the relative-gains problem to come into operation more often than might be expected on the basis of Powell's model."[41]

Grieco, along with Robert Jervis and Kenneth Waltz, argues that since there always exists some degree of uncertainty concerning the future intentions and actions of others, cooperation leading to gaps in gains even among allies may prove difficult. As Jervis states, "minds can be changed, new leaders can come to power, values can shift, new opportunities and dangers can arise."[42] This uncertainty also extends to future military capabilities and perceptions about that capability. Modern realists argue that even though the use of force may be currently too costly to employ, there is no guarantee that innovations will not occur to lower costs to an acceptable level or that leaders will not somehow become convinced that the costs of war are diminishing.

Concern for relative gains, according to Grieco, is produced by so many sources that cooperation is unlikely unless it generates equitable absolute gains *and* a guarantee that the opportunity to cheat cannot produce significant relative gains. Modern realists are less concerned about obtaining guarantees against cheating, since this is very difficult, than about making sure that if cheating occurs, it cannot lead to any exploitable advantage. While cooperation may occur short of these two conditions, finding a solution to *both* the exploitable cheating *and* relative gains problems is modern realism's "tough case."

The act of going to war ultimately challenges a state's ability to act independently. If a state is deciding to initiate a war, relative assessments must be carefully made concerning, among other factors, the opponent's military defenses and retaliatory capabilities, political stability, natural resources, potential allies, and economic strength. A state fearing an attack must engage in a similar set of calculations. An intense focus on relative power guides states in assessing the potential costs of going to war and makes cooperation in avoiding armed conflict all the more difficult.

The concern over relative power, however, can be constrained or exacerbated depending on the type of strategic environment in which states find themselves. This environment is greatly influenced by the weapons relied upon for deterrence.[43] What Grieco and Powell fail to do is explicitly distinguish between conventional and nuclear environments and their respective effects on state security concerns. Both Powell and Grieco focus on how state preferences are affected by the aggregate level of military costs (that is, death and destruction in war).[44] In the context of deterrence security environments, however, it is not the aggregate level of potential losses in battle, but the degree to which costs are contestable that creates distinct security dynamics.

The concept of contestability differs subtly, but importantly, from the discussion concerning the dominance of offensive versus defensive weapons. It is argued that when defensive weapons dominate, the security dilemma can be mitigated. John Mearsheimer has pointed to the stabilizing effects of nuclear weapons due to their nonoffensive characteristics.[45] The problem of clearly distinguishing between offensive and defensive weapons has always proven difficult (recall Soviet views of President Reagan's Strategic Defense Initiative as a first-strike offensive weapon).[46] This makes using the distinction problematic for analysis. A focus on contestable costs, however, captures the effect alluded to by the distinction between offensive and defensive weapons without suffering from a definitional lack of clarity. This is important because the intermediate structural effects are critical. It is not the cost of war that is at issue, but whether the infliction of cost can be contested in such a fashion as to produce an exploitable advantage.

States relying on a strategy of conventional deterrence will tend to have an intense focus on relative power because the retaliatory costs that they can threaten are ultimately contestable. With conventional deterrents, there exists the potential for finding technical, tactical, and operational solutions that may reduce or completely circumvent the threatened level of retaliatory costs.[47] This prospect fuels the intensity of relative calculations since both the state considering the initiation of war and the one trying to deter it know they must react quickly to each other's moves. While the costs of modern conventional warfare may be extremely high, the concept of winning still endures. The calculation driving the decision to go to war is not necessarily whether a state will be better off in absolute terms (given the destructive rather than constructive nature of war, this has been rare in history). The critical question is whether a state will be in a better position in relative terms after fighting other states in the system. The calculations of the Iraqi leadership during 1990–91 are interesting in this regard. Although faced with an overwhelming opposing force, Saddam Hussein was rationally able to ignore the compellent threat behind the UN coalition's demand that he withdraw from Kuwait. It was a reasonable roll of the dice, if one accepts the three assumptions that

divided American public opinion was highly sensitive to casualties;
Israel's entry into the war would fracture the coalition;
victory would be defined not by retention of Kuwait, but through regime survival.

The first two assumptions go to the heart of contesting the destructive potential of the coalition by an indirect strategy. Given their demonstrated ability to defend against larger forces during the eight-year war with Iran, it was not unreasonable to expect Iraqi troops to be able to inflict a level of casualties on the coalition that an American public might find unacceptable. Iraqi officials, after the war, stressed that the United States avoided direct combat, and there is evidence that the strange and brief Iraqi advance toward the Saudi city of Khafji was attempted solely to engage American ground troops into direct combat—as Iraqi Foreign Minister Tariq Aziz put it, to create "a touch" between armies.[48] The Scud attacks on Israel very nearly provoked an Israeli response.[49] This would have created an untenable position for the Saudis, Syrians, and Egyptians and put in jeopardy the entire coalition. Since time was required to inflict enough damage on Iraq to cause its surrender, Saddam Hussein could attempt to contest the coalition's firepower indirectly in the hope that the coalition would have to quit before it could inflict its full destructive potential. While in the end he may have miscalculated, the strategic environment of conventional war did nothing to preclude such thinking.[50]

In fact, the nature of the conventional battlefield encouraged such relative calculations on the part of Hussein. Contest on the conventional battlefield is the ultimate arbiter in the distribution of power across the international system.[51] A conventional military environment does nothing to moderate the concern for relative gains. In the end, conventional war determines whose relative assessments were more correct.[52] Thus, cooperation in mutual strategies of war avoidance is difficult.

Military threats represent proposals of future action. There is a reasonable degree of uncertainty that can be attached to conventional threats. Whether the level of destruction threatened can actually be reached is suspect. Given the possibility of adaptation, the destructive potential of a conventional weapon can go from being high to negligible or even counterproductive in fairly short order. British bombers that were equipped with rearward-looking radar had an enhanced ability to reach and bomb their targets when first introduced during the Second World War. The Germans were able to circumvent the radars and negate their advantage within months. Eventually, the radar itself became detectable, which increased the Germans' ability to find and shoot down the British bombers.[53] Through German adaptation, the radar actually decreased the destructive potential of the British Bomber Command.

The costs to be inflicted by a conventional deterrent capability can be contested by an opponent. This fact encourages the search for countermeasures. In a nuclear environment, the military capability itself is not open to circumvention. The calculation of gains and losses is constrained considerably in a nuclear deterrence environment. Unlike with conventional weapons, the retaliatory costs associated with nuclear weapons are clear. If nuclear weapons are used, the level of destruction threatened can be reached. There is a "reliability of effect" that can be associated with nuclear use.[54] Uncertainty exists only at the level of whether the weapons *will* be used. This is a much less vexing problem, despite much concern about the credibility of threats voiced in the deterrence literature.[55] When it comes to the issue of national security, states are likely to be risk-averse in their calculations, erring in the direction of worst-case planning.[56] The type of strategic environment states find themselves in will affect their risk-averse behavior. In a conventional deterrence environment where concern over relative power is high, risk-averse states will find cooperation difficult. While it may be viewed as a mutual gain, agreeing to avoid war in one instance may produce an uneven outcome. War avoidance might be sought only to obtain the time necessary to build the forces or find the appropriate strategy needed to make the use of force an attractive future option. In a nuclear deterrence environment in which certainty exists about the absolute loss that would result from nuclear attack, however, the cautious calculus of a risk-averse state should incline that state to cooperate to produce the *absolute gain* of avoiding a nuclear exchange.

In a conventional deterrence environment, relative calculations are intense, and thus small differences may have a significant impact. It is appropriate for states to "assume that there is at least some chance that force" could be used.[57] The overwhelming power of nuclear weapons, however, tends to overshadow small differences. Potential gaps in power, which may translate into relative advantage, are not sufficient in a nuclear environment to provide military opportunity. Once a secure second-strike force is available, the focus of assessments becomes political will rather than capabilities. Here, risk aversion leads a state considering the use of force to assume that there is a chance that the other side will use its nuclear weapons. Since nuclear retaliation would outweigh any conceivable benefit, war initiation is likely to be avoided. The slight chance of a response involving a guaranteed level of unacceptable destruction is more likely to produce war avoidance than a great chance of a response involving a high but suspect level of destruction. This is the difference between state security calculations in nuclear and conventional deterrence environments. Relative calculations might have driven the development of nuclear forces, but when it comes to actual use of nuclear forces, states are faced with a strong sense of absolute loss. The difference in framing is significant. Whereas conventional warfare can be discussed in terms of relative gains, nuclear war must be conceived of in the context of absolute loss.[58] Grieco's defensive positionalist state is concerned with maintaining independence. Nuclear weapons provide unconditional support from external threats to state territorial integrity. While gaps in gains and power may be exploited in nonmilitary areas and extended military environments, national territorial security is enhanced by central nuclear deterrence.[59]

Anarchy creates structural incentives for states to act as if "relative gain is more important than absolute gain."[60] Nuclear weapons, however, place significant constraints on the effects of this anarchical structure. Nuclear possession, while viewed as a unit-level attribute (an enhancement to military power), must also be recognized for its intermediary impact. The strategic interaction between states armed with nuclear weapons is fundamentally different from that between conventionally armed states. While still attempting to better themselves relative to other states, nuclear opponents must make their calculations without viewing the recourse to war as a viable option. In a nuclear context, one question guides decisions concerning peace and war: How can I achieve my objectives without provoking a military response from my opponent? This differs significantly from the strategic questions that can be asked in a conventional environment. There, the possibility of achieving objectives exists even after an opponent responds militarily. In the former situation, alternatives are constrained by a focus on the possibility of absolute losses; in the latter, relative gains remain relevant.

The avoidance of military engagement when conflicts of interests arise requires some degree of coordination, if not cooperation. International security relations can be viewed as an ongoing bargaining process. States may still seek the best national results in the competition for gains, but cooperation on the objective of avoiding war is consistently supported by the absolute nature of nuclear conflict. Competition is not eliminated, but rather channeled away from the military battlefield. The incontestable nature of nuclear weapons holds out the prospect of a security environment in which significant relative calculation is reduced, if not eliminated, by creating incentives to focus on absolute losses. Where nuclear weapons are possessed by all combatants, war avoidance becomes a cooperative action producing mutual, if not equitable, advantage. In the specific situation of MAD—an environment in which destruction is mutually assured—cheating, which might amount to a first strike, does not lead to an exploitable advantage.[61] Thus, there exists a symmetrical benefit (avoidance of annihilation) with no concern about cheating. In essence, MAD seems to qualify as the solution to modern realism's tough case. The problem of both relative gains and exploitable cheating are overcome in such a strategic environment. While nothing is guaranteed in the future, the costs of nuclear war are clear. This clarity supports sufficient confidence that cooperation in nuclear war avoidance will enhance security. Brodie's reconceptualization of security is captured by the absolute context of nuclear war.

Contestability and the Future of Security

The structural imperative of a strategic environment in which exploitable advantages cannot be produced through contesting the actual use of weapons requires, to paraphrase Brodie, military preparations that seek to avoid rather than fight war. Why fight if there is no relative gain? William T. R. Fox's reference to nuclear weapons as absolute is apt in the sense that these state assets create an intermediary set of constraints within an overall anarchical system that reduce, if not mitigate, concerns over relative power.

Where nuclear weapons are present, international security operates under a different set of practices and suggests a different set of problems and solutions. It challenges the expectations, theories, and policies that assume relative power and relative gains and losses in war are the key to state security and independence. The nuclear paradigm portends a major shift in the conduct of international security relations as well as our understanding of state interaction. Intellectual and political resistance to its laws, logic, required practices, and spread is likely to continue, if for no other reason than that international security relations under the conventional paradigm highlight the importance of leading states.

Great power policy, supported by general international opinion, reached a near consensus in the immediate aftermath of the Cold War concerning movement back toward a system in which the conventional paradigm was unchallenged.[62] The extension of the Nuclear Non-proliferation Treaty in 1995, the conclusion of negotiations for a Comprehensive Test Ban Treaty, and American pursuit of counterproliferation strategies all can be seen as restorative prescriptions.[63] Each, in its bid to reduce the role and influence of nuclear weapons in state security relations, attempts to restore and promote a system of security relations in which relative power calculations are key.[64] From a great power perspective, pursuit of such restorative policies is perfectly in line with traditional realist notions of national interest defined by political power.[65]

The term *great power* is not simply based on an assessment of such factors as territory, population size, economic capacity, natural resources, political stability, and military capability.[66] "Great" power is defined by the widening set of interests such power allows states to consider vital. Great power status has always been defined in terms of extent of interests. All states define their national interest, minimally, in terms of securing their own territorial integrity. The extension of the national interest to include a broader range of interests must be linked to an expansion of political power. At a minimum, therefore, a great power can be categorized as a state that defines its national interests beyond its own territorial integrity across the spectrum of political, economic, and military relations. Ultimately, it is the ability to project power across these three broad issue areas that sets apart certain states from the rest in an international system.[67] In a self-help anarchic system, projection of military power has been perceived as most crucial. While dominance in the realms of economic or political regional and international relations is important, the use or threat of military force has proven to be the ultimate arbiter of state affairs. The capacity of military power projection is what distinguishes the great power from the non–great power. In the Thucydidean tradition, "the strong do what they have the power to do and the weak accept what they have to accept."[68]

The push by the United States and other leading nuclear powers for nonproliferation can be understood as an effort to retain the traditional distinction between strong and weak states. In Thucydides' account of the Melian dialogue, we are told that the generals of Athens presented the inhabitants of Melos with a choice: surrender to imperial control or accept annihilation. Placing their hopes in the gods and a slow-moving Sparta, the Melians resisted to their death. But what if Melos had possessed nuclear weapons? Would the overwhelming conventional military superiority of the Athenian empire have been brought to bear if the city-state of Athens had been laid open to a threat of retaliation? Could a great power brazenly threaten the existence of a weak power, if that weak power possessed the capability to threaten massive destruction?

Weak states,[69] such as ancient Melos or present-day Pakistan, cannot hope to compete with great powers in the general struggle across issue areas. However, if they attain "equality" in the power to hurt, they may alter the traditional dynamic that has existed between weak and great power states. Realist logic holds that the independence of weak states is primarily based on exogenous factors such as the distribution of power, the presence of a great power benefactor, or great power disinterest.[70] Possession of an invulnerable second-strike force of only a small size by a weak state may serve as a sufficient equalizer to secure state territorial integrity and thus basic independence.[71] Weak states may be able to look out for themselves. They may be able to prevent the projection of military power.

Thus, nonproliferation and disarmament goals are logical policy outgrowths of a concern to maintain the most distinctive feature of great power status. Nuclear weapons are not effective tools of offensive force.[72] They cannot conquer territory, but they do add to national power the ability to deter. Deterrence power enhances territorial integrity by creating what might be conceptualized as a soft shell of protection through threat of retaliation.[73] This is a contribution which is at the same time limited and limitless. It is limited in the sense that direct attack on one's own territory can be considered a rare event in international politics. It is limitless in the context that confidence in securing one's own territory is the elusive goal of every unit in an anarchical system. Territorial security is the foundation for conducting relations across all other issue areas. Nuclear possession carves out a particular realm of international activity—direct territorial aggression—from the traditional logic that has dominated international politics for centuries.

It does this for great power, aspiring great power, and weak power relations alike. The nuclear paradigm does not recognize as significant what makes great powers distinctive; the conventional paradigm does. We should expect, therefore, that states that find themselves on the short end of intense security competition for relative power will be most interested in escaping such a strategic environment (if capable of doing so). India's refusal to allow the Comprehensive Test Ban Treaty to move forward in the summer of 1996 might be better understood with this notion in mind.[74] However, for states who find the competition over relative power to forward their security interests, we should expect an effort to limit the spread of nuclear weapons, and for the top military power to seek their total elimination.

Nuclear weapons create a fundamental problem for those states concerned with extending influence beyond their borders because they create imperatives for cooperation in war avoidance. They are tools of state power that actually create an environment for strategic interaction that itself constrains state power. And yet, in twentieth-century world politics, possession of nuclear weapons has been associated with great power status. In line with the counterintuitive logic of much of the nuclear paradigm, great power is both enhanced and constrained by nuclear possession. The independent ability of weaker states to create incentives for larger states to avoid military confrontation with them is a new phenomenon. The implications for international politics have yet to be fully appreciated. Given the conceptual and practical difficulty of dealing with such an outcome, pervasive acceptance of the nuclear paradigm is doubtful anytime soon. Brodie's first words on the nuclear era are unlikely to be the last.

NOTES

1. Thomas Kuhn, *The Structure of Scientific Revolutions,* 2d ed. (Chicago: University of Chicago Press, 1970), 7.

2. Bernard Brodie, ed., *The Absolute Weapon: Atomic Power and World Order* (New York: Harcourt, Brace, 1946), 76.

3. The central thesis of Clausewitz is that war, as organized violence, must serve some political end. Since no political end could justify all-out nuclear war, retaining Clausewitz's premise requires war avoidance. For a similar point on Brodie and Clausewitz, see Robert Jervis, *The Meaning of the Nuclear Revolution* (Ithaca, N.Y.: Cornell University Press, 1989), 251–57.

4. See Eric Mlyn's contribution to this book and his *The State, Society and Limited Nuclear War* (Albany: SUNY Press, 1995).

5. My use of the term *paradigm* is taken from Kuhn, *Scientific Revolutions,* viii, where he defines *paradigm* as a universally recognized practice consisting of laws, theories, and applications that provides model problems and solutions to a community of practitioners.

6. The term *conventional paradigm* is meant to capture a similar, yet broader sense than the term *conventionalization,* which is used by Robert Jervis and Hans Morgenthau. See Jervis's discussion and citation of Morgenthau in *Nuclear Revolution,* 15–19; and Jervis, *The Illogic of American Nuclear Strategy* (Ithaca, N.Y.: Cornell University Press), 56–63.

7. The most intense academic debate over the future of security relations revolves around the promise or peril of nuclear proliferation. For an excellent review of this literature, see Peter Lavoy, "The Strategic Consequences of Nuclear Proliferation: A Review Essay," *Security Studies* 4 (Summer 1995): 695–753.

8. In this chapter, the term *military deterrence environment* corresponds with Patrick Morgan's definition of an immediate deterrence environment. See Patrick Morgan, *Deterrence: A Conceptual Approach* (Beverly Hills, Calif.: Sage, 1977), chaps. 1–2.

9. Authors have noted the fact that nuclear weapons can quickly destroy much and through implication that this disadvantages those trying to respond. The concept of contestability makes explicit what, I believe, has been primarily implicit in the works of Bernard Brodie, Kenneth Waltz, and Robert Jervis. See Bernard Brodie, *Strategy in the Missile Age* (Princeton, N.J.: Princeton University Press, 1959); Kenneth Waltz, "Nuclear Myths and Political Realities," *American Political Science Review* 84 (September 1990): 731–45; and Robert Jervis, "The Political

Effects of Nuclear Weapons," *International Security* 13 (Fall 1988): 87. Jervis's explicit discussion tends to focus on how lack of time eliminates possibilities for bargaining. Contestability focuses on how the potential for adapting to the costs of war can undermine deterrence of war and how the inability to contest can enhance it.

10. William T. R. Fox anticipated the relative versus absolute gains debate when he coined the phrase *the absolute weapon:* "When dealing with the absolute weapon, arguments based on relative advantage lose their point." Fox, "International Control of Atomic Weapons," in Brodie, *The Absolute Weapon,* 181. Jervis also noted this connection but focuses primarily on relative assessments of capabilities, rather than gains and losses. *Illogic,* 59–63. Nuclear weapons threaten absolute costs in the sense that differences in the level of destruction after mutual strategic nuclear use are not exploitable and thus of no relative significance.

11. See Geoffrey Blainey, *The Causes of War* (New York: The Free Press, 1973).

12. Richard Ned Lebow, "Windows of Opportunity: Do States Jump through Them?" *International Security* 9 (Summer 1984): 147–86.

13. See Basil Liddell Hart, *Strategy* (New York: Praeger, 1972).

14. Edward Rhodes, *Power and MADness* (New York: Columbia University Press, 1989), chap. 2; Irving Janis and Leon Mann, *Decision-Making: A Psychological Analysis of Conflict* (New York: The Free Press, 1977).

15. For the classic discussion on the "fog of war," see Carl von Clausewitz, *On War* (Princeton, N.J.: Princeton University Press, 1976).

16. See Robert O'Connell, *Of Arms and Men: A History of War, Weapons, and Aggression* (New York: Oxford University Press, 1989); Martin van Crevald, *Technology and War* (New York: The Free Press, 1987); and William H. McNeill, *The Pursuit of Power: Technology, Armed Force and Society* (Chicago: University of Chicago Press, 1982).

17. Lost and damaged planes totaled 730, 463, and 685 in the first three months of 1944, respectively. Edward Luttwak, *Strategy* (Cambridge: Belknap, 1987), 257 n. 16.

18. See summary report of the *Gulf War Air Power Survey* (Washington, D.C.: Office of the Secretary of the Air Force, 1993), in particular 5, 7, 13, 15.

19. General Wafic al Samarrai, former head of Iraqi military intelligence, reported that no Scud launchers were destroyed. American analysis after the war seems to confirm this contention. <http://www.pbs.org/pages/frontline/gulf/oral/samarrai/7.html>

20. Robert Jervis, "Cooperation under the Security Dilemma," *World Politics* 30 (January 1978): 167–214.

21. R. Ernest Dupuy and Trevor Dupuy, *The Encyclopedia of Military History,* 2d ed. (New York: Harper and Row, 1986), 959–60.

22. See Rhodes, *Power and MADness,* chap. 2, esp. 77–81, for discussion of incremental decision making and rationality.

23. Civil defense can make some difference, but ultimately it can be easily overwhelmed. The classic on nuclear civil defense, its promise, and problems is Herman Kahn, *On Thermonuclear War* (Princeton, N.J.: Princeton University Press, 1960). It is important to note that the United States and Russia, with their geographical

size, represent a dispersion of population not seen in most of the rest of the world.

24. One of the problems facing deterrence theorists is the limited empirical base of nuclear deterrence cases. If nuclear and conventional deterrence are fundamentally distinct, then much of the critical empirical literature on deterrence, which is based on conventional cases, may have limited relevance for understanding nuclear deterrence. I examine this argument in detail in "Nuclear Prominence" (unpublished manuscript).

25. Fox, "International Control," 198–203; Michael Howard, "Deterrence and Reassurance," *Foreign Affairs* (Winter 1982–83). For a somewhat critical view, see Richard Ned Lebow and Janice Gross Stein, "Beyond Deterrence," *Journal of Social Issues* 43, 4 (1987): 5–71.

26. Denial of gains can also serve as a basis for dissuasion, but it has been viewed as a weaker form than retaliation. See Glenn Snyder, *Deterrence and Defense* (Princeton, N.J.: Princeton University Press, 1961); Robert Art, "To What Ends Military Power," *International Security* 4 (Spring 1980): 4–35; and Samuel Huntington, "Conventional Deterrence and Conventional Retaliation," *International Security* 8 (Winter 1983–84): 32–56.

27. See Joseph Grieco, "Anarchy and the Limits of Cooperation: A Realist Critique of the Newest Liberal Institutionalism," *International Organization* 42 (Summer 1988): 485–507. For a neoliberal institutionalist clarification, see Robert Keohane and Lisa Martin, "The Promise of Institutionalist Theory," *International Security* 20 (Summer 1995): 39–52.

28. See Stephen Krasner, ed., *International Regimes* (Ithaca, N.Y.: Cornell University Press, 1983); Robert O. Keohane, *After Hegemony: Cooperation and Discord in the World Political Economy* (Princeton, N.J.: Princeton University Press, 1984); and Charles W. Kegley, ed., *Controversies in International Relations Theory: Realism and the Neoliberal Challenge* (New York: St. Martin's Press, 1995).

29. See Kenneth Oye, ed., *Cooperation under Anarchy* (Princeton, N.J.: Princeton University Press, 1986). For an overview of the general debate on cooperation, see David Baldwin, ed., *Neorealism and Neoliberalism: The Contemporary Debate* (New York: Columbia University Press, 1993).

30. For example, see Robert Keohane, *International Institutions and State Power: Essays in International Theory* (Boulder, Colo.: Westview Press, 1989); Arthur Stein, *Why Nations Cooperate: Circumstance and Choice in International Relations* (Ithaca, N.Y.: Cornell University Press, 1990); and Oran Young, *International Cooperation: Building Regimes for Natural Resources and the Environment* (Ithaca, N.Y.: Cornell University Press, 1989). For a recent challenge to this literature, see John Mearsheimer, "The False Promise of International Institutions," *International Security* 19 (Winter 1994–95): 5–49.

31. See in particular Robert Axelrod and Robert Keohane, "Achieving Cooperation under Anarchy," in Oye, *Cooperation under Anarchy*, 226–54.

32. For the classic neorealist perspective, see Kenneth N. Waltz, *Theory of International Politics* (New York: Random House, 1979). Further analysis of the perspective can be found in Robert Keohane, *Neorealism and Its Critics* (New York: Columbia University Press, 1986); and Barry Buzan, Charles Jones, and Richard

Little, *The Logic of Anarchy: Neorealism to Structural Realism* (New York: Columbia University Press, 1993).

33. See John Mearsheimer, "Back to the Future: Instability in Europe after the Cold War," *International Security* 15 (Summer 1990): 5–56; Kenneth Waltz, "The Emerging Structure of International Politics," *International Security* 18 (Fall 1993): 44–79; and, for a broader view, Robert Gilpin, "The Richness of the Tradition of Political Realism," in Keohane, *Neorealism and Its Critics*, 301–21.

34. Waltz, *Theory of International Politics*, 105.

35. Joseph Grieco, "The Relative-Gains Problem for International Cooperation: Comment," *American Political Science Review* 87 (September 1993): 729.

36. Robert Powell, "The Relative-Gains Problem for International Cooperation: Response," *American Political Science Review* 87 (September 1993): 735–37; Robert Powell, "Absolute and Relative Gains in International Relations Theory," *American Political Science Review* 85 (September 1991): 1303–20.

37. Waltz, *Theory of International Politics*, 102–28.

38. See Hans J. Morgenthau, *Politics among Nations: The Struggle for Power and Peace*, 5th ed. (New York: Knopf, 1973); Robert Gilpin, "The Theory of Hegemonic War," in Robert Rotblat and Theodore Rabb, eds., *The Origin and Prevention of Major Wars* (New York: Cambridge University Press, 1989), 15–38; and Kenneth Waltz, "The Origins of War in Neorealist Theory," in Rotblat and Rabb, *Origin and Prevention*, 39–52.

39. Powell, "Absolute and Relative Gains," 1306.

40. Powell notes this in "Absolute and Relative Gains," 1317 n. 5. Waltz suggests that this is the distinction offered, as well as sometimes confused, by Morgenthau. Waltz, *Man, the State, and War: A Theoretical Analysis* (New York: Columbia University Press, 1959), 35–37. The distinction in focus is also noted in the work of John Herz.

41. Grieco, "Comment," 733.

42. Jervis, "Cooperation under the Security Dilemma," 168; Waltz, *Theory of International Politics*, 104–6.

43. I focus on deterrence rather than defense because of the simple fact that no impenetrable defense has ever been created historically. Defense implies a competing offense and focuses on limiting the damage caused by aggression.

44. For a similar assessment, see Keohane and Martin, "Promise of Institutionalist Theory," 44.

45. Mearsheimer, "Back to the Future," 20.

46. For an excellent overview of this literature, see Sean Lynn-Jones, "Offense-Defense Theory and Its Critics," *Security Studies* 4 (Summer 1995): 660–91; Mearsheimer, "False Promise," 22–23, makes a similar assessment of Powell's implicit assumption concerning offensive and defensive weapons.

47. For a more detailed discussion, see Richard J. Harknett, "The Logic of Conventional Deterrence and the End of the Cold War," *Security Studies* 4 (Autumn 1994): 86–114.

48. When asked, "You wanted to see if you could inflict some casualties, a little like Vietnam?" Aziz responded, "Yes, . . . but they withdrew from Khafji, it was

almost vacant...." <http://www.pbs.org/pages/frontline/gulf/oral/aziz/3.html>

49. American Secretary of State James Baker concluded that the Israelis came very close to entering the war. Baker stressed that the United States refused to give the Israeli air force codes that would have helped them distinguish between coalition forces and Iraqi defenders. This presented the risk that the Israelis might mistakenly shoot down an American or allied plane. <http://www.pbs.org/pages/frontline/gulf/oral/baker/2.html>

50. It is interesting to note that Iraq was careful not to cross the conventional threshold by employing its chemical weapons. General Samarrai is quite explicit: "We told [Saddam] very clearly that should he use chemical weapons they will use their nuclear weapons. You saw for yourselves that Iraq used these chemical weapons on Iran because Iran did not have a nuclear deterrent force.... the [deterrent] warning was quite severe and quite effective." <http://www.pbs.org/pages/frontline/gulf/oral/samarrai/7.html, 1.html> Aziz is a bit more subtle: "It was not wise to use such weapons [chemical] in such kind of war, with such an enemy. *Question:* Because they had nuclear weapons? You can make your own conclusions." <aziz/3.html>

51. On war as a mechanism of change and distribution, see Robert Gilpin, *War and Change in World Politics* (Cambridge: Cambridge University Press, 1981), 15. For a more recent nonrealist analysis that views war as an "allocation mechanism," see John A. Vasquez, *The War Puzzle* (New York: Cambridge University Press, 1993), 46.

52. Georg Simmel writes, "to be sure, the most effective presupposition for preventing struggle, the exact knowledge of the comparative strength of the two parties, is very often only to be attained by the actual fighting out of the conflict." "The Sociology of Conflict," part 1, *American Journal of Sociology* 9 (January 1904): 501.

53. Luttwak, *Strategy,* 28.

54. I am indebted to Colin Gray for the phrase *reliability of effect.* See his contribution to this volume for a brief discussion of my argument concerning contestable costs.

55. This issue of credibility was a major focus of the early works on deterrence. See, for example, Thomas C. Schelling, *The Strategy of Conflict* (Cambridge: Harvard University Press, 1960); William W. Kaufmann, ed., *Military Policy and National Security* (Princeton, N.J.: Princeton University Press, 1956); and Morton Kaplan, "The Calculus of Nuclear Deterrence," *World Politics* 11 (October 1958): 20–43. The focus of this work was on political will. The problem with conventional deterrence is that it suffers from a credibility problem concerning capability as well as will.

56. Grieco refers to it as "a low tolerance for risk." "Comment," 734.

57. Joseph Grieco, "Understanding the Problem of International Cooperation: The Limits of Neoliberal Institutionalism and the Future of Realist Theory," in Baldwin, ed., *Neorealism and Neoliberalism,* 314.

58. On the significant difference in framing between loss and gain, see Amos Tversky and Daniel Kahneman, "Choices, Values and Frames," *American Psychologist* 39 (April 1984): 341–50.

59. Central deterrence focuses on the relationship between vital national objectives and the necessity to protect them. Extended deterrence deals with interests beyond what can be considered absolute central interests. Philip Bobbitt, *Democracy and Deterrence: The History and Future of Nuclear Strategy* (New York: St. Martin's Press, 1988), 9. The experience of the Soviet Union is interesting. There was no advantage gained immediately from the possession of nuclear weapons that could save the Soviet Union from internal collapse. However, the influence nuclear possession may have had on the relatively peaceful nature of this collapse of empire and the willingness of adversaries to help rather than exploit the emerging remnant states is worth study.

60. Waltz, *Man, the State, and War,* 198.

61. During the Cold War, there were concerns about windows of vulnerability. Where such windows exist, a MAD condition does not hold. Much of the debate about first strikes from the Soviet Union rested on a conventionalized view of nuclear conflict.

62. See the Clinton administration's *National Security Strategy of Enlargement and Engagement,* July 1994 (Washington, D.C.: GPO, 1994); Office of the Deputy Secretary of Defense, *Report on Nonproliferation and Counterproliferation Activities,* May 1994 (Washington, D.C.: GPO, 1994); Counterproliferation Program Review Committee, *Report on Activities and Programs on Countering Proliferation,* May 1995 (Washington, D.C.: GPO, 1995). The award of the Nobel Peace Prize for 1995 to Joseph Rotblat was made to "encourage world leaders to intensify their efforts to rid the world of nuclear weapons." <http://www.nobel.se/announcement-95/peace.html>

63. See Richard J. Harknett, "Nuclear Weapons and Territorial Integrity," in Ken Dark, ed., *New Studies in Post–Cold War Security* (Brookfield, Vt.: Dartmouth Publishing, 1996), 29–69. The rhetoric of the United States is taken from the normative/moral oppositions to nuclear weapons that advocate complete nuclear disarmament, even though the underlying motivation is pure power politics.

64. For example, see Glenn C. Buchan, *U.S. Nuclear Strategy for the Post–Cold War Era,* Rand MR-420-RC (Santa Monica, Calif.: Rand, 1994). Post–Cold War pursuit of nonproliferation is a natural outgrowth of superpower policy during the Cold War that spent enormous sums of money and intellectual energy attempting to escape the condition of MAD. Their failure to do so might be instructive.

65. Morgenthau, *Politics among Nations,* 3–17. John Lewis Gaddis points to the development of great power mechanisms for deterring aggression during the Cold War. See "Toward the Post-Cold War World," *Foreign Affairs* 70 (Spring 1991); see also Bobbitt, *Democracy and Deterrence.*

66. Waltz, "Emerging Structure," 50–52. William T. R. Fox argued that one of the more difficult hurdles to international control would be convincing great powers to abstain from a great power asset. Fox, "International Control," 169–203.

67. The ability to project social and cultural norms might also be added to a great power capability list. See the idea of "soft power" in Joseph Nye, *Bound to Lead: The Changing Nature of American Power* (New York: Basic Books, 1990).

68. Thucydides, *The Peloponnesian War* (Middlesex, United Kingdom: Penguin Classics, 1985), 402.

69. I use *weak* in the context of capabilities, in particular the capability to extend beyond one's border and defend against attack. For more on the definitional literature on weak states, see Miriam Fendius Elam, "The Foreign Policies of Small States," *British Journal of Political Science* 25 (1995): 171–217.

70. Morgenthau, *Politics among Nations,* 196.

71. Kissinger refers to nuclear weapons as "the great equalizer." Henry Kissinger, "How to Achieve the New World Order," *Time* (14 March 1994): 76.

72. Waltz, "Emerging Structure," 53; Mearsheimer, "Back to the Future," 20.

73. For a discussion of territoriality and the idea of a soft shell of deterrence, see Richard J. Harknett, "Territoriality in the Nuclear Era," in Eleonore Kofman and Gillian Youngs, eds., *Globalization: Theory and Practice* (London: Pinter, 1996), 138–49.

74. John Burns, "Anti-Nuclear Pioneer India Blocks a Test Ban," *New York Times* (17 August 1996), <http://www.nytimes.com/india-nukes.html> 1–4. Indian commentators emphasized the "future threat from China" as the main reason to keep a "nuclear option."

The Escalating Irrelevance of Nuclear Weapons

JOHN MUELLER

It may not be entirely fair to characterize disarmament as an effort to cure a fever by destroying the thermometer.[1] However, insofar as that expression suggests that weapons are more nearly the measure of international tension than its cause, it is instructive and useful. During the Cold War, there were often great international tensions between East and West, and as a result substantial arms were amassed. Among these arms were nuclear weapons, which were so impressive that it was commonly held that they were dominant influences on politics. A generation of theorists, thinkers, strategists, pundits, and politicians, beginning with Bernard Brodie's eloquent essays in *The Absolute Weapon* of 1946, spun out a huge literature about the military potential of nuclear weapons, sometimes justifying or rationalizing their existence, sometimes pointing to the possibilities for catastrophe. Accordingly, we lived, as we were continually told, in the nuclear age, in the atomic era.

When a fever subsides, the instrument designed to measure it loses its usefulness and is often soon misplaced. Hans J. Morgenthau once proclaimed that "men do not fight because they have arms"; rather, "they have arms because they deem it necessary to fight."[2] If that is so, it follows that when countries no longer deem it necessary to fight, they will get rid of their arms. As Winston Churchill put it in a House of Commons speech on July 13, 1934, "It is the greatest possible mistake to mix up disarmament with peace. When you have peace, you will have disarmament." And, on cue, as tensions eased at the end of the Cold War, many of the arms that had struck such deep fear for so long were quietly allowed—as the bumper sticker would have it—to rust in peace. Former enemies have embarked on a negative arms race in which weapons often are abandoned faster than treaty makers can fashion orderly agreements to sanction the abandonment.[3] This interesting development has left many theorists in an intellectual vacuum where their skills seem increasingly out of demand— even to have become quaint and obsolete. Nonetheless, rather than abandoning the enterprise, many have taken the nuclear theories that were so painstakingly developed for a former era and have sought to redevelop and refashion them to fit a new one.

This chapter sketches a set of propositions about the value and historical relevance of nuclear weapons. It allows that they have certainly added a new element to international politics: new pieces for the players to move around the board, new terrors to contemplate. But it seems that, despite all the sound and fury, things would have turned out much the same had nuclear weapons never been invented. In counter to Albert Einstein's famous remark that "the atom has changed everything save our way of thinking,"[4] it seems rather that nuclear weapons changed little except our way of talking, gesturing, and spending money. Nor, it seems, did they have anything to do with the demise of the Cold War.

Moreover, in the wake of the Cold War, it is becoming more difficult to identify the value, importance, and relevance of nuclear weapons. There may be imaginable circumstances under which they could be useful. However, as stockpiles are reduced, as international status becomes determined more by economic and other nonmilitary factors, and as the world becomes dominated by nonthreatening, wealth-seeking countries, nuclear weapons seem to be fading even as an object of discussion as policymakers reorient their perspectives for a new era. Like the thermometer, nuclear weapons have essentially been ancillary or marginal to the main course of international events. In the present era, that seems to be increasingly true.

Nuclear Weapons Have Not Been Necessary to Prevent a Major War

There have been no major wars—wars among developed countries—since 1945, and nuclear weapons have been developed and deployed in part to deter such a conflict. It does not follow, however, that the weapons have prevented the war—that peace has been, in Winston Churchill's memorable construction, the "sturdy child" of nuclear "terror."[5]

Kenneth Waltz suggests that "nuclear weapons have drastically reduced the probability of [a war] being fought by the states that have them."[6] John Mearsheimer notes that nuclear deterrence is "much more robust than conventional deterrence."[7] Robert Jervis stresses that nuclear weapons can cause destruction that is "unimaginably enormous" to *both* sides and can do so extremely quickly.[8] John Lewis Gaddis argues that "the vision of future war that Hiroshima burned into everyone's mind was vastly more frightening than any that had existed before."[9] And Carl Kaysen concludes that "[t]hese new technologies of war have amplified the message of this century's war experiences by many decibels, and set it firmly in the minds of the wide public as well as those of political and military leaders."[10]

Nuclear weapons can do a whole lot of damage extremely quickly. And it is appropriate to compare probabilities and degrees of robustness and to calibrate burning visions or decibel levels. But it is important as well to consider what those levels and degrees were before they were changed. A jump from a fiftieth-story window is more terrifying to think about than a jump from a fifth-story one, and quite a bit more destructive as well; but anyone who finds life even minimally satisfying is readily deterred from either adventure. Nuclear weapons may well have "reinforced an already declining propensity on the part of great powers to fight one another," as Gaddis puts it.[11] But this is similar to the way a $1,000 gift reinforces a millionaire's wealth or a straitjacket reinforces a Quaker's propensity to shun violence. While nuclear weapons may have been *sufficient* to prevent another major war, they have not been *necessary* to do so.[12]

Much of my argument on this score applies a counterfactual approach: if nuclear weapons had never been invented, the history of the postwar world would have come out much the same. But this counterfactual is in response to another, older counterfactual that is implicit in much of the literature about our "atomic age" and "nuclear era." It essentially holds that, because of the bomb, world affairs look a great deal different than they would otherwise. This venerable counterfactual suffers on close examination.

To assert that the ominous presence of nuclear weapons prevented a war between the two power blocs, one must assume that there would have been a war had these weapons not existed. This assumption ignores several important war-discouraging factors in the postwar world: the memory of the Second World War, the general postwar contentment of the victors, the cautious emphasis of Soviet ideology—the chief unsettling element in the postwar world—on lesser kinds of warfare, and the fear of escalation.

The Memory of the Second World War

The people who have been in charge of world affairs since the Second World War have been the same people, or the intellectual heirs of the people, who tried assiduously, frantically, desperately, and, as it turned out, pathetically, to prevent the Second World War. And when, despite their best efforts, world war was forced upon them, they found the experience to be horrible, just as they had anticipated. To expect these people somehow to allow themselves to tumble into anything resembling a repetition of that experience—whether embellished with nuclear weapons or not—seems almost bizarre. Although the people who have been running world politics since 1945 have had plenty of disagreements, they have not been so obtuse, depraved, flaky, or desperate as to need visions of mushroom clouds to conclude that major war, win or lose, could be a distinctly unpleasant experience.

They might be expected to be even *more* hostile to a nuclear war, but for the most part nuclear weapons simply dramatize a military reality that by 1945 had already become appalling: few who experienced the Second World War would contemplate a repetition without horror. Even before the bomb had been perfected, world war had become spectacularly costly and destructive, killing some fifty million worldwide. As former Secretary of State Alexander Haig put it in 1982: "The catastrophic consequences of another world war—with or without nuclear weapons—make deterrence our highest objective and our only rational military strategy."[13]

Postwar Contentment

For many of the combatants, the First World War was as destructive as the second, but its memory did not prevent another world war. Of course, most nations *did* conclude from the horrors of the First World War that such an event must never be repeated: if the only nations capable of starting the Second World War had been Britain, France, the USSR, and the United States, the war would probably never have occurred. Unfortunately, other major nations sought direct territorial expansion, and conflicts over these desires finally led to war.

Unlike the situation after the First World War, however, the only countries capable of creating another world war after 1945 were the big victors, the United States and the Soviet Union, each of which emerged comfortably dominant in its respective sphere: as Waltz has observed, "The United States, and the Soviet Union as well, have more reason to be satisfied with the status quo than most earlier great powers had."[14] While there have been many disputes since the war, neither power has had a grievance so essential as to make a world war—whether nuclear or not—an attractive means for removing the grievance.

Soviet Ideology

Although the Soviet Union, and the international Communist movement, had visions of changing the world in a direction they preferred, their ideology stressed revolutionary procedures over major war. The Soviet Union may have had hegemonic desires, but its tactics, inspired by the cautiously pragmatic Lenin, stressed subversion, revolution, diplomatic and economic pressure, seduction, guerrilla warfare, local uprising, and civil war—levels of conflict at which nuclear weapons have little relevance.[15] The Communist powers never—before and after the invention of nuclear weapons—subscribed to a Hitler-style theory of direct, Armageddon-risking conquest, and they were extremely wary of provoking Western powers into large-scale war.[16] Moreover, if the memory of the Second World War deters anyone, it probably did so to an extreme degree for the Soviets. Officially and unofficially, they seemed obsessed by the memory of the destruction they suffered. In 1953 Ambassador Averell Harriman, certainly no admirer of Stalin, observed that the Soviet dictator "was determined, if he could avoid it, never again to go through the horrors of another protracted world war."[17]

The Belief in Escalation

Those who started the First and Second World Wars did so not because they believed that costly wars of attrition were desirable, but because they thought that escalation to wars of attrition could be avoided. In the First World War, the offensive was believed to be dominant, and it was widely assumed that conflict would be short and decisive. In the Second World War, both Germany and Japan experienced repeated success with bluster, short wars in peripheral areas, and blitzkrieg, augmented by the counterproductive effects of their opponents' appeasement and inaction.[18]

As suggested above, military deterrence was probably not necessary to prevent a major war during the Cold War: while hostile to each other, no contestant ever saw war—whether nuclear or not—as a sensible way to carry out its policy. However, to the degree that military deterrence was helpful, world war in the post-1945 era has been prevented not so much by visions of nuclear horror as by the generally accepted belief that conflict can easily escalate to a level, nuclear or not, that the essentially satisfied major powers would find intolerably costly.

The notion that it is the fear of nuclear war that has kept behavior restrained looks far less convincing when its underlying assumption is directly confronted: the rather preposterous notion that the major countries would have allowed their various crises to escalate if all they had to fear at the end of the escalatory ladder was a sweet little exercise like the Second World War. Whatever the rhetoric in these crises, it is difficult to see why the unaugmented horror of repeating the Second World War, combined with a considerable comfort with the status quo, would not have been enough to inspire restraint. What deters under these circumstances is the belief that escalation to something intolerable will occur, not so much the details of the ultimate unbearable punishment. Where the belief that the conflict will escalate is absent, nuclear countries *have* been militarily challenged with war—as in Korea, Vietnam, the Middle East, Afghanistan, Algeria, and the Falklands.

This is not meant to deny that the sheer horror of nuclear war is impressive or mind-concentratingly dramatic, particularly in the speed with which it could bring about massive destruction. Nor is it meant to deny that decision makers, both in times of crisis and otherwise, have been fully conscious of how horribly destructive a nuclear war could be. It is simply to stress that the sheer horror of repeating the Second World War is not all that much less impressive or dramatic, and that powers essentially satisfied with the status quo will strive to avoid anything that they believe could lead to *either* calamity. The Second World War did not cause total destruction in the world, but it did utterly annihilate the three national regimes that brought it about. People remember things like that.[19]

Nuclear Weapons Did Not Notably Affect the Demise of the Cold War

The Cold War ended primarily because of a change of ideas. Weaponry, including nuclear weaponry, had little to do with it. In the late 1980s, the Soviet Union abandoned its threateningly expansionary ideology. Its love affair with revolution in the advanced capitalist world, frustrated for decades, ceased to have even theological relevance, and its venerable and once-visceral attachment to revolution and to "wars of national liberation" in the Third World no longer even inspired much lip service. As Francis Fukuyama has observed, "the role of ideology in defining Soviet foreign policy objectives and in providing political instruments for expansion has been steadily declining in the postwar period," and Mikhail Gorbachev "further accelerated that decline."[20]

In 1986, Gorbachev began undercutting Communist ideology about the "class struggle" and about the Soviet Union's "internationalist duty" as the leader of world socialism.[21] By 1988, the Soviets were admitting the "inadequacy of the thesis that peaceful coexistence is a form of class struggle" and began referring to the "world socialist system" or the "socialist community of nations" rather than to the "socialist camp."[22] The Kremlin's chief ideologist explicitly rejected the notion that a world struggle was going on between capitalism and communism.[23] Then, in a major speech in December 1988, Gorbachev called for "de-ideologizing relations among states" and, while referring to the Communist revolution in Russia as "a most precious spiritual heritage," proclaimed that "today we face a different world, from which we must seek a different road to the future."[24] Most impressively, by February 1989, Gorbachev had matched deeds to words by removing Soviet troops from Afghanistan.[25]

The United States was quick to react favorably. The possibility emerged that the United States and the Soviet Union could again become allies as they were during the Second World War. In December 1988, in his last presidential press conference, Ronald Reagan was specifically asked about this, and, stressing the ideological nature of the contest, he responded: "If it can be definitely established that they no longer are following the expansionary policy that was instituted in the Communist revolution, that their goal must be a one-world Communist state . . . [then] they might want to join the family of nations and join them with the idea of bringing about or establishing peace."[26] Six months later (but still before the East European changes) his successor, George Bush, was urging in a series of speeches that "it is now time to move beyond containment to a new policy" to "seek the integration of the Soviet Union into the community of nations."[27]

With these changes—which took place *before* the unexpected disintegration of the Soviet empire in Eastern Europe and long before the crumbling of the Soviet Union itself—the structure of world politics changed profoundly: the Cold War evaporated. The *New York Times* editorially proclaimed on April 2, 1989, that the Cold War was over, and on May 24 the *Wall Street Journal* added, "We won!" Later in the year, even staunchly anti-Communist commentators were agreeing: the Cold War was indeed "coming to an end. . . . The Soviet leaders have for all intents and purposes given up the ideological struggle. . . . [They] have retreated from the basic doctrine of international class struggle—the doctrine that gave rise to the Cold War in the first place."[28]

Thus, the key element in the demise of the Cold War derived from changes in ideas. Nuclear weapons were irrelevant to the process. Indeed, about the only thing that *did not* change very much at the time was the balance of weaponry, particularly the supposedly crucial nuclear weaponry, arrayed on both sides.[29]

Nuclear Proliferation Is Not Inevitable

Over the last half century, alarmists about nuclear proliferation have not shown a great deal of prescience. In 1958 the National Planning Association predicted "a rapid rise in the number of atomic powers . . . by the mid-1960s."[30] A couple of years later, C. P. Snow sagely predicted that "[w]ithin, at the most, six years, China and several other states [will] have a stock of nuclear bombs";[31] and John Kennedy observed that there might be "ten, fifteen, twenty" countries with a nuclear capacity by 1964.[32] Britain's sometime defense minister, Denis Healey, remarked at the time that "[s]o far, no country has resisted the temptation to make its own atomic weapons once it has acquired the physical ability to do so."[33] British defense commentator F. W. Mulley observed: "All the arguments which led Britain to decide to develop her own independent nuclear weapons are equally valid . . . for France herself, and there is no reason why other members of NATO should not decide to follow suit."[34]

Many assumed that nuclear weapons would continue to be important status—or virility—symbols and therefore that all advanced countries would want to have them to show how "powerful" they were. Thus, France's de Gaulle opined in 1965, "No country without an atom bomb could properly consider itself independent,"[35] and Robert Gilpin concludes that "the possession of nuclear weapons largely determines a nation's rank in the hierarchy of international prestige."[36] In Gilpinian tradition, some analysts who describe themselves as "realists" insist that Germany and Japan must soon surely come to their senses and quest after nuclear weapons.[37]

These observers extrapolate from the wrong cases. A more pertinent prototype would have been Canada, a country that could easily have had nuclear weapons by the 1960s but declined to make the effort.[38] Indeed, one of the most interesting developments in the postwar world has been the slow pace with which nuclear weapons have proliferated. In fact, several nations—Brazil, Argentina, South Africa, South Korea, and Taiwan—have actually backed away from or reversed nuclear weapons programs.[39] Some of this is no doubt due to the hostility of the nuclear nations, but the Canadian case seems to have general relevance.

As Stephen Meyer has shown, there is no "technological imperative" for countries to obtain nuclear weapons once they have achieved the technical capacity to do so.[40] Insofar as countries have considered acquiring the weapons, many came, like Canada, to appreciate several problems: the weapons are dangerous, distasteful, and costly. If one values economic growth and prosperity, the sensible thing is to avoid the weapons unless they seem vital for security.

Moreover, like military prowess in general, the weapons have *not* proved to be crucial status symbols. States like India, China, and Israel have not increased their general prestige. What, after all, is the value of the weapons? What problems would such an expensive venture solve? How much more status would Japan have if it possessed nuclear weapons? Would anybody pay a great deal more attention to Britain or France if they possessed 50,000 nuclear weapons, or would anybody pay much less if they possessed none? Does anybody even remember anymore whether China has nuclear weapons?

When France exploded its first bomb in 1960, President Charles de Gaulle was jubilant: "Hoorah for France!" he bellowed, "Since this morning she is stronger and prouder."[41] But de Gaulle had several hang-ups about status; today, most countries can obtain status in other ways, and the costs and travails of nuclear ownership only hamper that process.[42] When de Gaulle's successors carried out a modest set of underground nuclear tests in the Pacific in 1995 and 1996, their actions mainly attracted international disgust, condemnation, and outrage (as well as economic boycotts), not admiration or awe.

At best, nuclear weapons seem to have only a kind of "naughty child" effect: nuclear behavior can attract notice. Thus, North Korea can get people to pay more attention to it by developing a bomb than if it doesn't, and Russia's nuclear arsenal perhaps causes people to be concerned about its destiny more than they would if it had no bombs. But this phenomenon hardly generates real status or respect, and it is nothing compared to the kind of respect either country would attract if it were to become an important player in the international economy.[43]

The Minimal Usefulness of Nuclear Weapons

Nuclear weapons have not been very important thus far in shaping the course of international history. However, there are imaginable circumstances under which it might be useful to have nuclear weapons around, such as the rise in a major country of another lucky, clever, risk-acceptant, aggressive fanatic like Hitler. Thus, even if one concludes that nuclear weapons have not been necessary to preserve peace, it might still make sense to have some for added insurance against severe anachronism. Insofar as a military deterrent was necessary, the fear of another Second World War has been quite sufficient (indeed, more than sufficient, I expect) for the *particular countries* that have actually existed since 1945. But it does not follow that fear alone could prevent all imaginable wars. Why didn't Israel's nuclear weapons keep the Arabs from attacking in 1973? Why didn't Britain's prevent Argentina's seizure of the Falklands in 1982? Why didn't fear of the tens of thousands of nuclear weapons in the hands of the enveloping allied forces cause Saddam Hussein to order his occupying forces out of Kuwait in 1990? What good, after all, are they?

Central to all this is the issue of escalation. If a would-be aggressor thinks a move might very well escalate to something terrible like a world war (with or without nuclear weapons), caution is likely to ensue. Where that fear is lacking, war can come about. Waltz argues that "contemplating war when the use of nuclear weapons is possible focuses one's attention not on the probability of victory but on the possibility of annihilation. . . . The problem of the credibility of deterrence, a big worry in a conventional world, disappears in a nuclear one."[44] But when the Argentines launched military action against the interests of the nuclear-armed United Kingdom in 1982, they obviously knew that British nuclear retaliation was possible, yet they clearly did not find it credible that the war could escalate to this level.[45]

As this suggests, the belief in escalation may often be something of a myth. The Cuban missile crisis suggests that the major countries during the Cold War were remarkably good at carrying out—and working out—their various tangles and disagreements far below the level of major war.[46] I think the trends with respect to major war are very favorable.[47] However, since peace could be shattered by an appropriately fanatical, hyperskilled, and anachronistic leader who is willing and able to probe those parameters of restraint, it would be sensible to maintain vigilance. Still, as Robert Jervis has pointed out, "Hitlers are very rare."[48] It may be sensible to hedge against the danger, but that does not mean the danger is a very severe one.

As for lesser Hitlers—comparatively small-time aggressors—it is conceivable that nuclear weapons could sometimes have a beneficially deterring effect. It seems unlikely that Saddam Hussein would have invaded Khomeini's Iran in 1980 if the fanatical Iranian religious leader had had a few nuclear weapons at his disposal, and perhaps a repeat of that sort of circumstance can be imagined somewhere in the future. And, since they had a very low tolerance for casualties, it seems unlikely that the Americans and their allies would have attacked Iraqi forces in the Gulf War of 1991 if there had been a danger that a nuclear weapon or two would have been lobbed on them—particularly when there was another method, sanctions, to pressure Hussein to leave Kuwait. Whether a Kuwaiti bomb could have prevented Hussein's invasion of 1990 is more questionable. Iraq quickly took the country over and essentially held the entire Kuwaiti population hostage.

Some suggest that nuclear weapons might be useful to deter annihilation or even turn the war around when a country is going down to defeat in a conventional war—something like the position British strategists apparently assigned to gas in the Second World War.[49] For example, if an invasion by Arabs were leading to the eradication of Israel, the idea would be that the Israelis could prevent this by threatening a nuclear attack on Cairo, Damascus, Baghdad, or somewhere. The problem is that, by the time it came to considering "last resorts," the use of nuclear weapons could easily become patently suicidal. Even if the winners did not have nuclear weapons of their own with which to retaliate, they would be able, because of their winning position, credibly to counterthreaten that any nuclear explosions would be met with massacres of enemy civilians under their control: they would have hostages.

Therefore, although there may be some imaginable circumstances under which nuclear weapons could have value, these scenarios tend to be rather strained. Moreover, with the possible exception of the curious events surrounding the Yom Kippur War of 1973, there has been no clear militarized crisis among major countries since 1962. And conventional international wars between India and Pakistan and between Israel and the Arab states, once so common, have been absent from the world scene for decades. Indeed, international wars are quite rare: most armed conflicts—including ones currently taking place—are civil wars. Dropping a nuclear bomb on one's neighbor doesn't make a great deal of sense. Civil wars do not usually present military targets that might make nuclear weapons very helpful, although a nuclear attack on an enemy city could appeal to an appropriately fanatical leader as the ultimate in ethnic cleansing.

Foreign Policy and the Irrelevance of Nuclear Weapons

The general approach of most of the discussion so far has been essentially negative: nuclear weapons have not had this or that sort of consequence. It may be useful now to approach the issue positively and to sketch out what seems to be the shape of an emerging set of policy principles guiding major countries. Policy after the Cold War, like policy during it, will be improvised from issue to issue and from crisis to crisis; but by actions more than by explicit policy pronouncements, the United States and its major allies are developing a set of guiding policies that are at least as coherent and consensual as anything found during the Cold War.[50] Nuclear weapons, as it happens, scarcely matter to any of them.

Confront Major Immediate Problems with Determination and Dispatch

The principle of rapidly responding to international challenges is hypothetical. In fact, our era is most extraordinary: if we apply conventional standards, there are today no major immediate problems or threats. Militarily, the developed counties are wallowing in stability; a war between Russia and the United States is about as likely as one between the United States and Canada. Indeed, in the last few years the world has retreated so far from "doomsday" that the word, once so fashionable (remember those scorpions in a bottle?), has picked up a patina of quaintness. There remain minor immediate problems and major long-range problems, but no major immediate ones.

Seek Wealth

The absence of major immediate problems makes it possible to luxuriate in the quest for economic prosperity. Historically, this is a remarkable change. Increasingly, countries have prosperity as their central goal, and status derives from economic prowess, not from empire, military capacity, or triumph in war. By contrast, Leo Tolstoy observed in *War and Peace* in 1869 that "[a]ll historians agree that the external activity of states and nations in their conflicts with one another is expressed in wars, and that as a direct result of greater or less success in war the political strength of states and nations increases or decreases." But today, militarily unimpressive Japan and Germany, the big *losers* in the last war, today enjoy great "political strength"—even, of course, without nuclear weapons.[51]

The concept of leadership may undergo significant evisceration as the pursuit of wealth becomes a dominant motivation in world affairs. Continental Airlines at one time enjoyed "price leadership" in the industry but registered poor profits—something unlikely to impress stockholders. The United States is still overwhelmingly the world leader by almost any conventional standard, yet it has sometimes been consumed with a jealousy of follower Japan that approaches paranoia. In principle, pure economic actors do not care about influence or prestige. They care about getting rich. (Admittedly, as Japan has found, influence, status, and prestige tend to accompany the accumulation of wealth, but this is just an ancillary effect.) Suppose the president of a company could choose between two stories to tell the stockholders. One message would be, "We enjoy great status, prestige, and influence in the industry. When we talk, everybody listens. Our profits are nil." The other would be, "No one in the industry pays the slightest attention to us or ever asks our advice. We are, in fact, the butt of jokes in the trade. We are making money hand over fist." There is no doubt about which story would most thoroughly warm the stockholders' hearts. Moreover, it is not clear what benefits "leadership" or "primacy" bring. If it means a country must be the first to risk lives and capital for a venture of little importance to it, leadership is clearly of questionable value.

Chip Away Judiciously at Major Problems

There are two concerns in carrying out the principle of incrementally responding to enduring international issues: identifying what the major long-term problems are and doping out plausible solutions. Both tasks are tricky. In my view, the most important long-term concern today is helping to guide Russia and China toward international good citizenship. After the Second World War, Germany and Japan were converted from violent and intensely destructive enemies into prosperous friends, allies, and peaceful competitors whose perspective on the world is now similar to that of the Western victors. As policies go, this may well be among the greatest triumphs of enlightened self-interest in history, and there is a broad consensus that it is important now to do the same thing for Russia and China. No one knows exactly how to do this, of course, but policy agonies are made easier by the fact that, as with Germany and Japan, the Russians and the Chinese will have to do most of the work themselves.

There are other long-range problems that are held to be of major concern: for example, nuclear proliferation, international terrorism, pollution, global warming, migration, ethnic conflict, population growth, religious fundamentalism, and unemployment caused by rampant robotics. These bear watching. Perhaps it also is not a complete waste of money for the Defense Intelligence Agency to study the rapid growth of the water hyacinth in Africa's Lake Victoria on the grounds that the plant can kill fish, leading in turn to a famine that might somehow threaten "global security."[52] But how crucial many such concerns are is open to question. As Calvin Coolidge is alleged to have observed, when you see ten problems coming down the road, you can be pretty sure nine of them will wind up in the ditch before they reach you.[53]

Thus, pundits have been emptily heralding the supposed dangers of overpopulation for some 2,000 years. Global warmers are now arguing that the phenomenon will raise the sea level by one-tenth of an inch per year, making it a notable annoyance in about 600 years (during which time, presumably, one can fill a rather large number of sandbags).[54] And whatever happened to that Latin American debt crisis that inspired so much hand-wringing a while back? Remember those two winters in the early 1990s during which the population of Russia was supposed to starve to death? What of those famines that were going to engulf the globe in the 1970s? How about those many wars that were supposed to spread south, east, and north from the ones in Croatia and Bosnia? What about all those resources that were supposed to be exhausted unrenewably by the 1990s? And what about that nuclear war over the Crimea that was supposed to take place between Russia and Ukraine?

A few years ago, we were being urged that "economics is the continuation of war by other means," and Japan was said to be on the verge of a veritable takeover of the American economy.[55] This concern has been muted now as Japan's economy has gone into retreat and as incautious Japanese firms find themselves saddled with American properties worth half what they foolishly paid for them.

Another problem that alarmed many just a few years ago was the apparent rise in extreme nationalism in Central and Eastern Europe. But, while still a valid concern, hypernationalism seems to have been notably reduced recently in many places—even, it seems, in Serbia, where a policy of essentially cutting off the Bosnian Serbs has found few public opponents. Hypernationalism was dangerous only if it had some real demagogic appeal. It did for a while, but—perhaps—no longer.[56]

As noted earlier, by the standards raised by doomsayers, nuclear proliferation has been astoundingly slow. But it is natural that people whose life revolves around international affairs should strain to generate things to worry about as general interest in foreign policy sags. And, since the danger associated with nuclear weapons proliferation still generates reaction, it gets big play and occasionally inspires notice by the public and by policymakers.[57] Thus, we have been worrying now about what would happen if a terrorist got a bomb ever since nuclear weapons became small enough—*in the 1950s*—for this to become a possibility. It is perhaps inconvenient for this point of view that the number of Americans killed by international terrorists is quite a bit smaller than the number killed by lightning, and that the number of international terrorist incidents has been in decline for a decade.[58] Nonetheless, worry, even alarm, can still be inspired by easily imagined but unlikely developments.

Also notable is the fear generated when an unstable rogue state like North Korea seems about to get nuclear weapons. We would all prefer, I suspect, that North Korea not get the bomb, but it is not entirely clear that all the hysteria about the subject is justified. Apart from possibly deterring an attack from South Korea, an eventuality that hardly seems likely, the advantage that would accrue to the North Koreans from owning a nuclear weapon is not terribly obvious. To start a war or to lob their bomb on Seoul to send some sort of message would be suicidal. James Blight and David Welch argue that Fidel Castro may have been in an appropriately suicidal frame of mind during the Cuban missile crisis,[59] and so some degree of concern on this score may be justified. But we are clearly dealing with very remote conditions in this case—indeed, as Blight and Welch stress, Castro advocated a nuclear attack not preemptively or casually, but only if his island were invaded.

As long as nuclear weapons exist, we can also continue to worry about an accident.[60] We have been doing that for quite a while now. In a speech published in 1961, C. P. Snow grandly and sagely predicted that some nuclear bombs would go off by 1970 ("I am saying this as responsibly as I can; *that* is the certainty"),[61] and he was hardly the first. At the time, we had all that hysteria about accidents that led to such movies as

Fail Safe and the wonderful *Dr. Strangelove*. And then we went through it all over again for several years in the mid-1980s after the publication of such tracts as Jonathan Schell's *The Fate of the Earth*. Accidents do and can happen, of course, but the remarkably long record of nuclear weapons safety does suggest that they are far from inevitable. Moreover, an accident, nuclear or otherwise, need not necessarily lead to bigger things like war—indeed, wars do not seem to come about by accident.[62]

Facilitate Transitions to the Developed World

When a less developed country gets its act together and can make a constructive contribution, leading states often work to facilitate its transition into the developed world. Although there has been much talk about potential conflicts between "North and South" or between "the West and the rest,"[63] the wealthy countries of the world do not run an exclusive club. On the contrary, they have shown a considerable willingness not only to admit new members, but to expend resources to assist in the transition. It is to everybody's advantage that South Korea has come from devastation to productivity and growing prosperity. As South Korea and others like it (such as Mexico, Chile, Argentina, Taiwan, Singapore, and Thailand) advance, they have been welcomed into the ranks of prosperous states. Once they arrive, the developed countries—as the United States has recently shown with Mexico—will often spend money and take risks to help keep them there.

Seek Cooperation

Most day-to-day press attention has been focused on knotty immediate problems that are rather minor from the perspective of the major countries—though not, of course, from the perspective of those who are in the midst of them. For such concerns, policymakers and the public seem to be following the principle of acting when costs are low and prospects for gain are high. Whereas cooperation was extremely difficult to bring about during the Cold War because East and West were locked in an intensely competitive struggle, all sides now have a strong incentive in most places to cooperate to generate peace and stability. Thus, the major countries are free as never before to work together to establish an orderly and productive world. The curiosity is that, whereas they found during the Cold War that almost every place in the world was important as an arena of conflict, they are now unable to see that many areas are of much importance at all.

As a case in point, the mission to Somalia helped bring a degree of order to a deadly situation that was causing a major famine, and credible estimates of lives saved range into the hundreds of thousands. The economic cost of this international mission has been put at $2 billion, and some scores of peacekeepers lost their lives in the process. A carefully calibrated comparison would be difficult, but it seems likely that never in human history has so much been done for so many at such little cost. Yet this spectacular success is remembered, particularly in the United States, as a failure. This is chiefly because of an incident in October 1993 in which a mission went awry and some eighteen Americans (and 300 Somalis) lost their lives in a daylong firefight. The reaction of American politicians and the American public to this misguided episode is instructive: the political demand rose to pull U.S. troops out of Somalia. In essence, when Americans asked themselves how many American lives it was worth to save hundreds of thousands of Somali lives, the answer came out rather close to zero.

The general reluctance to become involved in the actual fighting in Bosnia, despite years of the supposed "CNN effect," suggests that Americans reached a similar conclusion for that trouble spot—as have the British, French, Canadians, and others in their own terms.[64] Since they could not figure out a way to police the situation at an acceptably low cost in lives, the big countries fairly successfully sought to isolate the conflict to keep it from spreading, particularly to the north. The reluctance to intervene should not be seen as some sort of new isolationist impulse. Americans were willing, at least at the outset, to send troops to die in Korea and Vietnam, but that was because they subscribed to the containment notion holding communism to be a genuine threat to the United States that needed to be stopped wherever it was advancing. Polls from the time make it clear they had little interest in losing American lives simply to help out the besieged South Koreans or South Vietnamese.[65] Thus, an unwillingness to send Americans to die for purposes that are essentially humanitarian—even when promoted as advancing democracy or freedom—is hardly new. There is not now, and never has been, much political will among nonthreatened wealth-seeking countries to send troops to lose their lives refereeing deadly quarrels in distant and essentially unimportant arenas. That reality sets limits to such interventions, but it does not necessarily make them impossible or paralyze policy.

Samuel Huntington has challenged critics of his notion that the central dynamic of world politics will be a "clash of civilizations" to produce "a better explanation for what is going on in the world."[66] One that suggests itself is Thomas Friedman's observation in a *New York Times* column[67] that the world is being divided into forward-looking states like Japan, which produce superb products like the Lexus automobile, and backward-looking ones like Serbia, which fight over who owns which cherry tree. The Lexus builders of the world are willing to spend money and a very small number of lives to help the cherry-tree battlers settle their disputes; but they are determined, failing coherent resolution of these disputes, to contain and isolate such conflicts while they continue pursuing their primary goal in life—to become even richer. The role nuclear weapons play in all this is minor at best.

Conclusion

The declining importance of nuclear weapons conceivably poses terminal problems for "realism," insofar as anybody can figure out what realism is. The concept of power has been at the center of realist theorizing about international affairs, particularly after Morgenthau grandly declared in 1948 that "international politics, like all politics, is a struggle for power."[68] Morgenthau defines "power" as "man's control over the minds and actions of others,"[69] while realist Kenneth Waltz offers "the old and simple notion that an agent is powerful to the extent that he affects others more than they affect him."[70] In the international context, the use of the word *power* tends to imply military strength.[71] And in our era, that obviously implies nuclear weapons. Morgenthau and Waltz make the connection quite explicit. "The dependence of national power upon military preparedness," declares Morgenthau without much elaboration, "is too obvious to need much elaboration."[72] Because of the "weight" of American "capabilities," observes Waltz, "American actions have tremendous impact."[73] The notion that a disarmed country could possess great "power" is all but inconceivable under these patterns of thought. As Robert Art and Waltz conclude, "the seriousness of a state's fundamental intentions is conveyed fundamentally by its having a credible military posture. Without it, a state's diplomacy generally lacks effectiveness."[74]

But if "power" essentially means "influence" or "status," contemporary Japan has become a "powerful" state as discussed above. It happens to have rather substantial "self-defense forces," but it is not respect for these forces that makes Japan's diplomacy effective, gives it weight in world affairs, or allows it to "set the scene of action for others," in Waltz's expression.[75] Thus, international developments have undermined a key component of realist theory. Although nuclear weapons seem unlikely to be of any greater relevance in our newly transformed world than they were in the old one, their gradual diminution in numbers could conceivably supply one notable benefit. Asked at the 1992 meeting of the Midwest Political Science Association "What would happen if Ukraine were to give up nuclear weapons?" hyperrealist John Mearsheimer responded, "That would be a tremendous blow to realist theory." I suspect, however, that nuclear weapons won't have much of an impact even here. More likely, realism will rebound by cleverly rolling with the punch, as it has done so often in the past.

This is greatly facilitated by the fact that no one really, deep down, seems to know what realism actually *is*. Richard Lieber, in a valiant attempt to define realism with some degree of precision, argues that realists believe three propositions: "states exist in an international system without an authority to provide order; this 'self-help' system creates imperatives that shape foreign policy behavior, especially in security matters, and sometimes in other realms; conflicts, which are inevitable in human affairs, and for which externally devised solutions are unavailable, have the potential for erupting into violence and war."[76] If that is what realism is all about, it would appear that everyone from St. Francis to Attila the Hun is a realist. Indeed, Charles Glaser[77] would presumably go out of his way to welcome St. Francis to the fold, since he finds that realism can, after all, imply cooperation rather than conflict and distrust.[78] This is in distinction to Mearsheimer's argument that, in our terrible condition of anarchy, "there is little room for trust among states" and "security will often be scarce,"[79] or to the declarations of realists Robert Art and Kenneth Waltz that international politics tends toward "pure coercion," that "no state can confidently rely on the goodwill of other states over the long term," that "trust is hard to come by," that "all states all of the time must make provisions for their defense," that statesmen "must be short-sighted," that states "cannot afford to be moral," that "military power is necessary for survival," and that states "need force" because "they cannot get along without it."[80]

Two analysts who claim to be applying a realist approach to the Japanese case come to opposite conclusions. Huntington argues that, even though it has no important military capability, Japan is seeking to "maximize its power"—and has become an alarming threat to U.S. "primacy"—by accepting "all the assumptions of realism" but applying "them purely in the economic realm."[81] Christopher Layne, by contrast, concludes that Japan cannot today be considered a great power because it lacks "the requisite military capabilities, especially strategic nuclear arsenals"; he confidently predicts, however, that Japan will soon "acquire the full spectrum of great power capabilities, including nuclear weapons"[82]—a notion that may come as a surprise to many Japanese.[83]

Realism seems to be infinitely malleable and may actually prove to be quite a bit like nuclear weaponry. Although fundamentally irrelevant, both will likely remain with us forever as nagging irritants.

NOTES

1. William E. Rappard, *The Quest for Peace since the World War* (Cambridge: Harvard University Press, 1940), 490.
2. Hans J. Morgenthau, *Politics among Nations: The Struggle for Power and Peace* (New York: Knopf, 1948), 327.
3. Something similar happened with the once-rancorous rivalry between the United States and British Canada. John Mueller, *Quiet Cataclysm: Reflections on the Recent Transformation of World Politics* (New York: HarperCollins, 1995), chap. 3.
4. Albert Einstein, *Einstein on Peace,* ed. Otto Nathan and Heinz Norden (New York: Simon and Schuster, 1960), 426.
5. Some of this discussion updates and reformulates arguments made in John Mueller, "The Bomb's Pretense as Peacemaker," *Wall Street Journal* (4 June 1985): 32; "The Essential Irrelevance of Nuclear Weapons: Stability in the Postwar World," *International Security* 13 (Fall 1988): 55–79; *Retreat from Doomsday: The Obsolescence of Major War* (New York: Basic Books, 1989); and *Quiet Cataclysm.* It also deals with some of the counterarguments made to my perspective by Robert Jervis, "The Political Effects of Nuclear Weapons," *International Security* 13 (Fall 1988): 28–38; Carl Kaysen, "Is War Obsolete?" *International Security* 14 (Spring 1990): 42–64; John J. Mearsheimer, "Back to the Future: Instability in Europe after the Cold War," *International Security* 15 (Summer 1990): 5–56; John Lewis Gaddis, *The United States and the Cold War: Implications, Reconsiderations, Provocations* (New York: Oxford University Press, 1992); and Godfried van Benthem van dem Bergh, *The Nuclear Revolution and the End of the Cold War* (London: Macmillan, 1992). On some of these issues, see also John A. Vasquez, "The Deterrence Myth: Nuclear Weapons and the Prevention of Nuclear War," in Charles W. Kegley, Jr., ed., *The Long Postwar Peace: Contending Explanations and Projections* (New York: HarperCollins, 1991), 205–23; and Evan Luard, *War in International Society* (New Haven, Conn.: Yale University Press, 1986), 396.
6. Kenneth N. Waltz, "Nuclear Myths and Political Realities," *American Political Science Review* 84 (September 1990): 731–45.
7. Mearsheimer, "Back to the Future," 31.
8. Jervis, "Political Effects," 31–36.
9. Gaddis, *The United States and the Cold War,* 109.
10. Kaysen, "Is War Obsolete?" 61.
11. Gaddis, *The United States and the Cold War,* 108.
12. This formulation derives from Carl Kaysen, Robert S. McNamara, and George W. Rathjens, "Nuclear Weapons after the Cold War," *Foreign Affairs* 70 (Fall 1991): 95–110.
13. *New York Times* (7 April 1982). See also Michael Mandelbaum's comment in a book that in this respect has a curious title, *The Nuclear Revolution:* "The tanks and artillery of the Second World War, and especially the aircraft that reduced Dresden and Tokyo to rubble might have been terrifying enough by themselves to

keep the peace between the United States and the Soviet Union." Mandelbaum, *The Nuclear Revolution* (Cambridge: Cambridge University Press, 1981), 21. And, of course, given weapons advances, a full-scale *conventional* third world war could be expected to be even more destructive than the Second World War.

14. Kenneth N. Waltz, *Theory of International Politics* (Reading, Mass.: Addison-Wesley, 1979), 190; see also Joseph S. Nye Jr., "Nuclear Learning and U.S.-Soviet Security Regimes," *International Organization* 41 (Summer 1987): 377.

15. The chief exception to this seems to be the Korean War, a limited military probe that got out of hand and was never tried again. See Mueller, *Retreat from Doomsday,* chap. 6.

16. At a conference of the Nuclear History Program in Washington, D.C., in September 1990, Georgy Kornienko, a member of the Soviet foreign ministry since 1947, said he was "absolutely sure" the Soviets would never have initiated a major war even in a non-nuclear world. The weapons, he thought, were an "additional factor" or "supplementary," and "not a major reason." In his memoirs, Nikita Khrushchev is quite straightforward about the issue: "We've always considered war to be against our own interests"; he says he "never once heard Stalin say anything about preparing to commit aggression against another [presumably major] country"; and "we Communists must hasten" the "struggle" against capitalism "by any means at our disposal, *excluding war."* Strobe Talbott, ed., *Khrushchev Remembers: The Last Testament* (Boston: Little, Brown, 1974), 511, 533, 531 (emphasis in the original). The Soviets have always been concerned about wars launched *against* them by a decaying capitalist world, but after 1935 at the latest, they held such wars to be potentially avoidable because of Soviet military strength and because of international working class solidarity. Frederick S. Burin, "The Communist Doctrine of the Inevitability of War," *American Political Science Review* 57 (June 1963): 339. For the argument that the Soviets never contemplated, much less planned for, "a military offensive against the West," see Stephen E. Ambrose, "Secrets of the Cold War," *New York Times* (27 December 1990): A19. For a study stressing the Soviet Union's "cautious opportunism" in the Third World, see Stephen T. Hosmer and Thomas W. Wolfe, *Soviet Policy and Practice toward Third World Countries* (Lexington, Mass.: Lexington Books, 1983).

17. *Newsweek* (16 March 1953): 31. The Soviets presumably picked up a few things from the First World War as well; as Taubman notes, they learned the "crucial lesson . . . that world war . . . can destroy the Russian regime." William Taubman, *Stalin's American Policy* (New York: Norton, 1982), 11.

18. Hitler, however, may have anticipated (or at any rate was planning for) a total war once he had established his expanded empire—a part of his grand scheme he carefully kept from military and industrial leaders who he knew would find it unthinkable. See R. J. Overy, "Hitler's War and the German Economy: A Reinterpretation," *Economic History Review* 35 (May 1982): 272–91. The Japanese did not want a major war, but they were willing to risk it when their anticipated short war in China became a lengthy, enervating one, and they were forced to choose between wider war and the abandonment of the empire to which they were ideo-

logically committed. See Robert J. C. Butow, *Japan's Decision to Surrender* (Stanford, Calif.: Stanford University Press), chap. 11.

19. See also McGeorge Bundy, "The Unimpressive Record of Atomic Diplomacy," in Gwyn Prins, ed., *The Nuclear Crisis Reader* (New York: Vintage, 1984), 42–54; and *Danger and Survival: Choices about the Bomb in the First Fifty Years* (New York: Random House, 1988). For arguments that nuclear weapons did not cause the bipolar structure of the postwar world, see Mueller, *Quiet Cataclysm*, 70–71.

20. Francis Fukuyama, "Patterns of Soviet Third World Policy," *Problems of Communism* 36 (September–October 1987): 12.

21. Dan Oberdorfer, *The Turn: From the Cold War to a New Era* (New York: Touchstone, 1992), 158–64.

22. David Binder, "Soviet and Allies Shift on Doctrine," *New York Times* (25 May 1988): A13.

23. Bill Keller, "New Soviet Ideologist Rejects Idea of World Struggle against West," *New York Times* (6 October 1988): A1.

24. *New York Times* (8 December 1988): A16; (9 December 1988): A18.

25. On the Gorbachev transformation, see also Raymond L. Garthoff, "Why Did the Cold War Arise, and Why Did It End?" *Diplomatic History* 16 (Spring 1992): 287–93; Mueller, *Quiet Cataclysm,* chap. 2.

26. *New York Times* (9 December 1988): A18. Notably, Reagan tied this development to an end of the Soviet expansionary threat, not to the reform of its domestic system. That is, cooperation, even alliance, was not contingent on the progress of Soviet domestic reform. As long as the Soviet Union, like China in the 1970s or Yugoslavia after 1949, continued to neglect its expansionary and revolutionary ideology, it could be embraced by the West. Illiberal, nonexpansionist Portugal, after all, was a founding member of NATO.

27. George Bush, *Public Papers of the Presidents of the United States: George Bush, 1989* (Washington, D.C.: U.S. Government Printing Office, 1990), 541; see also 546, 553, 602, 606, 617, 667. Interestingly, much of this was anticipated in a comment made decades earlier by the quintessential cold warrior, John Foster Dulles: "The basic change we need to look forward to isn't necessarily a change from Communism to another form of government. The question is whether you can have Communism in one country or whether it has to be for the world. If the Soviets had national Communism we could do business with their government." John Lewis Gaddis, *Strategies of Containment* (New York: Oxford University Press, 1982), 143.

28. Owen Harries, "Is the Cold War Really Over?" *National Review* 41, 21 (10 November 1989): 40.

29. Economic difficulties exacerbated by military expenditures may have helped to bring these changes about; the failure of the Soviet economic and administrative system doubtless encouraged Gorbachev and others to reexamine their basic ideology. However, as Myron Rush observes, these problems by no means required a doctrinal change: had the Soviet Union done nothing about its problems, "its survival to the end of the century would have been likely," and "by cutting defense

spending sharply . . . a prudent conservative leader in 1985 could have improved the Soviet economy markedly." Myron Rush, "Fortune and Fate," *National Interest* (Spring 1993): 21. Thus, faced with the same economic strains, a Soviet leader other than Gorbachev might have maintained basic ideology.

30. National Planning Association, *1970 without Arms Control* (Washington, D.C.: National Planning Association, 1958), 42.

31. C. P. Snow, "The Moral Un-Neutrality of Science," *Science* (27 January 1961): 259.

32. Sidney Kraus, ed., *The Great Debates: Kennedy vs. Nixon, 1960* (Bloomington, Ind.: University of Indiana Press, 1962), 394.

33. Denis Healey, *The Race against the H-Bomb*, Fabian Tract 322 (London, 1960), 3.

34. F. W. Mulley, *The Politics of Western Defense* (New York: Praeger, 1962), 79–80.

35. Charles de Gaulle, "The Thoughts of Charles de Gaulle," *New York Times Magazine* (12 May 1968): 102–3.

36. Robert Gilpin, *War and Change in World Politics* (New York: Cambridge University Press, 1981), 215.

37. Christopher Layne confidently insists that Japan by natural impulse must soon come to yearn for nuclear weapons. Layne, "The Unipolar Illusion: Why New Great Powers Will Rise," *International Security* 17 (Spring 1993): 5–51. John Mearsheimer equally confidently argues that "Germany will feel insecure without nuclear weapons" (Mearsheimer, "Back to the Future," 38), even though the Japanese and the Germans themselves continue, uncooperatively, to seem viscerally uninterested. On Japan, see Thomas U. Berger, "From Sword to Chrysanthemum: Japan's Culture of Anti-militarism," *International Security* 17 (Spring 1993): 119–50; and Peter J. Katzenstein and Nobuo Okawara, "Japan's National Security: Structures, Norms, and Policies," *International Security* 17 (Spring 1993): 115–16. John Gaddis has suggested that Mearsheimer's position is that the only countries that should get nuclear weapons are the ones who don't want them.

38. For a discussion of the relevance of the Canadian case, concluding from it that the issue of nuclear proliferation—then often known as the "Nth country problem"—was approaching "a finite solution," see John Mueller, "Incentives for Restraint: Canada as a Nonnuclear Power," *Orbis* 11 (Fall 1967): 864–84.

39. Thomas W. Graham, "Winning the Nonproliferation Battle," *Arms Control Today* (September 1991): 8–13; Mitchell Reiss, *Bridled Ambition: Why Countries Constrain Their Nuclear Capabilities* (Washington, D.C.: Woodrow Wilson Center Press, 1995).

40. Stephen M. Meyer, *The Dynamics of Nuclear Proliferation* (Chicago: University of Chicago Press, 1984). See also Kaysen, McNamara, and Rathjens, "Nuclear Weapons after the Cold War," 98.

41. De Gaulle, "Thoughts," 103; see also Paul Kennedy, *The Rise and Fall of the Great Powers* (New York: Random House, 1987), 370, 401.

42. Status, like beauty, rather seems to lie in the eye of the beholder. China's quest to host the Olympics in the year 2000 stemmed in part from the belief that it

would be a "mark of entry into the big league of world powers." Sheryl WuDunn, "Beijing Goes All Out to Get Olympics in 2000," *New York Times* (11 March 1993): A12. And some Koreans have apparently come to believe that status is achieved when a country has many entries in the *Guinness Book of World Records*: says one, "The more records we have leads to world power." *Wall Street Journal* (17 May 1990): A1. Although China does have a nuclear arsenal, some people are now hailing it as "a great power" (even without the Olympics) because its economy has pushed, by some measures, into third place in the world. Thomas Greenhouse, "New Tally of World's Economies Catapults China into Third Place," *New York Times* (20 May 1993): A1. On this issue, see also Richard Rosecrance, *The Rise of the Trading State: Conquest and Commerce in the Modern World* (New York: Basic Books, 1986).

43. Thomas McNaugher has arrestingly observed that, since missiles are expensive and vastly inferior to aircraft for delivering ordnance, it may be wiser and safer to encourage countries to waste their money on missiles rather than on cheaper and more effective airplanes. Thomas L. McNaugher, "Ballistic Missiles and Chemical Weapons: The Legacy of the Iran-Iraq War," *International Security* 15 (Fall 1990): 32–33. It seems conceivable that a similar argument could be made about nuclear weapons. If a potentially dangerous country foolishly expends scarce resources on expensive nuclear weapons, it won't have nearly as much money to spend on conventional ones. It would now have the capacity, of course, satisfyingly to scare the easily traumatized major countries (whose fondest desire, of course, is to continue to waste their resources on these weapons monopolistically), but it would be less able to cause actual trouble.

44. Waltz, "Nuclear Myths," 734.

45. Robert Jervis, *Implications of the Nuclear Revolution* (Ithaca, N.Y.: Cornell University Press, 1989), 28–29; T. V. Paul, *Asymmetric Conflicts: War Initiation by Weaker Powers* (New York: Cambridge University Press, 1994), chap. 8. See also T. V. Paul, "Nuclear Taboo and War Initiation: Nuclear Weapons in Regional Conflicts," *Journal of Conflict Resolution* 39 (December 1995): 696–17.

46. Mueller, *Retreat from Doomsday*, chap. 7.

47. Mueller, *Retreat from Doomsday; Quiet Cataclysm*, chap. 9. See also Bernard Brodie, ed., *The Absolute Weapon: Atomic Power and World Order* (New York: Harcourt, Brace, 1946).

48. Robert Jervis, *The Illogic of American Nuclear Strategy* (Ithaca, N.Y.: Cornell University Press, 1984), 156–57.

49. Frederick J. Brown, *Chemical Warfare: A Study in Restraints* (Princeton, N.J.: Princeton University Press, 1968), 229.

50. For a more extended discussion, see John Mueller, "Policy Principles for Unthreatened Wealth-Seekers," *Foreign Policy* (Spring 1996): 22–33.

51. Another important development in our age has been the decline of the age-old notion of empire—quite a notable historical change, because empire seems to have been an essential element in international affairs since the dawn of the human race. See Neta C. Crawford, "Decolonization as an International Norm: The Evolution of Practices, Arguments, and Beliefs," in Laura W. Reed and Carl Kaysen,

eds., *Emerging Norms of Justified Intervention* (Cambridge, Mass.: American Academy of Arts and Sciences, 1993), 37–61. Major countries no longer vie for colonies (are there any circumstances under which England would take India, "the jewel in the crown," back?), and the imperial manipulation that often accompanied that process no longer exists.

52. Greenhouse, "New Tally."

53. George F. Will, "The Tenth Problem: The Dangerous Reticence of Clinton the UnCoolidge," *Newsweek* (27 June 1994): 62.

54. Malcolm W. Browne, "Most Precise Gauge Yet Points to Global Warming," *New York Times* (20 December 1994): C4.

55. Samuel P. Huntington, "America's Changing Strategic Interests," *Survival* (January/February 1991): 3–17; Huntington, "Why International Primacy Matters," *International Security* 17 (Spring 1993): 68–83.

56. A recent study by Ellen Gordon and Luan Troxel notes that Turkey opened its borders to Bulgarian Turks in 1989—but soon closed them again when the new immigrants caused so many problems. Thus, they find, "Turkey, while being supportive of the Turkish minority in Bulgaria, has little interest in inflaming internal ethnic relations in Bulgaria." Ellen J. Gordon and Luan Troxel, "Minority Mobilization without War," paper delivered at the Conference on Post-Communism and Ethnic Mobilization, Cornell University, 21–22 April 1995. Poland, they also note, has come to a similar conclusion with respect to the Polish minority in Lithuania. Similarly, Russia has done remarkably little about Russians living in other countries. And in the 1994 election in Hungary, politicians found that calls to help Hungarians in other countries were ineffective with a troubled electorate that responded, "What about the Hungarians *within* Hungary?"

57. But not too much. Public opinion data demonstrate that Americans only worry about international affairs when they espy a clear and present danger. The last time foreign events outweighed domestic ones in American concerns was in February 1968.

58. For data, see Mueller, *Quiet Cataclysm*, 23.

59. James Blight and David A. Welch, "The Cuban Missile Crisis and New Nuclear States," *Security Studies* 4 (Summer 1995): 841–45.

60. See Scott S. Sagan, *The Limits of Safety: Organizations, Accidents, and Nuclear Weapons* (Princeton, N.J.: Princeton University Press, 1993).

61. Snow, "Moral Un-Neutrality of Science."

62. See Mueller, *Retreat from Doomsday*, 227–32.

63. Samuel P. Huntington, "The Clash of Civilizations?" *Foreign Affairs* 72 (Summer 1993): 22–49; and James Kurth, "The *Real* Clash," *National Interest* (Fall 1994): 3–15.

64. The "CNN effect" essentially holds that people are so unimaginative that they only react when they see something visualized. However, Americans were outraged at and mobilized over the Pearl Harbor attack weeks—or even months—before they saw pictures of the event. Moreover, the Vietnam War was not noticeably more unpopular than the Korean War for the period in which the wars were comparable in American casualties, despite the fact that the later war is often seen

to be a "television war" while the earlier was fought during the medium's infancy. See John Mueller, *War, Presidents and Public Opinion* (New York: Wiley, 1973), 167; Michael Mandelbaum, "Vietnam: The Television War," *Daedalus* (Fall 1981): 157–69. See also Daniel C. Hallin, *The "Uncensored War": The Media and Vietnam* (New York: Oxford University Press, 1986). On those rare occasions when pictures have—or seem to have—an effect, as in Ethiopia in the mid-1980s, people espy the effect. When pictures fail to have any effect, they fail to notice—or come up with other, tortured explanations. The process is illustrated by the case of journalist Jack Germond. As the Haitian crisis was heating up in 1994, he observed, "We're seeing the coverage of children starving and ill and so forth—the effects of the sanctions. Which means there is much more pressure on Clinton to do something different—radically different—than what he's been doing." When it was pointed out to him that "the best polls are saying that the consensus in the country—two thirds—don't want U.S. GI's in Haiti in combat because they don't see it as in the vital national interest of the United States," Germond responded, "The numbers might change if we keep getting all this film about the starving kids there." *McLaughlin Group*, PBS, July 1, 1994. However, when they didn't change, he later mused, "It's interesting that three or four years ago in Somalia, for example, television film of starving children was enough to make the country act. Now, television film of starving children in Haiti and atrocities is not enough." Groping for an explanation for this remarkable phenomenon, Germond philosophized, "No one wants to say so, but there's a race factor here. There's no question about that." *McLaughlin Group*, PBS, September 16, 1994. That the starving children in Haiti happened to be of the same race as those in Somalia did not dampen his punditry in the slightest.

65. Mueller, *War, Presidents and Public Opinion*, 44, 58, 100–101.

66. Samuel Huntington, "If Not Civilizations, What? Paradigms of the Post–Cold War World," *Foreign Affairs* 72 (November–December 1993): 186–94.

67. Thomas L. Friedman, "As Some Nations Build, the Past Devours Others," *New York Times* (12 July 1992): D1.

68. Morgenthau, *Politics among Nations*, 13.

69. Morgenthau, *Politics among Nations*, 13.

70. Waltz, *Theory of International Politics*, 192.

71. See John M. Rothgeb Jr., *Defining Power: Influence and Force in the Contemporary International System* (New York: St. Martin's Press, 1993), 18.

72. Morgenthau, *Politics among Nations*, 183.

73. Waltz, *Theory of International Politics*, 192.

74. Robert J. Art and Kenneth N. Waltz, *The Use of Force* (Lanham, Md.: University Press of America, 1983), 7.

75. Waltz, *Theory of International Politics*, 72.

76. Richard J. Lieber, "Existential Realism after the Cold War," *Washington Quarterly* 16 (Winter 1993): 166.

77. Charles L. Glaser, "Realists as Optimists: Cooperation as Self-Help," *International Security* 19 (Winter 1994–95): 50–90.

78. For exasperation with endless, shifting definitions of what "realism" actually

is, see Paul W. Schroeder, "Reply," *International Security* 20 (Summer 1995): 193–95.

79. Mearsheimer, "Back to the Future," 12, 45.
80. Art and Waltz, *Use of Force,* 3–8.
81. Huntington, "Why International Primacy Matters," 72.
82. Layne, "Unipolar Illusion," 5 n. 1, 37.
83. On the other hand, the realists' record for predictions is somewhat flawed. The venerable Hans J. Morgenthau intoned in 1979: "In my opinion the world is moving ineluctably towards a third world war—a strategic nuclear war. I do not believe that anything can be done to prevent it. The international system is simply too unstable to survive for long." Quoted in Francis Anthony Boyle, *World Politics and International Law* (Durham, N.C.: Duke University Press, 1985), 73.

Nuclear Weapons and the Revolution in Military Affairs

COLIN S. GRAY

"Third-wave" warfare is upon us.[1] "Cyberwar is coming."[2] The age of the information warrior has dawned. Claims such as these—arresting yesterday, the stuff of cliché today—command attention, but require examination. What does the dawning of the age of cyberspace mean for the future significance of nuclear weapons?[3] In a summary of the Clinton administration's "Nuclear Posture Review," Secretary of Defense William J. Perry has written that "nuclear weapons are playing a smaller role in U.S. security than at any other time in the nuclear age."[4] The future roles and strategic significance of nuclear weapons are deeply uncertain at present.[5] Is what we think we know, or need to know, about the roles of nuclear weapons scheduled for profound change as the world moves from one age to another? Is the nuclear age going to be replaced, or perhaps overlaid, by the information age with its own distinctive way of war?

The information age, whatever that grand concept may be agreed to mean, has burst upon the world before the world even has made full sense of the nuclear age. The rich variety of potential future conflicts renders broad-gauged analysis of their character a perilously ambitious enterprise. The method adapted here is as straightforward as the difficulties of the subject allow. The discussion begins by examining the elements needed to understand trends and change in modern strategic history. The essay employs and analyzes the concept of a first nuclear age (coterminous with the Cold War), of a second nuclear age (the post–Cold War period),[6] of an information age, and of revolutions in military affairs (RMAs). The discussion explores the character of an RMA, interrogates the concept for its utility, and inquires as to whether information (age) warfare constitutes such a revolution. The essay then considers the strategic advantages and disadvantages of nuclear weapons in this new "age of free silicon."[7]

The concepts of an RMA and an information age—and such derivative ideas as information warfare and information warriors—are eminently contestable and, indeed, are being contested today. Detailed consideration of these concepts is presented below. It is now sufficient to register the proposition that, in the opinion of some scholars, strategic history proceeds through a series of RMAs, the defining characteristic of which is some advance in technology and probably military method that radically alters the character and conduct of war. The rapidly evolving microchip with its consequent computing power is, allegedly, effecting the latest such revolution. This most recent RMA is the product and expression preeminently of the modern computer, which is defining an age of information. In the information age, so the argument goes, the acquisition or denial of information is the key to victory. Whereas in times past styles in warfare were characterized principally by attrition or maneuver, today and in the future warfare will be about information control. Victory will be sought via the paralysis of the enemy.[8]

The analysis ranges widely and sometimes rides roughshod over apparently familiar terrain. The principal propositions explored here are the speculative notions, first, that a new model, or models, of warfare currently is emerging and, second, that the weapons most characteristic of the new style in warfare will be able to locate and strike targets over great distances with a degree of precision that obviates all but any practical need to employ nuclear warheads.[9] The third-wave, cyberwar weapon of today is the Tomahawk land-attack missile (TLAM), which achieves precise navigation for extreme accuracy by receiving data in flight from the NAVSTAR GPS satellite constellation.[10] Of course, there is much more to information-age warfare than this.[11] For example, the extended statement of U.S. Marine Corps philosophy, *Warfighting,* focuses on the concept of maneuver rather than on exploration of particular technologies, but it is supportive of the broad notion of information-age warfare.[12] Nonetheless, it is appropriate for readers to note that the sharp end of warfare in the information age is a pilotless vehicle delivering non-nuclear ordnance with great precision far over the horizon. What does the arrival of this, and closely related military capabilities, imply for the future strategic value of nuclear weapons? Will the information age enable the United States and others to procure so lethal a conventional, precision-strike capability that the nuclear age of warfare will be all but over? Will nuclear weapons be consigned to the garbage heap of history as yesterday's weapons? This is the question that binds this analysis.[13]

Two recent advocacy pieces can serve as useful terms of reference. Few significant doubts trouble John Arquilla about information warfare. He advises that the opportunity exists to transform knowledge into capability (quoting Clausewitz) via information dominance. For Arquilla, the nature of war fighting will undergo radical changes because of the consequences of information dominance, which will succeed, subsume, and transform many of the effects derived from its principal predecessors, seapower and airpower.[14]

Arquilla also offers the thought that "[a]s British naval mastery once made possible the conquest and consolidation of a global empire by small forces, so information dominance will allow a similarly lean American military to serve and protect its country's still-extensive interests in a world fraught with peril."[15] These are extensive claims indeed. Arquilla is comparing capabilities for information warfare with seapower and airpower, and he even identifies a distinctive paradigm of war—control (as contrasted with attrition or maneuver)—for information-rich armed forces.

By contrast, Captain Warren Caldwell Jr., USN, speaks with admirable directness for those who find advocacy of information-warfare techniques to contain technobabble and general gee-whizzery. Captain Caldwell judges "the supposed technical revolution in military affairs" to be "overly optimistic and inappropriate," and he finds advanced technology presented as a panacea—"a substitute for sound, cogent, and incisive strategic thought and analysis."[16] After describing what the advocates of the new RMA envisage as the army, navy, and air force of the information-age future, Caldwell delivers his summary body blow. None of this is truly revolutionary. The current RMA mantra simply updates an old agenda and adds a few more microchips.

These ideas are popular because they conform to American concepts of war, but they often lead us to ignore basic issues regarding the nature of warfare or encourage the notion that we can alter or control a conflict exclusively through the application of advanced technology and military power.[17] But actual policymakers, and people like this author who advised them for many years, are obliged to behave in accordance with Bernard Brodie's wise reminder that strategy, *au profond*, is a practical subject.[18]

Strategic Concepts for Grand Theory

From time to time in world politics a breathing space occurs.[19] The mid-1990s are such a pause. Notwithstanding some murderous proclivities among nations, tribes, and communities on the periphery of the former USSR and from the Maghreb to South Asia,[20] in addition to the nastiness of much of sub-Saharan Africa's political life,[21] for the super and medium powers of the West these are interwar years.[22] In these periods military effectiveness in future wars, great and small, is forged.[23] While these years are not a time-out from strategic history, they do provide an opportunity for deliberate consideration of fundamental matters of statecraft and strategy. This kind of thinking was pushed aside by the exigencies of the Cold

War. The strategic concepts examined in this section, however, have the holistic qualities essential for grand theory. The concepts of nuclear ages, of an information age, and of RMAs can all provide coherence to otherwise disorganized material.

The starting point for this inquiry is the working proposition that scholars may not understand statecraft or strategy. It could follow from this speculative proposition that a catastrophic outcome to the Soviet-American Cold War was avoided more by luck than by good judgment.[24] There may be some good grounds, however, for self-congratulation over the relatively peaceful outcome to the Cold War. After all, official behavior on all sides undeniably was compatible with the avoidance of war. But it is all too easy to draw fragile conclusions for policy and strategic theory from the non–great war history of East-West relations from 1945 to 1991. My argument suggests the possible breadth and depth of ignorance about the following nonmarginal subjects:

The character of the first phase of the nuclear age (1945–91)
The character of the second phase of the nuclear age (1992–?)
The character of the information age
The implications of RMAs[25]

Given the grand theory that is needed to make sense of strategic history and the emerging strategic condition, there are serious problems with the largest conceptual building blocks. The literature that is focusing upon the significance of nuclear weapons for this new post–Cold War security environment faces a far more difficult task than many of its authors appreciate. Not only is there uncertainty about emerging strategic conditions, let alone about the more distant consequences of these contemporary conditions (for example, if they are akin to those of the mid-1920s, is there a 1930s over the horizon?), but there also is uncertainty about the Cold War. The first phase of the nuclear age has many secrets still to reveal. The "golden age" of modern Western strategic theory, from 1954 to 1966, erected three main "pillars": deterrence theory, limited war theory, and arms control theory. Limited war theory went missing in action in Vietnam in the second half of the 1960s; arms control theory was substantially evidence-challenged by the course of the Soviet-American arms competition in the 1970s; but deterrence theory, the jewel in the crown of the postwar nuclear-oriented strategic theorist, was a source of much professional pride and not a little self-satisfaction.

For example, no less an authority than Michael Howard, a founder of the International Institute for Strategic Studies, has offered the bold and quite unsubstantiated judgment that "[w]hat is beyond doubt, however, is that we effectively deterred the Soviet Union from using military force to achieve its political objectives."[26] Later on, Howard is pleased to register the rather self-congratulatory claim that "[w]e have become rather expert at deterrence."[27] Alas, Howard's judgment and claim are both thoroughly contestable. The fall of the Soviet Union truly was a famous victory for the U.S.-led Western alliance. But we do not know that particular victory was a victory for an evolving strategy of deterrence.

The analysis in this section rests upon a skeptical view of much of the merit in the exact content claimed to define the four organizing concepts that have influenced much Cold War thinking.

The First Phase of the Nuclear Age (1945–91)

Historians still debate the reasons for the decline and fall of the Western Roman Empire, and it is not obvious that more evidence would settle the argument. It is scarcely surprising that an event—the Cold War, completed so recently with the formal demise of the USSR in December 1991—should lend itself to a range of powerful alternative explanations. With the benefit of a little perspective (and it *is* only a little perspective), it becomes apparent that much of what we thought we knew well enough for navigation in statecraft in the Cold War was in fact navigation by dead reckoning, by instruments of uncertain reliability, or by guesswork.[28]

An obvious advantage of analysis today of the first nuclear age—the Cold War decades of East-West competition under the nuclear shadow— is that there are legions of people, East and West, who were "there" during the history in dispute. Scholars today can retain a firsthand knowledge of the Cold War that subsequent generations will be unable to replicate. The no less obvious disadvantage of this temporal proximity is that current interpretations of the course and outcome of the Cold War are provided by noticeably interested parties. But we all have a substantial stake in how that history is written, because ideas for policy in the immediate future will be influenced by fashionable interpretation of the recent past.

To dramatize the argument somewhat: did nuclear Armageddon not occur because of or despite U.S.-NATO and Soviet policies? Or, for another example, did the policies pursued by the Reagan presidency trigger, delay, accelerate, or function in ways irrelevant to the process of imperial decline and collapse in the East? Was "the balance of terror" ever truly "delicate"?[29] Even if the balance was in a delicate condition, would that ever-arguable fact (in whose calculations was it delicate?) have mattered much? As I have suggested in detail elsewhere,[30] the U.S. defense community in practice did achieve an enduring and workable rough consensus on rules of prudence for nuclear weapons policy, strategy, and posture.

Administration after administration endorsed the prudential rules that nuclear-armed forces should be large rather than small, should be diversely rather than simply postured (that is, a triad-plus), and should be contingently directed by war plans that allowed for an ever-greater measure of flexibility in employment. Rules such as these were demonstrated to be correct only in the sense that the guidance they provided coincided with the persisting fact of nonwar. There continues to be deep uncertainty about the strategic history of the Cold War and the role of nuclear weapons in that history. Every argument about strategy and policy in this new nuclear age that rests to any noteworthy degree upon a claim to understand what "worked" from 1945 to 1991 is vulnerable to lacunae in that understanding. Whether a theorist is proposing continuity or discontinuity from Cold War practice, the quality of historical understanding could be critical. It is commonplace today to hear the claim that what worked well enough to deter during the Cold War may not deter different kinds of adversaries today. This claim is sensible, with the vital qualification that our knowledge of what worked well enough to deter during the Cold War remains overwhelmingly conjectural.

The Second Phase of the Nuclear Age (1992–?)

Today we are underinformed about how and why peace with security generally was preserved in the first phase of the nuclear age. It also is necessary to come to grips both with the inherent uncertainties concerning the future and, in particular, with the ramifications of an emerging information age. The structure and functioning of this second part of the nuclear age are likely to be more opaque than the structure and dynamic of the Cold War decades.

Certainly, we remain in the nuclear era, no matter how "virtual" nuclear capabilities may become.[31] But this post–Cold War period should be regarded as a second, very different stage. By no means was all of the nuclear context to world history from 1945 to 1991 Soviet-American and East-West Cold War in content, but that orientation was dominant. Whatever the nuclear tragedies that might have occurred for regional reasons in the Middle East, South and East Asia, and Southern Africa in the 1970s and 1980s, those hypothetical tragedies were dwarfed in their potential for global damage by the weight of menace in the nuclear arsenals of East and West. Of course, a regional nuclear accident or purposive use could have had appalling catalytic consequences along powder trails to superpower arsenals; but still, in West and East the problem of nuclear proliferation was subordinate to the central global competition. Indeed, that competition variably proved either restrictive or permissive of regional bids for nuclear capability, as superordinate foreign policy needs commanded. For example, U.S. policy toward Pakistan's nuclear weapons program in 1979–80 underwent an abrupt shift following the Soviet invasion of Afghanistan.

The structure and functioning of this second phase of the nuclear age are mysterious. In terms of historical periodicity, is this age best described as being of a postwar, interwar, or prewar character? If strategic history is more cyclical than arrowlike in its structure, then the future, like the past, will comprise a succession of great power struggles separated by periods of recovery (weapons technology, military usage, and war plans permitting). Unfortunately for neatness and manageability of analysis, everything about the subjects under discussion here is related to everything else. This second stage connects to a predictable third nuclear epoch of nuclear-armed great-power struggle on the highway of strategic consequences.[32] In other words, the next great-power struggle must grow out of the insecurity fostered by the trends of these post–Cold War years. In that sense, the interwar conditions of the 1920s and 1930s produced the context wherein the Second World War became ever more certain. The twentieth century has registered no fewer than four periods between great wars of very different duration (1871–1914, 1918–39, 1945–47, and 1992–?). There is no overwhelmingly persuasive reason evident today why this fourth such period should have a character and eventual outcome radically different from its predecessors.

Unfortunately, uncertainty over the duration of this hypothetical interwar period is connected to uncertainty over how best to prolong the interwar condition and postpone the onset of an undesirable prewar context. NATO determines to allow for its eastward "enlargement" (that is, expansion),[33] but there is no internal agreement on just what are the problems to which its continued existence, its reform, its enlargement, and even its new strategic concept are relevant. It is difficult to provide good enough answers to imprecise, let alone unknown, questions.[34] Today there is no settled architecture of international security. Some Cold War–era security ties and military deployments still persist, but they are under increasing challenge. Collective defense on the traditional NATO model has been eroded by the demise of the great Soviet threat, while collective security suffers from its own inherent contradictions.[35]

The United States is the only superpower, but it is a superpower less and less motivated by cold calculation of a national interest to lead posses for international peace. Moreover, as weapons of mass destruction (WMD) and their associated delivery vehicles proliferate, the cost-benefit calculus that must shape U.S. policy choice will show diminishing advantage accruing from the pursuit of protection duties. U.S. forces will be sent in harm's way, including potential harm from WMD, when the survival of the American polity is believed to be at stake. U.S. forces will be dispatched, similarly, in support of vital national interests. Those forces will not be dispatched, however, when nonvital stakes are at issue. In this second phase of the nuclear age, even the high lethality expected of information-age weaponry should not be expected to neutralize American fears for the safety of U.S. forces in regions well sown with WMD.

First, WMD are proliferating, albeit at a slow trot rather than at a canter. Second, the ballistic and cruise missile means for potential delivery of those WMD also are proliferating.[36] Third, deterrence (by the United States or NATO) of "rogue," or simply unexpected, behavior is much more problematical even than it was during the Cold War (when, as recent research reveals, it fell distinctly short of reliable).[37] Fourth, responsibility for order in world politics becomes ever more uncertain as the East-West Cold War fades into memory. Fifth, security problems and agendas have broadened to a zone wherein the traditional military instruments exercised by a super or great power are not obviously able to act to decisive military effect.[38] The postmodern wave of ethnic, religious, tribal, national, and even criminal violence does not lend itself to the Patton, LeMay, or Schwarzkopf treatment for clear military resolution. Sixth, information technology and the new methods of operation and organizational forms that it spawns are part founder and shaper and part simply accidental features of this second phase of the nuclear age. The emerging information-age character of the United States may well have played a critical triggering role in the Soviet demise, since recognition of that character prompted the advancing of impracticable demands for reform in the interest of military-industrial competitiveness. But now, with the Cold War concluded, it seems likely that the age of information is both cohabiting globally with the nuclear age and even underlining the strategic value of WMD to those polities and groups who expect to remain cyberchallenged. Finally, notwithstanding periodic reminders of times past—some discussion of START II, for example, or evidence that late-model Russian Akula SSNs are up to their old shadowing tricks in the North Atlantic[39]—the second phase of the nuclear age does not have a central strategic relationship to provide structure and terms of reference. For the time being, the absence of such a central relationship is a negative defining feature of this new era. Will the nuclear age coexist with the information age? Indeed, can the late 1990s and immediately beyond belong to both ages, or must one age consume the other?

The Character and Implications of the Information Age

I have argued elsewhere that familiarity with the concepts of arms race and arms control can dull the critical senses.[40] As the literature proliferates promiscuously on the information age, on information-age warfare, and on an information-keyed hypothesized RMA, fundamental existential questions also tend to be displaced.[41] Surely hundreds of conferences, dozens of study contracts and grants, an upsurge of Ph.D. theses, and a raft of publications cannot be thoroughly in error?

The information age and information-age warfare certainly exist as a composite topic that currently is exciting scholars and officials. A poor idea, however, does not miraculously become a good idea just because a small library of studies, books, and articles debate it in detail. One would be more inclined to be credulous of the information-age hypothesis were one less well informed on the historical sociology of defense debate in the United States.

There is a kind of "wave train" of successive hot new (or refurbished old) concepts that surge and pass only to be followed inexorably, if irregularly, by later concepts. The size of the extended U.S. defense policy community all but guarantees that a new idea, especially if fired from an authoritative launchpad,[42] is likely to attain escape velocity for entry into scholarly orbit. Naturally, the orbit will decay rapidly as the concept becomes exhausted and the frontier theorists turn their attention to a new concept.

It would be foolish to ignore possible connections between process and content. In the case of information-age warfare, not only is there a process among "networked" institutions and individuals eager to latch on to the latest fashion; in addition there is a hardware/software industry of awesome proportions ready and willing to encourage the process to celebrate change with the commitment of tax dollars.

To characterize today as the information age would seem to be a truth so self-evident as to be trivial. The evidence is all around us and, indeed, is often an intrusive reality. The question the strategic theorist must pose, however, is "so what?" To recite the marvels of communication achievable through the exploitation of cyberspace does not answer the question. Strategists must guard against giving tactical answers to strategic questions. The proliferation of computers, the growth of networks that allow extremely rapid dissemination of information, and the adaptation of institutions and processes to this blossoming of information-rich nodes are not in question. The issue, rather, is what it means.

There are two approaches to the concepts of an information age and information-age warfare. The first approach is that which has launched the current excitement about information-age warfare and a possible RMA: it focuses typically—though not exclusively—upon technology and machines as driving influences. This focus suggests that the computer, essentially the microchip, is redefining military relationships. The claim is that the computer is changing the character of warfare in discontinuous ways. However, more sophisticated advocates and commentators are aware of the limitations of information-age-warfare weapons and technology. For example, in a distinctly cool and balanced analysis, the authors of the summary volume to the *Gulf War Air Power Survey* offer the pithy thought that "technology alone does not a revolution [in warfare] make."[43] They proceed to explain, unexceptionably, that "how military organizations adapt and shape new technology, military systems, and operational concepts matter much more."[44]

It is possible that even a richly detailed and diverse appreciation of military innovation that views technology and weapons only as components vital to a process of revolution still may be in error. The second approach to the concepts of an information age and of information-age warfare eschews any particular technological dependency. Without hostility toward technology in general, or toward any kinds of weapons or weapon-support systems in particular, one can see the struggle for information as a permanent dimension of statecraft and war at all levels.

One among several possible useful ways to conceptualize the second approach is via the Boyd theory, or Boyd cycle. Presenting the logic of effectiveness in an aerial dogfight, Colonel Boyd, USAF, postulates that the acquisition and exploration of information at a rate more speedy than could be accomplished by a foe enables you to turn inside his circle and score a kill. The Boyd cycle comprises four stages: observation, orientation, decision, and action (OODA).[45] The OODA cycle can be used to elucidate an approach to what has long been termed maneuver warfare;[46] or, as here, the cycle may help explain the information-warfare dimension to all conflict.

The Boyd cycle could be applied by anybody engaged in statecraft or warfare in any period and in virtually any circumstance. It is no insult to the would-be cyberwarrior of the 1990s, and it is certainly not demeaning to the military promise of the microchip, to argue that the pursuit of information superiority or dominance is as old as human conflict. From this perspective, information warfare should be thought of not as a new era in conflict, triggered and fueled by the maturing of computer technologies, but rather as a permanent dimension of war (the quest to obtain and to deny intelligence). Whether or not information dominance is more reliably and thoroughly achievable today than in the past depends upon considerations little analyzed in discussions of information warfare. It is not necessary for this essay to register a choice between the technology-weapon-machine approach to information warfare and the approach that prefers to see the struggle for information as what Stalin would have termed a permanently operating factor. I lean toward the second view, though I believe that there are some serious perils that could beset rejection of the information-warfare thesis. To be skeptical of information warfare as a distinctive, historically delimited phenomenon is not to be skeptical of either the significance of information in war or the valuable roles that computers can play in the persisting struggle to control information in war.

Politically minded scholars may be excused some alienation from writings that appear to offer more technobabble and razzle-dazzle than strategic analysis and political judgment. But the words of the more thoughtful would-be information warrior need to be considered at face value. For example, Martin Libicki advises that vast improvements in information technology are happening now and will continue to happen; that these improvements will change the conduct and context of national security is virtually certain. Other technologies do not seem to offer as much in the way of change these days and thus do not offer large, cumulative advances of deep significance. According to Libicki, technologies that alter society radically tend to result from a long chain of small discoveries and incremental improvements. The radio, in the hands of charismatic thugs, fomented wars. Future changes in informational technology will as certainly rewrite the assumptions—both political and military—upon which national security rests.[47]

Elsewhere, Libicki has argued that geography is "rapidly fading" in its strategic significance. "The race may not necessarily go to those who grasp the new pride of placelessness, but, in cyberspace [the sum of the globe's communications links and computational nodes], that's the increasingly obvious place to be."[48]

The Implications of RMAs

To consider the future significance of nuclear weapons in an information age that allegedly is triggering an RMA, one must make sure that RMA is an intelligible and useful concept well rooted in historical experience. Just because scholars can conceive of the exciting concept of an RMA does not guarantee that the concept is more than a chimera.

There is no question but that nuclear weapons are meeting an age wherein information technologies and networks are burgeoning. But is it true that "today we confront a revolution in information technologies"?[49] More relevant still is the familiar strategists' question, "so what?" In the words of one leading theorist: What is a military revolution? It is what occurs when the application of new technologies into a significant number of military systems combines with innovative operational concepts and organizational adaptation in a way that fundamentally alters the character and conduct of conflict. It does so by producing a dramatic increase— often an order of magnitude or greater—in the combat potential and military effectiveness of armed forces.[50]

Three basic questions beg for answers: what is an RMA; is the concept useful, does it have considerable explanatory power; and is the current exponential development and growth in information technologies producing an RMA?

1. What Is an RMA?

The definition quoted above appeals to common sense, which is no small virtue in a potentially key idea. The problem with this definition is that its author inadvertently conflates the tactical-operational and the strategic. Of course, strategic effectiveness rests upon tactical prowess (that is, we have a strategy, but people have to try to do tactics at the sharp end of conflict).[51] Developments that produce an arguably fundamental alteration in the character and conduct of conflict attract notice. One is troubled, however, by the consequentialist claim in the second half of the answer by Andrew Krepinevich quoted above. Is it true that the military-revolutionary polity or coalition achieves "a dramatic increase in the combat potential and military effectiveness of armed forces?" It stands to reason that this should be so, but did not Clausewitz (and Sun-tzu and every other great theorist on war) note the fact that war is a duel?[52] In other words, there is an intelligent enemy out there with an independent will who is strongly motivated, and variably able, to thwart our cunning plans.

It is one thing to claim an RMA on the evidence of profound change in the character and conduct of war; it is quite another to claim that RMAs produce a dramatic increase in military effectiveness. Even though there is a sense in which Krepinevich's Napoleonic, Nineteenth-Century Land Warfare, and Interwar (1919–39) Revolutions did improve dramatically the fighting power of their implementing military organizations, that improvement was, alas, eventually multilateral and therefore of much-reduced net benefit to each would-be revolutionary.[53] It may be eccentric on my part, but I interpret a claim for an order of magnitude increase in military effectiveness to imply the ability of truly modern armed forces to achieve favorable decision in war at a price that their proprietor societies deem tolerable. The two world wars of this century, both purportedly shaped in their character and conduct by RMAs, manifestly did not demonstrate any net dramatic increase in military effectiveness by the combatants. The reasons were both that there is more to strategic history than RMAs and that each major belligerent, in its own style, adopted, or adapted to, the RMA of the period.

The hollowness of the claim that an RMA produces a dramatic increase in military effectiveness is demonstrated with particular clarity with reference to the nuclear revolution. "The absolute weapon" has proved to be all but absolutely unusable, save in the most terminal of last resorts.[54] The bedrock of that unusability lies, as suggested above, in the inexorable fact of inconvenient possession of nuclear weapons by several other polities. RMAs have a way of appearing revolutionary and effective when they pit Maxim guns against tribal swordsmen or panzer divisions against horse cavalry. Those same RMAs, however, through the generality of adoption of some of their features—or the adoption of counterrevolutionary tactics—also helped shape two of the greatest protracted wars of attrition in history.

Information warriors, conducting information warfare (I-war), will be uniquely vulnerable to tailored counter-I-war means and methods.[55] Warriors have always known that war is not a game of solitaire, but still they have repeatedly found ways to ignore that knowledge. The greater the enthusiasm with which a community of advocates seeks to sell its RMA—for information warfare, in this case—the less likely is it to be open to imaginative recognition of the new vulnerabilities that could well offset its strategic virtues. The conduct of cyberwar, in particular, for denial of reliable control via information dominance, is a mode of conflict that many groups and polities could wage.[56] However, not all of those groups and polities will be equally at risk in the event of failure in cyberspace.

2. Is the Concept of an RMA Useful?

No matter which answer one prefers, the question is important. As the Director of Net Assessment in the Office of the Secretary of Defense has stated: "We do not yet fully know what the next revolution will bring about, or certainly that a new revolution is in the offing; but a military revolution would be a development of fundamental importance to DOD, so it is important to try to understand the possibilities as best we can."[57] Quite so.

Although the two world wars do not show that competent innovation in accordance with a revolutionary paradigm of war produces ultimate victory, those wars do show that poor innovators get beaten (for example,

Poland in 1939, Britain and France in 1940) and that sound innovators at least win for a while. Progress in implementation of an RMA can help produce definitive victory over foes unable to recover and learn from the bitter experience of defeat.

Geography limited the military effectiveness of the interwar revolutions in mechanization, aviation, and information, whose combat cutting edge was the panzer division and the Luftwaffe in army support roles. Had Britain been continentally contiguous to France and had the USSR been a country of more modest physical dimensions, the German way of war of 1940–41 would have secured complete victory.[58]

The quotation offered earlier that "technology alone does not a revolution [in warfare] make" needs augmentation with the thought that RMAs alone do not drive or explain strategic history. Even if the concept and pre-theory of RMAs is deemed useful, in that it does help make orderly what otherwise is chaotic, does it focus attention on principal historical dynamics? Is it useful to seek to understand history as a series of irregularly occurring great transformations? Sometimes, perhaps, continuity rather than change is more important in preparation for future war. It is commonplace to berate generals for preparing to fight the last war. No less often it would be fair to berate generals for forgetting sound lessons of the past. Warfare always is a process of adaptation, but that adaptation has to involve both the management of novelty, including the timely rejection of harebrained novelty, and the rediscovery of practices and ideas known to be sound by previous generations of warriors. Charles E. Callwell wrote in 1900 in the light of the initially shocking experience of the Anglo-Boer War, "[t]actics are perpetually changing."[59] That advice beckons the observation, *plus ça change*. Still on this elevated plain, note Captain Alfred Thayer Mahan's Jominian thought that although "[f]rom time to time the superstructure of tactics has to be altered or wholly torn down; the old foundations of strategy so far remain, as though laid down upon a rock."[60] By definition, the RMA concept focuses attention upon change. But are the elements of change more important than the elements that do not change, or that change only slowly?

Even if an RMA framework of analysis is judged helpful in explaining change, it tends to discourage focus on supporting elements of defense preparation and war. The RMA paradigm has a lot to say about Napoleon's victories, but what can it contribute to an understanding of Wellington's victories with an emphatically nonrevolutionary instrument for land warfare (the British Army)? Again, the RMA paradigm speaks volumes to Nazi Germany's early victories, but does it contribute negatively to our understanding of why Germany eventually lost? It is right and proper to take prominent notice of some variant of what J. F. C. Fuller

Nuclear Weapons and the Revolution in Military Affairs / 113

called "the dominant weapon,"[61] but might that notice blind us to the fact that Hitler's army overwhelmingly was logistically dependent not upon the internal combustion engine, but rather upon horsepower and steam engines?[62] Paradoxically, in the nuclear age "the dominant weapon" is the one weapon that has not been used, inter alia because of its lethality (ironically) and because—as always, eventually—several polities acquired it.

Given that the strategic world is always changing, is it not sensible to be cautious in welcoming the RMA paradigm because of what that program tends to exclude? Experience suggests that for an RMA to have radical strategic consequences (for example, the fall of France in May–June 1940), conditions have to be permissive: the victim should lack assets (say, geography, high morale, inspired leadership, powerful allies able to lend timely assistance) that can compensate for the disadvantage of being at the wrong end of an RMA. It is not quite the case that an RMA is another way of saying strategic, operational, tactical, or technical surprise. The advantage secured by an RMA lies more in the realm of surprise effect than surprise itself.

If a "revolution" occurs not over the course of years or decades, but perhaps over a century or longer, does it not assume more the character of a slowly emerging condition than of a revolution? The cumulative effect of the introduction of gunpowder, or of sailing ships with sides pierced for the delivery of broadsides by gunpowder naval ordnance, may well warrant ascription as "revolutions." But might not the long duration of the periods of adaptation deny in practice some of the commonsense implications of the claim for revolution?

The concept of an RMA is akin to the concept of crisis: a time of challenge, peril, but also a time of great opportunity. If, as suggested here, RMAs make their strategic mark by surprise effect rather than surprise, long familiarity with particular military tools or methods need not necessarily negate their revolutionary potential. Even if long duration is no absolute barrier to RMA status for a weapon or military method, that lengthy passage of time provides opportunity for the diffusion of elements of that RMA abroad, and for yet another RMA to creep from fertile brains to drawing board, to factories, and then into military practice.

Does it follow that the RMA paradigm is liable to mislead? Perhaps it is liable to mislead only the unwary. If the concept of "the nuclear age," or "the nuclear revolution," does not explain the whole character and conduct of conflict from 1945 to the present, is it likely that the postulate of an RMA geared to progress in the military adoption of information technologies similarly could be seriously flawed? This possibility merits respect.

3. Is the Information Age Heralding an Information-Oriented RMA?

For there to be a profound change in the character and conduct of war—a military revolution—there must be general agreement on what needs to be altered. Consensus attends claims that an RMA requires (a) new technology; (b) new weapon systems; (c) new operational concepts; and (d) new forms of military organization, including new institutions. In addition, one might speculate about an item (e) new strategic concepts, but that would pass beyond the pale typical of current debate.[63]

It is not hard to locate extravagant-sounding claims for an RMA keyed to information control or dominance. For example, Alvin Toffler reveals that "[w]hat is happening now is the emergence of a new, third-wave war form that has its own special characteristics [for example, demassification, desynchronization, soft war, deep battle, and so forth] and is highly dependent upon the application of knowledge."[64] Or consider the claim that "[t]he new battlefield is the battlefield for knowledge."[65] We are told that "[t]he post-modern battlefield stands to be fundamentally altered by the information technology revolution, at both the strategic and tactical levels."[66] It is useful to contrast such claims with the more measured thoughts of Andrew W. Marshall. The information dimension or aspect of warfare may become increasingly central to the outcome of battles and campaigns. Therefore, protecting the effective and continuous operation of one's own information systems and being able to degrade, destroy, or disrupt the functioning of the opponent's will become a major focus of the operational art. Much as over the last sixty to seventy years one wished to obtain air superiority to better conduct all other military operations, in the future obtaining early superiority in the information area may become central to doing well in warfare.[67]

Marshall's thoughts here are as wise as they are utterly nonrevolutionary. Indeed, information warfare, as Marshall so sensibly characterizes it, is as long familiar as was the notion, say, of "competitive strategy(ies)."[68] Allied lack of knowledge of the location of the German *Schwerpunkt* in 1914 (north of the Sambre and Meuse)[69] and 1940 (through the Ardennes to the Meuse at Sedan)[70] had dire operational, strategic, and political consequences. The struggle for information dominance over the war at sea in the Second World War may have been a realm of decision for the contest as a whole.[71] It looks as if today's theorists of information-based warfare are rediscovering the obvious, though, as Mahan demonstrated with seapower, such rediscovery can be valuable.

Whereas the nuclear dimension to security is in the process of rapidly being reduced to the complex problem of rogue proliferants,[72] the information warfare–RMA basket of challenges and opportunities is attracting more and more of the short supply of intellectual horsepower in the defense community. The information-oriented RMA that some analysts judge somewhat casually to be supplanting the nuclear RMA lends itself to what may be enlightening disaggregation. Instead of conceiving of current developments holistically as an RMA, it is plausible to postulate that three streams of military-technical advance are coinciding historically and functioning synergistically. Today we are witnessing

> the full maturing of airpower;
> systematic operational exploitation of (military and civil) space systems (spacepower);
> exponential improvement in electronics in general, in computers for rapid data processing in particular, and in electronic forms of communication.

Maybe the RMA really under way today is not so much a shift to knowledge-based defense systems and warfare, as if the struggle for knowledge usable in war were something novel, but rather a slow adjustment to the challenge of war in the geographical fourth dimension of space. Of course space systems, to date, only perform enabling functions on behalf of military executive agents on land, at sea, and in the air. In that sense, spacepower could be regarded as an increasingly vital contributor to prowess in the conduct of information warfare. Nonetheless, if one is interested in profound changes in the character and conduct of warfare, the quest for control of information is much less revolutionary than is either the arrival of the military space age or the demonstration in 1991 that dominant airpower can be "the leading edge" or "key force" in war in open terrain.[73] The rise of essentially placeless, antigeographical cyberspace as the latest "environment" for conflict has had the effect of demoting space from the top rung of the hierarchy of fashionably new frontiers. Americans have become more and more cyber-minded as computers have become less and less costly and therefore more and more accessible. America's love affair with information technology bears some nontrivial relation both to the country's long-standing cultural affinity for machines and to the still strong national appeal of aviation.[74] But, unlike ships and spacecraft, airplanes and computers are part of the everyday lives of Americans.

Scholars excited by the information-warfare thesis might profit from asking themselves whether what they are postulating as the driving force of an RMA is not simply an example of what Clausewitz eloquently identified as a possible "center of gravity . . . the hub of all power and movement, on which everything depends. That is the point against which all our energies should be directed."[75] Whatever an enemy's center of gravity is judged to be, its identification and the feasibility of menacing it require accurate information.

This discussion is not generically skeptical of the RMA hypothesis pertaining to the practicability today of struggling to achieve information dominance. If the Mongols regularly could achieve such dominance in the thirteenth century,[76] and the Allies achieved it often enough in the Second World War, why should not great polities succeed similarly in the late 1990s and beyond? The contrary notes sounded here both signal the relative neglect in public debate of the significance of the geographically distinctive advances in spacepower and suggest that a claim for the importance of knowledge in defense planning and war is anything but revolutionary.

From Age to Age?

I have focused mainly upon the elements that allegedly are moving strategic history via an RMA into the historically new territory of an information age. This section, by contrast, reviews key arguments about the utility and disutility of nuclear weapons in the future. The discussion is organized to answer the heroic question: what are the unique advantages and disadvantages of nuclear weapons? Lurking none too subtly in the wings are two related questions: will information-age conventional weapons replace nuclear weapons as the instruments of choice for deterrence and war fighting? And will nuclear proliferation proceed further?

Because the broad purpose of this inquiry is conceptual and general, the analysis that follows is as detached from specific polities, places, issues, and weapon systems as is compatible with the integrity and force of the argument. First, what are the advantages arguably unique to nuclear weapon capabilities in an information age?

Crystal-Ball Effect

The horror that nuclear weapons could inflict quickly is beyond dispute. Friends and foes alike already are persuaded both that nuclear weapons work and that they would work, in action, to produce an all but historically unparalleled (in speed of occurrence) catastrophe. From time to time, polities will find it useful to be able to command disaster on a scale beyond dispute. The sheer enormity of the catastrophe indicated may compensate for the low likelihood that a sane and sober leader actually would choose either to provoke it or to issue threats "that leave something to chance."[77]

As Richard J. Harknett argues persuasively in his contribution to this volume, "[w]hat is clearly distinctive about conventional and nuclear weapons is how contestable the former is compared to the latter. Measured on a scale of contestability—the degree to which technical, tactical, or operational effects can impact the actual destruction to be borne in combat—the destructive potential of nuclear weapons tends to be highly resilient. At a low level of possession, nuclear weapons can maintain a relatively incontestable level of military force."[78] In practice, there is likely to be a great deal to contest about the probable scale of nuclear damage, but at the level of political discourse there is an essential quality of awesome potential to cause disaster promised by nuclear possession—arguably, the existential deterrent—that brooks scant dispute.

"Anti-Friction" Arsenal

There is a simplicity to the proposition that the *ultima ratio regis* is a stock of more or less battle-ready nuclear weapons, not necessarily the latest models, which is reassuring to policymakers who must cope with a very uncertain world in which a great many things can go wrong. A nuclear arsenal may be regarded as an insurance policy against potentially significant errors in other regions of defense planning. Nuclear weapons may compensate for Clausewitzian friction.[79] Can one know how much is enough, especially as an information-led RMA gathers pace globally?[80] A nuclear arsenal may have limited utility, but, like an air bag in the car, it could just make the difference between national survival or destruction. By way of a distinctly imperfect analogy, there are many ways to kill a rattlesnake, but the potential lethality of the bite commands respect. There may be little of a positive character that the threat of a nuclear bite can deliver, but that threat is likely to protect core national values; that, at least, is the consensus among declared and nondeclared nuclear-weapon states today.

Reliable Strategic Answer to Clever Enemies

Readers may recall the memorable scene in *Raiders of the Lost Ark* wherein Indiana Jones's answer to a threat of fancy swordplay is to draw his revolver and shoot the swordsman. The answer is elegant in its simple brutality. Polities far less advanced in the information age than is the United States, and much less I-war capable, may believe with some good reason that brutal nuclear capabilities can provide a strategically adequate offset to cunning plans and sophisticated conventional weaponry. Whether or not America's I-war-shaped arsenal, in military-technical principle, could paralyze a lesser foe "inside-outside,"[81] would U.S. I-warriors be unleashed in time, and would they be preclusively successful?

Information warfare has the mixed blessing of being non–platform and non–environment specific. The incontestable reliability—to accept some oversimplification—of nuclear-armed forces likely will contrast advantageously with the deeply uncertain benefits for fighting power and overall strategic effect yielded by an information-led RMA. As with morale, for example, there is something intangible and uncertain about I-war prowess for which prudent leaders will seek brute-force compensation. Just how "clever" will friendly and unfriendly forces prove to be? A nuclear arsenal reduces the need to be improbably accurate in guessing the right answer to that question.

Status

Admittedly, nuclear status is not an unmixed blessing, but even notoriety can be advantageous in statecraft for deterrence and especially compellence.[82] The negative singularization of a taboo on nuclear acquisition induces an awe that is of benefit to national influence. Any taboo proclaims the significance of the behavior or object declared objectionable.[83] It may well be that the status pertaining to nuclear possession is substantially only negative. Lack of status attends an absence of such possession. In this view, nuclear weapons matter principally if a polity does not have them. By analogy, an honors degree may confer no benefit in a society where such degrees are commonplace. But the lack of an honors degree in that society might impose all but crippling limitations upon personal advancement.

It is not obvious what "use" Japan and Germany could make of national nuclear arsenals. But it is scarcely debatable that their lack of nuclear armament seriously limits their roles and behavior in regional and international security.[84]

Preservation of Order among Great Powers

Smart conventional weapons that exploit the cutting edge of I-war technologies will not substitute for a "classical" strategic nuclear posture in relations among super states (or close-to-super states). Notwithstanding the reality today of some approximation to political peace in the relations among those states, the current interwar period eventually will be transformed by a revival of great-power conflicts. The open-source literature advises that Russia has deployed at present approximately 13,500 tactical and 8,000 strategic nuclear weapons. The figure for China is in the zone of

300–500.[85] It is possible that Russia may yet ratify and actually implement the START II agreement, which would require a strategic weapon reduction to 3,500, but one should not hold one's breath waiting on that event. No matter how arms control and disarmament proceed over the next decade, it will remain a fact that nuclear-proliferant polities will acquire and retain nuclear arsenals ranging from the tens (India, Pakistan) to the low hundreds (Israel). Declared nuclear weapon states will keep arsenals ranging from the low hundreds (Britain) to the several thousands (Russia), at least. As the last line of defense for international order, the United States will need a nuclear force posture that is survivable, lethal, able to penetrate defenses, and reliably commanded and controlled.

Those in search of exemplary statements of strategic dogma would be hard-pressed to improve upon the hubristic 1994 claim by Ashton Carter, the cochairman of the Clinton administration's "Nuclear Posture Review," that "[w]e can use conventional forces to prevail anywhere in the world."[86] There will be rare occasions in the future, as in the past, when only a large and war-fighting-lethal nuclear posture will appear to fit the bill for prewar deterrence, intrawar deterrence, and possibly just plain denial. Nuclear weapons are not obsolescent or obsolete either for super and great powers or for regional rogues. Precise conventional capabilities on the requisite scale will not be available to all possible nuclear players; inferior conventional capabilities must encourage interest in WMD as an I-war offset; and I-war lacks the reliability of effect that is all but guaranteed by a tolerably survivable nuclear force posture.[87]

Taboo

In contrast to the advantages of nuclear possession, what are the disadvantages arguably unique to nuclear weapon capabilities? Antiproliferation theorists in the West have postulated unconvincingly the growth over the past quarter century of a nuclear taboo. The postulate is that nuclear weapons, as capability, as overt menace, let alone as action force, have been anathematized by the decent opinion of humankind. In this view, nuclear weapons have lost much of their legitimacy and hence much of their political and strategic value to actual and potential proliferants. Proof of this postulate allegedly may be found in the slow pace of proliferation, in the reluctance of new proliferants to declare their arsenals, in the supposed value of "virtual" nuclear arsenals, and in the apparently ever-smaller visible and practical roles of nuclear weapons in world politics.

The postulate of a nuclear taboo is an ethnocentric delusion on the part of Western theorists.[88] The desirability of such a taboo for the protection of our values is generally as obvious in the post-Soviet context as it is strategically irrelevant. Forbidden fruit is all the sweeter for being forbidden. The number of polities that today sign up for variably antinuclear propositions and sentiments is beside the point. The scale of the nuclear dimension to the future is no more going to be determined by the length of the list of nuclear abstainers than the risk of a Second World War could be measured in the 1930s by the number of people who found war abhorrent, or of polities who genuinely sought a lasting peace.

There is some danger that American theorists may persuade themselves that a nuclear taboo has achieved legal (or quasi-legal) and moral authority courtesy of the Nuclear Non-proliferation Treaty and the lengthening period of history that has witnessed no nuclear use. Fact and value are confused. A nuclear taboo is a value. It is especially attractive as a value to American culture, which loves the latest technology, believes it enjoys a long lead in exploiting that technology, and yearns to find clean, discriminate, (American)-casualty-minimal modes of war. Cyberwar is particularly appealing to a mind-set that seeks to avoid war's brutal realities, instead striving to find ways to play at war in cyberspace.[89] Needless to say, "virtual" war is appealing, just as deterrence is appealing. If war reliably can be advanced, or reduced, to the mode of a video conflict, there would be much worth saying in favor of such a trend. After all, it is not so long ago that the U.S. defense community was debating the scientific vagaries of a horrific potential "nuclear winter." In the future, though, not all of America's foes will be ready, able, and willing to play at cyberwar; moreover, some of those foes will be asked or obliged to acquiesce in prompt catastrophic defeat at the hands of the cyberproficient.

Martin Libicki notices rightly that in the Gulf War in 1991, "[w]e were on one side of a revolution and they were on the other." No less correctly, he proceeds to warn, "[y]et consider how differently we would have had to operate if they had had but a fraction of our capabilities (alternatively, what a conventional war against the Soviets in the 1990s would have been like). Virtually everything we used on the battlefield would have been vulnerable had it been visible."[90] To take Libicki's caveat still further, imagine how one would need to prepare for regional conflict were the foe thoroughly unpersuaded of the authority of a nuclear taboo.

Nuclear Weapons Are Too Destructive

Harnessing the power of the atom, nuclear weapons are uniquely efficient in converting mass to destructive energy in a variety of weapon effects. Paradoxically, the scale of energy released renders nuclear weapons singularly disadvantageous in that they deliver more destruction than is compatible with the control and desired outcome of war. In a tactical sense, nuclear weapons are liable to deliver "overkill," a fact that sharply diminishes their strategic value.

Nuclear Weapons Lack Credibility

The very destructiveness of nuclear weapons can sever the bridge between policy and military power known as strategy. The residual menace of Armageddon that lurks in a nuclear arsenal has obvious "last resort" merit in protection of core national values, but that arsenal can have little positive or even negative instrumental value in support of the protecting role of a superpower. At most, so the argument proceeds, nuclear capability discourages the political or military use of nuclear weapons (or other WMD) by others.[91] Such discouragement is not a minor benefit, one should add. WMD in support of the large conventional forces of a regional power would pose a nightmare scenario for the efficacy of U.S. extended deterrence or effective regional defense.

Opportunity Costs

Nuclear weapons are not cheap to acquire and operate.[92] They are cheap relative to the conventional arsenals of super and great powers, but they are anything but cheap for regional polities. In fact, the opportunity costs to a regional nuclear proliferant are likely to include an order of magnitude reduction in the quality and quantity of its non-nuclear forces. By way of analogy, consider the opportunity cost to the Imperial German Army of Grand Admiral Alfred von Tirpitz's High Seas Fleet.[93]

More broadly considered, the opportunity costs of a successful nuclear weapons program could include foreign goodwill, material hardships if sanctions are suffered, and diplomatic support sacrificed. Whether or not these burdens are worth bearing along with the cost of a smaller and less modern non-nuclear arsenal than could have been purchased would depend upon the local circumstances.

Yesterday's Weapon

If the cutting edge of global military proficiency is the ability to strike over the horizon with great precision and achieve desired effects by non-nuclear means, what price nuclear weapons?[94] Even if a nuclear arsenal probably continues to "work" in a narrow military sense—though one can never be sure without trying—nuclear weapons are out of fashion; they are yesterday's weapons. Whatever the military reality in some specific case, the wave of I-war speculation, argument, investment, peaceable demonstration, and even periodic punitive employment (for example, against Iraq and the Bosnian Serbs) has devalued the worth and the reputation of nuclear capabilities. If policy elites around the world join the bandwagon of those who rhetorically celebrate an information age and an associated style in warfare, nuclear weapons must appear crude, backward, and ever less desirable.

To move from political and cultural perception to narrowly military matters, it is probable that state-of-the-art conventional weapons with a strong I-war flavor to them may be able to defeat nuclear capabilities directly. Nuclear threats should be discouraged, devalued, and even outright negated by a general expectation that an information-dominant United States could on the one hand paralyze or destroy an enemy's nuclear arsenal preventively or preemptively, while on the other hand support strategic defense. Multilayered air and missile defenses, cued and guided by sensors in space, would command passage through the relevant geographical environments. In the words of two confident theorists:

> [E]ven a successful proliferator will prefer to keep conflicts conventional, as the United States will continue to maintain overwhelming counterforce and countervalue advantages over all nascent nuclear adversaries. Therefore, the likelihood that future wars, even nuclear ones, will be non-nuclear adds all the more reason to make an effort to optimize our capabilities for conventional and unconventional wars by developing a cyberwar doctrine.[95]

All of which is well and good, except that it both amounts to posing a severity of challenge analogous to a one-foot putt and neglects the role of friction in the fog of crisis and the accidents and uncertainties of war. If a cyberwarrior is confronting a non-cyberwarrior in a war wherein cyberpower is trumps, guess who is likely to win? But what if the foe either is another cyberwarrior or is able to shape the terms of engagement so as to place cyberprowess at a discount? In addition, even if I-war excellence should rule, what if friction hampers performance markedly? Indeed, the less cybercompetent combatant would be strongly motivated to seek out and exploit vulnerabilities peculiar to those who are heavily cyberdependent.[96]

Becoming a Nuclear Target

As good sportsmen, the world's statesmen allegedly have signed on for a taboo against the issuing of nuclear threats to, or the imposition of nuclear damage upon, non-nuclear polities. After all, it would "not be cricket" to visit nuclear menace upon those who are not nuclear armed.

It follows that a significant cost of nuclear weapons acquisition is the possible consequential acquisition of an honored place in the nuclear war plans of other nuclear-weapon states. This possibly substantial cost needs to be placed in context, however, no matter how hypothetical. It is difficult to price an option if alternatives do not carry price tags. A probable alternative option to the nuclear status that could license nuclear peril is a non-nuclear defense posture that assuredly would go down like corn before the harvesting equipment of America's conventional I-warriors.

In the calculations of some regional powers, the practicable alternative to a nuclear posture, with its attendant special risks, would be a non-nuclear defense that will work. Witness what the U.S.-led coalition wrought upon Iraq in 1991. I-war-challenged polities will be motivated to find strategic answers to the menace of an information-dominant United States. On the one hand, they will seek the I-war equivalent of the options open to a second-class naval power (for example, mines or torpedo boats). On the other hand, they will endeavor to defeat U.S. strategy by threatening to unleash WMD from mobile missile launchers that will be extremely hard to locate, track, and kill.

The huge literature on nuclear issues has yet to be amended, or even seriously interrogated, by the emerging speculation about an information age, information-age warfare, or an I-war-focused RMA.[97] The discussion here is a contribution to the intellectual equipment for the safe management of that historic encounter. Speculative analysis, idea spinning, concept floating, and the like are the state of play today. With proper acknowledgment for the misquotation from Winston Churchill, it is all too appropriate to observe that the debate pursued in these pages has yet to see the end of the beginning.[98] It is not even certain that we should be thinking in terms of an information age, information-age warfare, an RMA—or even RMAs as a general paradigm for relevant historical change—or a first or second phase to a nuclear age.

The Fallacy of the Golden Key

Accepting some risk of undue parsimony, five themes emerge from this analysis. First, there is an understandable tendency for tactics to be confused with strategy. The unquestionably burgeoning activity of an information-age character often is assumed to be self-explanatory in its strategic implications. But evidence of activity toward the achievement of excellence in the conduct of I-war is not synonymous with strategic meaning.

Second, the contemporary I-war hypothesis and its associate notion of an RMA probably constitute "discovery" of a permanent dimension to statecraft and war: the struggle to secure and deny usable knowledge. There is little that is truly novel about this contemporary discussion.

Third, a sociological sensibility among Western, and especially American, strategic theorists should alert us to the perils of intellectual fashion and the pull of cultural yearnings. The quest for novelty can have several motives, including intellectual curiosity, commercial advantage, and the public good. But the particular dynamics of strategic debate in the United States are wont to encourage the headlong and uncritical pursuit of that which sounds novel. When that which sounds novel appeals strongly to the preferred American way in warfare, the prospects for sensible analysis and prudent judgment are reduced yet further.

Fourth, it is distinctly possible that the excitement over information-age technologies has blinded many people to the change in the character of defense preparation and warfare effected by the development of space-power. It may be an error to subsume spacepower as a lesser category of joint military activity in an information age.

Finally, for all their promise of much-enhanced military effectiveness, information warriors with a conventional bite will not pose a lethal menace to the strategic value of nuclear weapons in the eyes of the policymakers of polities great and small. There is a brutal certainty about nuclear danger that will continue to find wide appeal, almost no matter how persuasive in principle are the items of nuclear disadvantage. A doctrinaire strategic devaluation of nuclear weapons is popular today in the senior ranks of the U.S. defense community, and particularly among the relevant top policymakers of the Clinton administration. The military promise of I-war excellence is the frosting on the cake of current U.S. superiority in conventional power projection. A U.S. defense community that fifty-five years ago saw in the Norden bombsight the golden key to a precision bombing that would deliver victory through airpower[99] today identifies cyberspace controlled by America's information warriors as the golden key to quick and decisive success. Similar fallacies attend the belief in a golden key in both historical cases.

NOTES

1. A thesis developed in Alvin Toffler and Heidi Toffler, *War and Anti-War: Survival at the Dawn of the 21st Century* (Boston: Little, Brown, 1993), especially chap. 9.

2. John Arquilla and David Ronfeldt, "Cyberwar Is Coming!" *Comparative Strategy* 12 (April–June 1993): 141–65.

3. Cyberspace "may be understood as the sum of the globe's communications

links and computational nodes." Martin Libicki, "Why Information Matters More than Geography," *Orbis* (Spring 1996): 261–76.

4. William J. Perry, Secretary of Defense, *Annual Report to the President and the Congress* (Washington, D.C.: U.S. Government Printing Office, February 1995), 83. A superior unfriendly critique of the "Nuclear Posture Review" is Michael R. Boldrick, "The Nuclear Posture Review: Liabilities and Risks," *Parameters* 25 (Winter 1995–96): 80–91.

5. The better examples of recent speculative inquiry include Michael J. Mazarr, "Nuclear Weapons after the Cold War," *Washington Quarterly* 15 (Summer 1992): 185–201; Stephen J. Cimbala, "Nuclear Weapons in the New World Order," *Journal of Strategic Studies* 16 (June 1993): 173–99; Michael McGwire, "Is There a Future for Nuclear Weapons?" *International Affairs* 70 (April 1994): 211–28; Ivo H. Daalder, "What Vision for the Nuclear Future?" *Washington Quarterly* 18 (Spring 1995): 127–42; Dean Wilkening and Kenneth Watman, *Nuclear Deterrence in a Regional Conflict* (Santa Monica, Calif.: RAND, 1995); David Gompert, Kenneth Watman, and Dean Wilkening, "Nuclear First Use Revisited," *Survival* 37 (Autumn 1995): 27–44; Patrick J. Garrity, "The Next Nuclear Questions," *Parameters* 25 (Winter 1995–96): 92–111; and Fred Iklé, "The Second Coming of the Nuclear Age," *Foreign Affairs* 75 (January–February 1996): 119–28.

6. A distinction explained and developed in Colin S. Gray, "The Second Nuclear Age: Insecurity, Proliferation, and the Control of Arms," in Williamson Murray, ed., *Brassey's Mershon American Defense Annual, 1995–96* (Washington, D.C.: Brassey's, 1995), 135–56.

7. See Martin Libicki, *The Mesh and the Net: Speculation on Armed Conflict in an Age of Free Silicon,* McNair Paper 28 (Washington, D.C.: National Defense University, Institute of National Strategic Studies, March 1994).

8. An admirably clear and uncompromising statement of this argument is John Arquilla, "The Strategic Implications of Information Dominance," *Strategic Review* 22 (Summer 1994): 24–30.

9. See Andrew F. Krepinevich Jr., "The Military Revolution: Restructuring Defense for the 21st Century," prepared testimony presented to the Senate Armed Services Subcommittee on Acquisition and Technology, 5 May 1995, 3.

10. Irving Lachow, "The GPS Dilemma: Balancing Military Risks and Economic Benefits," *International Security* 20 (Summer 1995): 126–48, is useful.

11. The most useful introduction is provided in two studies by Martin Libicki: *Mesh and the Net;* and *What Is Information Warfare?* ACIS Paper 3 (Washington, D.C.: National Defense University, August 1995).

12. U.S. Marine Corps, *Warfighting* (New York: Doubleday, 1994; first pub. 1989). Alternatively, see H. T. Hayden, *Warfighting: Maneuver Warfare in the U.S. Marine Corps* (London: Greenhill Books, 1995).

13. As the references to this chapter attest, there is no shortage of speculative inquiry about either nuclear weapons after the Cold War or information-age warfare. But, as of this date (early 1996), there is next to no literature available that attempts to treat the inevitable historical strategic encounter between the information and nuclear ages.

14. Arquilla, "Strategic Implications of Information Dominance," 29.
15. Arquilla, "Strategic Implications of Information Dominance," 25.
16. Warren Caldwell Jr., "Promises, Promises," *U.S. Naval Institute Proceedings* 122 (January 1996): 54.
17. Caldwell, "Promises, Promises," 56.
18. Bernard Brodie, *War and Politics* (New York: Macmillan, 1973), 452.
19. It is interesting to note that John Arquilla also favors this concept. He writes: "America's signal victories in recent years have reduced, in the aggregate, the relative power of its potential adversaries. This provides a strategic 'breathing space' for the United States." "Strategic Implications of Information Dominance," 30.
20. For speculation about conflict along intercivilizational fault lines, see Samuel P. Huntington, "The Clash of Civilizations," *Foreign Affairs* 72 (Summer 1993): 22–49. No less grim is the analysis in Ralph Peters, "The Culture of Future Conflict," *Parameters* 25 (Winter 1995–96): 18–27.
21. For an instant classic in analysis, see the deeply disturbing essay by Robert D. Kaplan, "The Coming Anarchy," *Atlantic Monthly* (February 1994): 44–76.
22. This is my thesis in "Villains, Victims, and Sheriffs: Strategic Studies and Security for an Interwar Period," *Comparative Strategy* 13 (October–December 1994): 353–69.
23. See Stephen Peter Rosen, *Winning the Next War: Innovation and the Modern Military* (Ithaca, N.Y.: Cornell University Press, 1991).
24. This possibility finds powerful support in three recent persuasive texts: Richard Ned Lebow and Janice Gross Stein, *We All Lost the Cold War* (Princeton, N.J.: Princeton University Press, 1994); Iklé, "Second Coming of the Nuclear Age"; and Keith B. Payne, *Deterrence in the Second Nuclear Age: Transcending the Valor of Ignorance*, forthcoming.
25. Iklé refers to "the new nuclear age" and to "a more volatile second act." "Second Coming of the Nuclear Age," 123, 126.
26. Michael Howard, "Lessons of the Cold War," *Survival* 36 (Winter 1994–95): 161.
27. Howard, "Lessons of the Cold War," 164.
28. With reference to the dangers of nuclear accidents, only one dimension to the security challenge of the Cold War, see Bruce G. Blair, *The Logic of Accidental Nuclear War* (Washington, D.C.: Brookings Institution, 1993); and Scott D. Sagan, *The Limits of Safety: Organizations, Accidents, and Nuclear Weapons* (Princeton, N.J.: Princeton University Press, 1993). Serious revisionist histories of deterrence in the Cold War are only beginning to appear.
29. As affirmed in Albert Wohlstetter, "The Delicate Balance of Terror," *Foreign Affairs* 37 (January 1959): 211–34.
30. Colin S. Gray, "Strategy in the Nuclear Age: The United States, 1945–1991," in Williamson Murray, MacGregor Knox, and Alvin Bernstein, eds., *The Making of Strategy: Rulers, States, and War* (Cambridge: Cambridge University Press, 1994), especially 606–10.
31. For development of this intriguing concept, see Michael J. Mazarr, "Virtual Nuclear Arsenals," *Survival* 37 (Autumn 1995): 7–26.

32. Fred Iklé provides the complementary judgment that "[w]ith the Cold War now over, the drama of the nuclear age has entered a more volatile second act. While one cannot yet predict when this act will end, or whether it will conclude peacefully or with the destructive use of nuclear weapons, one can readily recognize that it is transitory." "Second Coming of the Nuclear Age," 126.

33. NATO, *Study on NATO Enlargement* (Brussels: NATO, September 1995), currently is authoritative. This is a dynamic subject. Ronald D. Asmus, Richard L. Kugler, and F. Stephen Larrabee, "Building a New NATO," *Foreign Affairs* 72 (September/October 1993): 28–40, was a key period piece; while Jeffrey Simon, ed., *NATO Enlargement: Opinions and Options* (Washington, D.C.: National Defense University, 1995), also is useful.

34. It would be premature to proclaim that a new NATO is alive and functioning. For just such a view, see Javier Solana, "Bosnia: A Defining Moment for NATO," *International Herald Tribune* (29 December 1995): 6.

35. Richard K. Betts, "Systems for Peace or Causes of War? Collective Security, Arms Control, and the New Europe," *International Security* 17 (Summer 1992): 5–43, hits the mark.

36. These claims are not controversial. Secretary of Defense William J. Perry advised that "[w]eapons of mass destruction—nuclear, biological, and chemical—along with the ballistic missiles that deliver them, pose a major threat to U.S. security and that of U.S. allies and other friendly nations. Thus, a key part of the U.S. strategy is to stem the proliferation of such weapons and to develop an effective capability to deter, prevent, and defend against their use. Currently, more than 25 countries possess or are developing nuclear, chemical, or biological weapons, and more than 15 nations have ballistic missiles. This situation is exacerbated by the continuing spread of sensitive technologies that contribute to the development and improvement of ballistic missiles." *Annual Report* (1995), 239. In addition, see Humphrey Crum Ewing, *Ballistic Missiles: The Approaching Threat,* Bailrigg Memorandum 9 (Lancaster, England: Lancaster University, Centre for Defense and International Security Studies, 1994). It is not alarmist simply to note that the clear trend is for ever-longer-range ballistic missiles to find their way into the hands of regional polities that are more and more likely to be able to acquire WMD.

37. See Lebow and Stein, *We All Lost the Cold War.* Problems of cross-cultural communication are treated sensitively in Ken Booth, *Strategy and Ethnocentrism* (London: Croom, Helm, 1979); and Alastair Iain Johnston, *Cultural Realism: Strategic Culture and Grand Strategy in Chinese History* (Princeton, N.J.: Princeton University Press, 1995).

38. A particularly bold venture in theory down this particular track is Martin van Creveld, *The Transformation of War* (New York: Free Press, 1991). John Keegan, *A History of Warfare* (London: Hutchinson, 1993), also proclaims the end of an era in war making in a study that emphasizes war as a culture-based activity. See also Ralph Peters, "The New Warrior Class," *Parameters* 24 (Summer 1994): 16–26.

39. See, for example, James Adams, "New Russian Subs Outsmart Royal Navy," *The Sunday Times* (London) (18 February 1996): 19.

40. Colin S. Gray, *House of Cards: Why Arms Control Must Fail* (Ithaca, N.Y.: Cornell University Press, 1992); and "Arms Races and Other Pathetic Fallacies: A Case for Deconstruction," *Review of International Studies* (U.K.), forthcoming.

41. For a small sample of the explosion of literature on these topics, see van Creveld, *Transformation of War;* William E. Odom, *America's Military Revolution: Strategy and Structure after the Cold War* (Washington, D.C.: American University Press, 1993); Arquilla and Ronfeldt, "Cyberwar Is Coming!"; James R. FitzSimmonds and Jan M. van Tol, "Revolutions in Military Affairs," *Joint Force Quarterly* 4 (Spring 1994): 24–31; Libicki, *Mesh and the Net* and *What Is Information Warfare?*; Andrew F. Krepinevich, "Cavalry to Computer: The Pattern of Military Revolutions," *The National Interest* 37 (Fall 1994): 30–42; "Perspectives on the Revolution in Military Affairs," *Parameters* 25 (Summer 1995): 7–54; William A. Owens, *High Seas: The Naval Passage to an Uncharted World* (Annapolis, Md.: Naval Institute Press, 1995); and Eliot A. Cohen, "A Revolution in Warfare," *Foreign Affairs* 75 (March–April 1996): 37–54.

42. The idea of a revolution in military affairs has been endorsed as interesting by no less a scholar and interpreter for policymakers than Andrew W. Marshall, the Director of Net Assessment in the Office of the Secretary of Defense. See Marshall, "Revolutions in Military Affairs," prepared testimony presented to the Senate Armed Services Subcommittee on Acquisition and Technology, 5 May 1995.

43. Thomas A. Keaney and Eliot A. Cohen, *Gulf War Air Power Survey, Summary Report* (Washington, D.C.: U.S. Government Printing Office, 1993), 238.

44. Keaney and Cohen, *Gulf War Air Power Survey.* Eliot A. Cohen, "The Mystique of U.S. Air Power," *Foreign Affairs* 73 (January–February 1994): 109–24, conveys the same message.

45. The origins and development of Colonel Boyd's theory, a theory deriving largely from study of the reasons for the high kill ratios achieved by F-86s against MIG-15s in Korea, are explained clearly in William S. Lind, *Maneuver Warfare Handbook* (Boulder, Colo.: Westview Press, 1985), 4–6.

46. In addition to Lind, *Maneuver Warfare Handbook,* see Robert Leonhard, *The Art of Maneuver: Maneuver-Warfare Theory and AirLand Battle* (Novato, Calif.: Presidio Press, 1991); and Richard D. Hauser Jr., ed., *An Anthology of Maneuver Warfare* (Novato, Calif.: Presidio Press, 1993).

47. Libicki, *Mesh and the Net,* chap. 1, <http://www.ndu.edu/ndu/inss/macnair/mcnair28/m028cont.html>.

48. Libicki, "Why Information Matters More than Geography."

49. Krepinevich, "The Military Revolution," 3.

50. Krepinevich, "Cavalry to Computer," 30.

51. I am indebted to Wayne P. Hughes Jr. for the rigor of his logic in *Fleet Tactics: Theory and Practice* (Annapolis, Md.: Naval Institute Press, 1986). Hughes advises that "strategists *plan,* tacticians *do,"* 10.

52. Carl von Clausewitz, *On War,* ed. Michael Howard and Peter Paret (Princeton, N.J.: Princeton University Press, 1976; first pub. 1832), 75.

53. Krepinevich, "Cavalry to Computer," identifies ten candidate RMAs since the fourteenth century (pp. 31–36). These comprise (1) an Infantry Revolution

(Hundred Years' War); (2) an Artillery Revolution (Hundred Years' War); (3) a Revolution of Sail and Shot (sixteenth century); (4) a Fortress Revolution (sixteenth and seventeenth centuries); (5) an infantry firearms Gunpowder Revolution (sixteenth century); (6) the Napoleonic Revolution (1790s and 1800s, to 1815); (7) a Land Warfare Revolution introduced by railroads, the telegraph, the rifling of muskets, and artillery (1810s–1860s); (8) a Naval Revolution (1840s–1900s); (9) an Interwar Revolution in Mechanization, Aviation, and Information (1919–39); and, of course, (10) a Nuclear Revolution after 1945. A problem with grand theories that embrace several centuries is that the pursuit of regularity of form can allow content to suffer. For example, the Infantry Revolution of the fourteenth century may have been no revolution at all. In fact, the critical role of infantry and dismounted knights and men-at-arms in medieval warfare probably has been systematically underappreciated by many scholars for more than a century. See R. Allen Brown, "The Battle of Hastings," in Matthew Strickland, ed., *Anglo-Norman Warfare: Studies in Late Anglo-Saxon and Anglo-Norman Military Organization and Warfare* (Woodbridge, U.K.: Boydell Press, 1992), 171. For historical controversies, see especially Clifford J. Rogers, ed., *The Military Revolution Debate: Readings on the Military Transformation of Early Modern Europe* (Boulder, Colo.: Westview Press, 1995). Also useful are Michael Duffy, ed., *The Military Revolution and the State, 1500–1800* (Exeter, U.K.: Department of History and Archaeology, University of Exeter, 1980); Peter Paret, "Revolutions in Warfare: An Earlier Generation of Interpreters," in Bernard Brodie, Michael D. Intriligator, and Roman Kolkowicz, eds., *National Security and International Stability* (Cambridge, Mass.: Oelgeschlager, Gunn, and Hain, 1983), 157–69; Geoffrey Parker, *The Military Revolution: Military Innovation and the Rise of the West, 1500–1800* (Cambridge: Cambridge University Press, 1988); David Eltis, *The Military Revolution in Sixteenth-Century Europe* (London: Tauris Academic Studies, 1995); and Andrew Ayton and J. L. Price, eds., *The Medieval Military Revolution: State, Society and Military Change in Medieval and Early Modern Europe* (London: Tauris Academic Studies, 1995).

54. With a bow to Bernard Brodie, ed., *The Absolute Weapon: Atomic Power and World Order* (New York: Harcourt, Brace, 1946). Also see his *War and Politics,* chap. 9. A more recent outstanding analysis is Robert Jervis, *The Meaning of the Nuclear Revolution: Statecraft and the Prospect of Armageddon* (Ithaca, N.Y.: Cornell University Press, 1989). Sharing Brodie's conviction that nuclear weapons have utility only in nonuse (*War and Politics,* chap. 9), Jervis advises that "[a]lthough *military* victory is impossible, victory is not: nuclear weapons can help reach many important political goals" (22).

55. Libicki's studies, especially *Mesh and the Net* and *What Is Information Warfare?* are the stuff out of which national and international nightmares can be made.

56. See Arquilla and Ronfeldt, "Cyberwar Is Coming!"; and Arquilla, "Strategic Implications of Information Dominance."

57. Marshall, "Revolutions in Military Affairs," 1.

58. Richard Overy, *Why the Allies Won* (London: Jonathan Cape, 1995), explains persuasively just how formidable German power was by 1942.

59. Charles E. Callwell, *The Tactics of Today* (Edinburgh: William Blackwood and Sons, 1902), 1. The book was written "from the field" in South Africa in 1900.

60. Alfred Thayer Mahan, *The Influence of Sea Power upon History, 1660–1783* (Boston: Little, Brown, 1890), 88. For the leading source of Mahan's inspiration, see Antoine Henri de Jomini, *The Art of War* (London: Greenhill Books, 1992; reprint of 1862 ed.), 48.

61. J. F. C. Fuller, *Armament and History: A Study of the Influence of Armament on History from the Dawn of Classical Warfare to the Second World War* (London: Eyre and Spotiswoode, 1946).

62. See Martin van Creveld, *Supplying War, Logistics from Wallenstein to Patton* (Cambridge: Cambridge University Press, 1977), chap. 5. The tenuousness of the transportation provided to sustain the Wehrmacht in its great advance to the east is a major theme of Albert Seaton, *The Russo-German War, 1941–45* (New York: Praeger, 1971). As the war proceeded, the Red Army became more modern in its transportation, the German Army much less so.

63. Perhaps there are no truly new strategic concepts.

64. Alvin Toffler in *Horizon*, "The I-Bomb," text adapted from the program transmitted on 27 March 1995 (London: BBC Publications, 1995), 6.

65. Alvin Toffler in *Horizon*, 22.

66. Arquilla and Ronfeldt, "Cyberwar Is Coming!" 147.

67. Marshall, "Revolutions in Military Affairs," 1.

68. In 1989, Secretary of Defense Frank C. Carlucci explained that "[a] competitive strategy analysis employs a three-step chess match methodology designed to align enduring U.S. strengths against enduring Soviet weaknesses in a move-countermove-countercountermove sequence." Carlucci, *Annual Report to the Congress*, fiscal year 1990 (Washington, D.C.: U.S. Government Printing Office, 17 January 1989), 47. A useful end-of-period piece that provides valuable detail on the NATO orientation of much of the analysis conducted in pursuit of competitive strategies is David M. Abshire and Michael Moodie, "Competitive Strategies," *Washington Quarterly* 13 (Winter 1990): 29–42. The idea of competitive strategy suffers from a central redundancy that has the unfortunate effect of inviting derision for a sound, if obvious, idea. In the field of conflict, I cannot imagine a kind of strategy other than the genus intended to be competitive. The discovery, celebration, and institutionalization of competitive strategy and strategies (most notably in a Competitive Strategies Task Force, a Competitive Strategies Council, and a Competitive Strategies Senior Intelligence Committee) in the late 1980s could hardly help but suggest that the Department of Defense somehow had previously neglected the enemy in its planning. To heed the significance of information and knowledge for defense planning and the conduct of war is, similarly, to risk overdiscovery of the obvious and the enduring. This is not to deny that although there is a permanent need for strategy to be competitive, it is exceedingly difficult to pursue the chess analogy if the opponent, the particular game, the value of the "pieces," and even the rules are unknown and unknowable. Nineteen-eighties vintage "competitive strategies" was conceived as an effort to be competitive for a unique contingency: preparation for war with the Soviet Union. In his brilliant history of the British Army's Staff Col-

lege, Brian Bond commented thus on the strategic context after 1906: "at long last staff officers could be trained with a specific and realistic contingency in mind." *The Victorian Army and the Staff College, 1856–1914* (London: Eyre Methuen, 1972), 245.

69. See Samuel R. Williamson Jr., *The Politics of Grand Strategy: Britain and France Prepare for War, 1904–1914* (Cambridge, Mass.: Harvard University Press, 1969), especially 122, 169, 176; John Gooch, *The Plans of War: The General Staff and British Military Strategy, c. 1900–1916* (London: Routledge and Kegan Paul, 1974), 280, 282–84; and L. C. F. Turner, "The Significance of the Schlieffen Plan," in Paul Kennedy, ed., *The War Plans of the Great Powers, 1880–1914* (London: George Allen and Unwin, 1979), 199–221.

70. See Robert Allan Doughty, *The Breaking Point: Sedan and the Fall of France, 1940* (Hamden, Conn.: Archon Books, 1990); and Telford Taylor, *The March of Conquest: The German Victories in Western Europe, 1940* (Baltimore: The Nautical and Aviation Publishing Company of America, 1991; first pub. 1958), chaps. 5, 7.

71. A good popular overview is John Winton, *Ultra at Sea* (London: Leo Cooper, 1988). For an assessment somewhat skeptical of the decisive value of Ultra intelligence, see Dan van der Vat, *The Atlantic Campaign: The Great Struggle at Sea, 1939–1945* (London: Hodder and Stoughton, 1988), 259–60, 316. Also see Gerhard L. Weinberg, *A World at Arms: A Global History of World War II* (Cambridge: Cambridge University Press, 1994), 551–52; and especially Overy, *Why the Allies Won*, chap. 2, for well-balanced judgments.

72. On the debate over nuclear proliferation in the context of nuclear-focused strategic studies overall, see Gray, "Second Nuclear Age." Outstanding from the huge and generally exceedingly dire and dreary literature on nuclear proliferation is the following short list of useful items: Kathleen C. Bailey, *Strengthening Nuclear Proliferation* (Boulder, Colo.: Westview Press, 1993); Richard K. Betts, "Paranoids, Pygmies, Pariahs and Nonproliferation Revisited," *Security Studies* 2 (Spring–Summer 1993): 100–124; Office of Technology Assessment, U.S. Congress, *Proliferation of Weapons of Mass Destruction: Assessing the Risks*, OTA-ISC-559 (Washington, D.C.: U.S. Government Printing Office, August 1993); Office of Technology Assessment, U.S. Congress, *Technologies Underlying Weapons of Mass Destruction*, OTA-BP-ISC-115 (Washington, D.C.: U.S. Government Printing Office, December 1993); Scott D. Sagan, "The Perils of Proliferation: Organization Theory, Deterrence Theory, and the Spread of Nuclear Weapons," *International Security* 18 (Spring 1994): 66–107; for the "basics," see Gary T. Gardner, *Nuclear Proliferation: A Primer* (Boulder, Colo.: Lynne Reinner Publishers, 1994); Michael Mandelbaum, "Lessons of the Next Nuclear War," *Foreign Affairs* 74 (March–April 1995): 22–37; and Scott D. Sagan and Kenneth N. Waltz, *The Spread of Nuclear Weapons: A Debate* (New York: W. W. Norton, 1995).

73. The argument for spacepower as a candidate revolutionary development is developed in Colin S. Gray, "The Influence of Space Power upon History," *Comparative Strategy* 15 (July–September 1996). Also see David E. Lupton, *On Space*

132 / The Absolute Weapon Revisited

Warfare: A Space Power Doctrine (Maxwell AFB, Ala.: Air University Press, June 1988); and Steven Lambakis, "Space Control in Desert Storm and Beyond," *Orbis* 39 (Summer 1995): 417–33. On airpower as the "key force," see John A. Warden III, *The Air Campaign: Planning for Combat* (Washington, D.C.: Pergamon-Brassey's, 1989; first pub. 1988), 7, 123–27. On the question of the maturity of airpower in the 1990s, see Richard P. Hallion, *Storm over Iraq: Air Power in the Gulf War* (Washington, D.C.: Smithsonian Institution Press, 1992); "The Role of Aerospace Power in U.S. National Security Policy in the Next Quarter Century," special section in *Comparative Strategy* 12 (July–September 1993): 249–338; *Gulf War Air Power Survey*, 6 vols. (Director, Eliot A. Cohen) (Washington, D.C.: U.S. Government Printing Office, 1993); Carl H. Builder, *The Icarus Syndrome: The Role of Air Power Theory in the Evolution and Fate of the U.S. Air Force* (New Brunswick, N.J.: Transaction Publishers, 1994); Williamson Murray, *Air War in the Persian Gulf* (Baltimore: The Nautical and Aviation Publishing Company of America, 1995); Eliot A. Cohen, "The Meaning and Influence of Air Power," *Orbis* 39 (Spring 1995): 189–200; and Andrew G. B. Vallance, *The Air Weapon: Doctrines of Air Power Strategy and Operational Art* (London: Macmillan, 1996).

74. I develop this argument in my *Explorations in Strategy* (Westport, Conn.: Greenwood Press, 1996), chap. 5, "The United States as an Air Power."

75. Clausewitz, *On War*, 595–96. Unsurprisingly, Sun-tzu had the same idea, albeit with a different rank ordering of objectives. *The Art of War*, trans. Ralph D. Sawyer (Boulder, Colo.: Westview Press, 1994), 177. Whereas Clausewitz advised a focus, in descending order of desirability, upon the enemy's (1) army, (2) capital city, and (3) principal ally, Sun-tzu preferred to attack the enemy's (1) plans, (2) alliances, (3) army, and (4) fortified cities.

76. With good reason, the Mongol case is a favorite among would-be cyberwarriors. See Arquilla and Ronfeldt, "Cyberwar Is Coming!" 148–50. See also David Morgan, *The Mongols* (Oxford: Basil Blackwell, 1986).

77. See Thomas C. Schelling, *The Strategy of Conflict* (Cambridge, Mass.: Harvard University Press, 1960), chap. 8.

78. This is developed in Richard J. Harknett's contribution to this volume. See also his "The Logic of Conventional Weapons and the End of the Cold War," *Security Studies* 4 (Autumn 1994): 83–114.

79. Clausewitz, *On War*, 119–21.

80. Defense planning is an inexact art. See my "Off the Map: Defense Planning after the Soviet Threat," *Strategic Review* 22 (Spring 1994): 26–35. Paul K. Davis, ed., *New Challenges for Defense Planning: Rethinking How Much Is Enough* (Santa Monica, Calif.: RAND, 1994), contains essays both rigorous and imaginative, but as the Olympic trainer commented in the movie *Chariots of Fire,* he could not put in (to an athlete) what God left out. The problems with planning for the future are that the future has yet to happen and the future is not determinable by our decisions alone. Absent a reliable crystal ball, there is no way to know how much is enough for national defense in the future.

81. "Inside-outside" is the concept of operations realized in the Gulf War. The concept envisages assaulting the enemy's center of gravity immediately on the out-

break of war without having first to wage an extensive campaign to fight one's way through the enemy's protective layers. The immediate achievement of air superiority by the coalition allowed stealthy F-117s to go to downtown Baghdad on the first night of the war in pursuit of the enemy's strategic command structure. See John A. Warden III, "Employing Air Power in the Twenty-First Century," in Richard H. Shultz Jr. and Robert L. Pfaltzgraff Jr., *The Future of Air Power in the Aftermath of the Gulf War* (Maxwell AFB, Ala.: Air University Press, July 1992), 78.

82. Whereas the would-be deterrer seeks to prevent inimical behavior, the would-be compeller seeks to undo misdeeds already perpetrated. Once Saddam Hussein had seized Kuwait, the problem for the international community changed from deterrence to compellence. The classic statement of the relevant logic is Thomas C. Schelling, *Arms and Influence* (New Haven, Conn.: Yale University Press, 1966), 69–91.

83. Arguments in praise of a "global nuclear taboo" permeate Lewis A. Dunn, *Containing Nuclear Proliferation,* Adelphi Paper 263 (London: IISS, Winter 1991), and are criticized in Gray, "Second Nuclear Age," 145–48.

84. See the analysis in Garrity, "Next Nuclear Questions," 96–97.

85. Boldrick, "Nuclear Posture Review," 90 fn. 4, 91 fn. 48.

86. Quoted in Boldrick, "Nuclear Posture Review," 81.

87. Given the scale of latent menace in a nuclear arsenal, the military-technical requirements for a credible nuclear posture in practice are rather low. We may be less than certain that our nuclear weapons would "work" as intended, but our enemies could not be certain that they would not. To be credible enough to yield sufficient deterrent effect—if foes are deterrable, that is—a nuclear force posture does not have to meet rigorously the standards set by Albert Wohlstetter in his famous 1959 article. Indeed, it is not obvious that U.S. forces really needed to meet RAND's "particularly stringent conditions for deterrence which affect forces based close to the enemy." It may be recalled that, canonically, a credible (or second-strike) deterrent has to be (1) affordable; (2) survivable against enemy attacks; (3) reliably commanded and controlled; (4) able to reach enemy targets; (5) able to penetrate enemy active defenses; and (6) able to destroy the targets despite passive protection measures. Wohlstetter, "Delicate Balance of Terror." To be good enough, a proliferant's nuclear force posture need only pose an awesome menace to its regional foes and possibly to one or several of those foes' distant friends and allies. Even a nuclear posture that might pose a credible threat to deliver only a handful or less of nuclear weapons in retaliation most probably would translate as a second-strike capability apt to transform the risk-benefit calculus of distant would-be guardian powers.

88. On this subject, see Martin van Creveld, *Nuclear Proliferation and the Future of Conflict* (New York: Free Press, 1993), chaps. 3–4; but see also Gerald Segal, "Strategy and Ethnic Chic," *International Affairs* 60 (Winter 1983–84): 15–30.

89. I am grateful to Jim Wirtz for encouraging me to develop this thought.

90. Libicki, *Mesh and the Net,* chap. 2.

91. We know now from Iraqi sources that Saddam Hussein's decision not to

launch some of his Scud missiles with chemical or biological warheads was motivated by fear of U.S. nuclear retaliation. In his pioneering critique of the theory and practice of deterrence, Keith B. Payne notes wryly that "Saddam Hussein's decision making appears not to have been shaped by an appreciation of this nuclear taboo by U.S. leaders—the exploitation of it by a challenger more familiar with the United States political culture may affect a future regional crisis." *Deterrence in the Second Nuclear Age.*

92. See Bailey, *Strengthening Nuclear Nonproliferation,* chap. 11; and Etel Solingen, "The Political Economy of Nuclear Restraint," *International Security* 19 (Fall 1994): 126–69.

93. This is not to suggest that nuclear arsenals would be a "luxury fleet," as Winston Churchill once commented: "The British Navy is to us a necessity and, from some points of view, the German Navy is to them more in the nature of a luxury." *The World Crisis, 1911–1918,* vol. 1 of 2 (London: Odhams, 1938), 76. See Holger H. Herwig, *"Luxury" Fleet: The Imperial German Navy, 1888–1918* (London: George Allen and Unwin, 1980). Whether or not the High Seas Fleet was the appropriate answer to the Royal Navy, Germany's strategic condition in the twentieth century obliged it to seek to neutralize the multifaceted "enabling" roles of British seapower.

94. The answer on the part of a regional or declining great power most probably would be "at almost any payable price," if that power could not acquire armed forces on the cutting edge of global military proficiency.

95. Arquilla and Ronfeldt, "Cyberwar Is Coming!" 157.

96. For an analysis strongly critical of the "techno-chic image" sought by today's information warriors, see A. J. Bacevich, "Preserving the Well-Bred Horse," *The National Interest* 37 (Fall 1994): 43–49.

97. For example, a recent collection of essays on the frontier of nuclear reevaluation does not even contain an index reference to information warfare, cyberspace or cyberwar, computers, or RMAs. Jorn Gjelstad and Olav Njolstad, eds., *Nuclear Rivalry and International Order* (London: SAGE Publications, 1996). Such absence is the norm today, not the exception.

98. Winston Churchill told an audience in London on 10 November 1942 that "this is not the end. It is not even the beginning of the end. But it is, perhaps, the end of the beginning." Quoted in Martin Gilbert, *Churchill: A Life* (London: BCA, 1992; first pub. 1991), 734.

99. See Stephen L. McFarland, *America's Pursuit of Precision Bombing, 1910–1945* (Washington, D.C.: Smithsonian Institution Press, 1995).

Part 2

Deterrence: Fifty Years Later

Beyond Bipolarity: Prospects for
Nuclear Stability after the Cold War

JAMES J. WIRTZ

Although the Cold War specter of mutual assured destruction (MAD) no longer preoccupies American strategic thought, U.S. policymakers might again confront highly demanding nuclear threats by the early twenty-first century. There are indications that despite the successful extension of the Non-proliferation Treaty (NPT), the spread of nuclear weapons and advanced delivery systems will continue, or possibly accelerate, in the decades ahead. Instead of one nation constituting the primary nuclear threat to Americans, policymakers could confront several potential adversaries capable of using nuclear weapons to attack the continental United States, U.S. forces deployed overseas, or U.S. allies. Simultaneously, if the START II agreements are implemented, a strategic relationship approximating minimum deterrence will emerge between the United States and Russia.[1] When combined, these trends suggest that in contrast to the "nuclear abundance" of the Cold War, the United States will have to rely on a relatively small nuclear arsenal and related infrastructure to counter emerging proliferation threats.

A series of bilateral deterrence relationships might come to dominate a future international landscape populated by an increasing number of relatively small nuclear arsenals. As John Weltman noted some time ago, "beneath the rhetoric of 'omnidimensionality' [of nuclear threats], there has been little significant doubt about the direction in which [nuclear] weapons were and are pointed."[2] Despite the military characteristics of the strategic balance that leaves virtually all states open to nuclear devastation, political conflict is needed to make salient the potential for nuclear attack. Policymakers, according to Weltman, care little about hypothetical groupings of potential adversaries and instead focus on existing antagonists, which gives calculations of the nuclear balance a bilateral flavor. But if one abandoned this bilateral assumption, the strategic pressures inherent in multilateral or multipolar nuclear relationships—strategic situations suggested by current trends—could be explored. By resorting to a sort of "primitive realism," the potential military characteristics of various "multiple" nuclear balances could be identified.

This chapter explores the opportunities and pitfalls created by future strategic nuclear balances comprising at least a dozen states, each possessing a somewhat different level of nuclear capability. It begins by surveying arguments about bipolarity, MAD, and idiosyncratic sources of Cold War stability. It then explores the likelihood that these factors will contribute to arms-race and crisis stability in nuclear balances characterized by a variety of states armed with various levels of nuclear capability. The chapter then evaluates three political-military perspectives that might animate these multiple nuclear balances: nuclear multilateralism, nuclear multipolarity, and the conventionalization of nuclear war. In a multilateral nuclear world, the nuclear balance will seem to form a seamless web: changes in one state's nuclear arsenal will be perceived to have a direct impact on every nuclear state's security. In a multipolar nuclear world, policymakers will become preoccupied with the formation and maintenance of nuclear alliances: the nuclear balance will be based on calculations of the strength of competing coalitions. Conventionalization generally refers to the act of treating nuclear weapons and nuclear war as if they possessed the qualities and produced the effects of conventional weapons and war. The chapter then offers a description of how nuclear-armed states might behave in a world in which an escape from MAD is likely.

Nuclear Weapons and Cold War Stability

The gradual increase in the number of nuclear-armed states combined with the recent reduction in the size and capabilities of Russian and American arsenals highlights one of the great issues left unresolved at the end of the Cold War: What were the causes of stability—the absence of great power conflict—over the last forty-eight years? For example, some scholars have argued that Cold War bipolarity was inherently stable. In a bipolar world, alliances are of limited military significance, policymakers can concentrate on a single, and quite obvious, security problem, and average statesmen and officials can usually handle the diplomatic and strategic challenges created by one peer adversary. Bipolarity created relatively simple problems for the superpowers, reducing the potential for miscalculations, misunderstandings, or accidents that can lead to war.[3] From the perspective of structural realism, the number of great powers was decisive in producing Cold War stability. The reduction or elimination of bipolarity would be decidedly less stable.[4]

Others have argued that nuclear deterrence, especially the situation of MAD, greatly reduced the chance of war between the United States and the Soviet Union.[5] "The ghost of Pyrrhus," according to Colin Gray, "moves as a dire warning through the halls of nuclear-armed governments."[6] Since neither side could realistically hope to escape the potentially cataclysmic consequences of nuclear escalation, mutual restraint characterized Soviet-American military confrontations and diplomatic disputes.[7] Again, using the language of structural realism, the number of great powers is not particularly important; instead, whether or not the offense or the defense is the dominant form of warfare greatly influences systemic stability. And since assured destruction can be viewed as "the ultimate in strategic defensive advantage," MAD will foster stability even as nuclear-armed states proliferate.[8] Defined in this manner, MAD eliminates the security dilemma, but only if leaders perceive the defensive dominance of nuclear arsenals.[9]

Extrapolating from the superpower experience, some analysts have even argued that the proliferation of nuclear capabilities is a positive development. Other states will worry less about their security and will be restrained in their military and diplomatic activities once they obtain nuclear weapons; it would be especially desirable if nascent nuclear powers developed a secure second-strike capability.[10] If nuclear weapons take the guesswork and sources of optimism (hope for a cheap and quick victory) out of war, only prophets and the insane would engage in nuclear hostilities.

A third group of analysts suggest that bipolarity and MAD are largely superfluous in explaining the stability that characterized the Cold War. In the West, and for that matter the Soviet Union, there was never really much incentive for a showdown: both superpowers benefited from the status quo. War was viewed by the superpowers as a necessary evil, an instrument of statecraft used only in the direst circumstances. With democracy now spreading throughout the world, war, except in the so-called uncivilized portions of the planet, will become an anachronism. As democracies proliferate and are perfected not just in form but in substance, nuclear weapons will be discarded into civilization's ash heap, along with slavery, piracy, dueling, genocide, racism, sexism, and capital punishment.[11] Democracies are unlikely to fight each other and would have little use for nuclear weapons.[12] For these theorists, the factors identified by structural realism are irrelevant in explaining postwar stability.

Mercifully, history did not resolve the debate about the causes of Cold War stability: the Soviet empire collapsed with a whimper, not with a bang. But theorists are still left to struggle with the issue of whether the number of great powers (in this case, states possessing a large nuclear capability) or the fact that some states are capable of inflicting assured destruction on their opponents contributes to stability, or if the sources of Cold War stability were largely idiosyncratic. Further complicating the issue, however, are general questions about nuclear deterrence when nuclear arsenals are proliferating. For example, if a state seeks to deter more than one nuclear adversary, does it need specific forces to deter each adversary? Do nuclear threats need to be made against particular adversaries, or will potential nuclear opponents be deterred through "existential deterrence"—a recognition of the dire consequences of a full-scale nuclear war, consequences that are relatively insensitive to the specifics of nuclear strategy?[13] What will be the reaction of relatively benign nuclear powers to threats and deployments intended to deter a particularly dangerous regime? Most importantly, is the success of nuclear deterrence somehow linked to the bipolarity of the Cold War? Is deterrence a fundamentally bilateral relationship that will break down if states must consider multiple nuclear threats?

A New Nuclear Landscape

If current trends continue, the global nuclear balance will be different than the one that existed during the Cold War: Russian and American nuclear forces will continue to shrink in size while increasing numbers of states might deploy small nuclear arsenals or develop capabilities to field nuclear weapons quickly. The existence and implications of multiple nuclear "decision centers" could become increasingly salient to policymakers. These centers have long existed, but because the bipolar superpower relationship of MAD so dominated strategic perceptions, cross-cutting nuclear relationships remained relatively latent in the minds of policymakers. In the future, multiple strategic balances and competing perceptions of these balances could become more pronounced and important.[14] The idea that many nuclear powers will lack secure second-strike capabilities also raises the possibility that the threat of nuclear retaliation, let alone MAD, might not govern future nuclear relations between states.

This view of the emerging nuclear balance captures the strategic situation facing the United States. It acknowledges that START II will reduce the number of deployed warheads in the U.S. and Russian (Soviet) strategic arsenals by approximately 70 percent. Because the treaty will eliminate multiple independently-targetable reentry vehicles from intercontinental ballistic missiles, it also will reduce the number of Russian and U.S. prompt hard-target kill weapons. This reduction in hard-target kill capabilities will increase confidence in the survivability of retaliatory forces, even while the overall size of secure second-strike forces shrinks. But a situation of MAD between Russia and the United States will continue to exist, albeit at reduced force levels.

This conception of the nuclear future also contains a disturbing paradox: Russian-American nuclear retrenchment has not been accompanied by similar trends globally. On the one hand, policymakers and the public in both Russia and the United States no longer view "nuclear deterrence" as much of a problem. Leon Sigal recently summarized this prevailing mood: "The Soviet threat has disappeared, and with it the reason for nearly all the American nuclear arsenal."[15] And, in terms of the current Russian-American détente, this observation is justified. Relatively small arsenals, by Cold War standards, are sufficient to reduce greatly the risk of war under these circumstances. Only a few nuclear weapons are needed to deter possible adventurism between states that have no motivation to engage in hostilities. START II, by signaling that both nations no longer view each other as much of a nuclear threat, not only codifies the new political relationship between Russia and the United States, but also will diminish the urgency behind formal arms control efforts between these states. Indeed, it would be an act of folly for nascent allies (states that have no motivation to engage in hostilities) to limit each other's armaments while potential opponents were left free to develop their arsenals.[16]

On the other hand, nuclear proliferation has not slowed much in the aftermath of the Cold War. Great Britain and France appear committed to maintaining a limited second-strike capability, while the People's Republic of China seems interested in increasing the overall size and capability of its nuclear arsenal. India, Israel, and Pakistan probably lack an ability to retaliate after suffering a major nuclear attack but at a minimum appear committed to keeping their existing nuclear capabilities and infrastructure. A host of states now possess a very limited nuclear capability. Iraq, Iran, North Korea, Algeria, and Libya are on or have already crossed the nuclear threshold.[17] Other states, for instance Japan, seem to be developing a virtual nuclear deterrent; they possess a highly advanced nuclear infrastructure capable of fabricating nuclear weapons, a reserve of plutonium, and access to sophisticated delivery systems.

Prospects for Arms-Race Stability

In this new nuclear environment, however, arms-race stability—defined as "the rate of change in competitive armaments and the strength of the incentives discerned by each 'racing' party to introduce new, or more, armaments"—might be difficult to cultivate, for several reasons.[18] START II, for example, has lowered the price of admission to the superpower club. Admittedly, most observers agree that regional rivalries are largely responsible for the efforts of most threshold states to acquire nuclear weapons. For that matter, regional tensions are often identified as the reason "instant" nuclear powers (for example, Ukraine), at least for a period of time, had expressed interest in retaining their inherited capabilities. But as Russia and the United States reduce their nuclear forces, an incentive might be created for other nuclear powers to increase the size of their nuclear arsenals. If the United States and Russia significantly downsize their nuclear inventories, why would states limit their nuclear arsenals to a few hundred weapons when a few thousand would make them a major, if not the major, nuclear power? After all, it was not so long ago that Americans were inordinately preoccupied with quantitative measures of the nuclear balance and the possibility that minor quantitative imbalances could create unpleasant, if militarily unjustified, political consequences.[19] Greatly reducing U.S. and Russian nuclear capabilities eliminates a possible impediment to those engaged in regional rivalry, as in the case of India or Pakistan, or even to would-be nuclear powers—for example, Germany and Japan—to acquire a superpower nuclear capability.

If START II opens the door to would-be nuclear superpowers, why would a state take advantage of this opportunity?[20] Several reasons can be suggested, ranging from the benign to the apocalyptic. For example, acquiring a large nuclear capability would increase the diplomatic and military status of a nation. In practice, this would make a state a player in virtually any conflict, an attractive ally to be courted or a potential "spoiler" to be enticed to remain aloof from a brewing dispute.[21] Similarly, some states might attempt to replicate the stability that characterized the Cold War superpower relationship; they would seek a large nuclear capability for deterrence. More disturbing is the notion that states might acquire a large nuclear capability to make nuclear *threats* to intimidate their nonnuclear neighbors or to deter outside intervention as they settle scores with regional rivals in conventional combat. In other words, states might seek to practice an aggressive form of brinkmanship or bank on the stability-instability paradox to pave the way for conquest using conventional forces.[22]

Verging on the realm of the apocalyptic is the possibility that some states would consider using nuclear weapons to achieve their objectives quickly by simply substituting nuclear firepower for conventional weaponry. Even more threatening would be the emergence of a "millenarian" state, to borrow William Martel's term. This possibility was often dismissed during the Cold War with the observation that "Hitlers are relatively rare in world history."[23] Yet tyrants with unlimited ambitions are commonplace. In effect, what makes "Hitlers" unique is not their ambition or evil nature, but their ability to harness resource-rich nations to do their bidding. If the proliferation of advanced delivery systems and nuclear weapons continues, however, it is likely that more prophets (individuals whose "significant reality is the world which they are striving to bring about, not the world they are fighting to overcome") than in the past will come to possess enormous military power.[24] In the future, it might be easier and cheaper for visionaries to build nuclear arsenals than to harness the ideological, economic, or conventional military resources necessary to convert nations to their cause.

Nuclear weapons could offer a way for even run-of-the-mill megalomaniacs to pursue their ambitions. The implications of this type of development have been recognized for decades. According to Herman Kahn,

> Today, a Hitler of the type we picture now, one who is reckless, absolutely determined, and who is crazy or realistically simulates madness, would have an important negotiating edge. If somebody says to you, "One of us has to be reasonable and it is not going to be me, so it has to be you," he has a very effective bargaining advantage, if he is armed with thermonuclear bombs. If he can convince you he is stark, staring mad, and if he has enough destructive power, you will also be persuaded that deterrence alone will not work. You must then give in or accept the possibility of being annihilated.[25]

At a minimum, the potential of a "nuclear-armed Hitler" now raises the issue of whether deterrence works best when least needed; at worst, it raises the issues of preemption and preventive war.[26]

Arms-race stability thus appears likely if new nuclear powers adopt relatively benign political or strategic objectives. As the number of states possessing large nuclear arsenals grows, however, it is increasingly likely that at least one nascent nuclear power will attempt to harness its newly developed arsenal to support expansionist goals. The fact that Russians and Americans now see diminished utility in their nuclear arsenals in no way guarantees that others will view nuclear threats and intimidation as lacking in political, or military, effectiveness. Americans, or Russians for that matter, could not ignore the emergence of a third major nuclear power that embraces an ideologically or militarily expansionist foreign policy. From a political perspective, arms-race stability appears unlikely in the years ahead.

Prospects for Crisis Stability

There are at least three threats to crisis stability (defined as a measure of countries' incentives not to preempt in a crisis)[27] in the general nuclear situation posited by this analysis: (1) small nuclear arsenals are sensitive to qualitative and quantitative changes in opponents' arsenals; (2) some leaders might be deemed to be beyond the reach of deterrent threats; and (3) problems related to the issue of nuclear learning.

A traditional concern about small nuclear arsenals is that they are not particularly robust.[28] According to Glenn Snyder,

> [a nuclear] balance would be very unstable if both sides barely had a minimum strike-back capability and if the attacker-to-target ratio were low, so that only a slight increase in one side's forces, or a minor technical breakthrough, or a small rise in political tension, would create a situation in which one side felt it could rationally strike first.[29]

Problems related to the survivability, reliability, or penetrability of strategic forces become acute as the size of nuclear arsenals shrinks: quantity can no longer compensate for technological innovation or failure, or for quick changes in the size or makeup of an opponent's arsenal. For example, survivability could be called into question by a rapid quantitative or qualitative increase in an opponent's hard-target kill capabilities. Weapons systems, or their associated command and control networks, are also subject to catastrophic failure: systemwide mechanical problems or unforeseen bloc obsolescence, for instance, could render large segments of a nation's arsenal (for example, a bomber force) inoperable. Weapons must also be capable of penetrating an opponent's defenses. This latter problem, however, is more likely to be encountered by America's adversaries, especially if the United States proceeds with the development of theater ballistic missile defenses.[30]

Admittedly, these concerns would not particularly complicate Russian-American relations, although concerns about catastrophic failures in Russian nuclear systems could increase among Russians and Americans if the disintegration of Russian society is mirrored in its strategic nuclear forces. But within a decade, new nuclear powers could be capable of launching countervalue attacks against the United States; already, the U.S. military must come to terms with new nuclear adversaries armed with "regional" nuclear capabilities. Strategic systems do not last forever; eventually, Americans also will have to decide how to modernize an aging triad before the peacetime safety of these systems declines. At the moment, there is no follow-on program to develop a replacement for the Minuteman III intercontinental ballistic missile (ICBM) or the Trident D-5 submarine-launched ballistic missile (SLBM). And even the Air Force has not outlined its plans for a B-3. Regardless of events in Russia, developments on the "nuclear periphery" and an aging triad will eventually raise the issue of robustness in the U.S. strategic debate.

Crisis stability could be undermined as existing nuclear arsenals become less robust and as nuclear weapons proliferate. Two conditions are necessary for crisis instability (preemption) to occur. According to Charles Glaser,

> Each country must believe it has a first-strike advantage, that is, there is some advantage to attacking first rather than letting its adversary do so. Second, due to a crisis or ongoing war, each country fears that its adversary might launch a first strike to reap the relative benefits of going first.[31]

It is possible to imagine how these conditions might emerge with nuclear arsenals that are not particularly robust. Military/technical assessments of the strategic nuclear balance could indicate that some states are about to lose, while others are about to gain, a first-strike advantage. The obsolescence or modernization of delivery systems becomes increasingly important as arsenals become decreasingly robust. If accompanied by a less-than-benign political situation, these technical assessments, by definition, would produce crisis instability.

A second threat to crisis stability might be produced by a general loss of faith in nuclear deterrence when nuclear weapons proliferate. As Colin Gray has repeatedly insisted, crisis stability is not simply a function of the technical characteristics or size of nuclear arsenals. Instead, it is related to judgments national leaders make about the intentions of their competitors and the real intentions of potential adversaries.[32] During the Cold War, however, this distinction was masked by the fact that the Soviets were extremely cautious competitors.[33] The assumption of rationality, if not caution, that characterized both sides' perception of their competitor simply highlighted the importance of the qualitative and quantitative balance between their arsenals.

If one considers the nature of the regimes that might acquire nuclear weapons, it is easy to envision situations in which the characteristics of arsenals no longer provide much insight into the stability of a nuclear balance. If one adopts the ideas offered by the strategists of stable conflict, for example, then an Iraq armed with survivable nuclear weapons capable of reaching the United States would demonstrate relatively benign intentions. An aggressive Iraq would divert resources away from survivability to maximize its ability to strike its opponents; the only hope of winning a nuclear war lies in firing first. But it is unlikely that Americans would find this argument comforting. After all, Iraq could be banking on the stability-instability paradox (or, in less ethnocentric terms, divine intervention or Saddam Hussein's political savvy) to open a path for limited aggression. Given Iraq's recent behavior, and Hussein's continued leadership, the existence, not the characteristics, of an Iraqi nuclear capability would drive threat assessments. As Gray would observe, intentions, not the specific capabilities of an arsenal, influence perceptions of crisis stability. Concerns could emerge that particular millenarian states are beyond the reach of deterrent threats and that defense is only possible through a denial strategy based on preemption.

Third, it is difficult to predict which strategic ideas will guide the procurement, employment, deployment, and declaratory policies of nascent nuclear powers. But the full implications of this observation are not well understood in Moscow or Washington. It is unlikely that these new nuclear states will share Russian and American views about nuclear weapons.

Both Americans and Russians (Soviets) have engaged in a sustained strategic competition for nearly fifty years. During this competition, it appears that a process of "nuclear learning" occurred. Over time, the sophistication of "nuclear thinking" (for example, recognition of the "nuclear revolution") on both sides of the Cold War divide increased, making Americans and Russians the world's leading experts on nuclear weapons.[34] This sustained interaction created an epistemic community, defined by Peter Haas as "a network of professionals with recognized expertise and competence in a particular domain and an authoritative claim to policy-relevant knowledge within that domain or issue area."[35] As a result, policymakers, academics, and officers in both the Soviet Union and the United States eventually came to share similar expertise and concerns, if not always the same policies, in their dealings with nuclear weapons.[36] This epistemic community made it possible to communicate clearly about nuclear strategy and intentions; some analysts even argue that by repeatedly and publicly sharing negative images of nuclear war, epistemic communities made deterrence possible.[37]

At the moment, it is impossible to determine the sources of this nuclear learning. A process of convergence could have been at work: during the Cold War, phenomena at several levels of analysis were identified as responsible for a growing similarity in the nuclear policies embraced by the United States and the USSR. At the systemic level, for example, Kenneth Waltz suggested that "market forces" drove both sides to imitate the more successful or useful policies of their adversary, leading to a growing similarity in both nuclear outlooks and arsenals over time.[38] In terms of unit-level attributes, Zbigniew Brzezinski and Samuel Huntington suggested that the exigencies of technology, economics, and bureaucracy would eventually overwhelm ideological differences, producing convergence.[39] And in terms of human behavior, Robert O'Connell has recently observed that throughout history, sociological factors have led to convergence in the field of armaments.[40] One might thus expect that just as long as international relations remains anarchical, or modern technology or bureaucracy continues to proliferate, or human nature does not change, one of these factors will force nascent nuclear powers to imitate successful nuclear states. In a sense, nuclear proliferation itself suggests that some form of convergence is taking place.

Alternatively, both sides might have found themselves in a situation described by game theorists as prisoner's dilemma. By following tit-for-tat strategies, the superpowers might have modified each other's behavior until implicitly accepted rules of the game developed between them.[41] But it might be difficult to replicate the conditions necessary for this kind of learning—an iterated, bilateral prisoner's dilemma—as the number of nuclear-armed states increases. Indeed, as Scott Sagan has noted, instant nuclear powers have already acquired substantial nuclear arsenals without the benefit of nuclear learning; the secrecy that surrounds the efforts of current proliferators also hinders noncrisis interaction that might foster nuclear learning.[42] Conversely, the objective physical and strategic reality of nuclear weapons, compared to other military instrumentalities, might be relatively accessible; this observation is at the heart of Bernard Brodie's initial analysis of the impact of nuclear weapons on war and international politics. In other words, given sustained scientific or strategic study, people, regardless of ideological predispositions, will reach similar conclusions about the political and military utility, or disutility, of nuclear weapons. This "Brodie effect" might occur because individuals can easily recognize the obvious limitations of nuclear technology, or because a general understanding of the physics underlying nuclear weapons will spread among policymakers.[43] This hypothesis also would generally fit the tenets of learning theory, which suggest that when technical considerations limit policy alternatives or, for that matter, when threats to security are high, political factors are unlikely to interfere in the learning process.[44] The law of the instrument might apply to nuclear weapons; the Soviets, after all, did state that the atomic bomb did not obey the class principle.

Even if one accepts the proposition that nuclear learning occurred, the history of the superpower nuclear relationship still raises troubling questions. For example, exactly what were the behavioral consequences of nuclear learning? The superpowers continued to modernize arsenals and take foreign policy risks despite an image of nuclear holocaust shared by both epistemic communities and average citizens. Were Americans and Soviets simply lucky, avoiding Armageddon long enough so that nuclear learning could develop by chance? Members of epistemic communities are always with us, but a rather unique set of international, domestic-political, institutional, and personal (entrepreneurial) developments might have to occur before the ideas that they champion can triumph politically over existing dogma.[45] And it might have been the technical straitjacket produced by MAD that made nuclear learning possible: given the duration of the Cold War, the simple existence of nuclear weapons seems to have little effect on the emergence of nuclear learning. If that is the case, it is unlikely that leaders who might have high hopes for their new nuclear arsenals will embrace epistemic communities that offer solutions to nuclear dilemmas that have yet to be discovered by nascent nuclear powers. Indeed, it is more likely that existing military doctrines and organizational interests will shape the way states integrate nuclear weapons into their arsenals.[46]

Additionally, the history of nuclear learning is itself disturbing. Several lessons, which offer a potential guide to the behavior of "immature" nuclear states, readily come to mind: (1) in times of extreme conflict, new nuclear powers will use nuclear weapons against non-nuclear opponents (the Hiroshima lesson); (2) nuclear weapons will be viewed as a usable substitute for conventional capabilities (the Davy Crockett lesson); (3) nuclear threats, bluster, and bluff will be the preferred strategy of states lacking a second-strike capability (the Suez lesson); (4) states will undertake risky efforts to improve first-strike capabilities but will be slower to improve second-strike capabilities (the Cuban missile crisis lesson); and (5) accidents with nuclear facilities, weapons, and warning systems will occur.[47] Clearly, this is a past we would not wish to replicate in the future.

Ultimately, the issue of nuclear learning raises the possibility that a new image of nuclear war could come to dominate the emerging strategic landscape.[48] Through ignorance, belligerence, or simply the difficulty of communicating clearly in a setting where many parties are involved, a new global image of nuclear weapons might take on increasingly conventional qualities.[49] And this image, which is similar to conventionalizing nuclear weapons in a situation of MAD, makes nuclear war more likely for three reasons.[50] First, states are more likely to acquire nuclear weapons and to use them not to deter opponents, but to eliminate long-standing and deeply hated rivals.[51] Second, this conventional image of nuclear war is likely to spread to status quo powers because of a loss of faith in nuclear deterrence: preemption, if not preventive war, might be viewed as the only defense against extremely hostile opponents who treat nuclear weapons simply as more powerful conventional munitions. Third, images of war—its necessity, consequences, and inevitability—matter. It is the leaders and polities that irrationally view war as either inevitable, necessary, or winnable who define their age.[52] Status quo industrial states that value economic interdependence and democracy and have a healthy fear of nuclear war will not be the source of post–Cold War instability; but their behavior, shaped by the security dilemma or by an accurate recognition of a growing threat on the nuclear periphery, eventually will come to mirror that of their more reckless opponents.[53]

New Nuclear Politics

So far this assessment of the new nuclear landscape has been decidedly pessimistic; prospects for arms-race and crisis stability seem dismal. This negative assessment is largely produced by assuming that the factors that helped preserve stability during the Cold War might be lacking in the future nuclear balance. During the Cold War, for instance, status quo powers were unlikely to engage in hostilities, especially given the prevalence of second-strike capabilities that would remove most conceivable benefits from warfare. Bipolarity increased the likelihood that policymakers on both sides of the Cold War divide would recognize and be able to cope with this situation. It also was extremely unlikely that status quo powers (states that do not want to fight) would engage in wars that cannot be won. The surge in studies of "accidental" or "inadvertent" nuclear war that emerged toward the end of the Cold War, for example, was simply a sign of the times: given the dominant theories of international relations, this was literally the only conceivable way war could have erupted between the superpowers.[54]

Critics might charge, however, that by concentrating on these structural or military factors, this analysis ignores the political forces that fuel arms-race or crisis instability and the current political climate. In other words, the trends identified by this analysis have not produced full-blown arms races, nuclear crises, or nuclear wars. Nuclear weapons systems continue to proliferate, but in a decidedly matter-of-fact way. Admittedly, if one assumes that states will generally prefer the status quo or embrace relatively benign political intentions, then the nuclear balance will not exert much influence on international affairs. But what if deteriorating political relations quickly increase the salience of the nuclear balance? Three types of political relations might animate the future nuclear balance: multilateral and multipolar interactions and the conventionalization of nuclear war.

Nuclear Multilateralism

Multilateralism, defined not as aggregate bilateralism but as a situation in which actions taken by one state imply collective consequences, is an idea that has recently preoccupied those interested in international political economy.[55] It can also offer insights into the way policymakers might perceive nuclear threats. If policymakers come to adopt a multilateral view of a global nuclear balance, they would believe that changes in the nuclear arsenal of any one state would have direct implications for the security interests of all other nuclear-armed states. As a result, one state's activities might influence the international political climate that affects the way all nuclear states perceive their security concerns.

A multilateral nuclear balance can be viewed as a seamless web in international politics in two distinct ways. First, changes in one state's arsenal would spread across the international community like ripples on a pond as states adjusted their nuclear arsenals to an increase or decrease in a potential competitor's nuclear capability. If the People's Republic of China, for example, made a concerted effort to deploy a large ICBM force, the nuclear policies of the United States, Russia, Britain, France, India, Pakistan, Japan, and North Korea would unlikely remain unchanged. Second, states might begin to calculate the nuclear balance based on a variety of scenarios related to their ability to deal with several primary and secondary threats simultaneously. American policymakers, for example, might believe that their START II arsenal could deter an increasingly hostile and well-armed China but would hold little residual capability against a resurgent Russian, North Korean, or Iranian nuclear threat.

Nuclear multilateralism undermines the prospects for arms-race stability. Arms-race stability is possible in a multilateral situation if strategic interactions are broken down into their constituent bilateral relationships; the bipolar superpower competition, for instance, overshadowed a degree of nuclear multilateralism during the Cold War. But if one views the strategic relationships in a multilateral situation collectively, then the security dilemma becomes acute. Worst-case assumptions would dictate that states plan not only to deter a single adversary, but to maintain a secure second-strike capability against the most demanding set imaginable of current and future adversaries.

Another source of arms-race instability could emerge over concerns about an inability to cover an expanding target set in a second-strike situation. For example, as additional nuclear states emerge or existing nuclear states expand the size and capabilities of their arsenals, American forces intended to deter a militarily significant but politically nonexistent Russian threat could appear inadequate. The possibility that the United States might need to retaliate against several opponents after suffering a coordinated nuclear attack could create pressures for an increase in the size of the U.S. arsenal. But new strategic deployments under these circumstances would exacerbate the security dilemma. It would be difficult for other statesmen to believe that additional weapons, intended to deter several nations, would not be employed in a concentrated attack against a single state. Moreover, this situation would be exacerbated if hard-target kill capabilities are increased in nuclear arsenals or if states fail to emphasize survivability in their nuclear forces. A large prompt hard-target kill capability intended to cover extensive target sets in several countries might be viewed with alarm by some leaders because these weapons could be used in a concentrated counterforce attack against a single nation. Even if a state just sought a robust assured destruction capability against all potential nuclear antagonists, it would be difficult, if not politically impossible, to demonstrate how this capability did not threaten the retaliatory forces of individual states.

Additionally, it might be difficult for states to engage in the coordination of activities necessary to ameliorate the security dilemma in a multilateral situation. As the recent works of neorealists and game theorists studying collective action indicate, there is an "increased difficulty of conditional cooperation in larger groups."[56] Kenneth Oye notes that the declining feasibility of sanctioning, recognition and control problems (declining transparency regarding the actions of other players), and a limited ability to identify common interests would make multilateral cooperation—in this case, to stop a heated arms competition—unlikely.[57] Multilateral security cooperation is possible, but as John Ruggie has observed, some overarching threat must first emerge that overshadows the "usual risks and uncertainties that plague cooperation in the security realm."[58] Whether or not a "nuclear sword of Damocles" will produce this effect in a multilateral setting remains to be seen.

In sum, it is impossible to avoid the conclusion that arms-race stability is unlikely until a robust situation of mutual assured destruction emerges between any possible combination of potential adversaries. Technical evaluations of nuclear capabilities, based on worst-case analyses, will identify requirements for additional forces. Political judgments, responsive to the security dilemma, will identify the need for additional weapons. States will encounter difficulty engaging in multilateral, as opposed to bilateral, action necessary to reduce pressures for increased armaments.

Nuclear Multipolarity

Nuclear multipolarity suggests that in the future, nuclear alliances might be formed by several nuclear powers to advance their interests or to increase their overall nuclear capability. These political relationships also might emerge if smaller nuclear powers attempt to link their arsenals to one of the nuclear great powers. If this occurred, nuclear weapons might take on an increasingly important role in global affairs; monitoring and adjusting the nuclear balance could become more salient to policymakers. And politics, especially alliance politics, could cast a long shadow in a multipolar nuclear world. Balance of power politics would be transformed into nuclear balance of power politics.

During the Cold War, alliances, at least from the superpower perspective, mattered little in the strategic nuclear balance, but nuclear alliances would matter in a future situation characterized by a growing number of relatively small nuclear powers. In other words, because nuclear arsenals would be less robust, changes brought about by shifting alliances would have a greater impact on the survivability or adequacy (an ability to cover an expanding target set) of nuclear forces. Moreover, politicians and officers might be forced to monitor a changing nuclear landscape not by calculating the nuclear forces that might be deployed by an opponent in the distant future, but by assessing the possibility that opposing coalitions could quickly form. Thus, there is a distinct possibility that nuclear multipolarity would be extremely crisis-unstable: literally overnight, a coalition could form that possesses a first-strike capability against a smaller coalition or a single state. Under these circumstances, the weaker party might consider starting a preventive war before the larger coalition could launch a coordinated attack. Alternatively, the stronger coalition might feel pressures to launch a preventive war or a preemptive attack before a weaker antagonist or coalition could rapidly increase its nuclear capabilities or place its nuclear forces on generated alert.[59] In effect, the politics of nuclear alliances might create opportunities for some states to secure quickly first-strike capabilities against an opponent or opposing coalition.

Contributing to crisis instability is the fact that alliance dynamics are likely to accelerate in times of acute international confrontations; the very emergence of new international alignments during a crisis might be interpreted as evidence of hostile intentions. Similarly, it might be difficult to anticipate the strategies that are likely to dominate the behavior of nuclear alliances. For example, Thomas Christensen and Jack Snyder have argued that multipolarity favors buck passing when the defense is thought to be dominant, but it favors unconditional alliances when policymakers believe that the offense is the dominant form of warfare.[60] Thus, perceptions of the utility and impact of nuclear arsenals, not just the quantitative or qualitative balance of forces, could drive alliance behavior. If Christensen and Snyder are correct in their reasoning, then relatively capable nuclear powers, or nations that are likely to view their retaliatory capabilities as defensively dominant, are unlikely to respond to nascent nuclear powers or alliances of states with small nuclear arsenals. The worst of all worlds could result: "mature" nuclear states with relatively large nuclear arsenals and a defensive view of nuclear war would be slow to respond to nascent nuclear powers that view preemption as their preferred nuclear strategy.

Indeed, American policymakers would have to have either nerves of steel or brains of lead to adopt deliberately a policy of "strategic independence" under these circumstances. Why should the United States act as an "offshore balancer" and take the chance that regional balance of power dynamics will contain aggressive states willing to use nuclear weapons to attain their objectives?[61]

On balance, nuclear multipolarity will appear far more volatile to policymakers than the nuclear balance during the Cold War. Significant change in the size and capability of potential opponents' nuclear arsenals, produced by the possibility of shifting alliances, will seem to be an ever-present possibility. As a result, it will be difficult to predict even the short-term nuclear balance. Over time, this kind of uncertainty will probably move states with the requisite capability to increase their own defensive efforts by relying less on alliances and more on their own increasingly large arsenals to meet their security needs.

Conventionalization

The logic of MAD might not govern strategic relationships in the future. Counterforce strategies, nonsurvivable delivery systems, waning robustness of arsenals, and the potential for "windows of vulnerability" would reduce the prospects for arms-race and crisis stability, at least until second-strike capabilities emerge between any potential combination of nuclear-armed antagonists. Additionally, bipolarity, or the more idiosyncratic sources of Cold War stability, will not exist to reduce the instability created by the absence of MAD. An extremely dynamic nuclear balance, possibly produced by the politics of nuclear alliances, will stand in stark contrast to the slow and relatively predictable pace of change in the superpowers' Cold War arsenals.[62] And even an overwhelming nuclear advantage appears incapable of deterring millenarian states; perceptions of the intensity of leaders' motivations for engaging in war, and the actual strength of those motivations, would have a greater impact on stability in deterrence situations not characterized by MAD. When combined, these developments indicate that future nuclear relations could be governed by the logic of conventional deterrence.

In the future, it might be possible to conceive of circumstances in which nuclear cataclysm is not inevitable if one belligerent launches a nuclear attack. The costs of nuclear war might be viewed as contestable; policymakers might believe that it is possible to avoid the most devastating consequences of nuclear war. The concept of contestable costs distinguishes conventional deterrence from nuclear deterrence in a situation of MAD. On the conventional battlefield, the costs of war, to use Richard

Harknett's phrase, are "contestable" in the sense that it is possible to win and avoid the destruction of countervalue targets in one's homeland.[63] Moreover, it is far more difficult to predict the outcome of conventional war, an observation that greatly undermines the effectiveness of conventional deterrence. The quantitative balance of forces, as Israelis, Germans, and the members of the coalition that fought the Gulf War demonstrated, does not always offer a clear guide to the outcome of battle. Instead, outcomes on a conventional battlefield are a function of a strategic interaction between adversaries, an interaction that can be driven by qualitative factors. Superior strategy, technology, tactics, troop morale, training, technological surprise, or even an especially gifted commander can overcome numerically superior forces. These kinds of qualitative factors, however, rarely entered into debates about nuclear strategy once a situation of MAD emerged. No one ever argued that the United States could win a nuclear war if only Americans had the benefit of General Dwight Eisenhower's diplomatic skills, General Curtis LeMay's determination, or Admiral Clifton Sprague's grace under pressure.[64]

By contrast, MAD implies a degree of certainty about the negative consequences of war; the costs of war, in this case cataclysmic societal damage, are well known and inescapable. In conventional war, however, it is generally necessary to defeat the opponent's military forces before a state can inflict countervalue punishment, thereby engaging in what Thomas Schelling has called the "diplomacy of violence."[65] Herein lies the source of potential disaster: throughout history, statesmen and officers have believed, often erroneously, that they could engage in hostilities and win the war, thereby preventing an opponent from engaging in the diplomacy of violence. Conventional wars can be won, unlike nuclear war in a situation of MAD. Efforts at conventional deterrence can fail if the opponent believes that it is possible to circumvent deterrent threats.[66] Thus, if the logic of conventional deterrence comes to dominate future nuclear relations, deterrent threats will lose much of their efficacy. Leaders could come to believe that it is possible to escape the potentially cataclysmic consequences of nuclear war by winning a nuclear conflict.

If MAD took the guesswork out of nuclear war, the notion of contestable costs will introduce major uncertainties into nuclear balances. Diplomacy, the need to maintain or respond to shifting alliances in a crisis, will matter more. It might be possible to engineer a winning nuclear coalition through diplomacy. Strategy, force structure, and intelligence will become increasingly important. It might be possible, through surprise, an arms race, or superior nuclear strategy, to win a nuclear war. If future nuclear relations are governed by the logic of conventional deterrence (contestable costs), the outcome could be disastrous. By definition, escapes from MAD would be possible. Statesmen and officers, "unschooled" in nuclear matters, could come to believe that nuclear war is winnable through some combination of superior alliance politics, military strategy, technology, leadership, or an arms buildup. Most disturbing is the fact that these prophets of nuclear victory might be right.

Conclusion

This chapter offers no more than Dickens's Ghost of Christmas Future, just a look at the way things *might be*. At least a decade will pass before the global nuclear balance fully reflects the situation outlined in this analysis. It also is impossible to predict with certainty if nuclear multilateralism, nuclear multipolarity, or conventionalization will come to animate this post–Cold War nuclear balance. It is equally clear, however, that since the end of the Cold War, nuclear proliferation and reductions in the size and capability of Russian and American nuclear forces are taking place in a relatively benign political environment. The potential for crisis and arms-race instability inherent in emerging nuclear balances is not particularly salient to policymakers. As a result, the crisis or arms-race instability of a future nuclear balance might become apparent at the worst possible time, when policymakers are confronting a serious international crisis.

Compared to the competing and shifting alliances of nuclear multipolarity or the conventionalization of nuclear war, nuclear multilateralism probably holds out the greatest prospect for future crisis and arms-race stability. If the leaders of all nuclear-capable states recognize that their activities and statements directly affect the climate of international nuclear relations, then a modicum of political restraint would greatly contribute to international stability despite inherently unstable nuclear balances. Conversely, because nuclear multilateralism suggests that one state's actions affect all other states' nuclear policies, it also can quickly propagate arms-race and crisis instability. If a state decides to free ride on the restraint of others, banking on the stability-instability paradox, for instance, to pave the way for conventional aggression or political intimidation, then even conventional combat among regional nuclear powers could produce significant global consequences.

This chapter also indicates that MAD would foster crisis and arms-race stability in multiple nuclear balances. A situation approximating MAD between any possible combination of combatants in a multilateral world would tend to ameliorate many of the negative consequences produced by the end of bipolarity and the possible evaporation of the idiosyncratic factors that contributed to Cold War stability. In a multipolar balance, alliances would be rendered largely superfluous by MAD.

Nuclear allies would not offer states a potential escape from assured destruction. In terms of idiosyncratic factors, even states that were more risk-acceptant than the old Soviet Union might be deterred by the prospect of assured destruction: since MAD takes the guesswork out of war, it would be difficult for policymakers contemplating aggression to envision positive war outcomes.

But in identifying the potentially positive role that MAD could play now that the Cold War is over, the analysis also suggests that some aspects of the superpower rivalry will soon be sorely missed. Bipolarity makes deterrence easier in a variety of ways. The simplicity of bipolarity makes both nuclear learning and the clear communication of deterrent threats more likely. Moreover, states' leaders, domestic structures, and international goals—idiosyncratic factors that influenced Cold War stability—will continue to exert an overwhelming influence on security relationships. After all, MAD would not add much stability to a multilateral or multipolar balance if the states involved were democracies or status quo powers.[67]

At best, one can conclude that arms-race and crisis stability are increasingly likely as emerging nuclear relationships begin to approximate MAD. In a sense, MAD alone can produce stability, even if other variables—for example, the nature of the regimes involved—are not particularly conducive to the establishment of stable deterrence relationships. But Cold War stability, as John Lewis Gaddis once noted, was not synonymous with politeness: the superpower relationship was often acrimonious and sometimes even downright dangerous.[68] Without the idiosyncrasies of the Cold War, however, stability could appear horrifying to future observers. MAD provided cold comfort to Soviets and Americans alike over the last twenty-five years; some millenarian would not have to be as risk-acceptant as Saddam Hussein to convince all concerned that despite MAD, security would ultimately fall victim to the stability-instability paradox.

If MAD fails to emerge in future nuclear relationships dominated by rising political tension, the urge to engage in preventative war or preemption might become overwhelming. Under these circumstances, the conventionalization of nuclear war becomes increasingly likely. There is one way—ignoring the possibility of world government or empire (Morton Kaplan's hierarchical systems)[69]—for policymakers to escape the consequences of a conventionalized nuclear world, however. If the possibility of contestable costs heavily influences perceptions of the future nuclear balance, then MAD becomes the only realistic path to stability.

NOTES

1. Proponents of minimum deterrence envisioned far fewer than 3,500 warheads as an adequate strategic arsenal. See James H. Lebovic, *Deadly Dilemmas: Deterrence in U.S. Nuclear Strategy* (New York: Columbia University Press, 1990), 34–35. But if one assumes that the eventual U.S. force of 500 intercontinental ballistic missiles (ICBMs) will be vulnerable to destruction and that the bomber force remains on day alert, then the survivable portion of the U.S. triad will be limited to submarine-launched ballistic missiles (SLBMs). U.S. day-to-day second-strike capability might soon be well below 3,500 warheads, a development that seems to reflect a strategic policy resembling minimum deterrence. Alternatively, one could argue that U.S. nuclear forces will be less robust than they were during the Cold War. In other words, U.S. strategic forces, especially on day alert, will have less redundancy to ensure against catastrophic failure in one leg of the triad.

2. John Weltman, "Managing Nuclear Multipolarity," *International Security* 6 (Winter 1981–82): 8.

3. Kenneth Waltz, "The Stability of a Bipolar World," *Daedalus* 93 (Summer 1964): 881–909; Kenneth Waltz, *Theory of International Politics* (Reading, Mass.: Addison-Wesley, 1979); John Lewis Gaddis, "The Long Peace: Elements of Stability in the Postwar International System," *International Security* 10 (Spring 1986): 105–10.

4. John J. Mearsheimer, "Back to the Future: Instability in Europe after the Cold War," *International Security* 15 (Summer 1990): 13–18. For a critique of the argument that bipolarity is more conducive to stability than multipolarity, see Stephen Van Evera, "Primed for Peace: Europe after the Cold War," *International Security* 15 (Winter 1990–91): 36–40.

5. Robert Jervis, *The Meaning of the Nuclear Revolution: Statecraft and the Prospect of Armageddon* (Ithaca, N.Y.: Cornell University Press, 1989), 1–16; Robert Jervis, "The Political Effects of Nuclear Weapons," *International Security* 13 (Fall 1988): 80–90; Gaddis, "The Long Peace," 105–10.

6. Colin S. Gray, *Weapons Don't Make War: Policy, Strategy, and Military Technology* (Lawrence: University of Kansas Press, 1993), 17.

7. Jervis, *Meaning of the Nuclear Revolution*, 23–38. An effort to identify behavioral evidence of this restraint during a crisis is James G. Blight, *The Shattered Crystal Ball: Fear and Learning in the Cuban Missile Crisis* (Savage, Md.: Rowman and Littlefield, 1990). Conversely, a recent assessment of the nuclear threats made by U.S. policymakers found that the emergence of MAD had only a modest impact on their willingness to threaten the use of nuclear weapons. See Richard K. Betts, *Nuclear Blackmail and Nuclear Balance* (Washington, D.C.: Brookings Institution, 1987).

8. Ted Hopf, "Polarity, the Offense-Defense Balance, and War," *American Political Science Review* 85 (June 1991): 475–93. In Hopf's view, nuclear weapons are defensive in the sense that they can destroy an opponent in virtually any conceivable circumstance. Colin Gray offers a somewhat different explanation of this counterintuitive insight: "in a truly strategic sense—bearing upon means *and*

ends—defense is the stronger form of war, *by way of countervailing offense*, in that offensive weapons cannot disarm an enemy of his like weapons. In principle though not necessarily in practice, two unstoppable strategic offensive instruments should have the same implications for statecraft as would a standoff between two impenetrable defenses." Gray, *Weapons Don't Make War*, 15.

9. On the security dilemma, see John Herz, "Idealist Internationalism and the Security Dilemma," *World Politics* 2 (January 1950): 157–80; and Robert Jervis, "Cooperation under the Security Dilemma," *World Politics* 30 (January 1978): 186–214.

10. Kenneth Waltz, *The Spread of Nuclear Weapons: More May Be Better*, Adelphi Paper 171 (London: IISS, 1981); John J. Mearsheimer, "The Case for a Ukrainian Nuclear Deterrent," *Foreign Affairs* 72 (Summer 1993): 50–66; and Mearsheimer, "Back to the Future," 37–40, 54. For a recent counterargument to this position, see Steven E. Miller, "The Case against a Ukrainian Nuclear Deterrent," *Foreign Affairs* 72 (Summer 1993): 67–80.

11. John Mueller, *Retreat from Doomsday: The Obsolescence of Major War* (New York: Basic Books, 1989); John Mueller, "The Essential Irrelevance of Nuclear Weapons: Stability in the Postwar World," *International Security* 13 (Fall 1988): 55–79; Francis Fukuyama, *The End of History and the Last Man* (New York: Free Press, 1992). Manus Midlarsky also has offered several less utopian factors, especially the notion of scarcity, that have a greater influence on stability than polarity. See Manus Midlarsky, "Polarity and International Stability," *American Political Science Review* 87 (March 1993): 173–77. Jack Snyder argues that the relationship between polarity and world war in this century could be largely spurious: "the multipolar periods were unstable because extraordinarily aggressive states, Germany and Japan, were poles in the system." Jack Snyder, *Myths of Empire: Domestic Politics and International Ambition* (Ithaca, N.Y.: Cornell University Press, 1991), 320. Similarly, in his survey of the factors leading to the "long peace," John Lewis Gaddis has identified "ideological moderation" and the reconnaissance revolution as factors that have contributed to postwar stability. See Gaddis, "The Long Peace," 99–142.

12. Carol R. Ember, Melvin Ember, and Bruce Russett, "Peace between Participatory Polities: A Cross-Cultural Test of the 'Democracies Rarely Fight Each Other' Hypothesis," *World Politics* 44 (July 1992): 573–99; David Lake, "Powerful Pacifists: Democratic States and War," *American Political Science Review* 86 (March 1992): 24–37.

13. McGeorge Bundy, "The Bishops and the Bomb," *New York Review of Books* (16 June 1983): 3–8.

14. I would like to thank Richard Harknett for emphasizing the importance of this observation.

15. Leon Sigal, "The Last Cold War Election," *Foreign Affairs* 71 (Winter 1992–93): 9.

16. As Robert Kaufman has noted, however, Great Britain and the United States committed this error during the interwar period. They succeeded in restricting their rearmament efforts but failed to do the same to their fascist competitors.

See Robert G. Kaufman, *Arms Control during the Pre-nuclear Era: The United States and Naval Limitation between the Two World Wars* (New York: Columbia University Press, 1990).

17. Deutch's concluding remarks are worth noting in this regard: "In the final analysis several nations are determined to seek nuclear weapons capability, and some may eventually attain that goal. The world will almost certainly confront additional nations that either overtly or covertly possess a nuclear capability." John Deutch, "The New Nuclear Threat," *Foreign Affairs* 71 (Fall 1992): 134.

18. This definition of arms-race stability is taken from Colin S. Gray, *House of Cards: Why Arms Control Must Fail* (Ithaca, N.Y.: Cornell University Press, 1992), 59.

19. Michael Salman, Kevin J. Sullivan, and Stephen Van Evera, "Analysis or Propaganda? Measuring American Strategic Nuclear Capability," in Lynn Eden and Steven E. Miller, eds., *Nuclear Arguments: Understanding the Strategic Nuclear Arms and Arms Control Debates* (Ithaca, N.Y.: Cornell University Press, 1989), 172–205; Warner Schilling, "U.S. Strategic Concepts in the 1970s: The Search for Sufficiently Equivalent Countervailing Parity," *International Security* 6 (Fall 1981): 67–68.

20. Why states might want a large ("superpower") nuclear arsenal is one issue, the systemic effects produced by the effort to attain one are another. Although "unit" level motivations for acquiring nuclear weapons could vary, the systemic effects of a multipolar nuclear world should apply equally to all of the great powers. Christopher Layne, in an otherwise fine analysis, overlooks this point when he argues that America may remain aloof from regional nuclear arms competitions, but others will not have that luxury. See Christopher Layne, "The Unipolar Illusion: Why New Great Powers Will Rise," *International Security* 17 (Spring 1993): 5–51.

21. Gray, *Weapons Don't Make War,* 54.

22. On the notion of brinkmanship, most often associated with the Eisenhower administration's policy of massive retaliation, see Betts, *Nuclear Blackmail and Nuclear Balance,* 1–16; Thomas Schelling, *Arms and Influence* (New Haven, Conn.: Yale University Press, 1966), 91–109; and Jerome H. Kahan, *Security in the Nuclear Age* (Washington, D.C.: Brookings Institution, 1975), 14–15. Townsend Hoopes describes John Foster Dulles's "standard formula" for brinkmanship: "(1) an overstatement of the threat; (2) the development of an elaborate framework of specific 'authority' within which the President could take or avoid action solely at his discretion; (3) ambiguous public warnings as to the likelihood of such action; and (4) extreme vagueness as to military means." Townsend Hoopes, *The Devil and John Foster Dulles* (Boston: Little, Brown, 1973), 407.

23. Herman Kahn, *Thinking about the Unthinkable* (New York: Horizon Press, 1962), 78; Robert Jervis, *The Illogic of American Nuclear Strategy* (Ithaca, N.Y.: Cornell University Press, 1984), 156–57; Gray, *Weapons Don't Make War,* 98.

24. Quotation from Henry Kissinger, *American Foreign Policy* (New York: W. W. Norton, 1977), 39. According to David Jablonsky, "Historically, nation states like Gadhafi's Libya have emerged from time to time. But the majority remained

isolated, local phenomena. Modern technology has changed this. . . . The communications revolution now allows these states to achieve notoriety. . . . technology offers the potential for these countries to build up significant power to influence regional, if not global, events." David Jablonsky, *Strategic Rationality Is Not Enough: Hitler and the Concept of Crazy States* (Carlisle Barracks, Pa.: Strategic Studies Institute, 1991), 2.

25. Kahn, *Thinking about the Unthinkable,* 78–79.

26. Louis Rene Beres provides a recent example of this type of thinking: "faced with an essentially 'irrational' adversary in Iran, Israel would have no choice but to abandon reliance on traditional models of nuclear deterrence. Here preemption would become obligatory; the only questions would center on matters of timing, targeting and configuration of ordnance." Louis Rene Beres, "Israel, Iran, and Prospects for Nuclear War in the Middle East," *Strategic Review* 21 (Spring 1993): 55.

27. Charles Glaser, "Why Do Strategists Disagree about the Requirements of Strategic Nuclear Deterrence?" in Eden and Miller, *Nuclear Arguments,* 157.

28. A robust nuclear force would be insensitive to qualitative or quantitative changes in opponents' nuclear arsenals or, for that matter, to catastrophic failures. See Charles Glaser, *Analyzing Strategic Nuclear Policy* (Princeton, N.J.: Princeton University Press, 1990), 112; and Michael Mandelbaum, *The Nuclear Future* (Ithaca, N.Y.: Cornell University Press, 1983), 79.

29. Glenn Snyder, *Deterrence and Defense* (Princeton, N.J.: Princeton University Press, 1961), 98.

30. Kahan, *Security in the Nuclear Age,* 205–11; John C. Toomay, "Strategic Forces Rationale—A Lost Discipline," *International Security* 12 (Fall 1987): 194–96. Charles Glaser links reduced robustness of strategic forces to arms-race instability. See Charles Glaser, "Nuclear Policy without an Adversary: U.S. Planning for the Post-Soviet Era," *International Security* 16 (Spring 1992): 77–78.

31. Glaser, "Why Do Strategists Disagree?" 157.

32. Gray, *Weapons Don't Make War,* 31; Gray, *House of Cards,* 66. Richard Ned Lebow has also offered a similar observation: "As war is an extension of politics by other means, its objectives and timing are generally determined by *political* considerations. Attempts to predict war on the basis of the military balance are therefore likely to be misleading." Richard Ned Lebow, "Windows of Opportunity: Do States Jump through Them?" *International Security* 9 (Summer 1984): 185.

33. In his fine overview of "schools of thought" concerning Soviet foreign policy motivation, Richard Hermann has noted that most of the scholars ascribe an inherent cautiousness to Soviet foreign behavior. See Richard Hermann, *Perceptions and Behavior in Soviet Foreign Policy* (Pittsburgh: University of Pittsburgh Press, 1985), 12–18.

34. For a discussion of the notion of nuclear revolution, see Jervis, *Meaning of the Nuclear Revolution.* Claims about the sophistication of Soviet and American nuclear strategists vary. For example, Stephen Kull found little evidence of sophistication in the analytical positions of the Soviet and American experts he interviewed during the mid-1980s. Alternatively, Steve Weber has noted extensive evi-

dence for relatively sophisticated analyses in Soviet and American nuclear thought by the late 1960s See Steven Kull, *Minds at War: Nuclear Reality and the Inner Conflicts of Defense Policymakers* (New York: Basic Books, 1988); and Steve Weber, *Cooperation and Discord in U.S.-Soviet Arms Control* (Princeton, N.J.: Princeton University Press, 1991). It would appear, however, that a Russian-American epistemic community now exists. Given the paucity of nuclear thought emanating from nascent nuclear powers and the fact that Russian and American strategists occasionally recognize the implications of the nuclear revolution, one could entertain the notion that nuclear expertise is more likely to reside in Moscow and Washington than in Tehran or Baghdad.

35. Peter M. Haas, "Introduction: Epistemic Communities and International Policy Coordination," *International Organization* 46 (Winter 1992): 3. Those working with this concept generally credit Michel Foucault for introducing it. See Michel Foucault, *The Order of Things* (New York: Vintage Books, 1973).

36. Emanuel Adler, for example, has traced the diffusion of the idea of nuclear arms control from an American epistemic community to Soviet experts. See Emanuel Adler, "The Emergence of Cooperation: National Epistemic Communities and the International Evolution of the Idea of Nuclear Arms Control," *International Organization* 46 (Winter 1992): 101–45. David Twining relies on similar notions of diffusion to explain the emergence of "new thinking" in Soviet defense policy. See David Twining, *Strategic Surprise in the Age of Glasnost* (New Brunswick, N.J.: Transaction Publishers, 1992).

37. According to Timothy Luke, "The ultimate basis of nuclear deterrence . . . is essentially embedded in aesthetic-practical knowledge drawn from the repeated dramaturgical image-rehearsals of nuclear weapons explosions and/or scenes from nuclear ground zeroes." See Timothy Luke, "Nuclear Security after the Moscow Coup: Deterrence after the Empire Strikes Back," paper presented at the Annual Meeting of the American Political Science Association, Chicago, Ill., 3–6 September 1992. Jervis makes a similar point about the symbolic uses of nuclear weapons. See Jervis, *Meaning of the Nuclear Revolution*, 201–2.

38. Waltz, *Theory of International Politics*, 127–28.

39. Zbigniew Brzezinski and Samuel Huntington, *Political Power: USA/USSR* (New York: Penguin Books, 1978).

40. Robert O'Connell, *Of Arms and Men: A History of War, Weapons, and Aggression* (New York: Oxford University Press, 1989).

41. Robert Axelrod, *The Evolution of Cooperation* (New York: Basic Books, 1984).

42. Scott D. Sagan, "The Perils of Proliferation: Organization Theory, Deterrence Theory, and the Spread of Nuclear Weapons," *International Security* 18 (Spring 1994): 97–100.

43. Roman Kolkowicz, Matthew Gallagher, and Benjamin Lambeth with Walter Clemens and Peter Cohn, *The Soviet Union and Arms Control: A Superpower Dilemma* (Baltimore: Johns Hopkins University Press, 1970), 37. By contrast, Ernst Haas would link this convergence not to the technical limitations of systems but to the "popularization" of science: "Science becomes a component of politics

because the scientific way of grasping reality is used to define the interests that political actors articulate and defend." Ernst Haas, *When Knowledge Is Power: Three Models of Change in International Organizations* (Berkeley: University of California Press, 1990), 11.

44. James Clay Moltz, "Divergent Learning and the Failed Politics of Soviet Economic Reform," *World Politics* 45 (January 1993): 304.

45. Jeff Checkel, "Ideas, Institutions, and the Gorbachev Foreign Policy Revolution," *World Politics* 45 (January 1993): 271–300; Moltz, "Soviet Economic Reform," 308.

46. Sagan, "Perils of Proliferation," 27–29.

47. The Davy Crockett was a short-range weapon (600–4,000 meters) with an explosive yield of about .02 kt. In the late 1950s, the Army hoped to deploy the weapon in mortar companies to give commanders at the battalion level and below control over what amounted to a divisional artillery barrage (in the 1950s, .02 kt was roughly the equivalent of one round fired from all divisional artillery pieces). According to John Midgley, the availability of Davy Crockett appeared to offer a low-cost extension of the firepower of the Army's combat units. However, the technical characteristics of the weapon would allow these advantages to accrue only if nuclear fires were controlled at the lowest possible level. See John Midgley, *Deadly Illusions: Army Policy for the Nuclear Battlefield* (Boulder, Colo.: Westview Press, 1986), 112. The Suez lesson refers to Soviet nuclear threats made against Britain and France in November 1956. According to Thomas Wolfe, "Foreshadowing what was later to become Khrushchev's standard rocket-rattling practice in crisis situations, the missile threat against Britain and France came at a time when the Soviet Union had only begun to deploy a few medium-range missiles in the Western USSR and had not yet tested its first ICBM. Its missile inventory was therefore still far too limited to lend much substance to Khrushchev's threat." Thomas Wolfe, *Soviet Power and Europe, 1945–1970* (Baltimore: Johns Hopkins University Press, 1970), 81. On the Cuban missile crisis, see Raymond L. Garthoff, *Reflections on the Cuban Missile Crisis* (Washington, D.C.: Brookings Institution, 1989), 6–42. On nuclear accidents, see Scott D. Sagan, *The Limits of Safety: Organizations, Accidents, and Nuclear Weapons* (Princeton, N.J.: Princeton University Press, 1993).

48. Luke, "Nuclear Security after the Moscow Coup," 31.

49. One could also add that this new image could emerge from plausible interpretations of history. For example, Michael Mandelbaum maintains that "[n]uclear war can be and has been all too readily imagined. It is, however, not more but rather less likely to occur for that reason. The world is well aware that as long as the weapons exist, it will be possible to use them. It is aware that the result of their use would be disaster. This awareness has tempered the foreign policies of the owners of these weapons with caution, especially in their relations with each other." Mandelbaum, *The Nuclear Future*, 21–22. In response—building on Mandelbaum's concluding caveat—one could say that nuclear war exists in the realm of history, not the imagination, and that its consequences are not necessarily equally disastrous for those involved.

50. Hans Morgenthau was apparently the first to call attention to the conventionalization of nuclear war. See Hans Morgenthau, "The Fallacy of Thinking Conventionally about Nuclear Weapons," in David Carlton and Carlo Schaerf, eds., *Arms Control and Technological Innovation* (New York: Wiley, 1976), 256–64. For further discussion of conventionalization, see Jervis, *Illogic of American Nuclear Strategy*, 56. MAD is a necessary condition for conventionalization to occur. See Erik Yesson, "Strategic Make-Believe and Strategic Reality: Psychology and the Implications of the Nuclear Revolution," *International Security* 14 (Winter 1989–90): 190.

51. Steven R. David, "Why the Third World Still Matters," *International Security* 17 (Winter 1992–93): 153–54.

52. For a compelling discussion of the impact of images of conflict on leaders' willingness to initiate war, see Snyder, *Myths of Empire*.

53. James Goldgeier and Michael McFaul do not lament the passing of bipolarity; in their analysis, post–Cold War stability will be preserved by shared norms and the fear of nuclear war among industrial powers. They admit, however, that in the periphery, war is as likely as ever. See James Goldgeier and Michael McFaul, "Core and Periphery in the Post–Cold War Era," *International Organization* 46 (Spring 1992): 467–91. By contrast, this analysis is starker: I have assumed that some members of the disgruntled periphery will obtain nuclear weapons and that MAD, not just the existence of nuclear weapons, induces caution. In my view, instability could return to the industrial core via a disgruntled periphery. For a similar argument, see David, "Why the Third World Still Matters," 127–59.

54. For example, see Paul Bracken, *The Command and Control of Nuclear Forces* (New Haven, Conn.: Yale University Press, 1983); Richard Ned Lebow, *Nuclear Crisis Management: A Dangerous Illusion* (Ithaca, N.Y.: Cornell University Press, 1987); Ashton B. Carter, John D. Steinbruner, and Charles A. Zraket, eds., *Managing Nuclear Operations* (Washington, D.C.: Brookings Institution, 1987); Barry Posen, *Inadvertent Escalation: Conventional War and Nuclear Risks* (Ithaca, N.Y.: Cornell University Press, 1991); Bruce G. Blair, *The Logic of Accidental Nuclear War* (Washington, D.C.: Brookings Institution, 1991); Peter Douglas Feaver, *Guarding the Guardians: Civilian Control of Nuclear Weapons in the United States* (Ithaca, N.Y.: Cornell University Press, 1992); and Sagan, *The Limits of Safety*.

55. Although he is primarily concerned with multilateralism as an institution, James Caporaso identifies three properties of multilateralism that give it unique qualities: "indivisibility, generalized principles of conduct, and diffuse reciprocity." Caporaso's description of indivisibility, however, is relevant because it captures the notion that individual state action can have collective consequences: "Indivisibility can be thought of as the scope (both geographic and functional) over which costs and benefits are spread, given an action initiated in or among component units. If Germany experiences recession, are there consequences for Germany alone, the French, the members of the EC, or nationals in every corner of the earth?" John Caporaso, "International Relations Theory and Multilateralism: The Search for Foundations," *International Organization* 46 (Summer 1992): 601–2.

56. Michael Taylor, *The Possibility of Cooperation* (Cambridge: Cambridge University Press, 1987), 12. On this point, also see Mancur Olsen, *The Logic of Collective Action* (New York: Shocken, 1968), 35.

57. Kenneth Oye, "Explaining Cooperation under Anarchy," in Kenneth Oye, ed., *Cooperation under Anarchy* (Princeton, N.J.: Princeton University Press, 1986), 19.

58. John Gerard Ruggie, "Multilateralism: The Anatomy of an Institution," *International Organization* 46 (Summer 1992): 578–80. The Concert of Europe demonstrates that extensive cooperation is possible in the face of even potential significant threats (that is, a resurgent France). See Robert Jervis, "From Balance to Concert: A Study of International Security Cooperation," *World Politics* 38 (October 1985): 60–61.

59. For a similar analysis, based not on nonrobust arsenals but on the integration of defenses into a multipolar situation, see Glaser, *Analyzing Strategic Nuclear Policy,* 129–31.

60. Thomas Christensen and Jack Snyder, "Chain Gangs and Passed Bucks: Predicting Alliance Patterns in Multipolarity," *International Organization* 44 (Spring 1990): 137–68.

61. The argument that American policymakers should adopt a strategy of strategic independence is made by Layne, "The Unipolar Illusion," 147–51. Under most circumstances, it would make sense for U.S. policymakers to follow Layne's prescriptions: there is no reason why Americans must feel compelled to intervene in every regional conflict.

62. Of course, change occurred during the Cold War, but significant military developments were largely produced through the internal efforts of the superpowers; improved allied military capabilities were unimportant. See Waltz, *Theory of International Politics,* 168–70.

63. On the notion of contestable costs as a crucial distinguishing characteristic of conventional deterrence, see Richard J. Harknett, "The Logic of Conventional Deterrence and the End of the Cold War," *Security Studies* 4 (Autumn 1994): 86–114. For further discussion of this point, see James J. Wirtz, "Strategic Conventional Deterrence: Lessons from the Maritime Strategy," *Security Studies* 3 (Fall 1993): 117–51.

64. Clifton Sprague was in command of Taffy 3, the escort carrier group that engaged a force of Japanese battleships during the Battle of Samar in October 1944. See Samuel Eliot Morison, *The Two-Ocean War* (Boston: Little, Brown, 1963), 451–63.

65. Schelling, *Arms and Influence,* 1–34. At the moment, cruise missiles offer a way to engage in the diplomacy of violence using conventional weapons. Their ability to inflict widespread countervalue damage, despite Iraqi claims, is limited.

66. On this point, see John J. Mearsheimer, *Conventional Deterrence* (Ithaca, N.Y.: Cornell University Press, 1983); and Jonathan Shimshoni, *Israel and Conventional Deterrence: Border Warfare from 1953 to 1970* (Ithaca, N.Y.: Cornell University Press, 1988).

67. For a similar argument about how status quo great powers can bring stabil-

ity even to a tripolar world, see Randall L. Schweller, "Tripolarity and the Second World War," *International Studies Quarterly* 37 (March 1993): 80.

68. Gaddis, "The Long Peace," 139.

69. Morton A. Kaplan, *System and Process in International Politics* (New York: John Wiley and Sons, 1957), 51–52.

The Continuing Debate on Minimal Deterrence

GEORGE H. QUESTER

The concept of "minimal deterrence" is probably equivalent to what was once also debated as "finite deterrence,"[1] a notion that there would have been gains for American national security, as well as for international security, if the United States had acquired only a smaller number of weapons of mass destruction, rather than opting to acquire tens of thousands of nuclear weapons.

The arguments advanced in the 1950s for limiting the size of nuclear arsenals include all the separate considerations that will be outlined below. The policy problem that the United States confronts in the post–Cold War era is whether any or all of these arguments will be relevant for a world where Moscow and Washington are not commanding alliances directed against each other and where many other states may be deciding about how many nuclear weapons to possess. In this post–Cold War world, the question is not how much nuclear arsenals should be expanded, of course, but rather how much they should be contracted.[2]

Since the Soviet and American arsenals grew to such enormous levels of "overkill," with long lists of targets to justify the numbers of warheads acquired (but with target planners then claiming that these arsenals might still not be sufficient to hit all the important targets), reductions offer little financial savings. Sunk costs have already been paid. At least in economic terms, the choice of shrinking to minimal numbers is thus not the same as in the original arguments for rising only to such levels and going no higher (a policy China may have adopted).

The economic gains of forgoing larger totals of nuclear weapons (to be discussed further below) were never the primary minimal deterrence argument. Bernard Brodie had already noted in 1946 that nuclear deterrence would be seen as the cheaper alternative to maintaining extensive conventional defenses.[3] Yet, for all the other arguments for minimal deterrence, the gains or losses may also no longer be the same, as the dynamics of having risen to high numbers of nuclear forces and then coming down again may create a different perspective on lower levels, as compared to a world where nothing above the minimal levels had ever been accumulated. Bernard Brodie's accomplishment in *The Absolute Weapon,* and then in one work after another,[4] was to explore an as yet unexplored world, the world of confrontations of weapons of mass destruction. After fifty years of experience with such confrontations, what we must explore and predict now is a rather different situation. If the world has learned how to "live with" the huge arsenals of Russian and American nuclear weapons, what will this do to attitudes about the size of these arsenals, or of other nuclear arsenals? What was possible between 1945 and 1955 may be only a very imperfect clue to what is possible by the year 2005.

The Arguments for Minimal Deterrence

There are several arguments for minimal deterrence that can capture substantial support. First, the larger the number of nuclear warheads, and/or of other weapons of mass destruction, the greater the destruction to the world, *if* there should ever be an all-out war in which the adversaries were trying to inflict maximum damage on each other.

At the extreme, we have had projections of what was labeled "nuclear winter."[5] The soot and dust thrown into the atmosphere by nuclear attacks on cities and on underground missile silos would block the earth from the sun enough to alter climate drastically for several years. This would disrupt food production, cause major famine, and lower temperatures substantially so that many people would freeze to death. The bottom line on thermonuclear war, by the analysis of nuclear winter theorists, would be that the launcher of the nuclear attacks would suffer alongside the victim, and so would everyone else around the globe.

One always is concerned in these matters with three major arms control goals laid out so clearly by Thomas Schelling and Morton Halperin more than thirty years ago in *Strategy and Arms Control:* reducing the likelihood of war, the destruction if war comes, and the costs in peacetime of being ready for war.[6] Analysts have differed about what the likelihoods of various levels of war were, including the likelihood of all-out war—a war with no limits, in which every weapon gets used and no target is regarded as exempt from attack. Large nuclear arsenals did not offer a clear-cut solution to these arms control issues. In the 1970s, despite the presence of these arsenals, the likelihood of war had never been so much in question in the course of the arms control debates. Bernard Brodie conjectured at the time that the "delicate balance of terror" described by Albert Wohlstetter had never been so "delicate."[7]

But, in any such all-out war, there is surely a difference in destructiveness if tens of thousands of nuclear warheads are in existence as compared with a world where only hundreds or tens of them are in place. Reducing the nuclear arsenals to the levels of minimum deterrence might thus erase the possibility of nuclear winter and might very substantially reduce the casualties and suffering of this very worst calamity that could ever befall humankind, a calamity people inflicted on themselves.

A second kind of argument against accumulating more than some minimum number of nuclear weapons relates to the temptation to apply them as "just another weapon," as "tactical" weapons to be applied to reverse the outcomes of battles being fought with conventional weapons.[8] The more warheads one has, the argument would go, the greater the temptation to lower the nuclear threshold, to escalate from conventional war to nuclear war.

This kind of distinction was crossed by the United States and the Soviet Union in the past, amid enormous investments in tactical nuclear weapons. As part of achieving extended nuclear deterrence, of deterring Warsaw Pact conventional attacks by the prospect of nuclear escalation, American nuclear weapons were moved forward into the likely path of advancing Communist tank forces. In Western Europe and in South Korea, a flexible-response doctrine was adopted. Nuclear weapons would blunt a Communist conventional armored attack or (though it was never admitted so openly) might produce an escalation to all-out nuclear war, with either prospect deterring any Communist aggression in the first place. Such "tactical" nuclear weapons were likely to have less stringent command and control; while this increased the risk of all-out nuclear war, it also increased the credibility of nuclear escalation and therefore helped to deter conventional war.[9]

The "battlefield use" of nuclear weapons thus involved some very complex interactions of theory and difficult choices among goals. And any enthusiasm about such use certainly required large arsenals. The distinction between strategic and tactical nuclear weapons may have been seen as real by some; for others, it was merely a device to make escalation to nuclear retaliation a more plausible deterrent to conventional aggression. Happily, the distinction between strategic and tactical nuclear weapons has not been incorporated into whatever nuclear forces may exist in Israel, India, and Pakistan. Whatever else is gained or lost by the policies of ambiguity and of relative restraint in nuclear weapons accumulation that have been in place in these "nth" countries, there is as yet little evidence of training and planning for early applications of nuclear weapons to "battlefield" situations.

A third argument for minimum deterrence shifts away from considerations of nuclear strategy to the political message that is carried by weapons deployments. If country A invests in thousands of weapons of mass destruction aimed at country B and vice versa, these are hardly signs of political friendship between the two, but rather continuing irritants and insults. By contrast, if such countries choose to rest content with a small nuclear force, this would reinforce détente and positive relations. The highest compliment of all would be total nuclear disarmament, of course, or indeed total disarmament in all categories, including conventional weapons. This is what Americans are taught to remember as the situation on their border with Canada, "the longest unfortified frontier in the world." Some Canadians have looked at this example of disarmament a little more closely and found too many U.S. violations of treaty provisions to make this a total compliment.[10] Yet even when the disarmament, conventional or nuclear, is less than total, the signals of *substantial* disarmament or arms restraint here can nonetheless amount to a very powerful political symbol. The example of how Canadians and Americans feel about each other suggests what might be accomplished among other pairs of countries. A fourth argument would seem straightforward enough: the final consideration introduced by Schelling and Halperin among the guidelines for "arms control," namely, that reducing nuclear arsenals to a minimum deterrent might save money. As noted at the outset, however, there will not be any great savings in reducing the nuclear arsenals, and even perhaps additional cost. Dismantling a nuclear warhead is almost as complicated a task as assembling it in the first place (in some cases, a more complicated and costly task, since the original warhead might not be designed with any thought to dismantlement).[11] Missiles can perhaps be disabled simply by breaking them in half, but their nuclear warheads would become a major ecological hazard if they were disabled in any such quick and dirty way.

Yet, in the long run, there would be costs in maintaining and renewing a massive nuclear weapons force, and thus there will also be longer-term savings in shrinking back. One could indeed design a reduction in overall nuclear arsenals driven entirely by minimizing the economic cost of such forces, freeing up maximum resources for civilian purposes. Such an economically determined level of deterrence would not drop as rapidly as some would recommend now for other reasons, but it surely would drop over time and, perhaps over a century, would fall to zero. Sooner or later, even the most difficult-to-disassemble nuclear warhead would pose more of a hazard to civilian life in its current state, as compared with the costs and hazards of neutralizing it. On the basis simply of avoiding unnecessary military spending, the world would have come down to minimal nuclear forces or even to zero nuclear forces.

A sizing of the nuclear arsenal driven by economic savings would accept the assumption that the world no longer has any need for nuclear weapons, so that considerations of breakout and renewal of nuclear forces would be put aside. If one accepts the possibility that nuclear weapons might indeed be needed, if only because some "renegade" state might reach for them, then arms reductions would again become more complicated.

There is a fifth kind of argument for a minimum deterrence policy that enters into more controversial territory. It introduces a consideration that could indeed become an argument *against* minimal arsenals, rather than in favor of them. As one accumulates more nuclear warheads, does it come to seem possible to use these to cripple the entire opposing nuclear force? Could it be that crisis stability declines as the nuclear arsenals grow, as each side, or at least one side, sees the opportunity for launching a "splendid first strike"?[12]

This relates to what has been the central problem of nuclear deterrence, as outlined by Brodie in *The Absolute Weapon*,[13] as worrisomely presented by Albert Wohlstetter in the 1950s in the face of prospective "bomber gaps" and "missile gaps,"[14] and then as again presented with serious concern by analysts like Paul Nitze in the face of a possible 1980s "window of vulnerability."[15] For nuclear deterrence to function, for nuclear war to be avoided, each side's central concern has been that it must have enough second-strike nuclear force to retaliate significantly after the opposing side's first strike. If either side can catch most of its adversary's nuclear forces by a counterforce first strike, so that the (countervalue) second strike is not so massive, nuclear deterrence would be in great danger.

How would one then argue that restraining or reducing our own nuclear forces will reinforce mutual deterrence? The important point is that we should not put the other side into a position of "use them or lose them," into a fear that their forces will be preemptively destroyed, leaving them unable to retaliate.[16] If the other side's nuclear arsenal was not growing, acquiring a substantially larger number of warheads would make a first-strike counterforce attack more attractive. The prospect would tempt us more, and it would alarm the other side more, as their briefers might spot opportunities for us that we would not have taken as real, in the mutual analysis of "the delicate balance of terror."

The dominant argument, however, will instead be that larger arsenals of nuclear weapons and/or of other weapons of mass destruction *reinforce* crisis stability, or mutual assured destruction (MAD), since the measure of whether second-strike deterrence is effective and reliable is always how many city-busting countervalue warheads survive the other side's counterforce first strike.[17] Advocates of minimal deterrence might come up with some complicated model by which a preventive war or preemptive attack is less feasible at lower levels, but their case will normally be seen as stronger in the first four of the categories we have noted above.

Arguments Against: Crisis Stability

In the aftermath of the Cold War, there are many advocates of deep cuts in nuclear forces, perhaps even of a total elimination of nuclear weapons and all weapons of mass destruction.[18] Given the inherent difficulties of policing total disarmament, they would favor a reduction to very minimum forces, perhaps 200 or 300 nuclear warheads for each of two to five nuclear weapons states—a force much less insulting and irritating, a force less capable of producing anything like nuclear winter.

The most powerful category of argument *against* such minimum deterrence is the consideration we have just noted: crisis stability might be *lowered* (rather than enhanced) when the retaliatory forces became small. If we reduce the destruction that would be inflicted in a nuclear war but in the process substantially increase the chances of such a war being fought (chances that may have been quite small as things have stood for the past decades), have we really served the goals of disarmament advocates? Crisis stability might be defined as the basic calculation of whether, if war seemed more imminent, we would want to be the first to launch it or rather would want to wait out a possible enemy first strike—that is, it is a measure of whether rumors of war are likely to become self-confirming, as perhaps was the case with the outbreak of the First World War and as was often enough projected to be the explanation of a possible third world war.[19]

The standard measure of whether weapons thus contribute to crisis stability or to an instability in which each side would want to rush to beat the other to the punch is not necessarily the available numbers of weapons, but rather whether they are effective counterforce instruments and in their use eliminate more of the enemy's arsenal than they expend of their own. If because of a crisis war seems more possible tomorrow, does each nation see an advantage in being the first to use military force? If so, crisis stability is low. Or could the weapons be of a form such that each side is better off if the other has to be the first to launch a military operation? If so, crisis stability (sometimes also called strategic stability) is high.[20]

Very accurate missiles are thus more destabilizing than those that are inaccurate because they have a better chance of destroying the enemy missile silo at which they are aimed. Multiple-warhead (MIRV) missiles are particularly destabilizing because they allow the contents of one missile silo to be fired to destroy the contents of several silos on the opposite side. Submarine-based forces have been viewed as particularly stabilizing, since their position is difficult or impossible for an enemy to know, so that these submarine-launched ballistic missiles (SLBMs) do not amount to tempting targets for a "splendid first strike." If the huge nuclear arsenals of the Soviet Union and the United States had been based entirely on submarines and *if* there had been no breakthroughs on either side in antisubmarine warfare (ASW), crisis stability would not be a problem. Because of the certainty of destruction, of retaliation from these sea-based forces, it would have been the height of folly, by narrow and selfish military calculations as well as by broader humane considerations, for either side to launch a first strike.

The significant feature of the reductions in strategic nuclear forces President Bush negotiated with Gorbachev and Yeltsin was not the reduction in the numbers of nuclear-armed missiles on each side, but the priority given to eliminating MIRVed missiles. These weapons pushed both sides to strike first when in doubt and offered whoever struck first the more favorable force ratio after the exchange.[21] Advocates of minimum deterrence have surely taken considerations of "a war nobody wanted" into account in the design of the small nuclear forces they would advocate. MIRVed missiles would presumably be banned, and the remaining nuclear forces might be based heavily or entirely on submarines. Yet one can never be sure of what technology will bring in any area of military weaponry. If ASW techniques do not seem up to the task of detecting missile-carrying submarines in the near future, can we be so sure that there will not be dramatic breakthroughs here in the next decade, or at least rumors of such breakthroughs, causing each side to worry about whether their sea-based deterrent has become vulnerable to a sneak attack by the other?

Our worst fear, to repeat, would be that an enemy would launch so effective a counterforce first strike at our nuclear forces that almost none of our forces could carry out a countervalue retaliatory second strike at the enemy's cities. If the retaliatory damage of our second strike was not devastating enough, the aggressor might be tempted to launch a third world war, with the prospect of achieving thereby a monopoly of weapons of mass destruction and thus world domination. Regrettably enough, such dreams of world domination through a perfectly or near-perfectly executed counterforce first strike, and/or fears that such dreams would be entertained by an adversary, may become more real when the numbers of nuclear warheads are lower. Where are such warheads stored? How many submarines have been kept in service to carry them? How much would either side have to cheat above its quota of 200 warheads to have a reasonable chance of destroying all or almost all of the other side's 200 warheads? Such might be the questions buzzing around the briefings being delivered to the political and military leaders of all the important powers, and the result could be cheating on the disarmament agreements, or it could even be the launching of a preemptive or preventive war. Our worst result could be that the risks of nuclear war have risen.

As noted by Bernard Brodie already in 1946,[22] the most important number, to which the number of nuclear weapons or other weapons of mass destruction has to be related, has been the number of cities each country has. For deterrence to work as it has worked (and one can indeed certify that mutual nuclear deterrence "worked" during all the years of nonminimum deterrence, in that such weapons were not exploded on any of these cities), enough of our cities have to be vulnerable to a second strike to make it very unrewarding for us to launch a first strike. Years of MAD made this calculation a foregone conclusion. If the size of nuclear forces is dramatically reduced, however, the calculations of percentages of forces that will survive an enemy attack, as compared with numbers of cities that have to be held hostage, may become less of a foregone conclusion. Even if one does not assign other tactical or counterforce roles to nuclear weapons but wishes (as former secretary of defense Robert McNamara has so often stated) to use such weapons *only* to deter their use,[23] there must be enough nuclear weapons to inflict assured destruction on enough cities to deter an opponent.

Arguments Against: Targeting Morality

A second major problem with minimum deterrence is that it may too readily bring us back to explications of what the remaining nuclear warheads are aimed at, with the answer having to be quite as explicit as above: cities. One of the "advantages" of allowing nuclear arsenals to grow as they did was that it allowed American and other target planners to pretend that they were not planning to kill innocent civilians, that they were not blatantly violating all the laws of war and all the moral traditions of Western civilization. The Roman Catholic Bishops' Letter of 1983 specifically condemned any kind of deterrence that kept the peace (a good end) by threatening the lives of millions of civilians (a bad means).[24] The Reagan administration responded, as other American administrations had responded through the 1950s, 1960s, and 1970s to any such moral challenges, by asserting that the intended target of an American "strategic" attack was never civilians, but rather the industry and military potential of the enemy.

Civilian deaths and suffering were unintended "collateral damage" from nuclear retaliation—the unhappy result of the ways that military and civilian targets were "co-located."

During the bombing campaigns of the Second World War in Europe, the U.S. Army Air Force had prided itself, in important part because of such considerations of American morality, on aiming its bombs more carefully, by daylight "precision" raids, than the British RAF Bomber Command, which flew by night and inflicted "area bombing" attacks.[25] When the United States shifted to night area attacks against Japan, as in the massive March 1945 firebombing of Tokyo, this was still rationalized in that "military targets" were being struck, as the Japanese had allegedly dispersed much of their war production across civilian neighborhoods. Even the choice of Hiroshima for the first nuclear attack was explained by the fact that this city was the "home base" for two Japanese infantry divisions.

A skeptic could argue that this euphemism always has been hypocritical. The real purpose of the nuclear arsenals has been to achieve what the Roman Catholic bishops were condemning: to deter war by threatening enormous civilian destruction, to deter the potentially guilty by threatening the innocent. One can disapprove on intellectual grounds of hypocrisy, the manner by which the U.S. nuclear target planners in Omaha thus discovered "military targets" in every Soviet city. But, aside from favoring truth for truth's sake, one could also worry that such target planners would after a while take their supposed morality too seriously, as they applied ever-improving missile accuracies to direct MIRVed warheads at more truly military targets—that is, at Soviet missile silos, thus pushing Moscow into a very unstable situation of "use them or lose them" with regard to its own intercontinental missiles.

If, as this author believes, "more clean" counterforce targeting threatened the peace, while the "collateral damage" countervalue destruction of cities preserved the peace, then it would be advantageous to have an explicit MAD targeting doctrine, and minimum deterrence would be desirable simply because this brought such doctrines finally to the surface. Yet the fact remains that this will require an open and honest refutation of the moral message of the Roman Catholic Bishops' Letter, and of all such morality. It will be necessary to tell one and all that, because this is the best way to keep nuclear war from happening in the first place, the laws of war are to be ignored here—the laws by which military targets should be aimed at, while civilian destruction should be avoided as much as possible. What academic strategists would welcome as a final honesty and clarity may not be as welcomed by threatened populations or by the theologians and other moral leaders that have taken an interest in nuclear weapons issues in the past.

Examples from the Past: The United States after 1945

If one wishes to explain why the United States did not utilize its monopoly of nuclear weapons at the end of the Second World War to impose its will on the Soviet Union or at the minimum preserve the monopoly by preventing Joseph Stalin from acquiring nuclear weapons of his own, many different explanations are possible. Most Americans would simply conclude that their own country, and indeed democracies in general, would never start a war.[26] Richard Ned Lebow has explained that nations more generally are not so prone to exploit "windows of opportunity."[27] But, more relevant to what we are discussing here, some analysts have accounted for the American nonexploitation of its nuclear monopoly by the belated discovery that the United States itself actually possessed very few such weapons in the years from 1945 to 1948.[28]

Since Nagasaki was attacked with an atomic bomb three days after Hiroshima, the impression was conveyed to the Japanese, and to the world thereafter, that the United States had a steady production run coming of such weapons. If such a bomb could be used every three days, the reasonable inference would have been that the United States could have produced 120 weapons a year. The Nagasaki bombing was actually a colossal bluff, for the next American atomic bomb would not have been available in 1945 until several weeks later.[29] Since the size of the American nuclear stockpile was indeed a closely held secret in the Truman administration, most outsiders would have assumed that the United States could have possessed hundreds and perhaps thousands of such bombs by the time of the Berlin blockade of 1948, for example.

In actuality, we know now that the United States' nuclear deterrent in 1946 and 1947 was indeed *minimal,* perhaps even nonexistent. Depending on one's notion of a nuclear weapon, the United States had fewer than 100 bombs and by some definitions had zero. The nuclear weapons of 1945 to 1947 were still very crude devices, requiring a great deal of constant attention to keep them ready for use as an explosive. It was hardly clear that the American arsenal, stored in New Mexico as components, amounted even to "bombs in the basement," rather than to the potential for assembly of nuclear weapons over some period of time. In other words, the United States might have been, by some measures, further away from possession of nuclear weapons than Sweden or Japan is today. The knowledge of how to make bombs is widely spread,[30] and many such countries now possess more plutonium than the United States possessed in 1947 or 1948.[31] Nuclear scarcity is sometimes then advanced as *the* explanation for why the United States did not take preventive action to keep the Soviet Union from getting nuclear weapons. It was not necessarily because of the liberal goodwill of a Western democracy or because of an inherent hesitation about exploiting "windows of opportunity," so the argument would go, but because our own arsenal was too small.

Yet this "explanation" only begs the further question of why the Truman administration did not take steps in 1945 and 1946 to build up a more substantial nuclear force, of the size that the outside world, perhaps including Stalin, was imputing to the United States. Rather than letting so many of the key nuclear physicists and engineers of the Manhattan Project return to more peaceful pursuits at their respective universities, the U.S. government could surely have drafted or induced them to remain at work, producing more bombs, keeping existing bombs in readiness, and designing new types of nuclear weapons. What we may have here is one historical example of a deliberate choice of minimal deterrence. The Truman administration *chose,* for international and possibly domestic reasons, to maintain a very small nuclear arsenal, one indeed verging on total nuclear disarmament.[32]

Two aspects of this historical example do not match contemporary proposals for minimal deterrence. First, the United States had a monopoly of nuclear weapons, and American officials expected that it might take ten years until the Soviet Union or another power broke this monopoly. All of our current proposals are tuned to something other than monopoly. Indeed, the greatest fear of the United States is that one or another power would try to sneak into possession of a monopoly by cheating on its nuclear arsenal. This extra capability could then be utilized in a sneak attack to wipe out the other side's minimal deterrent, thereby establishing a nuclear monopoly.

Second, while the United States displayed such enormous self-restraint (a restraint that it is difficult to assume Joseph Stalin or Winston Churchill would have displayed if Russia or Britain had been the first to acquire nuclear weapons), it did not advertise this restraint; it did not tell the world that it had only a dozen or so nuclear weapons—weapons that had been disassembled, at that, and hence were hardly ready for early use. Instead, the U.S. government allowed the vague impression to circulate that it had numbers of nuclear weapons sufficient to replicate the Hiroshima-Nagasaki experience of a nuclear attack every three days.

There is an interesting parallel, however, between the 1946 situation and current proposals, in that the "bombs" that existed were kept stored and disassembled as components. In addition to reducing the totals of nuclear weapons in the American, Russian, and other nuclear arsenals to the hundreds or below, such proposals often call for reducing or eliminating their capability for immediate use, so that the earliest any city in the world could be destroyed by a nuclear attack might be a week or more after the decision had been taken to do so.[33] At the minimum, this might eliminate all the lingering risk of missiles being fired and cities destroyed by accident, or by some freak of insubordination or craziness in a lower-ranking military officer. It also would slow down the more deliberate processes of escalation or preemption that might otherwise set the stage for nuclear devastation.

Was the United States practicing the same restraint in keeping what few nuclear weapons it possessed far from use in the years immediately after the Second World War? Such weapons were held in the legal custody of a civilian Atomic Energy Commission after the passing of the McMahon Act in 1946 and thus were not in the hands of military officers. We know now that all bomb components were for a time concentrated in a single location in New Mexico, while all the B-29 bombers that had been refitted to carry the heavy weight of these first-generation atomic bombs were also stationed at a single air base in New Mexico, perhaps 100 miles or so from where the "bombs" were held.[34]

In retrospect, especially since Stalin's Soviet Union was to acquire its own nuclear weapons in just four years rather than ten or more, this might have seemed a very dangerous deployment and storage arrangement, inviting Stalin and his associates to try some wild preventive-war gamble in which destruction of the two targets in New Mexico would have instantly transferred the nuclear monopoly from Washington to Moscow. It is interesting, in retrospect, to try to compare Bernard Brodie's analysis of the requirements of nuclear deterrence with what the actual U.S. policy was from 1946 to 1948. While Brodie was later to discount the worrisome scenarios that Albert Wohlstetter presented, he would surely not have regarded American deployment policies as optimally safe.[35]

Keeping American nuclear weapons disassembled, however, may not have been so much a matter of choice in 1945 or 1947. The designs of such weapons were crude, posing continuing safety concerns and leaving their readiness for detonation always somewhat uncertain and fragile. Even the first atomic bomb ever to be used in warfare, the uranium bomb dropped on Hiroshima, was not "assembled" until the B-29 carrying it had taken off from Tinian. It was feared that with its extra-heavy load, the plane might crash on takeoff and that the bomb might then detonate, destroying the entire American base on the island.

When discussing what the Israelis or Indians or Pakistanis may have put together thus far, one sometimes gets into fascinating semantic debates about whether any of these countries have already "assembled" a nuclear weapon. One prime minister or another might thus be able to look the American ambassador straight in the eye, declaring that "we have not assembled any nuclear weapons," and in some sense would be telling the truth, as long as what that country possessed was still disassembled components. Was what took off from Tinian a bomb, or did it only become a bomb on the way to Hiroshima? Was what the United States had stored in New Mexico an arsenal of "bombs"?

Some of the American "restraint" here was thus dictated by the primitive state of nuclear technology, and some by the desire of nuclear scientists to go back to their normal university campuses. Another portion was a reaction to the earlier American "lack of restraint" in the Manhattan Project, as the United States, feeling itself in a race with Nazi Germany (in actuality there was no "nuclear arms race" run here, because of German ineptitude or because of some restraint among German physicists like Heisenberg),[36] had acquired a monopoly of nuclear weapons. President Truman, on the day of the bombing of Hiroshima, announced the United States was not going to share this secret. Having a monopoly, the United States could perhaps afford to be slow about producing such weapons in great numbers. When a second nuclear power emerged, the Soviet Union, it seemingly became necessary for both the "superpowers" to acquire large nuclear arsenals. But the third, fourth, and fifth nuclear powers and then the "nths" in Israel, India, and Pakistan, in the shadow of these nuclear superpowers, have in turn found it less necessary to move beyond minimal nuclear forces. Where a nation sits in the sequence of nuclear proliferation will affect the attractiveness of a minimum nuclear posture.

If one wishes to sell Americans on minimal deterrence today, the lessons of 1945 to 1949 are not especially helpful. The United States had offered to disarm totally in nuclear weapons, under the Baruch Plan, in exchange for the Soviets' submitting to what would have been the most elementary and tight nonproliferation regime, as all of the world's nuclear resources and industry would have been held under international ownership and supervision. Stalin had rejected this proposal for a variety of possible reasons: his closed and secretive USSR could not have stood the strain of having international managers wandering about its uranium mines; he feared that the United States would always have a lead in the relevant technology of atomic bomb production; or because he very much wanted nuclear weapons for himself.

The Soviets then surprised the United States by the speed with which they acquired nuclear weapons, showing that closed societies can mislead open societies about both intentions and capabilities. Stalin did not announce the 1949 atomic test detonation that was detected by an American reconnaissance flight. The detection was somewhat accidental, since it was by an airplane doing cosmic ray research, which returned with some of its photographic plates fogged in a way that reflected a nuclear test; since there had been no recent test detonations of American bombs, the implication was that the Soviets had broken the monopoly.[37] Molotov had already claimed in 1947 that the secret of nuclear weapons was no longer possessed only by the United States,[38] but the 1949 experience suggested that Stalin would have been content to test nuclear weapons and then accumulate them without giving public notice for a time. Bernard Brodie's analysis in *The Absolute Weapon* had not attached much significance or hope to a retention of the American nuclear monopoly; once Hiroshima had demonstrated that such a weapon was possible, others would strive to duplicate the feat, and Brodie's analysis indeed related very much to the coming world of *mutual* assured destruction.[39]

The 1945 to 1949 American nuclear monopoly, if it was at all characterized by American restraint, thus had disappeared in a disappointingly short time, with the lesson being that restraint had hardly paid off. Many Americans carried a vague memory of this period into the future, with the implication that any abandonment of nuclear weapons, or even any restraint at minimum deterrence, would have to reckon with the fact that "the secret" of nuclear weapons is out. And the same Americans may well believe that other countries would have been less restrained with a monopoly, less to be trusted about what they would do with any comparable monopoly in the future.

Even before the Soviets had thus been definitely caught detonating a nuclear weapon, Stalin offered few returns for any American nuclear restraint. This was reflected in his decisions to blockade West Berlin, impose Communist rule on Czechoslovakia, and direct other political and military pressures at the West by the maintenance of very substantial conventional ground forces. As a result of these events, a substantial acceleration in the American production of nuclear warheads took place after 1947. The actual transfer of nuclear weapons to military custody occurred after the 1948 Soviet imposition of the blockade on West Berlin.

The decades that followed 1949 were to be decades of much more than minimal deterrence, and at the same time decades sometimes characterized nonetheless as a "delicate balance of terror"; only the submarine basing of nuclear-warhead missiles may finally have stabilized the balance away from this "delicacy." The post-1949 decades are inevitably the period with which we will be comparing any proposals now for minimal deterrence. Yet there is nonetheless some advantage to reflecting on the pre-1949 years, because our memories of this time, explicit or implicit, may play an important role in how we view the post–Cold War possibilities.

Minimal Deterrence: Britain, France, and China

Some very different examples of minimal deterrence can be found in the explicit nuclear powers beyond the first two—Britain, France, and China—and then in the nonexplicit nuclear proliferators: Israel, India, and Pakistan. China has somewhat surprised the world by the relative moderation it has displayed in the growth of its nuclear arsenal since its first detonation in 1964. Its immediate and many-times-renewed commitment to "no first use" of nuclear weapons can indeed be seen as very consistent with an emphasis on countervalue retaliation, rather than any military or counterforce applications of such weapons, and with the accumulation of nuclear warheads in the hundreds rather than the thousands. While one hears hints from Chinese defense intellectuals that the no-first-use policy is being rethought in Beijing, as China might begin talking about tactical nuclear weapons and flexible response, the official policy as stated has not yet changed.

France has *never* endorsed no first use. France's message is that its *force de frappe* would come into use very soon after French territory had been violated by a conventional invading force; but the targeting emphasis has also always been on the damage that can be inflicted on a target of value to the Soviet Union—that is, a city—rather than on grand expectations for reversing the outcome of a battle on the ground. While there is a significant difference from the Chinese position, in that what France seeks to deter has been the use of Soviet conventional forces as much as the use of Soviet nuclear forces, the aim-points are the same: what one would expect with minimal rather than enormous nuclear forces, the population centers of the prospective enemy.

As compared with the clarity of Chinese and French pronouncements, British statements on the roles and purposes of nuclear forces have always been somewhat more vague, supporting an impression that Britain has been as concerned with the prestige and political gains of possessing nuclear weapons as with the immediate strategic implications. Because of the high costs of investing in additional rounds of such weaponry, or because the political gains can be achieved with a minimal entrance into the nuclear weapons club, the British nuclear arsenal has been orders of magnitude smaller than those commanded from Moscow and Washington.[40]

Yet an important part of the reasoning for the minimal, or at least restrained, nuclear arsenals in these three countries has been that the Soviet and American nuclear forces had indeed grown so large. First of all, the magnitude of these superpower forces might have seemed impossible to match or even to compete with. Second, this magnitude might have been seen as stabilizing and definitively deterring, so that China or France or Britain could exploit this stability to pursue their own purposes with national nuclear forces, reassured that a nuclear third world war was not going to break out. One of the bigger and more interesting questions about substantial superpower nuclear disarmament, whether or not it goes all the way down to what would be called minimal deterrence, thus pertains to what Paris, London, and Beijing will be asked to do, and will be willing to do, in the wake of major reductions in superpower forces.[41]

When asked to make percentage reductions comparable to the percentage reductions in the Russian and American strategic nuclear arsenals, each of these countries has responded with some indignation, in light of how much smaller their own arsenals were at the end of the Cold War. Some Chinese defense intellectuals responded with the suggestion that China should perhaps *increase* its nuclear arsenal as the Russian and American nuclear arsenals are reduced, in effect to meet the former superpowers "on the way down," with this being followed by parallel reductions from there on. One hears from French and British representatives no arguments for any increase in nuclear forces, because of the budgetary costs if for no other reasons, but at the same time arguments for no immediately drastic reductions, at least until Moscow and Washington have very much cut their forces.

All of these powers, of course, piously endorse the "ultimate" goal of total nuclear disarmament, a possibility that we are not addressing here and a possibility about which many or all of these leaders are being quite hypocritical; they never expect to see such a world free of nuclear weapons, because of all the problems of verification we have addressed. The three non-superpower nuclear states also can be tempted into endorsing fairness and parity, although they would be quick to assert that such fairness does not mean that Japan should have as many nuclear weapons as China, or that Germany and Italy should match Britain and France.

Leaving aside the symbolism of total disarmament and parity, the likely response of Britain, France, and China to deep cuts in Russian and American nuclear forces does pose one important question. Is it possible, is it even probable, that these nations would have invested in considerably larger nuclear forces, well above minimal deterrence, if the American and Soviet nuclear arsenals had not grown so large? We have to consider whether such a "minimal deterrent" makes more sense (or only makes sense) when two other powers have "shouldered the burden" of maintaining the enormous and decisively convincing overkill of MAD.

All of this is necessarily counterfactual and speculative, of course. We have no real experience with a world where large nuclear arsenals never get accumulated, and we have almost no experience (except for the brief periods that have been addressed above) with what would look like "minimum deterrent" forces. Yet one of the more powerful arguments against rapid reductions to very low levels in the U.S. nuclear stockpile is that the unknown may pose threats to peace as compared with the known. A world where the United States and Russia have settled at 300 total nuclear warheads might thus well *not* be a world where Britain, France, and China would be content to have fewer than the same total. The arguments for maintaining all five nuclear weapons states (and we will shortly turn to the "nth" states beyond these five) at 300 might come simply in a claim for justice and fairness. But they could also come as a reinforcement for strategic stability.

If there are only 300 American and 300 Russian strategic nuclear warheads, the temptations and fears may emerge of a counterforce first strike, in which either of these former nuclear superpowers is able to use fewer than the total of its nuclear weapons to eliminate *all* the opposing state's nuclear weapons and then to dictate world order from a position of nuclear monopoly. But what if, instead of having reduced to zero, the British, French, and Chinese have leveled at 300 weapons each as well? The dream of a monopoly-establishing first strike is then gone for either Washington or Moscow.

This is very much like the logic of the old balance of power model, by which the third, fourth, and fifth countries in the system would intervene if the first tried to dominate and conquer the second or vice versa, with this discouraging wars and conquests all around the loop as every power played the balancer in all the possible contests among all the others. Something like this was proposed as an "Air Locarno" in the 1930s, whereby the French, German, British, and Italian air forces would be so regulated in size that none could dream of disarming all three of the others.[42]

All of this might be summarized as follows: If the dream of minimal deterrence is also to minimize the total of separate nuclear forces, not only discouraging further horizontal nuclear proliferation but also inducing Paris, London, and Beijing to give up their independent nuclear forces, there may indeed be a major incompatibility among these goals. The restraint shown by these powers so far may have been a function of Washington's and Moscow's lack of restraint.

Recent Examples: The "Nth" Powers

India tested a "peaceful nuclear explosive" in 1974 and has day by day set the record ever since then for the duration until a second detonation. India is estimated to have enough plutonium for more than 100 nuclear warheads, and this has induced Pakistan, which has never detonated a device (it is unclear whether anyone needs to test-detonate anymore to be sure that a bomb will work in actual conflict), to accumulate enough enriched uranium for perhaps ten or fifteen nuclear warheads.[43] Israel, suspected to be working on nuclear weapons ever since the end of the 1950s, has also never detonated a device or admitted to having nuclear weapons and may now have more than 100 bombs.[44] All such nuclear proliferation is upsetting to the outside world, because of what would happen to Middle Eastern or South Asian cities if such bombs were ever to be used in war. Yet, at the same time, each such program, for financial or other reasons, can be seen as restrained, perhaps exemplifying minimal deterrence. Each of these countries, because of outside world pressure, has avoided openly claiming to possess nuclear weapons, merely letting the rumors do the job of transmitting a deterrent message. Only India has detonated, and one detonation seems to have served its deterrent needs.

The totals of nth-country weapons accumulated remain small. Because of the reluctance of the governments involved to admit to possessing nuclear weapons, and because the arsenals remain close to the minimal, there are few if any signs of an enthusiasm for battlefield or tactical applications of such weapons. This is welcome, of course, to those analysts who regard nuclear escalation during conventional battles as a trap because the damage produced by nuclear counterforce will exceed what is anticipated, causing further escalation. Small arsenals mean that the bombs that may exist "in a basement" will be assigned to a purely countervalue role—that is, that they are aimed at the adversary's cities.

A discussion has even emerged as to whether the Indian or Pakistani (or Israeli?) nuclear capability has been "weaponized," with skeptics questioning what this phrase could possibly mean when India has detonated and when everyone guesses that there are bombs ready at least in components, requiring some screwdriver assembly to be ready for use.[45] Perhaps the "weaponization" distinction refers to nothing more than what we saw in 1945 at Tinian, where the bomb was, for safety reasons, not assembled until the last minute. More importantly, it means that there is no extensive training of forces for battlefield use of nuclear weapons, that the number of officers who know about the warheads and are trained in how they will be used is kept very small, again just as with the first American atomic bombs used against Japan. The more general point, for *any* nuclear weapons state, would be that smaller arsenals generate fewer scenarios for nuclear escalation and less training for such contingencies. Limited arsenals push the professional military back toward conventional weapons.

Lest one attach too much importance to this "weaponization" distinction, however, one should also stipulate some basic nuclear deterrence functions that are now being served in these regions. If anyone drops a nuclear warhead on an Indian or Pakistani or Israeli city, we would have to anticipate a very immediate nuclear retaliation against the cities of the perpetrator of such an attack, this being the classic role of "basic nuclear deterrence." And if any conventional army were about to push one of these countries "into the sea," a fate much more plausible by geographic reasons for Israel than for India, this would also most certainly produce countercity nuclear retaliation. Minimal nuclear deterrence is classically sufficient to respond to nuclear attacks or to threats to one's very national existence. The perceived advantage of minimal deterrence is that it precludes ambitions to do more than this by nuclear means, that is, it precludes extending nuclear deterrence to protect allies (something China, for example, has never done for North Korea) or applying nuclear weapons to make up for conventional inferiorities on distant battlefields. Minimal deterrence is thus very compatible with "nonweaponized deterrence," even if they are not strictly the same thing.

Conclusions

The arguments for minimal deterrence are important, but there is at least one argument—that of preserving crisis stability and avoiding preemptive lunges into nuclear war—that may work against such a minimal approach to deterrence. The possibilities of minimal deterrence are more an unknown than a known, hence suggesting some elementary caution about any rapid adoption of minimalist policies. The nearest real experience we have in this field is buried in the early Cold War, when nuclear weapons seemed much more difficult to produce than they are today.

The tremendous growth of the American and Soviet nuclear arsenals in the 1950s and 1960s, far exceeding what any minimum or finite deterrence policy would have advocated, may have set a bad example for other nuclear powers—for Britain, France, and China, the states that openly possess nuclear weapons; for Israel, India, and Pakistan, the "opaque proliferators"; and for other nuclear weapons states in the future. But it is hardly obvious that issues of "example" and "fairness" will determine matters here. It is just as possible, in this world where we lack real experience and must work with inductive conjecture, that an American and Russian policy of staying well above minimum deterrence would make a greater contribution to discouraging nuclear proliferation and a greater contribution to holding the few states that do proliferate to a minimum deterrent level.

NOTES

1. A discussion of some of the "finite deterrence" arguments of earlier decades can be found in Henry A. Kissinger, *The Necessity for Choice* (New York: Harper, 1961), 15–40; and Herman Kahn, *On Thermonuclear War* (Princeton, N.J.: Princeton University Press, 1961), 7–36. Among the advocates of finite deterrence were

the U.S. Army and U.S. Navy, and even some "tactical" portions of the U.S. Air Force, together with civilians morally opposed to the "overkill" of nuclear weapons.

2. On the "how low to go" question, see Michael Mazarr, *Toward a Nuclear Peace* (Washington, D.C.: Center for Strategic and International Studies, 1993); and Jonathan Schell, *The Abolition* (New York: Knopf, 1984).

3. See Bernard Brodie, ed., *The Absolute Weapon* (New York: Harcourt, Brace, 1946), 44.

4. A very helpful and exhaustive overview analysis of all of Brodie's work, including some of his changes of view, is presented in Barry H. Steiner, *Bernard Brodie and the Foundations of American Nuclear Strategy* (Lawrence: University of Kansas Press, 1991).

5. The concept of nuclear winter was presented most tellingly by Carl Sagan et al., "Nuclear War and Climatic Catastrophe," *Foreign Affairs* 62 (Winter 1983–84): 257–90.

6. Thomas Schelling and Morton Halperin, *Strategy and Arms Control* (New York: Twentieth Century Fund, 1961), 2.

7. Bernard Brodie, *War and Politics* (New York: Macmillan, 1973), 379–81, responding to Albert Wohlstetter, "The Delicate Balance of Terror," *Foreign Affairs* 37 (January 1959): 211–34.

8. See Robert Jervis, *The Meaning of the Nuclear Revolution* (Ithaca, N.Y.: Cornell University Press, 1990).

9. An extended discussion of flexible response and extended nuclear deterrence can be found in Ivo Daalder, *The Nature and Practice of Flexible Response* (New York: Columbia University Press, 1991).

10. James Eayrs, *In Defense of Canada* (Toronto: University of Toronto Press, 1967).

11. For a discussion of some of the difficulties and costs of dismantling nuclear forces, see interview with William P. Burns, "Dismantling the Cold War's Arsenals," *Arms Control Today* 23 (September 1993): 3–7; Dunbar Lockwood, "The Nunn-Lugar Program: No Time to Pull the Plug," *Arms Control Today* 25 (June 1995): 8–13; and Stephen I. Schwartz, "Four Trillion and Counting," *Bulletin of the Atomic Scientists* 51 (November/December 1995): 32–52.

12. The crucial importance of crisis stability is outlined in Oskar Morgenstern, *The Question of National Defense* (New York: Random House, 1959).

13. See, in particular, Brodie, *The Absolute Weapon,* 76.

14. Wohlstetter, "The Delicate Balance of Terror."

15. Paul Nitze, "Assuring Stability in an Era of Detente," *Foreign Affairs* 54 (January 1976): 207–33.

16. A very elegant elaboration of this central argument about nuclear deterrence can be found in Morgenstern, *The Question of National Defense.*

17. For an early perception of this point by Bernard Brodie, see *The Absolute Weapon,* 47–48.

18. Among the more developed of such arguments, see Mazarr, *Toward a Nuclear Peace;* Harold Feiveson and Frank von Hippel, "Beyond START: How

to Make Much Deeper Cuts," *International Security* 15 (Summer 1990): 154–80; Carl Kaysen, Robert S. McNamara, and George Rathjens, "Nuclear Weapons after the Cold War," *Foreign Affairs* 70 (Autumn 1991): 95–110; and Michael May, George Bing, and John Steinbruner, *Strategic Arms Reductions* (Washington, D.C.: Brookings, 1988).

19. The impact of weapons in supporting or lowering crisis stability is analyzed in Schelling and Halperin, *Strategy and Arms Control.*

20. For a more extensive discussion of crisis stability, see Glenn H. Snyder, *Deterrence and Defense* (Princeton, N.J.: Princeton University Press, 1961), 97–110; and Kurt Gottfried and Bruce G. Blair, eds., *Crisis Stability and Nuclear War* (New York: Oxford, 1988).

21. On the details of the agreements President Bush reached with Gorbachev and Yeltsin, see Ivo Daalder, "The Future of Arms Control," *Survival* 30 (Spring 1992): 51–73.

22. Brodie, *The Absolute Weapon,* 47–48.

23. Robert S. McNamara, "The Military Role of Nuclear Weapons," *Foreign Affairs* 62 (Fall 1983): 59–80.

24. *The Challenge of Peace: God's Promise and Our Response* (Washington, D.C.: National Conference of Catholic Bishops, 1983).

25. A discussion of whether this distinction was very meaningful to those suffering the bombing can be found in Conrad C. Crane, *Bombs, Cities, and Civilians* (Lawrence: University Press of Kansas, 1993). An extended version of this author's views is presented in George H. Quester, *Deterrence before Hiroshima* (New York: John Wiley, 1966).

26. On the arguments about democracy and war, see Bruce Russett, *Grasping the Democratic Peace* (Princeton, N.J.: Princeton University Press, 1993); and articles by Christopher Layne, David E. Spiro, and John M. Owen, "Give Democratic Peace a Chance?" *International Security* 17 (Fall 1994): 5–125.

27. Richard Ned Lebow, "Windows of Opportunity: Do States Jump through Them?" *International Security* 9 (Summer 1984): 147–86.

28. See David Rosenberg, "U.S. Nuclear Stockpile: 1945 to 1950," *Bulletin of the Atomic Scientists* 38 (May 1982): 25–30.

29. The pace of nuclear weapons production is outlined in David Rosenberg, "The Origins of Overkill," *International Security* 7 (Spring 1983): 3–71.

30. Sweden indeed accomplished a great deal of advanced research in nuclear weapons design. See Christer Larssen, "Build a Bomb!" *Ny Teknik* (25 April 1985): 55–83.

31. On Japanese plutonium acquisition, see Paul Leventhal and Steven Dolley, *A Japanese Strategic Uranium Reserve: A Safe and Economic Alternative to Plutonium* (Washington, D.C.: Nuclear Control Institute, 1994).

32. The Truman administration's choices on nuclear weapons are discussed in Michael Amrine, *The Great Decision* (New York: Putnam, 1959). See also David Rosenberg, "Origins of Overkill"; and Marc Trachtenberg, "A 'Wasting Asset': American Strategy and the Shifting Nuclear Balance, 1949–1954," *International Security* 13 (Winter 1988–89): 5–49.

33. See Bruce Blair, *Global Zero Alert for Nuclear Forces* (Washington, D.C.: Brookings, 1995).

34. Details on this somewhat precarious deployment of the U.S. "nuclear force" are presented in Joel Larus, *Nuclear Weapons Safety and the Common Defense* (Columbus: Ohio State University Press, 1967), 46–47.

35. See, for example, Bernard Brodie, *Strategy in the Missile Age* (Princeton, N.J.: Princeton University Press, 1959), 281–86, 303–4.

36. For one interesting interpretation, see David Powers, *Heisenberg's War* (New York: Knopf, 1993).

37. The fortuitous nature of the American detection of the Soviet test is described in James R. Shepley and Clay Blair, *The Hydrogen Bomb* (New York: David McKay, 1954), 3–5.

38. For Molotov's speech, see *New York Times* (7 November 1947): 1.

39. See especially Brodie, *The Absolute Weapon,* 63–69.

40. See John Hopkins and Weixing Hu, eds., *Strategic Views from the Second Tier* (San Diego: Institute on Global Conflict and Cooperation, 1994).

41. These trends are discussed in Nicholas K. J. Witney, "British Nuclear Policy after the Cold War," *Survival* 36 (Winter 1994–95): 96–112; and David S. Yost, "Nuclear Debates in France," *Survival* 36 (Winter 1994–95): 113–39.

42. The proposal for an "Air Locarno" is outlined in Royal Institute for International Affairs, *Documents on International Affairs,* 1935, vol. 1 (London: Oxford University Press, 1936), 27, 36.

43. Indian and Pakistani nuclear weapons accumulations are discussed in George Perkovich, "A Nuclear Third Way in South Asia," *Foreign Policy* 91 (Summer 1993): 85–104.

44. On Israel, see Yair Evron, *Israel's Nuclear Dilemma* (Ithaca, N.Y.: Cornell University Press, 1994).

45. The background on such a conceptual distinction of "weaponization" is presented in Leonard Spector, *The Undeclared Bomb* (Cambridge, Mass.: Ballinger, 1988).

U.S. Nuclear Policy and the End of the Cold War

ERIC MLYN

Sometimes going back to the beginning can be the best way of thinking about how to move ahead to the future. Rereading Bernard Brodie's insightful assessment of the nuclear age makes it clear that Brodie immediately grasped the implications of the nuclear revolution. In *The Absolute Weapon: Atomic Power and World Order,* Brodie recognized that the chances for developing a defense against the bomb were exceedingly remote, that superiority in number of bombs would not ensure strategic advantage, and that increased accuracy of delivery vehicles would not make much strategic difference in nuclear warfare. In short, Brodie recognized the mutual assured destruction (MAD) revolution brought about by nuclear weapons.[1]

Not only did Brodie recognize the MAD implications of the nuclear revolution, he also realized that not everybody in the U.S. national security establishment would see things as he did. Presciently, Brodie wrote:

> The most dangerous situation of all would arise from a failure not only of the political leaders but especially of the military authorities of a nation like our own to adjust to the atomic bomb in their thinking and planning. The possibility of such a situation developing in the United States is very real and very grave.[2]

In elaborating on this urge to shift thinking, Brodie believed that the military would need to abandon military concepts from the past to avoid the conventionalization of nuclear weapons policy. Here, Brodie focused on thinking and planning in the military establishment. This is particularly important today. Although important changes have been made to U.S. nuclear weapons policy with the end of the Cold War, the way that defense officials think about nuclear weapons and plan to use them has not changed adequately to take advantage of post–Cold War opportunities.

Perhaps the most surprising realization in rereading Brodie is his static view of the nuclear situation. He seemed to think that because nuclear weapons were so revolutionary, little innovation would take place in the future. He wrote:

> The bomb is, to be sure, in its "infancy," but the statement is misleading if it implies that we may expect the kind of progress which we have witnessed over the past century in the steam engine. The bomb is new, but the people who developed it were able to avail themselves of the fabulously elaborate and advanced technology already existing. Any new device created today is already at birth a highly perfected instrument.[3]

Had those in the military establishment recognized the revolutionary nature of nuclear weapons as clearly as Brodie, his sense of the static nature of nuclear weapons would have been correct. But instead, Brodie's worst fear became reality: military and political leaders did not accept that revolutionary nature of nuclear weapons and continued to try to improve nuclear weapons with the development of the hydrogen bomb, multiple basing modes, MIRVs, MARVs, increased accuracy, cruise missiles, etc. They had in fact conventionalized nuclear weapons, as policymakers tended "to treat nuclear weapons as though they were conventional weapons, to apply the same way of thinking to them that applied to armaments in the pre-nuclear era."[4] This conventionalization was present at the outset of the nuclear age, when the bomb was fitted nicely into a Second World War style of strategic bombardment of industrial sites.[5] Later, as the Soviets developed their own nuclear capability and deterrence emerged, nuclear strategies continued to reflect conventional thinking.

Understanding why everybody did not come to the same realization as Brodie is central to understanding the present and perhaps even the future. This chapter will show that while the number, structure, and deployment of U.S. tactical and strategic nuclear weapons have in fact greatly changed since the Cold War, how policymakers think about nuclear weapons has not adequately responded to the collapse of the Soviet threat. The kind of thinking that led policymakers to treat nuclear weapons as useful military tools has not changed. Despite significant changes in the U.S. nuclear arsenal, U.S. policymakers continue to embrace the view that nuclear weapons are useful military tools. Though presented with an opportunity to denuclearize security policy, defense policymakers have instead embraced ambitious missions for the smaller U.S. arsenal.

Major changes have taken place since the end of the Cold War in the number of nuclear weapons deployed and the number of targets that these weapons could strike. Thus, if we compare the current nuclear posture to the Cold War posture, one could make the case that policy has significantly changed. In arguing that nuclear policy has not adequately changed, I compare the current nuclear policy to policies that have been advocated by those who either opposed the nuclear buildup of the Cold War or have envisioned significant changes given the end of the Cold War. The end of the rivalry between the United States and the Soviet Union created an opportunity to marginalize nuclear weapons—an opportunity that policymakers have not yet seized. Had the United States changed its nuclear policy as it did *during* the Cold War, we could indeed talk of the significance of these changes—we might even refer to them as radical changes. However, the end of the Cold War demands that we apply a different measure.

The emphasis on counterforce is a holdover from prenuclear days. This chapter, then, extends the type of argument made by Hans Morgenthau and Robert Jervis (and warned about by Brodie over fifty years ago). They argued persuasively during the Cold War that policymakers failed to perceive the revolutionary nature of nuclear weapons. Implicit in this conventionalization argument is that nuclear weapons did represent a change so significant that military strategies should no longer resemble the strategies of the prenuclear era. I take this argument one step further to update the conventionalization argument by showing that even a major structural change in the international system (the end of the Cold War) was not enough to change this way of thinking. The change in technology that came about at the end of the Second World War and now the change in structure that came with the end of the Cold War have not dislodged traditional ways of thinking about nuclear weapons. Part of the staying power of the conventionalization of nuclear weapons is due to the perception among policymakers and scholars that nuclear weapons had a positive and stabilizing effect on the Cold War and will continue to have the same effect in post–Cold War international security relations.

The issue of how policymakers think about nuclear weapons is important because the *number* of nuclear weapons is not nearly as important as the issue of *targeting* and *plans for their use*.[6] As tensions are reduced, the chance of an accident, miscalculation, or spiral resulting from large arsenals becomes more unlikely.[7] Now what is important is not how many weapons are in the U.S. arsenal or how they are deployed or even how they are targeted, but instead *how policymakers think about nuclear weapons*. Policymakers believe either that we need to move away from thinking about nuclear weapons as anything other than crude instruments of deterrence or that we need to think about them as integral and useful parts of the U.S. military arsenal.

Though some of those who gained key defense positions in the Clinton administration were at one time in favor of marginalizing nuclear arms, the Clinton administration remains firmly committed to the conventionalized view of nuclear weapons. The analysis in this chapter is also sensitive to the domestic political factors that have constrained the Clinton administration. President Clinton has not been forcefully involved in nuclear issues. He also lacks much credibility on matters of defense policy. From his lack of service in Vietnam to his misstep on the gays-in-the-military issue during the opening days of his first term, President Clinton has constantly had to guard against charges that he is soft on defense. As a result, radical changes in nuclear weapons policy might be difficult for this president to achieve.[8]

This chapter begins by describing the two competing approaches to conceptualizing the role of nuclear weapons in U.S. defense policy. A brief history of strategic nuclear weapons policy follows, which illustrates policymakers' efforts to build refined nuclear options so that the capability might make for a more credible nuclear deterrent or actually might be used in military conflict. Since the 1960s policymakers have looked at nuclear weapons as usable military tools. This history suggests U.S. policymakers have been engaged in the conventionalization of nuclear weapons. The chapter concludes that the way policymakers think about nuclear weapons has altered little following the end of the Cold War, despite the significant change in the international security environment.

MAD versus NUTs—or Traditionalists versus Marginalizers

At the core of nuclear issues during the Cold War was the debate between advocates of MAD and advocates of nuclear utilization theory (NUTs).[9] Though it has been assumed that U.S. nuclear targeting policy has been mutual assured destruction, the last ten years have seen the increasingly common recognition that this was not the case. Targeting policy has rarely targeted only cities. Instead, U.S. targeting policy, which became coordinated under the Single Integrated Operational Plan (SIOP) in 1960, has always called for a much higher level of counterforce targeting than would be called for by a MAD strategy.[10] This is referred to as NUTs.[11]

MAD and NUTs are ideal types. Strategists and policymakers rarely advocate a pure counterforce (NUTs) or pure countervalue (MAD) strategic nuclear policy. Instead, these are opposite poles on a continuum, with most policies falling somewhere between these points. Nevertheless, the underlying assumption behind specific strategic nuclear strategies usually reflects one of these schools.

A pure policy of MAD would target populations, or countervalue targets. Advocates of such a posture hold that the United States can maintain an effective and credible nuclear deterrent by holding only populations hostage. Opponents of this posture argue that such a threat, because of the condition of mutual vulnerability, is not credible and that the United States must have limited and flexible nuclear options. These latter options would include the targeting of nuclear forces and other military targets. Advocates of such postures claim that this type of targeting makes for a more credible nuclear deterrent and can, in case deterrence fails, enable policymakers to keep nuclear war limited. For advocates of MAD, there is little discussion of fighting a nuclear war, of "winning" or "prevailing." Deterrence rests on the threat of the destruction of civilization. Advocates of MAD do not move beyond thinking about what will deter. Instead, once nuclear weapons are used, this policy has failed.

Those who advocate counterforce options disagree with MAD advocates.[12] Advocates of counterforce options are skeptical that countervalue targeting is an effective and credible nuclear deterrent against an opponent's actions that are less than an attack on the U.S. homeland, and perhaps not even credible then. The credibility of the United States' extending deterrence to European allies had been the driving force behind the acquisition of limited counterforce nuclear options. It had never seemed credible to say that U.S. leaders would trade New York for Bonn if the Soviets attacked Western Europe.[13]

Those who advocated NUTs strategies believed that nuclear weapons could be used as military tools. Unlike advocates of MAD, NUTs advocates see nuclear weapons as having more utility than simply deterrence. NUTs strategies share the belief that nuclear wars could be fought short of total destruction. This position manifested itself in a variety of ways over the course of the nuclear age. Despite the different terms, all of the NUTs strategies targeted nuclear weapons against military assets and thus required accuracy. They also required options to use only small parts of the nuclear arsenal to meet a variety of contingencies short of all-out nuclear war between the United States and the Soviet Union.

Today this debate is between marginalizers and traditionalists, but it is essentially about the same issues.[14] The marginalizers believe that the end of the Cold War created an opportunity to stop looking at nuclear weapons as usable military tools—to delegitimize nuclear weapons. To move in this direction, marginalizers advocate that the United States should

> make a pledge of no first use, including a pledge not to use nuclear weapons against chemical and biological weapons;
> move quickly to ratify a Comprehensive Test Ban Treaty; eliminate remaining tactical nuclear weapons in Europe;

eliminate ICBMs;

move toward a posture of minimum or fundamental deterrence, leaving anywhere between 100 and 1,000 strategic nuclear warheads;

work toward enhancement of the nonproliferation regime, but not use nuclear weapons as part of the counterproliferation effort.

If most of these steps were adopted, the United States would make significant progress toward marginalizing nuclear weapons and would indicate that nuclear weapons had virtually no role in post–Cold War U.S. defense policy.[15]

The traditionalists, on the other hand, would leave nuclear weapons as central parts of U.S. security policy. They believe that the U.S. arsenal should not go below the 3,000–3,500 warheads permitted by the still unratified START II and that the United States needs a substantial and versatile nuclear arsenal to protect its interests in Europe and the Third World. From this perspective, the United States should reserve the right to use nuclear weapons for a variety of deterrence and defense purposes. Maintaining the nuclear triad is crucial for traditionalists. As the former chairman of the Joints Chiefs of Staff told the Senate Armed Services Committee, if the United States cut strategic nuclear warheads below the 3,500 level, it would become impossible to maintain the strategic triad.[16]

A Brief History

U.S. nuclear policy has shown an overwhelming commitment to NUTs, counterforce, and the belief that nuclear weapons could be used in a militarily meaningful way. What is remarkable about this historical record is that despite variations in the strategic environment, U.S. nuclear policy has remained highly constant. This legacy continues to influence policymakers since the end of the Cold War.

City Avoidance

Secretary of Defense Robert McNamara was horrified by the lack of discrimination in SIOP-62, which he had inherited from the Eisenhower administration.[17] The secretary went public with his concerns in discussions and later at a commencement address at the University of Michigan. McNamara stated that the United States would avoid targeting cities to keep a nuclear war limited and keep civilian damage to a minimum. This was recognized as a direct departure from the nuclear policy of massive retaliation announced by John Foster Dulles in 1954. McNamara wanted to add credibility to U.S. strategic nuclear policy and hoped that by moving U.S. targeting policy toward a no-city posture, the Soviets would do the same. In his announcement to the allies, McNamara said:

> The U.S. has come to the conclusion that to the extent feasible basic military strategy in general nuclear war should be approached in much the same way that more conventional military operations have been regarded in the past. That is to say, our principal military objective, in the event of a nuclear war stemming from a major attack on the Alliance, should be the destruction of the enemy's military forces while attempting to preserve the fabric as well as the integrity of allied society. Specifically, our studies indicate that a strategy which targets nuclear forces only against cities or a mixture of civilian and military targets has serious limitations for the purpose of deterrence and for the conduct of general war.[18]

The new policy met with some opposition at home and abroad. Many interpreted it as indicating that the United States was contemplating the fighting of a limited nuclear war. At worst, critics complained that the announcement of the no-cities doctrine made it sound as if the United States was seeking to gain a disarming first-strike capability against the USSR. This did not sit well with the public.

McNamara backed away from the rhetoric of cities avoidance at the declaratory level in favor of flexible response and MAD. By 1964, the Military Posture Statement did not refer to the cities-avoidance strategy. However, despite the public adherence to a policy of MAD, it is now clear that the SIOP contained targeting plans that were compatible with city avoidance. As an important participant recounted:

> Surely the SIOPs in the sixties did not fully reflect the declaratory policy of the Kennedy administration, they were very heavily oriented toward counterforce whereas the declaratory policy of MAD did not procure weapons for counterforce.[19]

The Department of Defense had developed SIOP-63, which had five targeting options: Soviet strategic nuclear forces, other elements of Soviet military forces away from cities, Soviet military forces and military resources near cities, Soviet command and control, and all-out industrial attack. Options 1 and 2, a pure counterforce attack, could be launched in a preemptive fashion in case of warning of Sino-Soviet attack.[20] The move toward counterforce targeting had begun. And weapons procurement at the time sought to provide these counterforce capabilities, with the development of intercontinental ballistic missiles (ICBMs), the beginning of

MIRV (multiple independently targetable reentry vehicle) research, the establishment of a secure triad, and debates over civil defense. The beginning of the decade saw the U.S. arsenal relying primarily on long-range heavy bombers, with only 54 ICBMs and 80 SLBMs (submarine-launched ballistic missiles). By 1968, the U.S. strategic triad was established with 1,054 ICBMs, 656 SLBMs, and 456 bombers.[21]

One of the most important developments was the advent of the MIRV, to add more counterforce capability to the strategic arsenal. As John Foster, director of research and engineering for the Department of Defense, testified, "[T]he MIRV concept was originally generated to increase our targeting capability rather than to penetrate ABM defenses."[22]

The accuracy of weapons had not yet developed to the point where policymakers could be confident in the strategic nuclear arsenal's counterforce capabilities. Furthermore, because of the great nuclear superiority that the United States enjoyed at the time, policymakers did not perceive that this endangered U.S. security. However, this period is important not only for the declaratory embrace of MAD that would become a habit for subsequent national security officials, but also for the funding of many strategic weapons systems that would eventually give the United States a significant counterforce capability.

Limited Nuclear Options

No major executive-branch official saw it as desirable to talk about limited nuclear options until James Schlesinger renewed this debate in the winter of 1974, when he announced that the president needed a more refined set of nuclear options.[23] Schlesinger said in part:

> There has taken place a change in the strategies of the United States with regard to the hypothetical deployment of the central strategic forces. A change in targeting strategy [to give the U.S. president] an option to hit a different set of targets—military targets . . . beyond an all out nuclear attack against cities.[24]

Numerous reasons have been given for this declaratory shift. Lynn Davis writes that while "no single objective lay behind the new doctrine, a remarkably widespread consensus in favor of change developed within the government."[25] A widespread consensus developed around the idea that the president should have multiple and flexible options if he chose to use nuclear weapons. However, by the end of the 1970s it was still not clear that the SIOP actually had the limited capabilities desired by civilian decision makers.

Changes to the SIOP were pushed forward by National Security Decision Memorandum 242 (NSDM-242), signed by President Nixon in 1974. NSDM-242 called for limited employment options within the SIOP. It also called for the targeting of Soviet recovery resources and sought to provide escalation control. NSDM-242 authorized the secretary of defense to put forward guidance for revising the SIOP. SIOP 5 was formally approved in December 1975 and took effect in January of 1976. This SIOP reemphasized the targeting of Soviet military forces and limited nuclear options.[26] However, the weapons to fulfill these plans were not fully available. As one participant recounted:

> What we discovered previously, the previous major study having been NSDM-242 in the mid-seventies, back in the Nixon administration, was that a lot of that didn't get implemented in the way that policymakers envisioned. And part of that was because it couldn't—there was not a willful failure to implement . . . they [the military] would say that we don't have the resources to do it, or we don't have the right kind of weapons, we don't have the right kind of command and control.[27]

This lack of capability that was perceived by the military resulted from a lack of counterforce capabilities. This partially arose from the belief that declaratory policy should not be linked to force development policy. One reason was that such an embrace over a decade earlier led to large funding requests from the military. Second, the change in doctrine and the request for funds for counterforce purposes pushed the issue of U.S. nuclear weapons strategy toward political salience. If the changes in doctrine did not require the appropriation of additional funds (as Schlesinger had initially maintained), Congress would have very little control over the course of U.S. nuclear strategy. As one participant put it:

> Schlesinger insisted, in a way that was understandable but totally illogical, that it be written into the report that this guidance is for deployment policy and not for acquisition policy. That's totally illogical, if you are going to have an employment policy that is totally divorced from acquisition policy.[28]

However, because the appropriation of funds became important for the implementation of this new policy, Schlesinger was forced to go before

Congress and explain in detail the changes he wished to make. It is the need for money for quantitative or qualitative improvements that forces these issues to a broader forum. Thus, after the Schlesinger announcement, he was forced to go before Congress to explain policy changes, in both open and closed sessions.[29]

PD-59

Though it was the Reagan administration that heard much of the public outcry regarding an increased emphasis on counterforce targeting in declaratory policy, moves toward this began during the Carter administration. They culminated in the summer of 1980 when President Carter signed Presidential Directive 59 (PD-59), which called for the targeting of Soviet military and political assets.[30] Though both Robert McNamara and James Schlesinger had made declaratory statements for the need for such capabilities in the U.S. nuclear arsenal, the embrace became clear, dominant, and unequivocal under both Presidents Carter (toward the end of his term) and Reagan. Both administrations embraced NUTs.

In the public explanations of this policy, Secretary of Defense Harold Brown was careful to note that he did not view PD-59 as a radical departure from previous U.S. nuclear policy. He stressed this point in August 1980 during his address at the Naval War College. Instead, he stressed that it was a refinement of previous U.S. targeting plans. He wrote in the DOD's *FY 1981 Annual Report:*

> For nearly 20 years, we have explicitly included a range of employment options—against military and nonmilitary targets—in our strategic nuclear employment planning. Indeed, U.S. nuclear forces have always been designed against military targets, as well as those comprising war-supporting industry and recovery resources.[31]

Though this renewed emphasis on counterforce targeting began in the Carter administration, it was the Reagan administration that began an all-out effort to procure the weapons systems that would be necessary for such a targeting scheme. The Reagan administration sought to implement NUTs fully. It sought to modernize ICBMs by developing the more accurate MX missile. It sought to add counterforce capability to SLBMs with the new Trident missile. It sought improvements in the command and control system, something very important for a true war-fighting strategy.

And the administration talked much more about nuclear war-fighting than other administrations. Caspar Weinberger talked of "prevailing" in a nuclear war.[32] Secretary of State Alexander Haig spoke of firing nuclear warning shots.[33] The administration's first complete defense guidance was leaked in May of 1982 and indicated that the U.S. was planning to acquire the capability to fight a protracted nuclear war with the Soviet Union.[34]

Nuclear Weapons after the Cold War

Central to U.S. nuclear policy during the Cold War was the mission of extending deterrence to Europe. The United States and its allies reserved the right to use nuclear weapons first and resisted pressure to declare a policy of no first use. Opposition to a no-first-use policy stemmed from the fear of a Soviet conventional invasion of Western Europe. Many U.S. policymakers perceived that Soviet conventional forces could overtake NATO conventional forces, and thus a policy of flexible response was necessary to assure deterrence.[35] However, with the dissolution of the Soviet Union and the Warsaw Pact, the fear of Soviet invasion disappeared. But the United States has not abandoned the threat to use nuclear weapons first. New extended deterrence scenarios have appeared in policy-making circles that continue to push policymakers toward making nuclear weapons a central part of U.S. strategy. For example, NATO expansion would probably require that the United States extend the nuclear umbrella to new NATO members.[36]

In addition to extending deterrence to Europe and other parts of the globe, U.S. policymakers seek to maintain a diverse and flexible nuclear arsenal to prevent nuclear proliferation. Policymakers stress that if the United States were to abandon extended deterrence, non-nuclear countries with existing or potential security threats would be more likely to acquire their own nuclear arsenals. And it is still U.S. policy to deter chemical and biological weapons attacks by threatening retaliation with nuclear weapons.

Though the United States and NATO have eliminated nearly all of the tactical nuclear weapons that were deployed during the Cold War, America has not yet taken the final step toward the denuclearization of U.S. deterrence policy—the adoption of a pledge of no first use.[37] Policymakers, despite all of the changes to be discussed in this chapter, have refused to stop looking at nuclear weapons as integral parts of U.S. defense forces. Threats in the Third World as well as the hedge against Russian resurgence have left policymakers committed to integrating nuclear weapons into U.S. defense policy. Old patterns have proven difficult to break.

In the summer of 1989, Robert Toth and Desmond Ball investigated revisions to the SIOP and U.S. strategic nuclear targeting. The title of their journal article the following year well described the revision plans: "Revising the SIOP: Taking War-Fighting to Dangerous Extremes."[38] The overall direction of the new SIOP-6F, which took effect in October 1989, was perfectly consistent with previous war-fighting doctrine that had since the 1960s dominated U.S. nuclear weapons targeting. Perhaps most significant was the seriousness with which the Bush administration had been taking the goal of destroying Soviet leadership early in a conflict.[39] The targeting and destruction of mobile targets was also taken seriously.[40]

The guidance that led to SIOP-6F found that the U.S. strategic arsenal did not contain adequate counterleadership capability and command and control to accomplish the goals of the overall policy. The study of earth-penetrating warheads, which had begun years earlier, was thus given renewed emphasis. And the ability of the B-2 Stealth bomber to locate and strike mobile ICBMs was seen as important in this regard, though this never really became the prime justification for the system.[41] Furthermore, according to a secret 1989 Pentagon document that had been issued by former chairman of the Joint Chiefs of Staff Admiral William T. Crowe:

> Our forces will hold at risk those assets that the Soviet leadership would need to prevail in a nuclear conflict and dominate a postnuclear world. These targets include the Soviet military forces, political leadership structure and war-supporting industry.[42]

At the end of 1989, the Bush administration launched a review of nuclear targeting that was completed in May of 1991. The group was headed by General Lee Butler and included many officials who would later become high-ranking members of the Clinton administration, including R. James Woolsey, John Deutch, Ashton Carter, Edward Warner, and Walter Slocombe.[43] This process eliminated up to 3,000 targets. Due to glasnost and an increase in accuracy in strategic warheads, the United States was able to cut redundant targets. Targets in Eastern Europe and former Soviet republics were also taken off the list. However, even after these changes, U.S. nuclear operations were still formally operating under National Security Decision Directive 13 (NSDD 13), signed by President Reagan in 1981.[44] There were other indications in the post–Cold War world about policymakers contemplating the use of nuclear weapons, particularly low-yield nuclear weapons for use against emerging nuclear powers in the Third World.[45]

START I was signed in July of 1991 and reduced strategic nuclear warheads by approximately 50 percent. This was followed by a bold move in September of 1991 when President George Bush announced that the United States would unilaterally cut most of its tactical nuclear weapons in Europe, including all artillery shells and short-range nuclear weapons.

Bush also took U.S. bombers off alert.[46] The only tactical nuclear weapons that would remain after these cuts were implemented would be nonstrategic aircraft deployed in Western Europe and South Korea. The following month, the elimination of tactical nuclear weapons continued as Soviet president Gorbachev matched the Bush cuts. In addition, NATO announced in October 1991 that it would cut NATO nuclear weapons by 80 percent, which in effect cut the tactical nuclear weapons that remained on bombers. The United States also announced that it was withdrawing its nuclear weapons from South Korea.

The move toward the reduction in the number of nuclear weapons continued when President Bush announced the end of production of the B-2, the MX, and the small ICBM in the beginning of 1992. Finally, with the signing of START II in the beginning of 1993, there were agreements to reduce approximately 70 percent of deployed strategic nuclear weapons and to eliminate nearly 90 percent of tactical nuclear weapons from the levels that existed at the height of the Cold War. Though START II had not yet been ratified as of December 1996 by the Russian Duma, in terms of the numbers of weapons deployed and planned procurement of nuclear weapons, there had been clear changes in the policies of the United States.

Through the fall of 1996, resistance within the Russian Duma to the ratification of START II remained firm. At the root of this opposition was the START II requirement to de-MIRV ICBMs, the part of the strategic triad that held almost 60 percent of Russian strategic nuclear strength. The treaty requires the Russians to eliminate these weapons and replace them with single-warhead ICBMs up to START II levels. Many in the Russian Duma are hesitant to do this because of the large financial outlay required. They would prefer to renegotiate the treaty. Uncertainty about the status of the ABM treaty along with strong Russian opposition to NATO expansion imperiled the ratification of START II.[47] Some have suggested that the Clinton administration move quickly to START III, thus allowing the Russians to avoid the cost of building new single-warhead ICBMs. Little has been done, however, to move forward on this idea.

The lack of a commitment to further cuts has been an obstacle to getting a consensus on a Comprehensive Test Ban Treaty (CTBT). Though the Clinton administration should be commended for its signing of a CTBT in September of 1996, the failure to get the agreement of India could result in an obstacle to the treaty's coming into force. Though over sixty countries have signed, without the approval of India and other potential nuclear states, the treaty's enforcement mechanisms will not come into force.[48] Although the implementation of START II reduces the number of deployed strategic warheads, the U.S. and Russian arsenals will be larger than the 3,000-warhead limits because many warheads have been transferred to a reserve status. If one includes spares, warheads remaining from nondeployed tactical systems, the strategic warheads reserve, and remaining fissile material, the reduction of warheads does not appear as impressive as it might at first glance.[49]

Policymakers also seem to want to leave nuclear weapons an integral part of U.S. defense policy. The Strategic Advisory Group of the Joint Strategic Target Planning Staff issued a report at the end of 1991.[50] The Reed-Wheeler report suggested maintaining levels of strategic nuclear weapons within the 5,000 range, explicitly rejected no first use or counter-city targeting, and urged that nuclear weapons be used to deter and potentially respond to biological and chemical attacks. Overall, the study had an expansive view of U.S. nuclear weapons policy and did not break with traditional views of the importance of nuclear weapons to U.S. national security. The report advocates that the United States reorient its nuclear strategy toward targeting "every reasonable adversary." When this became public in testimony before the Senate Armed Services Committee, the lack of real change was easily observed. The report explicitly ruled out more radical reductions in nuclear forces and rejected adopting a pure strategy of MAD (referred to here as vague threats to destroy cities) as "immoral and unwise." In rejecting MAD, the report said that the United States should not deliberately target populations. This is a distinction of critical importance for America's nuclear posture.[51]

There is also much evidence that policymakers continue to view nuclear weapons as usable across a wide variety of situations. In mid-1993, the Joint Chiefs of Staff issued the "Doctrine for Joint Nuclear Operations," which justified nuclear weapons for their ability to deter chemical, biological, and nuclear weapons of mass destruction. Reports indicated that Iran has also been added to the targeting plans of the United States.[52]

Another example of this trend came in April of 1996, when forty-three African countries signed the African Nuclear-Weapon-Free Zone (ANWFZ) Treaty. The U.S. signed a protocol pledging that it would not use or threaten to use nuclear weapons against any of the signatories of the treaty. Robert Bell of the National Security Council, however, later backed away from this position and moved away from the U.S. pledge made in 1978 that it would not use nuclear weapons against non-nuclear states.[53]

A focus on targeting and declaratory policy indicates that U.S. nuclear weapons policy has not embraced the changed realities of the post–Cold War international environment. Despite all of the important changes outlined above, the United States has not adopted a targeting or declaratory policy that rules out the first use of nuclear weapons or that recognizes that nuclear weapons have no military utility. This continues the long-standing policy of the United States to develop the capabilities and strategy that would allow nuclear weapons to be used in a "limited" way.

The Clinton Administration and the NPR

Changes to U.S. nuclear weapons policy that came with the Clinton administration followed a long series of actions since the end of the Cold War that significantly reduced the *number* of both strategic and tactical nuclear weapons in the U.S. arsenal but did not change the way policymakers thought about using these weapons. In October of 1993, Secretary of Defense Les Aspin announced the initiation of the Clinton administration's Nuclear Policy Review (NPR), which promised to be a thorough review of all aspects of U.S. nuclear weapons policy. This was the first such comprehensive review since 1978. In the briefing on the NPR, Aspin suggested that great changes to U.S. nuclear weapons policy might be forthcoming:

> One era has ended, and a new one begun. The world has fundamentally changed. We are responding with the first Nuclear Policy Review in 15 years. In fact, it is the first Defense Department revision ever to incorporate revisions of policy, doctrine, force structure, operations, safety, security, and arms control in one look.[54]

Initially chaired by Ashton Carter, Assistant Secretary of Defense for Nuclear Security and Counterproliferation, and Lieutenant General Barry McCaffrey, Director for Strategic Plans and Policy for the Joint Staff, the NPR was to consider the overall role of nuclear weapons, nuclear force structure and operations, nuclear safety and security, counterproliferation policy, and threat reduction in the former Soviet Union.[55] It was suggested by some that the NPR might conclude that the United States did not need the strategic triad, that it might adopt a no-first-use policy and abandon its right to use nuclear weapons in response to the use of biological and chemical weapons. Such changes would have indicated that the Clinton administration was moving toward marginalizing the role of nuclear weapons in U.S. defense policy. Only one year before the announcement of the NPR, Aspin, then chairman of the House Armed Services Committee, noted, "[I]f we now had the opportunity to ban all nuclear weapons, we would."[56]

Les Aspin was replaced by William Perry, and before the NPR was even completed, it was clear that the ambitious goals that Aspin had articulated were not going to be met. By the summer of 1994, Perry acknowledged that because of fear of a resurgent Russia, the NPR would not consider eliminating the land-based leg of the triad nor would it change the justification of possible use of nuclear weapons against chemical and biological weapons.[57] Finally, nearly one year after the NPR was announced, a half year after the report was originally scheduled to be completed, Perry announced the results, stating, "[N]ow it's time to alter the way we think about nuclear weapons, and the Nuclear Posture Review was conceived to do just that."[58] In testimony on the NPR, Deputy Secretary of Defense John Deutch said that the "posture review takes us to a smaller and safer nuclear force structure with *a changed role.*"[59] But how much of a change did the NPR really make to U.S. nuclear weapons policy? Did it really, as Perry initially claimed, change the way U.S. policymakers think about nuclear weapons?[60]

The *Washington Post* summarized the NPR with the headline "Clinton Decides to Retain Bush Nuclear Arms Policy." In fact, the NPR left U.S. strategic nuclear weapons policy virtually untouched. Strategic force levels would not move below the 3,000 to 3,500 deployed warheads already agreed to in START II. It left the strategic triad in place, failed to adopt a policy of no first use, and left open the option of using nuclear weapons in retaliation for the use of chemical or biological weapons. The NPR did decrease the number of Trident subs from eighteen to fourteen, but it called for retrofitting four of the Trident submarines that had C-4 missiles with the more accurate D-5 missile. Furthermore, the NPR kept limited tactical nuclear capabilities in Europe by maintaining 480 dual-capable tactical aircraft.

Reports on the NPR process indicate that bolder steps were considered, though these were rejected. Some involved in the process pushed for the elimination of the land-based leg of the triad.[61] However, the military intervened late in the process to prevent the reduction of the Minuteman force from 500 to 300 or 450. Policymakers justifying the results of the NPR emphasized that the United States had to maintain a hedge against political reversal in the former Soviet Union. As a result, the NPR allowed many dismantled forces to remain in storage that could be uploaded if necessary. Some estimates indicate that as many as 5,000 warheads would be in reserve.[62] For those who hoped the NPR might make significant changes to the U.S. arsenal, the process was a disappointment.[63]

In the beginning of 1994, Presidents Clinton and Yeltsin announced the "detargeting" of Russian and U.S. strategic nuclear weapons. This was a largely symbolic move since targets could be added to the weapons quickly, in some cases in minutes. Nonetheless, older weapons such as the Minuteman III were aimed at the ocean, since they need a target in their computer systems, and new weapons such as the D-5 were actually deployed without targets.[64] The NPR, however, did not change the philosophy behind U.S. targeting. It did not change the fact that thousands of targets in Russia would continue to be targeted, including military assets such as strategic and conventional forces, along with industrial and command and control assets.[65] In the press conference announcing the NPR, Deutch justified the ICBM leg of the triad because of "the ability of these weapons uniquely to be selectively used."[66] In testimony on the NPR, he confirmed that "our targeting includes distinction between target classes. We are not anticipating that deterrence is just threatening one massive retaliation."[67] Though there are many important changes here, there is no sense of moving away from the notion that nuclear weapons could in fact be used as military tools. This latter point is confirmed by the active program to improve the accuracy of the Minuteman force to achieve the same accuracy as the MX missile.[68] This, coupled with the fact that all SLBMs will be equipped with the accurate D-5 missile, gives the U.S. nuclear arsenal a significant counterforce capability. Thus, there was detargeting in numbers but not philosophy.

This lack of a shift in nuclear philosophy is paradoxically illustrated by a statement made by Secretary of Defense William Perry when announcing the NPR. He said of nuclear weapons policy during the Cold War that "it was characterized by a unique military strategy called mutual assured destruction, or MAD."[69] With this statement, Perry continued a long tradition of mischaracterizing U.S. nuclear weapons policy as MAD when in reality it has always embraced more limited options. As Perry's statement illustrates, many have believed or asserted that U.S. nuclear weapons policy has always embraced MAD, rather than the NUTs that was its operational policy.

Why the Unrelenting Pursuit of NUTs (Even Now)?

Why is there an unrelenting effort to make nuclear weapons usable? Considerations of this question are most useful if we ask two separate but related questions. First, why the pursuit of NUTs during the Cold War? Second, why the lack of far-reaching change with the dissolution of the Soviet Union and the end of the Cold War? The roots of such an explanation lie in the ideas associated with the conventionalization of nuclear weapons policy. This set of notions led policymakers to think about nuclear weapons as if they were conventional weapons. As a result, counterforce has dominated targeting. This is consistent with targeting philosophies that preceded the advent of nuclear weapons. Thinking of nuclear weapons as rational political instruments was thus perfectly consistent with how military and civilian leaders had always thought about using weapons. The privileged place of this idea in the minds of both civilian and military leaders is a partial explanation for the staying power of counterforce targeting in the nuclear age.[70] And it is the deep historical roots of this type of thinking that have made counterforce targeting a privileged idea adhered to by the state throughout the history of nuclear weapons policy. They have also made it a difficult habit to break.[71]

The history of U.S. nuclear weapons policy is clear: the entrenched bureaucracy shows a great deal of continuity. Whether administrations were Democratic or Republican, the same people have shaped U.S. nuclear weapons policy over the years. As is illustrated above, many of the very same people who did the nuclear review for President Bush in 1989 joined the Clinton administration in 1992 and became responsible for nuclear weapons policy. Historical accounts show the same phenomena to be true throughout the nuclear age. Officials such as Franklin Miller, Andrew Marshall, Leon Sloss, Walter Slocombe, William Perry, and John Deutch have influenced nuclear weapons policy for decades, and many of them continue to do so within the Clinton administration despite the end of the Cold War. One might imagine that Les Aspin, had he continued in the position of secretary of defense (and had he survived), might have been able to implement more substantial changes to overall U.S. strategic policy. But his resignation from office came about partly from his inability to fit into Pentagon culture. Perhaps the Pentagon bureaucracy is able to repel those whose ideas do not fit into longtime existing patterns of thinking.

There are other indications that the course of the NPR can be explained from this perspective. Ashton Carter, a longtime analyst of nuclear issues but somebody who has spent most of his career outside of the Pentagon bureaucracy, seems to have been the one in the NPR most forcefully pushing significant change. As the account above indicates, Carter, who cochaired the NPR, may have been the most supportive of eliminating or reducing the ICBM force. Reports indicate that Carter had proposed post–START II nuclear force postures of 1,700 nuclear warheads and the elimination of ICBMs. Much of the opposition to this has been attributed to the presence of Franklin Miller, a longtime member of the Pentagon's nuclear bureaucracy, who reportedly resisted the major changes that were under consideration.[72] Those who had been involved in making and keeping U.S. nuclear weapons policy committed to counterforce, NUTs, and usability have managed, despite some changes, to continue to dominate this policy.

The dominance of this way of thinking about nuclear weapons is also supported by the perception that nuclear weapons were responsible for the relative peace of the Cold War. U.S. policymakers widely perceive that nuclear weapons helped deter the Soviets in Europe and other areas of

U.S. interest. This pushes U.S. weapons policy today. There is no shortage of new ideas out there on how U.S. weapons should be deployed and used. In fact, the end of the Cold War has created a virtual cottage industry of analysts proposing significant changes in the arsenal. But these continue to remain outside the mainstream of nuclear deliberations.

There are two ways that ideas within the nuclear bureaucracy might change. One would be for those who have been around this issue for decades to change the way they think about nuclear weapons—to move them toward the margins of U.S. policy. Perhaps rereading Bernard Brodie would be a place to start. Given the argument presented here, this is unlikely. Or, those making policy in this area could be replaced by new faces. This also appears to be unlikely, as the new faces in the Clinton administration have been pushed to the sidelines in favor of the traditionalists. This analysis suggests that nuclear weapons will remain a central part of U.S. policy for years to come.

These reports also indicate that President Clinton has not provided the type of leadership that would be necessary to shift U.S. policy. Part of this is probably due to Clinton's lack of background in nuclear issues. In addition, the Clinton administration seems to have had very little to gain by attempting to move from NUTs or traditional views of nuclear weapons to embrace MAD or the views of marginalizers. This caution by the Clinton administration did not dislodge the dominant bureaucratic perspectives and ideas that have historically dominated U.S. nuclear weapons policy.

These domestic factors also include economic and budgetary considerations. The increasing pressure in the United States to cut defense spending may actually work to keep the central role of nuclear weapons in U.S. defense policy. We may think of the 1950s here, when the threat of massive retaliation served to extend U.S. interests abroad while at the same time demobilizing troops. Because nuclear weapons are usually viewed as relatively inexpensive, American policymakers in the post–Cold War era must rely on them even more than they did during the Cold War. There are clear economic motivations to continue to rely on nuclear weapons.

Thus, what we see is that a combination of ideas, bureaucratic interests, and domestic politics works toward policy continuity. Though changes in the international environment opened a crack in the Pentagon bureaucracy for real changes in the way the United States incorporates nuclear weapons into overall defense policy, the existing nuclear bureaucracy eventually repelled this challenge. Changes in the international environment would thus appear to be necessary but not sufficient conditions for a fundamental change to U.S. policy. One also can imagine an instance in which political and public pressure might open up cracks in the nuclear bureaucracy, as it did in the early 1980s with the nuclear freeze movement and increasing salience of nuclear debates. But today, with the end of the Cold War, issues of nuclear strategy rarely show up as a concern to citizens and politicians. Continuity seems to be a safe prediction.

NOTES

1. Bernard Brodie, ed., *The Absolute Weapon: Atomic Power and World Order* (New York: Harcourt, Brace, 1946). In particular, see 28, 36, and 46 for an elaboration of these points.
2. Brodie, *The Absolute Weapon*, 81.
3. Brodie, *The Absolute Weapon*, 62.
4. Robert Jervis, *The Illogic of American Nuclear Strategy* (Ithaca, N.Y.: Cornell University Press, 1984).
5. For more on this, see Robert W. Tucker and John J. Weltman, "The Nuclear Future," in Patrick J. Garrity and Steven A. Maaranen, *Nuclear Weapons in the Changing World* (New York: Plenum Press, 1992), 241–61.
6. Charles Glaser has made the interesting point that once tensions between the United States and the Soviet Union were reduced or eliminated, the need to disarm was greatly reduced. See Charles Glaser, *Analyzing Strategic Nuclear Policy* (Princeton, N.J.: Princeton University Press, 1990).
7. Of course, the chance of accident and/or unauthorized use in the former Soviet Union may be higher in the post–Cold War years.
8. For more on this and an account of the Clinton administration's Nuclear Posture Review, see Stephen A. Cambone and Patrick J. Garrity, "The Future of U.S. Nuclear Policy," *Survival* 36 (Winter 1994–95): 73–95.
9. This section is based on my book *The State, Society, and Limited Nuclear War* (Albany: SUNY Press, 1995).
10. I will not cover the period before the creation of the SIOP in 1960. For an excellent treatment of these issues for that period, see David Alan Rosenberg, "The Origins of Overkill: Nuclear Weapons and American Strategy," *International Security* (Spring 1983): 3–69.
11. For an unabashed endorsement of NUTs policy after the Cold War, see Baker Spring, "What the Pentagon's Nuclear Doctrine Review Should Say," *Heritage Foundation Reports* (26 May 1994).
12. The most well known advocate of such postures within the academic literature is Colin Gray. See his "Nuclear Strategy: A Case for a Theory of Victory," *International Security* 1 (Summer 1979): 66–90; Colin S. Gray and Keith Payne, "Victory Is Possible," *Foreign Policy* 39 (Summer 1980): 14–27; and Colin S. Gray, "Targeting Problems for Central War," *Naval War College Review* (January–February 1980): 3–21.
13. Central to this debate had been the notion of extending deterrence to Western Europe. The goal of deterring a Soviet conventional invasion of Western Europe was a major factor in the search for these implementable nuclear options.

And though the fear of a Soviet invasion of Western Europe is now virtually nonexistent, the United States may still be concerned with extended deterrence to stem the spread of nuclear weapons in Europe. See Edward Rhodes, "Hawks, Doves, Owls, and Loons: Extended Deterrence without Flexible Response," *Millennium: The Journal of International Studies* 19, no. 1 (1990): 37–57.

14. These categories are discussed by Cambone and Garrity, "Future of U.S. Nuclear Policy." The marginalizers are also discussed by Lawrence Freedman, "Great Powers, Vital Interests, and Nuclear Weapons," *Survival* 36 (Winter 1994–95): 35–52.

15. The marginalizers include Jonathan Dean, "The Final Stage of Nuclear Arms Control," *Washington Quarterly* 17 (Autumn 1994): 31–52; Jonathan Dean and Randall Forsberg, "The Road to Zero," *Technology Review* (August/September 1995): 74–76; Michael Mazarr, "Virtual Nuclear Arsenals," *Survival* 37 (Autumn 1995): 7–26; Ivo H. Daalder, "Stepping Down the Thermonuclear Ladder: How Low Can We Go?" *Center for International and Security Studies at Maryland* (1993); and Daalder, "What Vision for the Nuclear Future?" *Washington Quarterly* 18 (Spring 1995): 127–42. Accounts by the traditionalists include Walter B. Slocombe, "The Future of U.S. Nuclear Weapons in a Restructured World," in Garrity and Maaranen, *Nuclear Weapons in the Changing World.*

16. Theresa Hitchens, "Clinton Review Challenges Triad; Decision Tilts on Russian Relations," *Defense News* (28 February 1994): 3.

17. Fred Kaplan, *The Wizards of Armageddon* (New York: Simon and Schuster, 1983), 271; Scott D. Sagan, "SIOP-62: The Nuclear War Plan Briefing to President Kennedy," *International Security* 12 (Summer 1987): 22–51.

18. Robert S. McNamara, *Remarks by Secretary McNamara, NATO Ministerial Meeting* (5 May 1992), Office of the Secretary of Defense, Freedom of Information Act.

19. Confidential interview with high Defense Department official from the Pentagon who served during the McNamara years.

20. Desmond Ball, *Politics and Force Levels: The Strategic Missile Program of the Kennedy Administration* (Berkeley: University of California Press, 1980), 66.

21. These numbers are taken from Graham T. Allison and Frederic A. Morris, "The Determinants of Military Weapons," in Daniel J. Kaufman, Jeffrey S. Mikitrick, and Thomas J. Levy, eds., *U.S. National Security: A Framework for Analysis* (Boston: Lexington, 1983), 307–36.

22. See Alton Frye, *A Responsible Congress* (New York: McGraw-Hill, 1975), 49.

23. For a discussion of these changes, see Lynn Etheridge Davis, *Limited Nuclear Options: Deterrence and the New American Doctrine,* Adelphi Paper 191 (London: International Institute for Strategic Studies, 1974). Later, Schlesinger would acknowledge that other administrations had targeted military targets as well.

24. Davis, *Limited Nuclear Options,* 1.

25. Davis, *Limited Nuclear Options,* 4.

26. Desmond Ball, "U.S. Strategic Forces: How Would They Be Used?" *International Security* 7 (Winter 1982–83): 36–37.

27. Confidential interview with member of Foster Panel (the interagency task force on targeting policy) and JCS.

28. Confidential interview with member of Foster Panel.

29. Alan Platt, *The U.S. Senate and Strategic Arms Policy: 1969–1974* (Boulder, Colo.: Westview Press, 1978), 104.

30. For a discussion of this, see Jeffrey Richelson, "PD-59, NSDD-13, and the Reagan Strategic Modernization Program," *Journal of Strategic Studies* 8 (June 1983): 125–46.

31. Cited in Leon Sloss and Marc Dean Millot, "U.S. Nuclear Strategy in Evolution," *Strategic Review* 12 (Winter 1984): 20–21.

32. Richard Halloran, "Weinberger Angered by Reports on War Strategy," *New York Times* (24 August 1982): 8.

33. Bernard Gwertzman, "Haig Cites a Standing NATO Plan Envisioning a Warning A-Blast," *New York Times* (5 November 1981): 1.

34. Richard Halloran, "Pentagon Draws Up First Strategy for Fighting a Long Nuclear War," *New York Times* (30 May 1982): 1.

35. See Ivo Daalder, *The Nature and Practice of Flexible Response: NATO Strategy and Theater Nuclear Forces since 1967* (Ithaca, N.Y.: Cornell University Press, 1991).

36. With the end of the Cold War, NATO did announce a new strategic concept that stated that the chances of using nuclear weapons had become remote. See "The Alliance's New Strategic Concept," *NATO Press Communiqué*, S-1 (91) 85 (7 November 1991).

37. Though the no-first-use debate was most intense in the early 1980s, some analysts continue to advocate such a pledge in the post–Cold War years. For an example, see David Gompert, Kenneth Watman, and Dean Wilkening, "Nuclear First Use Revisited," *Survival* 37 (Autumn 1995): 27–44.

38. Desmond Ball and Robert Toth, "Revising the SIOP: Taking War-Fighting to Dangerous Extremes," *International Security* 14 (Spring 1990): 65–92.

39. See Robert Toth, "U.S. Shifts Nuclear Response Strategy: New Formula Designed to Eliminate Soviet Leadership Early in Conflict," *Los Angeles Times* (23 July 1989): 16.

40. As guidance was being prepared for the new SIOP, it was generally referred to as SIOP-7. However, the Bush administration decided to label the new SIOP 6F, to communicate its continuity with the existing SIOP-6. See Ball and Toth, "Revising the SIOP," 66, citing General John T. Chain, CINCSAC, from Richard Halloran, "U.S. Revises Its War Plan for a New Age," *New York Times* (2 November 1988): A7.

41. See Ball and Toth, "Revising the SIOP," 79–81.

42. R. Jeffrey Smith, "U.S. Trims List of Targets in Soviet Union," *Washington Post* (21 July 1991): 1.

43. When one looks at the history of U.S. nuclear weapons policy, it becomes readily apparent that many of the same figures who made policy in the 1960s and 1970s continue to have a great deal of influence today. The same people seem to maintain top-level positions through changes in administrations.

44. R. Jeffrey Smith, "Nuclear Arms Doctrine to Be Reviewed: Comprehensive Evaluation Will Be First since End of Cold War," *Washington Post* (19 October 1993): A17.

45. Paul Quinn-Judge, "US, Russia Strategists See Place for 'Mininukes,'" *Boston Globe* (12 July 1993). For a piece that favorably explores the role of small nuclear weapons, see Thomas W. Dowler and Joseph S. Howard II, "Countering the Threat of the Well-Armed Tyrant: A Modest Proposal for Small Nuclear Weapons," *Strategic Review* (Fall 1991): 34–39.

46. Andrew Rosenthal, "U.S. to Give Up Short-Range Nuclear Arms; Bush Seeks Soviet Cuts and Further Talks," *New York Times* (28 September 1991): 1, 4; Eric Schmitt, "Bush's Plan Would Sharply Cut Nuclear Arms for Battlefield Use," *New York Times* (28 September 1991): 5.

47. For a discussion of this, see Yuri K. Nazarkin and Rodney W. Jones, "Moscow's START II Ratification: Problems and Prospects," *Arms Control Today* (September 1995): 8–14.

48. Alison Mitchell, "Clinton, at U.N., Signs Treaty Banning All Nuclear Testing," *New York Times* (25 September 1996): A1.

49. Many of these points are made by Jonathan Dean, Adviser for International Security Issues, Union of Concerned Scientists, in comments presented to the Swedish War College, Stockholm (transcript in author's possession).

50. Thomas Reed and Michael Wheeler, *The Role of Nuclear Weapons in the New World Order* (Washington, D.C., December 1991), reprinted in U.S. Congress, Senate, *Threat Assessment, Military Strategy, and Defense Planning* (Hearings before the Committee on Armed Services, 102d Congress, 2d session, January–March 1992): 156–213.

51. The report and testimony on it can be found in "Future Nuclear Weapons Requirements" (Hearing before the Defense Policy Panel and the Department of Energy Defense Nuclear Facilities Panel of the Committee on Armed Services, House of Representatives, 102d Congress, 2d session, 2 April 1992).

52. This is based on William Arkin, "NPT—Back to Ground Zero," *The Nation* (24 April 1995): 553–56.

53. For details on this, see George Bunn, "Expanding Nuclear Options: Is the U.S. Negating Its Non-Use Pledges?" *Arms Control Today* (May–June 1996).

54. News briefing, Office of the Assistant Secretary of Defense (Public Affairs), 29 October 1993.

55. McCaffrey was later replaced by Army Lt. Gen. Wesley Clark.

56. "From Deterrence to Denuking: A New Nuclear Policy for the 1990s," draft working paper by Rep. Les Aspin, Chairman, House Armed Services Committee, in *Shaping Nuclear Policy for the 1990s: A Compendium of Views* (Report of the Defense Policy Panel of the Committee on Armed Services, House of Representatives, 102d Congress, 2d session, 17 December 1992), 10.

57. For a report on this, see Theresa Hitchens, "Uncertainty over Russia Clouds U.S. Nuclear Strategy," *Defense News* (20–26 June 1994).

58. Defense Department briefing, "Nuclear Posture Review—William Perry," 22 September 1994, Federal Information Systems Corporation, Federal News Service.

59. Hearing of the House Foreign Affairs Committee, Report for the 103d Congress, Federal Information Systems Corporation, 5 October 1994.

60. For an account that suggests the NPR left open the opportunity to "denuclearize" U.S. policy, see Cambone and Garrity, "Future of U.S. Nuclear Policy," 73–95.

61. Some reports indicate that Ashton Carter, cochair of the review, was pushing for elimination of the land-based leg of the triad. For one report, see "ICBM Controversy," *Aerospace Daily* (23 April 1994): 129.

62. See William Arkin and Robert Norris, "Nuclear Notebook: U.S. Strategic Nuclear Forces, End of 1994," *Bulletin of the Atomic Scientists* (January/February 1995): 69–71.

63. Some accounts of the process tell the story of hard-line DOD bureaucrats preventing real change from taking place. See William Arkin, "Bad Posture: The Nuclear Priesthood Slouches Onward," *Bulletin of the Atomic Scientists* (July/August 1995): 64; and William Arkin, "Inarticulating Nuclear Policy," *Bulletin of the Atomic Scientists* (January/February 1995): 72.

64. Accounts suggest that moves of this nature had begun to be considered under the Bush administration in the Strategic Stability Working Group. This group consisted of U.S. officials in the Department of Defense and Soviet officials from the Defense Ministry. It was this group that did the behind-the-scenes work on the detargeting issue. "Background Briefing by Senior Administration Officials," Moscow, Russia, Federal Information Systems Corporation, Federal News Service, 14 January 1994.

65. Dunbar Lockwood, "New Nuclear Posture Review Shows Little Change in Policies," *Arms Control Today* (November 1994): 27, 33.

66. Defense Department briefing, 22 September 1994.

67. See House Foreign Affairs Committee hearing, 5 October 1994.

68. See Arkin and Norris, "Nuclear Notebook," 70.

69. Defense Department briefing, 22 September 1994.

70. For this type of explanation, see Janne Nolan, *Guardians of the Arsenal* (New York: Basic Books, 1993).

71. This idea is further developed in Christopher McGrory Klyza and Eric Mlyn, "Privileged Ideas and State Interests: Bombs, Trees, and State Autonomy," *Policy Studies Journal* 23 (Summer 1995): 203–317.

72. This account is from Arkin, "Bad Posture," 64.

Deterrence and Alternative Images of Nuclear Possession

WILLIAM C. MARTEL

Deterrence, as it is presented in Bernard Brodie's *The Absolute Weapon*, universally applies to all states. Brodie et al. suggest that the threat of nuclear retaliation promises a level of massive destruction that leads policymakers facing such threats to avoid nuclear war. This chapter poses two hypotheses that question the universal applicability of deterrence. First, deterrence fundamentally involves the core values of societies; that is, societies have different notions of the relationship between the use of military force and political ends.[1] Second, the rational pursuit of political ends does not exclude risking the survival of society. Both of these points greatly complicate the current understanding of deterrence. The chapter concludes that, in contrast to Brodie, deterrence is best viewed as a particularistic rather than universal construct.

This chapter proceeds with three broad arguments. The first section explores the fact that most of the literature on deterrence during the Cold War viewed deterrence as universally applicable based on a single conception of what could be defined as rational behavior. The universal applicability of deterrence strategy was tied directly to an implicit assumption that avoiding societal destruction represented the instrumental limit on rational action. The universal view of deterrence can be challenged, therefore, by recognizing the possibility that there may be societal conceptions of rational behavior that instrumentally include the potential for societal destruction in the pursuit of societal goals. If it can be established that there are different conceptions of the fundamental limit to what might be defined as rational instrumental behavior, then the possibility of competing images[2] of nuclear possession emerges. (The use of the term *society* is meant to convey a coherent group that may or may not be in total control of a state's political and military structures. It is possible for separate societal groups to function within a single state.)[3] The second section discusses a "millenarian" image of nuclear war and deterrence. In millenarian societies, limits on rational behavior rest on beliefs about creating ideal societies through revolutionary action. The third section of the chapter examines the different international security dynamics that might be created when competing images interact between nuclear-armed societies.[4]

This inquiry into alternative images is not motivated by the desire to provoke reductio ad absurdum debates on the nuances of deterrence. Rather, the desire is to reexamine deterrence theoretically. In the end, all societies have a profound stake in the question of whether nuclear deterrence can be pursued based on a universally held conception that societal destruction is irrational or whether nuclear weapons may be possessed by some who see societal sacrifice as rational and instrumental in advancing their goals. This chapter is a theoretical examination of that latter possibility.

The Brodie Image of Deterrence

The threat of nuclear retaliation holds out the prospect of not merely massive damage, but national destruction. Ultimately, it is this possibility of catastrophe that makes nuclear deterrence so compelling. Actions that would bring about nuclear retaliation, therefore, would result from irrational decisions or loss of control. Leaving the second possibility aside, the idea that provoking nuclear retaliation (that is, defying a nuclear deterrent threat) is irrational rests on the assumption that while countries might be willing to expend great effort in the pursuit of political objectives in war, the loss of one's society in such pursuit cannot be justified. There is, thus, an implicit instrumental limit to what can be deemed rational behavior.[5]

The concept of deterrence prior to the end of the Cold War described an internally consistent and deductive model for understanding interactions among nuclear-armed societies in both peace and war.[6] While deterrence became a metaphor for describing the role of nuclear weapons in U.S.-Soviet relations, the more profound consequence of the Cold War was equating deterrence implicitly with a metaphysical construct for describing how nuclear weapons influence all societies.[7] Since the origins of the Cold War, the dominant construct for deterrence among policymakers has been an image that explicitly assumed that nuclear-armed societies strive to act in rational and risk-averse ways. Nuclear deterrence strategies have rested on a cost-benefit analysis that assumed that loss of one's society would outweigh any expected benefit. Any calculation beyond such a limit was deemed irrational.[8]

The literature on rationality in deterrence argues that the obvious benefit of acting rationally when armed with nuclear weapons—that is, in a deliberate fashion that follows a cost-benefit procedure for pursuing one's goals—is to promote and sustain peace and stability in international politics.[9] The fundamental belief in American diplomacy was that deterrence added immeasurably to international stability because it provided a framework for avoiding actions that might cause crises to escalate to the use of nuclear weapons.[10]

Deterrence was elevated to a metaphysical—that is, transcendent or supersensible—system of thought involving elaborate and subtle forms of expression. In the tradition of analytic philosophy, the implicit assumption was that deterrence bounded by the rational limit of avoiding societal destruction (what hereafter will be referred to as the Brodie image of deterrence) was a metaphysical concept that enveloped all conceivable conditions in which states might find themselves engaged in nuclear diplomacy.[11] The article of faith among theorists was that the Brodie image of deterrence transcended political, ideological, economic, cultural, and historical conditions in societies. This view of rationality was embedded as an assumption of deterrence in much the same way that economic rationality is embedded in microeconomic theories of the firm.[12]

The early nuclear states, and in particular the United States, elevated the Brodie image of deterrence to a grand strategic concept that was endowed with the rigor of logic and the certainty of mathematics. Scholars spoke of deterrence with the reverence of a physical principle, thus implicitly reaffirming the view that it controls coercively the actions of all nuclear-armed societies—whether they like it or not.[13] If we believe that deterrence is a universal construct in which the actions of nuclear societies are governed by "metaphysical" rules, then new nuclear societies will be governed deterministically by the rules of deterrence.

Elevating deterrence to a universal and metaphysical construct provides a context to understand and predict the actions of nuclear societies. The Brodie image is supported by a number of influences, which flow from the historical and philosophical traditions of the leading nuclear states. Rather than recognizing these influences as particular to the societies in possession of nuclear weapons, the arguments are presented as universally applicable. In large measure this is because three of these underlying influences rest on universal logics.

The first is the clear influence of the Platonic idea that rational or logical investigation will reveal a universal logic.[14] The Platonic influence expresses itself through the objective of constructing the best form of deterrence attainable by, or descriptive of, specified categories and then fitting deterrence to those categories. Because it could not be conceived that instrumental rational behavior could be pursued to the point of societal destruction, the logic of deterrence had to rest on the ideal of limited instrumental rational behavior.

The second influence is utilitarianism. In a practical sense, deterrence draws from classical utilitarianism, which avows that the "supreme good" produces the greatest happiness for the greatest number.[15] In deterrence, the utilitarian function is to produce the greatest degree of utility—measured in stability and war avoidance—for the greatest number of people and societies. Nothing has greater utilitarian value than a theory of deterrence that strengthens the illusion that security is possible for all societies.

Third, deterrence has clear normative overtones, given the fundamental presumption that all societies are driven by the desire to avoid nuclear war. For instance, the notion of war avoidance is embedded in the theory of deterrence even though, under certain circumstances, nuclear weapons may be what is needed to secure states' interests. This particular normative content, which is depicted as universally held, overshadows competing social, cultural, or historical traditions. Action leading to the destruction of one's society, therefore, is not only irrational but morally corrupt.

The final influence that supported the emergence of deterrence as a universal construct was the time period in which the concept was developed—the historically rare moment of a bipolar world.[16] As the leading nuclear powers, the United States and the Soviet Union dominated the discourse on deterrence and produced a rich source of data on the theory and practice of deterrence. The analytic efforts of deterrence theorists focused on understanding these particular superpower interactions. Seen from the perspective of the 1990s, it is not only possible, but probable, that the Cold War was representative of only one category of nuclear societies.[17] Bipolarity discouraged theorists from including alternative images of nuclear possession, simply because other societies ultimately did not matter in great power politics. This enhanced the rationale for applying deterrence universally.

The Case for a Particularistic View of Deterrence

Despite the emphasis throughout the Cold War on the Brodie image of deterrence, scholars and strategists occasionally expressed concerns that deterrence was one-dimensional. Patrick Morgan implicitly recognized this problem when he argued that "one must take into account the nature of the government that attempts deterrence."[18] The emphasis on two governments, those of the United States and the Soviet Union, reflected the fact that "deterrence theory was developed to improve our understanding of the burdens of statecraft in the nuclear age."[19] Richard Ned Lebow understood that Morgan was arguing that "deterrence, in theory and practice, is largely an expression of politics in the United States."[20] Deterrence theory matched the status quo orientation and risk-averse political interests of the United States and even the Soviet Union. Furthermore, this argument raises the possibility that alternative ideas might govern nuclear strategy in the future.[21]

But the literature on deterrence contains only vague references to specific societies other than the United States, the Soviet Union, their respective allies, and China.[22] That literature does not imagine, or at least fails to address directly the prospect of, a world in which a diverse array of societies someday might possess nuclear weapons. It often seemed, as Morton Halperin observed, that the Soviet Union constituted the limit of new thinking about what we meant by diverse societies.[23] And to complicate matters, the taxonomy of deterrent threats was based largely on Western examples, as Thomas Schelling noted.[24] The subtle presumption was that because the United States was the first society to possess nuclear weapons, there was an obligation to articulate a universalist construct of deterrence so that all nuclear-armed societies could manage their relationships without resorting to cataclysmic violence.

The existence of other nuclear-armed societies strengthens the case for alternative constructs of deterrence. It is not sufficient to base the theory of deterrence on the logic of diplomatic discourse that existed during the bipolar moment of the Cold War. As Lebow observed, "To base a universal theory of international relations upon such a singular experience [as the Cold War] seems foolish in the extreme."[25] By contrast, the more robust interpretation is to argue that "[i]f deterrence is not a universally applicable strategy, it is imperative for its proponents to reformulate the theory so that it specifies the kinds of conflicts or situations in which it is germane."[26]

The problem, of course, is the "difficulty of framing meaningful generalizations about . . . deterrence that apply to all periods of history."[27] While John Mearsheimer might have said "societies" instead of "periods of history," the point becomes more critical if we assume that any two antagonists operate with the same model of deterrence regardless of whether the weapons are nuclear or conventional ones. Independent of the argument that there ought to be different images of nuclear possession, the theory of deterrence would be more robust if such constructs existed—even though game theory suggests that rationality will prevail when facing a nonrational opponent.[28]

Paradoxically, differing societal images of nuclear possession existed implicitly during the early stages of the Cold War. Some scholars and strategists argued that the Soviet leadership might have had a different orientation to diplomacy and the use of force than that which existed in the West. Brodie himself, writing in *Strategy in the Missile Age* in the late 1950s, suggested that the attitude of the Soviet leadership might be one that is "indifferent to the loss of individual cities."[29] While the role of the Communist leadership in the Soviet Union and China probably was the closest that we came to alternative societal images of deterrence, this construct must be broadened to include the actions of societies vastly more diverse than those of China, Russia, and the United States. This is not to imply that China was irrational with nuclear weapons, for it might have been rational for China to make nuclear threats when its capabilities were decidedly inferior to those of the United States.[30]

While scholars of deterrence occasionally observed that the unique aspects of individual societies must be taken into account in deterrence policies, these ideas never amounted to serious thinking about alternative frameworks or images of nuclear possession. While John Mearsheimer noted that disparate societies may possess nuclear weapons, the prevailing notion of deterrence still retains the dominant Brodiesque orientation.[31] And in his observations about the centralized nature of governmental decision making, Thomas Schelling's argument that decisions reflect various internal processes and influences in a society strengthens the presumption that there may exist alternative images.[32]

It is legitimate to argue theoretically that different societies might possess alternative conceptions of deterrence. This prospect was raised indirectly by Raymond Aron several decades ago when he asked if deterrence belongs to the "traditional theoretical and practical categories of international politics"—that is, the tradition of the behavior of states.[33] By this reasoning, Aron implicitly defends particularistic constructs of deterrence that transcend the experiences of those societies whose behavior led to the construction of formal models of deterrence and international relations. This observation reflects the broader criticism that the strategy of deterrence may reflect a particularistic construct, which cannot be sustained through universal application.

This reasoning is critical for building the case that alternative images of nuclear possession should serve as the principal framework for constructing future deterrence strategies. Embracing the Brodie image of deterrence as an ideal form reinforces the argument that deterrence is an unchanging, predictable model for understanding the actions of nuclear-armed societies. Cold War deterrence strategy was comforting to scholars and practitioners because it was seen as an internally consistent model of state interactions that produced some degree of strategic stability. It is dangerous, however, to believe that the strategy applies equally well to all societies and all strategic conditions. The assumption that rational behavior is limited by the desire to preserve society lent theoretical predictability to the irregular and unpredictable features of international politics. The assumption also meant that deterrence theory ultimately could not describe the behavior of nuclear-armed societies that might be governed by a revolutionary ideology or leadership as anything but a deviation from rational behavior.

Millenarian Images of Nuclear Possession

Millenarianism is a form of eschatology, which itself is the branch of theology concerned with death and salvation, that ultimately focuses on prospects for the human condition. As such, millenarianism is related to various radical ideologies that promise to create a better condition for the members of its society. Millenarian ideologies tend to claim superiority in secular matters of the state. Thus, the intimate relationship that exists between political and religious ideas in millenarianism provides a natural connection to the behavior of societies that are governed by radical ideologies.[34]

A distinctive feature of millenarian societies is that they hold a different image of costs and benefits that may extend beyond the traditional conception of rational behavior. This means that millenarians may be willing to sacrifice their society, if such action advances their revolutionary ideology or theology. Such sacrifice of the society may be instrumentally rational. The Brodie image, however, rests on an implicit assumption that there is no greater good than preservation of society itself. War can be fought at great expense, but it is fought to forward the interests of the surviving society. What constitutes rational behavior is limited by what preserves society. For millenarian societies, there is no similar instrumental limit to what they regard as rational costs. The point needs to be stressed: millenarian societies are not irrational, but they place radically different standards on what constitutes the instrumental limits of permissible action.

The importance of a millenarian image of nuclear possession concerns its theoretical significance for deterrence. The hypothesis is that for millenarian societies, the "traditional" rules of deterrence carry no necessary relevance, because the secularism inherent in the Brodie image of deterrence (specifically, its limits on the use of force and the unwillingness to risk the destruction of society) is not necessarily pertinent to societies that define the human condition in broad cosmological or religious terms. If a millenarian society advocates the creation of a more perfect society in the future, then that society might see nuclear weapons as an acceptable instrument for the annihilation or decimation of enemies who impede progress.[35] For a millenarian society, the theoretical and "traditional" discourse on deterrence is of little concern.

If deterrence is the product of particular conditions in societies rather than universal rules, then state behavior is open to influences from a broad panoply of political, religious, ideological, and cultural systems of thought. Analyses of these factors have been the focus of the literature on military culture and its influence on strategic thinking.[36] In brief, this literature argues that culture bounds the realm of possible action and thus might explain why some plausible options are ignored by states. The concept of military culture remains useful if, in this case, it evolves into a broader paradigm of deterrence. Then it would bound the realm of possible action by focusing on rational deterrence through the stipulation that nuclear weapons should be used only as a last resort.

Thus, we move to the notion of particularistic images of nuclear possession. These rest on the principle that all societies—whether secular or religious, Western or Eastern—judge cultural, historical, and political values differently, employ dissimilar schemes for judging the proper ends of statecraft, and possess radically different images of security. A millenarian image, therefore, is important if the diverse nature and behavior of all societies affect the language of deterrence through alternative images of nuclear possession.

A millenarian image explicitly reintroduces several considerations into discussions of nuclear behavior by acknowledging, first, that the relevance of the Brodie view of rational behavior may decrease as the number of nuclear societies increases and, second, that these societies may have no particular allegiance to a tradition of rationalism that rejects societal sacrifice. In fact, such a limitation on rational behavior may be an anathema to their ideology and theology. Brodie's image of deterrence provided assurance that interactions among nuclear societies would be relatively predictable. It also downplayed the role of irrational actions. The theoretical justification for Brodie's reasoning was that systematic research about nuclear behavior is not possible if we admit the possibility that states may behave in ways that exceed traditionally recognized limits of rational behavior.[37] Thus, a millenarian image of nuclear possession explicitly broadens the universe of possible actions and motivations that influence the behavior of societies.

Revolutionary Societies and Images of Nuclear Possession

The possibility that deterrence is not necessarily a universal construct and that not all societies are equally deterred by nuclear weapons legitimizes the notion of particularistic constructs of nuclear possession.[38] While deterrence evolved into a pristine, abstract, and logical construct for the use of force, a contrary notion is imaginable: deterrence may be the product of millenarian concepts for the use of nuclear weapons that are unified by specific historical traditions and political experiences in revolutionary societies that possess nuclear weapons.

Revolutionary Societies

From the beginning, deterrence applied to a relatively small set of status quo societies—namely, the United States, Britain, and France—and two revisionist states, the Soviet Union and China. But we can imagine the case of a millenarian image of nuclear possession that is guided by a revolutionary ideology or personality. The operant belief is that an ideal society can be created through revolutionary actions.[39] Theoretically consistent with this notion of revolutionary ideology is the existence of new nuclear societies that act in accordance with strict religious, fundamentalist, or radical political ideologies that "clash" directly, to use Samuel Huntington's term,[40] with the traditions of most of the leading nuclear states.

If revolutionary societies have different approaches to decision making, they may not be inhibited by the same constraints on using nuclear weapons. One also could suspect that such societies might use nuclear weapons without regard to the likely costs of nuclear retaliation. A revolutionary society guided by a millenarian image of nuclear possession could be driven by fatalistic urges to destroy its adversary, and thus itself, rather than allow the enemy to prevail. Furthermore, revolutionary societies could justify the decision to use nuclear weapons as an act of martyrdom in service of their deity or because their adherence to a revolutionary ideology mandates radical actions against status quo powers.

The millenarian image of nuclear possession derives from the observation that ideological or religious forces in revolutionary societies could lead them to see nuclear weapons as an instrument for eradicating evil. There is no theoretical reason to exclude the possibility of revolutionary societies' using nuclear weapons to wage religious wars, or jihads, against infidels and pagans. But it is equally true that there is no necessary reason for revolutionary societies to have a fatal or fanatical tendency to use nuclear weapons. It is not clear that such action would necessarily stretch the limits of the prudent use of force if the adversary was seen not as a secular opponent, but as a transcendental evil or pagan force whose eradication was considered theologically permissible and morally correct.

There are several revolutionary societies today, including Iran, Iraq, and Libya, that could be drawn toward a millenarian image of nuclear possession based on radical political ideologies and beliefs that are animated by the desire to destroy status quo societies. There are also examples of revolutionary societies below the state level. Aum Shinrikyo is a millenarian society that existed within the Japanese state but did not control the Japanese government or people. The possession of nuclear weapons by such societies, however, would instantly propel them to a status of power traditionally ascribed only to states. Revolutionary societies may seek to destroy one another whether they are in control of an entire state or exist entirely within a state. The conventional war between Iran and Iraq—which lasted nearly a decade, killed roughly one million people, and produced no meaningful strategic gains—reveals the danger when millenarian principles begin to guide security interactions.[41]

The proper question is, how might revolutionary societies behave with nuclear weapons? We cannot argue with impunity that Iran clearly would hesitate to use nuclear weapons when the half million casualties that it suffered in the war with Iraq are quite comparable to the potential losses from an Iraqi nuclear attack against military, economic, and urban targets—or that Iraq would be deterred by the potential suffering if Iran used nuclear weapons against it. We also should note that Iraqi chemical attacks killed thousands of Iranians during this war[42] and that Iraq maintained its occupation of Kuwait despite the amassing of enormous military forces by the United States and its UN coalition partners. A question asked, yet insufficiently answered, is how Saddam Hussein failed to understand the determination of the international coalition,[43] or how Iraq's revolutionary leadership misinterpreted the signs of an impending war.

The millenarian image also suggests that it will be increasingly difficult to explain, manage, or predict the actions of a world populated by revolutionary societies whose images of nuclear possession are at variance with the Brodie image of rational behavior. As an example, we should consider the ability of the North Vietnamese to accept punishment and continue to fight during the Vietnam War. When one contemplates the level of casualties suffered by the North Vietnamese, it is interesting to speculate whether other societies subjected to similar levels of punishment would have surrendered rather than continue the armed struggle.[44] The unwillingness to surrender and the desire to exact costs implicit in the kamikaze suggest that millenarian constructs dominated the thinking of some groups during the Second World War.

The obvious caution that must be raised is that use of the term *millenarian image* should not be read as non-Western. Societies like the Branch Davidians reveal that millenarian imagery can arise even in the United States, and the final days of Hitler's rule over Germany also typify such imagery. Thus, raising the distinction that revolutionary societies may hold alternative images of nuclear possession is not an attempt to make value judgments about the relative worth or value of these societies;

Deterrence and Alternative Images of Nuclear Possession / 223

nor is it an imputation that culture defines rationality or that some societies have an inherent right, based on their imputed adherence to rational or millenarian images, to possess nuclear weapons.[45]

The consequence of understanding deterrence as a particularistic construct is to call into doubt the ability of nuclear-armed societies to control events before crises spiral out of control. More broadly, if revolutionary societies see nuclear possession through the lens of millenarianism, these societies may not feel obligated to adhere to the "rules" that governed the risk-averse behavior of the superpowers.

The development of nuclear weapons requires a sophisticated educational and technological infrastructure, and thus it might be argued that the process of development takes place in an environment likely to reinforce and help internalize the fact that using nuclear weapons entails risks in excess of any possible benefits. But when revolutionary societies buy rather than build nuclear weapons or acquire them swiftly, the people and leadership lose the opportunity to understand the immense consequences of possessing nuclear weapons. In the absence of such understanding, a fundamental disconnect between nuclear weapons and the revolutionary society could mean that these societies have a greater propensity to use nuclear weapons than the current members of the nuclear club.

As revolutionary societies learn to live with nuclear weapons, they gradually may come to realize that a Brodiesque image of deterrence strategy is more relevant to their decisions.[46] But there is considerable danger that, during the intervening period between the acquisition of nuclear weapons and the deepening of deterrence strategies, revolutionary societies may believe that the use of nuclear weapons is a plausible option.

Finally, it is important to understand the theoretical significance of millenarian images of nuclear possession. Positing the existence of a millenarian image of nuclear possession is equivalent to dismissing the argument that the systematic theory of deterrence applies with equal force to all societies. Using the example of the revolutionary state to focus on millenarian images of nuclear possession shifts the debate to the behavior of societies whose interests undermine the significance of universal models for political action. This is not a defense of the proposition that millenarian images of nuclear possession necessarily reflect the political conditions in societies, or that this image is not amenable to abstract analysis or rules. But if it is possible to envision a logic of millenarian images of nuclear possession, it leads to the observation that deterrence consists of more than the sum of the historical, political, and secular/nonsecular experiences of the first nuclear societies, and by inference that deterrence is more complex than the highly stylized constructs that evolved from Brodie's initial conceptualization.

Interaction among Images of Nuclear Possession

The critical question that remains to be addressed in this chapter is the interaction among different societal images of nuclear possession. This analysis focuses on the ways in which different images may affect the use of nuclear weapons.

Figure 1 provides an illustration of the likely forms of interaction among societies with similar and alternative images of nuclear possession. In each case, I examine how societies, whether acting as the initiator or defender in a crisis, might interact in crises involving the possession of nuclear weapons.

In box I, we have the case of the Brodie-image society that is the initiator of a nuclear crisis with another Brodiesque society that is acting as the defender. In this space, the rules and logic of deterrence strategy as we understood them during the Cold War are in effect. All of the theoretical literature and analyses for the last fifty years offer some guidance. As one might expect in such a crisis, it is very unlikely that nuclear weapons would be used when the antagonists are guided by the notion of mutual assured destruction.

Box II represents the interaction between a Brodie-image society that acts as the initiator of a crisis and a millenarian-image society in the role of the defender. This case represents a somewhat greater probability that nuclear weapons will be used, principally because the Brodie-image society may consider a preemptive or preventive attack against the millenarian-image society to forestall the chances of strikes against the initiator. The central objective in this case is for the initiator to defend the status quo through the use of force.

The chances of preemptive or preventive strikes are not as remote as some might suppose if we recall the debates in the United States as exemplified by the recommendations made by the Joint Chiefs of Staff to President Eisenhower that the United States conduct a preemptive nuclear strike against the Soviet Union in the early 1950s. At that time, the Strategic Air Command could have delivered a devastating blow against Soviet bomber bases and largely prevented the Soviets from launching a major retaliatory strike in their infancy as a nuclear power. At that time, the United States clearly saw the Soviet Union as a radical ideological opponent in ways that are quite similar to the postulated notion of a millenarian society. Talk of military action against North Korea in the early 1990s to forestall its nuclear capability also might serve as an example.

Box III represents the case of a millenarian-image society that acts as the initiator of a crisis in which a Brodie-image society is in the position of

Initiator	Defender	
	Brodie Image	Millenarian Image
Brodie Image	Classic Deterrence I	Preemptive/Preventive War II
Millenarian Image	Terrorism, War III	Revisionist Nuclear Use IV

Fig. 1. Interactions among nuclear possessors

the defender. In this case, the probability of nuclear use is even greater because the initiator sees nuclear weapons as an offensive instrument, perhaps in the form of an attack by state-sponsored nuclear terrorist groups against a nuclear power. Examples include Libya, Iran, or Iraq supporting nuclear terrorist attacks to deter further aggression by the United States. Such an attack could occur during the period of escalation prior to a major conventional war—for instance, one could have occurred during the summer and fall of 1990, when the United States deployed 500,000 troops to the Persian Gulf. Thus, in box III, the use of nuclear weapons is quite possible.

Finally, box IV examines the case of a millenarian-image society that initiates a crisis with another millenarian-image society in the role of the defender. Of the four cases, this space presents the highest probability of nuclear use as two millenarian-image societies seek to revise the status quo. However, the main point here is that boxes II, III, and IV represent environments in which the possibility of nuclear use is higher than the logic of box I allows. The most troubling aspect of these three other environments is that the crisis dynamics involving alternative-image antagonists remained essentially unexplored in the theoretical research on deterrence during the Cold War. The reason, of course, was that the United States and the Soviet Union were interested principally in crisis dynamics between nuclear-armed superpowers and expressed only peripheral concern with nuclear crises that were the product of third-power actions.[47]

Examples of Revolutionary Leaderships

Critics might note that millenarians are rare in world politics. There are, however, several historical examples of revolutionary societies that were willing to sustain losses for the sake of revolutionary or millenarian goals. Such examples make the theoretical notion worthy of exploration. To begin with, Joseph Stalin's explicit policies of forced collectivization of agriculture led to the deaths of millions of peasant and middle-class farmers in the 1930s. At the same time, Stalin directed purges of the Red Army leadership, which decimated the Soviet Union's officer corps, and ordered a policy of resistance to the German invasion that contributed to the loss of roughly twenty million people during the Second World War. A common, though heatedly debated, argument during the Cold War was whether, in view of the Soviet Union's record of forced collectivization and the Second World War casualties, the Soviets might have countenanced twenty or thirty million casualties to achieve strategic goals.[48]

During the same historical period, Adolf Hitler provoked the Second World War and the subsequent loss of roughly fifty million people. The German Army inflicted millions of casualties throughout Europe, and the German people suffered untold losses in the latter years of the war as a result of Hitler's refusal to surrender even when defeat was imminent. Nazi Germany did initiate an atomic bomb project, which, had it been successful, might have affected calculations at the end of the war.

Another interesting case of a revolutionary leadership that was willing to accept considerable losses for the purpose of revolutionary goals is that of North Vietnam during the war with the United States. Throughout the Vietnam War, the United States inflicted enormous casualties and physical destruction on North Vietnam's people and infrastructure. And during intense periods of negotiations—as, for example, during December 1972—the North Vietnamese leadership was willing to sustain the damage inflicted by the Christmas bombing campaign despite pressure from the Nixon administration. In the context of the war in Southeast Asia, we have the example of the genocidal policies of Pol Pot in Cambodia. In perhaps one of the most ruthless campaigns of genocide, Pol Pot ordered the physical extermination of more than one million Cambodians during 1975–76 to eliminate any potential opposition and purify the country of ideological resistance. Furthermore, we have the policies of Idi Amin in Uganda in the 1970s as another example of a revolutionary leadership that was willing to engage in genocidal policies. Finally, there is the case of the policies of Ayatollah Khomeini in Iran during the 1980s. With the destruction of the Shah's regime, Iran engaged in increasingly hostile policies toward the West, notably directed against the United States, as part of a strategy of returning Iran to a radical fundamentalism. In defense of this policy, Khomeini actively encouraged and supported terrorist organizations in the Middle East to destroy the "Great Satan." A significant number of acts of terrorism were committed under the tutelage of Iran, and Iran's revolutionary leadership continues to support policies that advocate confrontation with the West.

In contemporary terms, there are several examples of revolutionary leaderships that pursue dangerous and possibly self-destructive policies. The Serbian leadership in the former Yugoslavia seeks to destroy their ethnic and religious enemies through campaigns of genocide. In Rwanda in April 1994, roughly 500,000 Tutsi were slaughtered by the Hutu majority in a campaign of terror and murder that employed weapons no more sophisticated than knives and machetes. The radical terrorist sect in Japan, the Aum Shinrikyo, conducted an attack in Tokyo with sarin nerve gas in 1995 that killed several people and impaired thousands. Furthermore, Aum Shinrikyo planned to conduct additional attacks against cities in Japan with the significant supply of sarin gas at its disposal. In the United States, the Branch Davidians preferred suicide to surrender. One might suspect that if given the opportunity, this society would have attempted to kill their "tormentors" on a massive scale.

The question that arises from all of these cases is whether their actions transcend Brodie-image cost-benefit analysis. The deliberate policies of these revolutionary leaders demonstrate that some individuals are willing to run great risks, suffer enormous losses, and threaten global security, often on levels that are similar to moderate nuclear attacks, to achieve their political objectives. In the face of historical examples of revolutionary leaderships that sometimes are willing to run risks for ideological reasons,[49] the strategy of Brodie-image deterrence may not offer insights into this behavior. However, it is also the case that revolutionary societies not imbued with millenarian beliefs are likely to be risk-acceptant but limited by a desire to avoid societal destruction.

Conclusions

The use of nuclear weapons remains unlikely, but it is unlikely only insofar as decision makers in societies are governed by the Brodie image of deterrence that depicts political choices in terms of cost-benefit analyses and rational behavior limited by the desire to preserve society. Some societies, however, may not make decisions bounded by the same limitation. In particular, revolutionary societies or leaderships may be more likely to use nuclear weapons as we enter the twenty-first century.

The paradox is that the existence of revolutionary societies with millenarian images of nuclear possession may make the use of nuclear weapons more likely by societies that are governed by Brodie images of deterrence. Nor is this condition as far-fetched as it might seem. Consider, for instance, the late 1940s and early 1950s, when some circles in the

United States argued that the Strategic Air Command should preemptively strike the Soviet Union to forestall a future war in which Soviet nuclear capabilities would be more significant. Furthermore, the Soviet Union was dominated by a revolutionary ideology that openly predicted a conflict with the West. The empirical case in which U.S. policymakers, who were guided by a desire to preserve society, contemplated preemptive nuclear strikes against the Soviet Union strengthens the argument for rethinking the interactions between societies with alternative images of nuclear possession.

One positive outcome of the interactions between status quo and revolutionary societies in the opening days of the Cold War was that they gave these societies the opportunity to internalize the consequences of nuclear possession. It is conceivable that nuclear learning moderated the radical ideology of the Soviet Union and perhaps quelled the hostility between the two nuclear superpowers as they learned that errors of statecraft in the nuclear age have truly catastrophic consequences. And it is possible that the U.S. perception of the Soviet Union as a revolutionary state was strengthened by the existence of nuclear weapons and total war. A protracted period in which ideological adversaries coexist without using nuclear weapons offers the greatest source of optimism that nuclear war is not likely in the future.

There are several observations about the future of nuclear deterrence. To begin with, several generations of thinking about crises in the nuclear age were based on the Brodie image of deterrence because that was the only construct available. This image of deterrence necessarily reflects the various "theologies" about the employment of nuclear weapons that gained prominence in the 1950s and 1960s.[50] Not only is the actual empirical experience with nuclear crises extremely limited, but, worse, deterrence strategy is necessarily one-dimensional because it ignores the diverse historical factors that influence societal behavior.

There is no assurance that universal constructs of deterrence automatically guarantee that the new nuclear societies will behave in a risk-averse fashion. These societies may hold grievances that are not amenable to the traditional deterrence strategies that governed the conduct of the United States and the Soviet Union during potential nuclear crises. While none of these crises escalated to general war, we cannot dismiss the fact that both powers acted as if they held the Brodie image of nuclear possession. The problem, however, is that the consensus among potential nuclear antagonists on the need to prevent nuclear war does not translate into assurances that the universal construct of deterrence will govern behavior in an absolute fashion. This fact alone offers the most compelling reason to consider alternative images of nuclear possession.

NOTES

1. A generally useful definition of deterrence is offered by Richard Ned Lebow and Janice Gross Stein: "Deterrence seeks to prevent undesired behavior by convincing those who might contemplate such action that its costs would exceed its gains. In the area of security, deterrence usually attempts to prevent a military challenge; but it also can and has been used to try to prevent unacceptable military deployments (such as the deployment of Soviet missiles in Cuba) or nonmilitary actions that defenders perceive as threatening to their national security. Deterrence requires that the 'defender' define the behavior that is unacceptable, publicize the commitment to punish or restrain transgressors, demonstrate the resolve to do so, and possess the capabilities to implement the threat. General deterrence is based on the existing power relationship between adversaries; it attempts to prevent an adversary from seriously considering a military challenge of any kind because of the obviously adverse consequences." Richard Ned Lebow and Janice Gross Stein, "Deterrence: The Elusive Dependent Variable," *World Politics* 35 (April 1990): 336.

2. The notion of images figures prominently in this chapter. For a discussion of images, see Robert Jervis, *The Logic of Images of International Relations* (Princeton, N.J.: Princeton University Press, 1970).

3. On society, see Charles Andrain, *Political Life and Social Change* (Belmont, Calif.: Duxbury Press, 1974); Talcott Parsons, "Culture and Social Systems Revisited," *Social Sciences Quarterly* 53 (September 1972): 253–66; and Karl Deutsch, "Symbols of Political Community," in Lyman Bryson et al., *Symbols and Society* (New York: Harper and Row, 1953).

4. The most powerful argument in favor of deterrence as a universal theory of the actions of nuclear-armed societies is that the only common factor in all situations involving societies is human nature.

5. For American diplomacy, deterrence was the operational embodiment of the judgment that it was necessary to contain the Soviet Union and communism without permitting its political differences to escalate into a destructive nuclear war. The dominant writings on deterrence reflect this: Bernard Brodie, *Strategy in the Missile Age* (Princeton, N.J.: Princeton University Press, 1959); Herman Kahn, *On Thermonuclear War* (Princeton, N.J.: Princeton University Press, 1961); Alexander L. George and Richard Smoke, *Deterrence in American Foreign Policy: Theory and Practice* (New York: Columbia University Press, 1974); Philip Green, *Deadly Logic* (Columbus: Ohio State University Press, 1966); Morton Halperin and Thomas Schelling, *Strategy and Arms Control* (New York: Twentieth Century Fund, 1961); Henry A. Kissinger, *Nuclear Weapons and Foreign Policy* (New York: Harper and Row, 1957); and Thomas C. Schelling, *Arms and Influence* (New Haven, Conn.: Yale University Press, 1966).

6. The sources of evidence for deterrence theory are quite small. First, the evidence is derived from a small empirical database of the experiences of several nuclear powers—the United States, the Soviet Union, Great Britain, France, and China, as well as the smaller nuclear powers of Israel, India, and Pakistan. Second, the putative database for deterrence focuses on a small number of crisis situations

between nuclear-armed societies. Finally, deterrence theory is the victim of unexplained, and often unexplainable, assumptions about the behavior of states. Taken as a whole, these factors fundamentally constrain the universality or explanatory power of deterrence theory.

7. Metaphysics is defined as any abstract structure or proposition that is internally consistent, whose conclusions are arrived at deductively, and that admits of certitude. However, none of these conclusions have any demonstrable or necessary connection with empirical reality, and thus the construct possesses neither predictability nor testability in any methodological sense.

8. See Edward Rhodes, *Power and MADness: The Logic of Nuclear Coercion* (New York: Columbia University Press, 1989), in particular chap. 2.

9. There is an extensive literature on the role of rationality in deterrence theory. For instance, see Thomas C. Schelling, *The Strategy of Conflict* (Cambridge: Harvard University Press, 1960); Glenn H. Snyder, *Deterrence and Defense* (Princeton, N.J.: Princeton University Press, 1961); Stephen Maxwell, *Rationality in Deterrence*, Adelphi Paper No. 50 (London: International Institute for Strategic Studies, 1968); Patrick M. Morgan, *Deterrence: A Conceptual Analysis* (Beverly Hills, Calif.: Sage, 1977); Anatol Rapoport, *Fights, Games, and Debates* (Ann Arbor: University of Michigan Press, 1960); and John D. Steinbruner, *The Cybernetic Theory of Decision* (Princeton, N.J.: Princeton University Press, 1974).

10. This discussion of rationality involves Weber's definition of using ever more efficient means to achieve clearly defined goals. In this sense, the rational objective of deterrence is, fundamentally, to avoid nuclear war. Nor should we infer that the use of the word *rational* is suggestive of the only true interpretation of reality or politics. There is a danger if other societies believe that the emphasis on rationality signals that those who subscribe to the rational image have a monopoly on the truth. In fact, all societies believe that they have equal claims on the truth. See Reinhard Bendix, *Max Weber: An Intellectual Portrait* (Garden City, N.Y.: Doubleday Anchor, 1962); Arnold Brecht, *Political Theory: The Foundations of Twentieth-Century Political Thought* (Princeton, N.J.: Princeton University Press, 1970); and George H. Sabine, *A History of Political Theory* (Hinsdale, Ill.: Dryden Press, 1973).

11. William C. Martel, "Deterrence after the Cold War," in Stephen J. Cimbala and Sidney R. Waldman, eds., *Controlling and Ending Conflict: Issues before and after the Cold War* (Westport, Conn.: Greenwood Press, 1992), 41–63.

12. See Anthony Downs, *An Economic Theory of Democracy* (New York: Harper and Row, 1957).

13. While deterrence theory is largely associated with nuclear weapons, it is evident that deterrence is not a singularly "nuclear" concept because it has existed for as long as one state has been able to induce fear in another, only recently with nuclear weapons. Even though deterrence was a product of the clash between the United States and the Soviet Union, it might have been shaped differently if the United States and Great Britain had been the first and only nuclear powers. This argument is expressed by George Quester, "Nuclear Deterrence and Political Hostility," in Cimbala and Waldman, *Controlling and Ending Conflict,* 241–50. On the

application of deterrence theory to conventional weapons, see Richard J. Harknett, "The Logic of Conventional Deterrence and the End of the Cold War," *Security Studies* 4 (Autumn 1994): 86–114.

14. For the Greeks, words have intrinsic meaning because the force of reason compels us to understand. Aristotle, however, rejects the principle that ideas are real and the notion of transcendental ideal forms. These distinctions are important for rational-actor deterrence because that construct reveals the tendency to believe that the ability to imagine the idea of deterrence theory creates the intellectual reality of deterrence. But the logic of deterrence does not compel anything, including the behavior of societies that do not adhere necessarily to the rational-actor image of nuclear possession. See Sabine, *History of Political Theory;* and Brecht, *Political Theory.*

15. See Brecht, *Political Theory,* 139; Sabine, *History of Political Theory,* 640, 647; William T. Bluhm, *Theories of the Political System* (Englewood Cliffs, N.J.: Prentice-Hall, 1978), 445–50; and Antony Flew, *An Introduction to Western Philosophy* (New York: Bobbs-Merrill, 1971), 116–18.

16. While many bipolar relationships in international politics—Athens and Sparta, Rome and Carthage, England and France in the early nineteenth century, and the United States and the Soviet Union—usually concluded with the annihilation or defeat of one actor, the larger point for these purposes is that deterrence largely reflected the underlying bipolar structure of the international system during the Cold War.

17. I include the experiences of the United Kingdom and France under that rubric and do the same for China despite its strategically and culturally dissimilar positions. While the theoretical work on general deterrence focused essentially on the behavior of the superpowers and their allies, there is the notable exception of works on China. A recent study that changes this approach is Shu Guang Zhang, *Deterrence and Strategic Culture: Chinese-American Confrontations, 1949–1958* (Ithaca, N.Y.: Cornell University Press, 1992).

18. Patrick Morgan, "Saving Face for the Sake of Deterrence," in Robert Jervis, Richard Ned Lebow, and Janice Gross Stein, eds., *Psychology and Deterrence* (Baltimore: Johns Hopkins University Press, 1985), 151.

19. Morgan, "Saving Face," 131.

20. Richard Ned Lebow, "Conclusions," in Jervis, Lebow, and Stein, eds., *Psychology and Deterrence,* 204.

21. For example, one can make the argument that the Non-proliferation Treaty is simply a manifestation of U.S. political goals rather than some demonstrably objective, absolute, universal, or positive goal. See William C. Martel and William T. Pendley, *Nuclear Coexistence: Redefining U.S. Policy to Promote Stability in an Age of Proliferation,* Air War College Studies in National Security, no. 1 (Montgomery, Ala., 1994), 24–25, 165–77.

22. Glenn H. Snyder, *Deterrence and Defense: Toward a Theory of National Security* (Westport, Conn.: Greenwood Press, 1975), 10.

23. Morton Halperin, *Limited War in the Nuclear Age* (New York: John Wiley and Sons, 1963), 55.

24. Schelling, *Arms and Influence*, 37.
25. Lebow, "Conclusions," 221.
26. Lebow, "Conclusions," 223.
27. John J. Mearsheimer, *Conventional Deterrence* (Ithaca, N.Y.: Cornell University Press, 1983), 16.
28. See Martin Shubik, ed., *Readings in Game Theory and Political Behavior* (New York: Random House, 1954), 1–11, 43–46; Schelling, *The Strategy of Conflict;* Rapoport, *Fights, Games, and Debates;* and John von Neumann and Oskar Morgenstern, *Theory of Games and Economic Behavior,* 2d ed. (Princeton, N.J.: Princeton University Press, 1947).
29. Brodie, *Strategy in the Missile Age,* 280. Brodie also believed that the prospect of a societal "insensibility to human suffering . . . probably affects significantly the dynamics of deterrence."
30. For an examination of Chinese strategic culture, see Alastair Iain Johnston, "China's New 'Old Thinking': The Concept of Limited Deterrence," *International Security* 20 (Winter 1995–96): 5–42; and Banning N. Garrett and Bonnie S. Glaser, "Chinese Perspectives on Nuclear Arms Control," *International Security* 20 (Winter 1995–96): 43–78.
31. Mearsheimer, *Conventional Deterrence,* 44.
32. Schelling argued that any given decision "depends on the internal politics and bureaucracy of a government, on the chain of command and on lines of communication, on party structures and pressure groups, as well as on individual values and careers." Schelling, *The Strategy of Conflict,* 86.
33. Raymond Aron, *Peace and War* (Garden City, N.Y.: Doubleday, 1966), 434. He continued, "States, in our age as during the preceding centuries, reserve the right to make autonomous decisions, including the decisions of peace and war. They continue to aim at incompatible objectives, to regard their interests as opposed, to suspect each other of the darkest plots. Interstate relations are more than ever a test of wills. If we call power politics the peaceful or belligerent relations between states which acknowledge neither law nor arbitrator and attempt to constrain, seduce and convince each other, the politics of our period conforms more than ever to this age-old model."
34. Brecht, *Political Theory,* 460, describes the intellectual relationship between secular and religious ideas that fall under the domain of millenarianism, or what may be called chiliasm. Brecht goes on to observe that many of the "fundamental principles referred to in academic works on state and government until the end of the nineteenth century can easily be traced to the religious heritage. . . . Actually, even Comte and Marx remained under the influence of religious chiliastic ideas."
35. This was the argument raised by Kissinger, *Nuclear Weapons and Foreign Policy,* 316–61.
36. This is the argument about military culture. See Stephen Peter Rosen, "Military Effectiveness: Why Society Matters," *International Security* 19 (Spring 1995): 5–31, which examines "the impact of social structure on the amount of military power that can be generated by nations of different culture" (p. 5); Alastair Iain Johnston, "Thinking about Strategic Culture," *International Security* 19 (Spring 1995): 32–64, which argues that "elites socialized in different strategic cultures will

make different choices when placed in similar situations"; and Elizabeth Kier, "Culture and Military Doctrine: France between the Wars," *International Security* 19 (Spring 1995): 65–93.

37. See Schelling, *The Strategy of Conflict;* Rapoport, *Fights, Games, and Debates;* von Neumann and Morgenstern, *Theory of Games and Economic Behavior;* and Karl W. Deutsch, *The Nerves of Government* (New York: The Free Press, 1966), 66–71.

38. It is important to observe that the millenarian image of nuclear possession is but one example of a particularistic construct of deterrence. In theory, many such images may exist independently or operate together to shape alternative images of nuclear possession.

39. For an analysis of the nature and behavior of revolutionary ideologies, see Henry A. Kissinger, *American Foreign Policy* (New York: W. W. Norton, 1974), 23, 39, 53; Kissinger, *A World Restored: Metternich, Castlereagh, and the Problems of Peace, 1812–22* (Boston: Houghton Mifflin, 1973), 67–70; and Stephen M. Walt, "Revolution and War," *World Politics* 44 (April 1992): 321–68, which discusses revolutionary ideologies and personalities.

40. See Samuel Huntington, "The Clash of Civilizations," *Foreign Affairs* (Summer 1993): 22–49, which argues that "civilizational identity will be increasingly important in the future . . . differences among civilizations . . . are the product of centuries. . . . They are more fundamental than differences among political ideologies and political regimes" (p. 25). Also see James Kurth, "The Real Clash," *The National Interest* 37 (Fall 1994): 3–15, for an alternative perspective to Huntington's thesis.

41. For a discussion of the regional implications of the war between Iraq and Iran, see Richard Cottam, "Iran—Motives behind Its Foreign Policy," *Survival* 27 (November–December 1986): 483–95; and Charles Tripp, "Iraq—Ambitions Checked," *Survival* 27 (November–December 1986): 495–509.

42. Iraq's chemical weapons attacks killed roughly 7,000 people, or 2 percent of Iran's total casualties, and thus had a negligible effect on the outcome of the war; but its use of weapons of mass destruction raises questions about its behavior with nuclear weapons. For an analysis of the war, see Efraim Karsh, *The Iran-Iraq War: A Military Analysis,* Adelphi Paper No. 220 (London: International Institute for Strategic Studies, 1987), 56.

43. For the argument that the Iraqi leadership did not believe that the diplomatic signals from the United States were largely supportive of an invasion of Kuwait, see Janice Gross Stein, "Deterrence and Compellence in the Gulf, 1990–91: A Failed or Impossible Task?" *International Security* 17 (Fall 1992): 147–79.

44. This argument would support the notion that it was not that U.S. bombing per se was mistaken, but that the North Vietnamese were abnormally tough adversaries.

45. It is prudent to suspend judgment as to the matter of which societies should possess nuclear weapons, unless one believes that all societies must adhere to the norms and standards established by Western societies; but that would be equivalent to a Western-centric bias or imperialism.

46. Matthew Evangelista, "Cooperation Theory and Disarmament Negotiations in the 1960s," *World Politics* 42 (July 1990): 526–28.

47. There were concerns with the problem of catalytic nuclear war, in which the actions of allies or third powers could draw the United States and the Soviet Union into nuclear war. See Henry A. Kissinger, *The Necessity for Choice* (New York: Harper, 1960), 241–44.

48. Colin S. Gray, "Nuclear Strategy: A Case for a Theory of Victory," *International Security* 1 (Summer 1979): 54–87.

49. Timothy J. Lomperis, *The War Everyone Lost—But Won* (Baton Rouge: Louisiana State University Press, 1984).

50. The works of Brodie and Kissinger, among others, had a profound effect on the diplomatic strategy that the United States and Western Europe adopted and followed for decades. They were the chief architects of a theory and strategy of deterrence that manifested nearly metaphysical certitude about its correctness and applicability.

PART 3

Controlling the Absolute Weapon

New Nuclear States and the International Nuclear Order

ASHOK KAPUR

This chapter explains the attitudes and policies of three new nuclear states—Israel, India, and Pakistan—and the characteristics of the international nuclear order. The new nuclear states differ in salient ways from the old ones, and the characteristics of the international nuclear order are complex and different from what is depicted in the nonproliferation regime (NPR), whose main pillars are the Nuclear Non-proliferation Treaty (NPT) and the International Atomic Energy Agency (IAEA) safeguards system. This regime is part of a wider and enduring pattern of power relationships that evolved during the Cold War and continue to evolve in the context of an emerging multipolar international system. The chapter discusses the permanent tension between the NPR and the new nuclear states, as well as the salient differences between the regime and the foundations of the international nuclear order. The NPR has serious flaws despite its almost universal membership. These result from a failure of nonproliferation policies to reflect practical wisdom rather than narrow national interests. The contrast is stark between the orientation of the regime and the sound advice and admonitions in Bernard Brodie's classic work, *The Absolute Weapon*.[1]

This chapter critiques current Western and especially American nonproliferation policy. It revisits classical realism by endorsing the progressive outlook of *The Absolute Weapon,* criticizes the ethnocentric biases of scholars of proliferation, and argues that most of their analyses are popular and mundane and may not be intellectually significant. To remedy this deficit, this chapter offers an alternate view of the proliferation issue.

Differences between New and Old Nuclear Powers

There are four differences in the international position and the pattern of nuclear behavior of the new and the old nuclear powers. First, the international status of the old nuclear states is recognized by the NPT. The treaty accords them special rights, it protects their security and prestige by maintaining their latitude to act within the nuclear sphere, and it restricts their treaty obligations to a rhetorical declaration about eventual nuclear disarmament. The curbs on the sovereignty of the five nuclear powers are token gestures. The NPT accords legal recognition to the right of the old nuclear powers to possess and to use nuclear arms, in contrast with international conventions that ban the use of other types of weapons of mass destruction. By extending the NPT indefinitely, the right to possess and use nuclear arms is also extended indefinitely. This special international nuclear position is buttressed by the permanent seat and the veto power accorded to the Permanent Five (P-5) at the United Nations Security Council. The UN Charter froze the pattern of power relationships that was desired by the winning coalition of the Second World War. The NPT extended this pattern in the nuclear sphere and froze it using January 1, 1967, as the cutoff date for defining a legitimate nuclear power in the treaty.

Second, the old nuclear states are overt nuclear powers. They flaunt their nuclear weapons and justify their value for national defense; and their public opinion supports the military uses of nuclear weapons. Third, the old nuclear states seek to arrest the emergence of new nuclear states. They do so by national and international control measures, pressures, and inducements. The objective is to preserve the international nuclear status quo. The view is put forward that the old nuclear states are responsible and are driven by a desire to contain enemy threats. In contrast, the new nuclear states are seen as irresponsible, prone to nuclear accidents caused by irrational decisions of unstable decision makers. The objective behind these competing views of nuclear possession is self-serving. It is customary for great powers to ensure their primacy through international arrangements that serve their interests. Such reasoning supports these arrangements.

Behind the nonproliferation rhetoric lies a deeper issue. The old nuclear powers have a low or zero tolerance of upwardly mobile regional and middle powers, and conversely, they are reluctant to adjust international treaty arrangements to reflect the downward mobility of former great powers, in the present instance the United Kingdom, France, and Russia. This indicates incongruence between treaty rights and the evolving redistribution of power and influence in a changing world. The international system has a bias toward the status quo in treaties, and it lacks an automatic mechanism or methodology to adjust treaty arrangements to correspond to changes in the distribution of power and the pattern of relationships among major and minor state actors.

Finally, the NPT and other nonproliferation measures provide a legal and a political platform to mount pressure against the new nuclear states, although the timing and intensity of the pressure depend on the nature of the political and strategic relationship and interests on the governmental agenda of the established nuclear states. The pressure is suspended when other issues gain priority over nonproliferation issues; it is increased when other issues decline in importance. Despite these variations, the NPR increases the freedom of the old nuclear powers to pressure the new nuclear states as well as deviant members of the regime and enemy states like Iran and North Korea.

Realities versus Stereotypes: Behavior of the New Nuclear States

The NPT specifies January 1, 1967, as the basis of recognition of a legitimate nuclear power. The undeclared or new nuclear states are therefore beyond the pale of the treaty language; they are by definition rogues or outlaws and are often described as intransigent and a threat to regional and world peace. *The Absolute Weapon* cautions us not to rely on outlawry to deal with the nuclear problem, while the NPT and its promoters do precisely that.

The new nuclear states are portrayed as illegitimate nuclear players even though the modern international system is anarchical, as the realist school of international relations argues, and the principle of self-defense is recognized in the UN Charter. The NPT specifically derecognizes the right of the new nuclear states to acquire nuclear weapons for deterrence or defense, even though the possession and use of nuclear weapons are not banned by the world community and in international law. The old nuclear states explicitly reserve the right to possess and use nuclear weapons indefinitely, and they do not accept a specific obligation to sacrifice their sovereignty in this regard.

The NPT recognizes the principle of national sovereignty and national security by accepting the right of an NPT party to withdraw from the treaty with three months' notice if the supreme interests of the state require such an action. However, this right is rhetoric, and it is comparable to the right of the former Soviet republics to secede under the Stalinist constitution. North Korea followed the treaty rules and declared its intention to withdraw from the treaty. It was subsequently subjected to serious Western governmental pressure not to do so. The withdrawal right seems to be like the old Catholic marriage. Even if the marriage is bad, once in, there is no getting out. The NPT still relies on outlawry and inspection when the incentive (national interest) to stay in the treaty no longer exists. Compare this with the advice in *The Absolute Weapon:* an agreement must be self-enforcing, which is likely if there is an incentive to keep the agreement; outlawry and inspection alone are not enough.[2]

The international nuclear and political rights of the old nuclear states are recognized by the treaty and by the UN Charter; the nuclear and political rights of the new nuclear states are derecognized in the NPT, although the right to self-defense still exists for them through their membership in the UN and by the UN Charter. Furthermore, the NPT lacks mutuality of obligations between the old and the new nuclear states and between the nuclear and the non-nuclear states.

The new nuclear states have systematically, secretly, and incrementally acquired nuclear weapons and missile capability, but they have done so without a formal declaratory policy that would require weaponized nuclear deterrence. However, the official postures of the new nuclear states allude to nuclear possession or to nuclear option building along with declarations of a lack of desire to weaponize openly under prevailing regional security conditions. Unlike the old nuclear states, they do not flaunt their nuclear weapons capability; indeed, they keep the components in storage to avoid provoking enemies and friends unnecessarily. They avoid raising public expectations and/or concerns about the military value of nuclear deterrence and the costs of maintaining large nuclear and missile arsenals. These states practice nonweaponized nuclear deterrence. Several American scholars have recognized the value of this new approach.[3]

Undeclared nuclear weapons and delivery capabilities reflect practical domestic and international politics and the national diplomatic and military aims of new nuclear states. However, the uses of nuclear capability vary. The old nuclear states seek to deter general war, deter nuclear war, provide nuclear umbrellas to allies, maintain the existing distribution of power and the pattern of power relationships they desire, and offer a sense of safety to their respective publics. For the new nuclear states, the value of an undeclared nuclear weapons capability is multifaceted. Figure 1 summarizes these uses. The relative importance of each use varies among Israel, India, and Pakistan, depending on each country's domestic and external imperatives. Space limitation prevents a thorough examination of each use in the case histories of the three new nuclear states.

The new nuclear states do not seek international arrangements to curb horizontal proliferation. They are interested in restraining the warlike behaviors of their regional enemies. India hardly has a problem with a nuclear Pakistan. It has not had a serious problem with the Pakistani military since 1971. Pakistan's nuclear and military capabilities are known to Indian authorities, the maturity of Pakistan's post-1971 military leadership is appreciated, and there is a recognition that Pakistani generals are not presently inclined toward general war, although they will engage in low-risk proxy warfare in Kashmir. Indians, however, fear Pakistani interventionist urges that affect stability in India's border provinces. They

New Nuclear States and the International Nuclear Order / 241

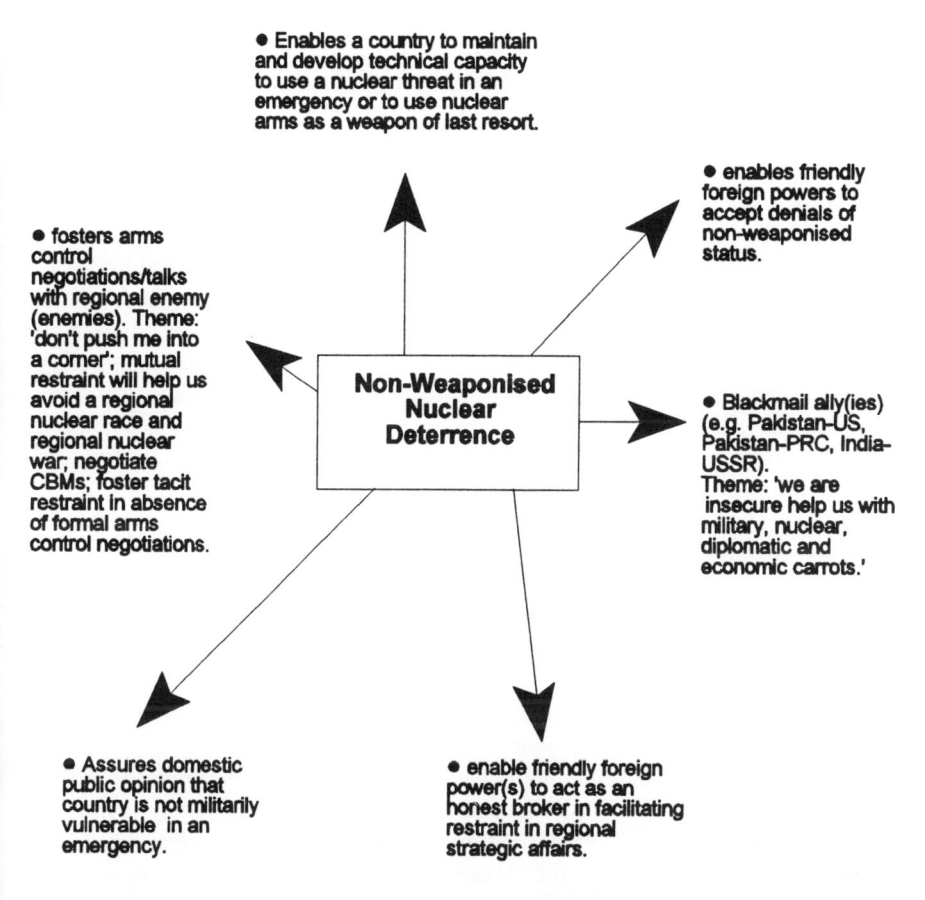

Fig. 1. Value of nonweaponized nuclear deterrence for India and Pakistan. (Reprinted from A. Kapur, "India and Pakistan: Nature and Elements of Nuclear Deterrence between Two Regional Rivals," University of Manitoba, Occasional Paper, 1995, 18A.)

are also concerned with instability in Pakistan that could lead to its balkanization and bring outside forces to fill the void. With China, India's focus is on its nuclear capabilities, the implications of Chinese nuclear and missile aid to Pakistan, and the pattern of Chinese activities in the Himalayan region and in the Burma (Myanmar)–Bay of Bengal sector. Considerations of military security and diplomatic prestige have led to a loss of Indian interest in nonproliferation and India's 1996 rejection of the Comprehensive Test Ban Treaty (CTBT).[4]

Pakistan's attitude toward international nonproliferation arrangements has wavered. Prime Minister Zulfikar Ali Bhutto opposed them, President Zia ul-Haq favored an Indo-Pakistani nuclear deal that was comparable to the NPT deal, and Prime Ministers Nawaz Sharif and Benazir Bhutto have maintained that stance. However, Pakistan is not a convinced nonproliferator. Its agenda historically has been to secure parity with India. This is a rational national interest for Pakistan, just as it is rational for India to oppose it. Pakistan has pursued its aims by mobilizing American pressure for Indian nuclear disarmament, by military and subversive action to balkanize India and to cut it down to size, and by a conventional and nuclear arms buildup. When Pakistan failed to gain parity by diplomatic and military means, and India persisted in its policy of seeking regional stability through a pattern of enduring military asymmetry, Pakistan sought a nuclear equalizer.[5] In sum, Pakistan's nuclear and diplomatic policies are governed by its security interests and domestic politics, rather than a concern for the international NPR or its norms.

Israel too rejects the NPT and the demand for full-scope international safeguards on its nuclear facilities. Instead, Israel suggests starting negotiations on a nuclear-weapons-free zone in the Middle East two years after the signing of a comprehensive peace agreement with its Arab neighbors, including Iraq and Iran. As a consequence of the Middle Eastern peace process and the agreements between Israel and Egypt and Jordan, Israel's nuclear and political situation is favorable. Israel has maintained its nuclear monopoly in the Middle East thus far, although Iran is not likely to leave itself unprotected in the nuclear sphere. Israel has maintained this monopoly by using military measures (for instance, the Iraqi Osiraq nuclear reactor attack in 1981)[6] and by the UN destruction of Iraq's mass destruction capability after the Desert Storm operations. Israel, however, remains under Egyptian pressure to join the NPT and to accept international safeguards. This pressure has been exerted at the meetings of the IAEA, at the NPT Extension conference in 1995, and at other UN forums.

Why is Egypt agitating against Israel in the nuclear sphere even when it has signed a peace treaty with Israel, enjoys the benefits of the NPT, and has gained in monetary and diplomatic terms by becoming an American ally? The answer lies in the Egyptian belief that it is a leader of the Arab world; it desires that the United States and Arab states should recognize its leadership. Egypt was a leader of the Arab world before the peace process gained momentum. After Yasser Arafat, leader of the Palestinian Liberation Organization (PLO), signed a peace deal with Israel, Jordan went its own way and Syria avoided Egyptian mediation; many Arab states moved toward Israel and the United States.

Cairo wants to make deals with Israel, but Egypt no longer has sufficient opportunities to lead the Arab Middle East. Arab leaders are making foreign policy in the context of unstable domestic political and economic situations. There also has been constant American pressure on the Arab states to join the NPT and to follow its rules without linking it to Israeli nuclear disarmament. The Middle East peace process shows that Israel is no longer the enemy of the Arabs. The Saudi regime worries about Iran in the religious, political, and military spheres, and it has joined the NPT. Egypt has tried to unify the Arabs on the nuclear issue, but Israel is no longer a unifying element. Consequently, neither the Americans nor the Arab leaders were behind the Egyptian campaign against Israeli nuclear armament, and the Egyptian campaign in international forums remains unsuccessful. The reality is that it is impossible to push Israel into the NPT; the political and economic realities show the context and limitations of universal nuclear nonproliferation in the Middle East.[7]

Finally, the new nuclear states have developed strategies to escape and contain the pressures of the old nuclear states. By retaining its nuclear monopoly in the region, for example, Israel has maintained its freedom of nuclear action if its physical survival is threatened. The existence of a secret nuclear arsenal and its military reputation (which is based on past threats to go to war in an emergency) give credence to its ambiguous nuclear stance. Israel has also been proactive in offering to negotiate a regional nuclear-weapon-free zone after the achievement of comprehensive peace in the region. The Egyptian and IAEA pressures to join the NPT and to accept international safeguards have been contained as well.

The Choices of the New Nuclear States

India has developed its freedom of nuclear action by the procurement of unsafeguarded plutonium, by its know-how in nuclear weapons technology, and by its acquisition of ballistic missiles and space capabilities. It has historically linked horizontal nonproliferation to vertical nonproliferation and nuclear disarmament. This position enjoys widespread support in Indian interparty politics and in Indian public opinion; no great power in the world today is willing to pressure a population of 900 million on this issue. In 1996, India distanced itself from the Western position on the CTBT by linking its position to nuclear disarmament.[8] This indicates an acute polarization between the Western powers and India because the expectations about the value of CTBT vary. It is meant to be a nonproliferation measure for the Western nuclear powers and their non-nuclear allies who want to maintain their privileged position in the nuclear sphere. From the Indian point of view, this sort of a CTBT is harmful for India's security interests and efforts at acquiring major power status. In June 1996, India voted against the CTBT, arguing that it was not comprehensive, that it was not a disarmament measure, and that India's position was dictated by national security considerations that include maintaining the nuclear weapons option.

Pakistan has also increased its freedom of nuclear choice by its acquisition of nuclear weapons capability using the sophisticated enriched-uranium route. That Pakistan did so even though it has enjoyed alliance relations with two nuclear powers (the United States and China) reveals the depth of its insecurity vis-à-vis India and the lack of faith in its great power allies' nuclear umbrellas. Pakistan also has developed a clever diplomatic stance to help it escape great power pressures to join the NPT: it has repeated its desire to join the NPT or its equivalent regional arrangements if India joins the treaty and disarms itself. In sum, the new nuclear states take their current status as regional powers seriously. They see themselves as upwardly mobile in economic and military affairs, and they recognize the multifaceted utility of the nuclear factor in external and domestic politics and national strategies. Their determination and capacity to increase their freedom of nuclear choice occurred during the Cold War, and they have been retained following its end in 1990. The Indian and Pakistani nuclear developments occurred primarily during the Cold War. The two were not simply American and Soviet clients. They did not rely on the leadership and protection of the so-called superpowers even as they benefited by their ties with them. Both demonstrated independence of thought and policy in the nuclear sphere despite intense pressures that have been brought to bear on them to conform to the dictates of the Western powers. Israel too developed an independent nuclear position during the Cold War, when it faced acute security pressures in its neighborhood and lacked complete confidence in Washington's protective umbrella.

The new nuclear powers demonstrate a strong preference for and expectation of change in the distribution of military and nuclear power in their favor; and they have confidence in their ability to manage the regional security agenda by creating a pattern of countervailing pressures in their respective security environments. The strategy and the ability to do so continued to work following the end of the Cold War. When India lost Soviet support and the U.S. government sensed an opportunity to increase the pressure on India in the nuclear sphere, India was able to strengthen its diplomatic and military ties with China, thereby deflecting American pressures and compensating for the loss of the Soviet card. Israel's strategic importance declined after the internal collapse of the Soviet Union. Yet Israel was able to achieve a psychological and political breakthrough with the Arab world and to keep Americans engaged in the peace process rather than focused on nuclear nonproliferation in the Middle East. However,

Pakistan lost its frontline status following the Soviet withdrawal from Afghanistan and the end of the Cold War. Nevertheless, it was able to deflect American pressure on the nonproliferation front by emphasizing a basket of issues on which American and Pakistani interests converged: Pakistan's value as a moderate Muslim state, its location next to "radical Iran," its utility as a bridge for American diplomacy in Central Asia, and its role as a line of pressure against India on the Kashmir and nuclear fronts. As the Western nuclear powers gained a platform to mount pressure against the new nuclear states, which was reinforced by the indefinite extension of the NPT, the new nuclear states have found ways to contain the pressures.

The NPT Bargain

The behavior (but not the rhetoric) of the old and the new nuclear states supports the suggestion in *The Absolute Weapon* that the proliferation issue is inseparable from the problem of political relations among states. The nuclear and nonproliferation policies of the declared nuclear states have constantly served a variety of great power interests. The NPT guaranteed their possession of and right to use nuclear weapons for self-defense. It maintained their freedom to engage in nuclear commerce. Finally, it enabled them to denuclearize or non-nuclearize their enemies or potential enemies outside the P-5 club.

For the old nuclear powers, the NPT was never divorced from great power politics. From its inception, the NPT was a product of Cold War politics especially as viewed by the United States and the Soviet Union. The NPT was a realpolitik bargain that recognized the necessity or the inevitability of asymmetrical multipolarity among the five nuclear powers. In classical realpolitik international relations theory,[9] strains in great power relations produce compensatory arrangements among the great powers; if great powers cannot be defeated militarily, then conflicting interests have to be adjusted or harmonized through great power bargains. The NPT sealed the bargain among the five nuclear powers by offering them a special position in the treaty; the status quo at January 1, 1967, confirmed the membership in the exclusive club. In essence, the five nuclear powers were like the horses that escaped through the open barn door—closing the door would not bring them back. This, however, was manageable because these horses were motivated by containment and security rather than victory or revolution. By contrast, other horses could be dangerous, and they had to be contained once and for all by closing the barn door via the NPT and the IAEA. The real bargain was an American-

Soviet tacit understanding to keep Germany non-nuclear as it became a good world citizen. Germany is now a convinced nonproliferator because of unique historical circumstances.

For the allies, the message was "stay non-nuclear because the bloc leader has a vital interest in your strategic well-being." For others, the message was "be good and we will give you modern atomic technology under safeguards (Article IV of the NPT) and conditional security assurances through the UN." This assurance was given only to NPT states. It put at risk the value of the UN Charter, which assured protection by the world community against aggression to all UN members. The NPT was not taken seriously by countries with serious disputes that involved regional and great powers. Finally, Article VI of the NPT offered negotiations in good faith relating to nuclear disarmament at an early date. Thus far (1968–96), the five nuclear states have not engaged in disarmament negotiations aimed at eliminating all of their weapons.

If the NPT was primarily an agency to serve the vital interests of the great powers, did it have a disarmament function? Several potential proliferators were stopped by unique circumstances or were co-opted by the Americans and Soviets through inducement (alliance protection and financial aid) or pressure. Other countries decided that nuclear weapons were unnecessary for their national defense in the foreseeable future. For the five nuclear powers, the endgame was not their own disarmament. In 1952, the United States rejected disarmament as a basis of national security, and it continues to do so even after the demise of the Cold War.[10] The disarmament impact of the NPT is marginal because the destructive atomic power in the possession of the five nuclear powers today remains high.

Furthermore, the old nuclear powers, especially the United States, only sought the disarmament of enemies and looked the other way when key regional allies proliferated. Here great power interests and not the benign goal of stopping or slowing proliferation determined the policy response. With political leaders looking the other way, Western, Russian, and Chinese authorities provided vital help for the nuclear and missile projects of their regional allies. Iraq received ample help when it was fighting Iran, America's enemy. As a frontline state against the Soviet Union in Afghanistan, Pakistan gained from Western and Chinese tolerance and aid for its nuclear activities. India gained much from its links with Western and Eastern countries. Western, especially French, help for Israeli nuclear projects is clouded in secrecy; however, its existence is undeniable. To the extent that nuclear supply relationships were extensive—and they existed even after the NPT and IAEA safeguards came into being—the relationship between great power interests and selective proliferation or nonproliferation is the significant determinant of nonproliferation policy. The end of the Cold War led to adjustments in targeting doctrine and the size of the nuclear arsenals of the five nuclear powers, but it did not affect the politicized basis of approaches of the great powers to the proliferation problem.[11]

The new nuclear states also adopted a political view of proliferation. What they say and do is tied to their interests. They do not believe that the NPT is capable of dealing with political conflicts, especially in the Middle East and South Asia. NPT advocates see the proliferation problem as a result of nuclear aspirations of the new nuclear states. This is not the way the new nuclear states define the problem. Countries go nuclear because they have regional and international security dilemmas. The old nuclear states see themselves as part of the solution of regional conflicts, but, in the views of the new nuclear states, they become a part of the problem when the interests of the old and the new nuclear states clash. Figure 1 shows why the interests of the new nuclear states are served by proliferation. For them, nonproliferation is costly if it leads to national insecurity.

The indefinite extension of the NPT in 1995 and the conclusion of the CTBT in 1996 indicate that the nonproliferation constituency is strong, but can it prevail in the Middle East and South Asia? Since the 1970s, the constituency has gained institutional strength by developing nuclear supply controls and full-scope safeguards. In addition, a post-NPT antinuclear and antimissile orientation has emerged in the thinking and policies of the old Western nuclear powers.[12] Adherence to the NPT is not enough; now the non-nuclear pledge requires a rollback of delivery capabilities, including dual-use space capabilities that have military and commercial applications. The Missile Technology Control Regime (MTCR) is meant to slow missile proliferation. The orientation of the Western nuclear powers is to combine the NPT and the MTCR philosophies, along with post-COCOM (Coordinating Committee on Export Controls) arrangements, to curb horizontal proliferation of weapons of mass destruction (WMD).

Despite its support among an overwhelming majority of states, the NPT lacks universal legitimacy. It faces a number of challenges. The new nuclear states are few in number, but they function as regional powers in two important zones of conflict since the end of the Second World War. Their voices are not heard in NPT conference diplomacy; however, they have a resonance in many capitals of the world. Their public defiance of American leadership reveals a chink in the American diplomatic armor; it reveals Washington's inability to win the minds and the hearts of the Israelis, Pakistanis, and Indians when their vital interests are concerned. Such a successful challenge by the new nuclear states that are outside the

NPT creates ideas and opportunities for some inside the NPT to rebel against P-5 authority in world affairs. That three medium powers—North Korea and Iran, not to mention Iraq—continue to resist American demands suggests that the old nuclear powers are helpless giants and the new nuclear powers outside and inside the NPT may not be helpless pygmies in select circumstances. It seems that countries that involve themselves in significant international issues acquire a leverage that exceeds their economic and military power.

The counterorganization of ideas and policies has challenged the legitimacy and the effectiveness of the antiproliferation constituency. The task is made easier by the reluctance of China to subscribe fully to the nonproliferation cause. China is one of the few independent voices in the international system. Even as it negotiated trade and political relations with the Western world, even as it joined the NPT and appeared to agree to subscribe to the MTCR, it maintained its supply relations in the nuclear and the missile sphere with Pakistan, Iran, and Syria, and it continued to blow the whistle against American hegemony. In December 1995, the Chinese ambassador showed remarkable understanding for India's nuclear policy when he stated that "[u]nlike the Americans, we will not pressurize India to sign the nuclear non-proliferation treaty (NPT) or the Comprehensive Test Ban Treaty (CTBT). We respect India's independence in the matter."[13] Although China insisted that the CTBT could not enter into force unless India accepted it, this was a sign of China's concern about India's nuclear capability and intentions, and it gave China an escape clause for itself.

Despite internal pressures and the pro-Western tilt in its foreign policy following the end of the Cold War, Russia, like China, developed its nuclear trade with Iran, a pariah in American thinking. Moscow's actions undermine current U.S. nonproliferation policy. Here Russian commercial and strategic interests and the value of ties with Iran, rather than its nonproliferation commitment, have shaped Russian nuclear trade. To a certain extent, the national sovereignty and national interests of Iran, Russia, and China challenge the nonproliferation regime. In January 1996, the new Russian foreign minister, Yevgeny Primakov, announced a desire to forge closer links with Asian and Middle Eastern countries (including Iraq) and to "correct" the "imbalance" of his predecessor Andrei Kozyrev's policies.[14] A sign of these "corrections" was the visit of the Russian defense minister to India in 1996. So the counterorganization to the nonproliferation constituency includes two non-Western nuclear powers. The P-5 appear disunited, and Washington's inability to consolidate the ranks of the P-5 creates bargaining opportunities for the proliferation camp.

The Absolute Weapon and Order

The term *order* indicates a predictable framework of interstate behavior that results in manageable instability; it does not imply equilibrium or status quo. Given a changing distribution of military and economic power and changing interstate strategic relationships at the global and the regional levels during 1945–95, an "evolving order" is a better description of reality. There is an absence of consensus about the meaning of the term, about whether reality consists of an interactive process of both "order" and "disorder" (i.e., consolidation in some areas and fragmentation in others), and about the causes of either condition. Classic British international relations scholarship does not favor the use of the term *order*. Order is a precise idea according to the dictionary, but it is often loosely used.[15] Some argue that the world today is disorderly, that it is a continuous story of manageable instability. In nuclear affairs, the Indians argue that the dominant nuclear order is discriminatory. The Chinese have also taken the view that the present international order is unjust.[16]

The Absolute Weapon has a rich menu of ideas. Frederick S. Dunn explored the dilemmas posed by atomic energy in interstate politics. Arms limitation agreements suffer strain and carry a heavy burden because the subject matter concerns the security of a state. Nuclear weapons create a special strain because of the enormous advantage gained through treaty violation. Historically, states have sought safeguards before renouncing a great source of power; these were in the form of solemn promises, the taking of hostages, territorial occupation, and international inspection. The security dilemma has been an enduring feature of the modern state system. Should the world get rid of war to avoid atomic warfare, or should it acquire the capability to resort to atomic warfare at short notice and "get rid of" (deter?) war? Bernard Brodie warned against "ethnocentric smugness" in addressing the nuclear issue. He was categorical in predicting proliferation and emphatic in the belief that loss of monopoly must be the basis of international control of atomic energy. He studied the value of the deterrence concept to guard against blackmail; the value rests in a reciprocal ability to retaliate in kind if the bomb is used rather than a reliance on treaty limitations. Brodie was making the case for national nuclear deterrence.[17]

Like Brodie, Arnold Wolfers expected proliferation to occur and predicted the end of the U.S. atomic monopoly. He doubted that possession of the bomb created diplomatic leverage if the issues under dispute were of secondary importance. He speculated that atomic warfare could lead to the enemy's defeat and enforced disarmament, but this would likely lead to a quest for revenge against an unjust peace. Wolfers looked at the issue in terms of the other side's psychology and interests and made an important point about "bargaining away" American monopoly and privileges. This is to be achieved not by U.S.-Soviet negotiations but by measures to "accelerate the advent of multiple possession of atomic armaments." This would place the Soviet Union in a position of equality. Then came the suggested bargain: to obtain Soviet consent to internationalize atomic energy in peacetime without losing the advantage of "dual possession" of atomic power in wartime.[18]

Wolfers distinguishes between three types of defense in atomic affairs. The first is to improve bilateral relations with the potential enemy. The second is to form international arrangements to eliminate or reduce the danger of atomic weapons. The third is to take military steps to deter war, not because the USSR is warlike but to avoid the danger of war by mistake. Here the threat of retaliation is important. Wolfers puts the atomic issue in the context of the international distribution of power. The United States and Soviet Union could reduce or cancel their power in a nuclear war, thereby enhancing other states' military strength. If some of the weaker nations acquired an atomic capability, their position would be strengthened and they would become worthwhile allies of the superpowers.[19]

William Fox's analysis is in tune with the Brodie and Wolfers chapters. Fox emphasized the value of "balancing interests," and he notes the limits of inspection mechanisms. He maintains that the great powers must accept a "substantial narrowing in the range of free choice of policy" and that the control issue is inseparable from the general problem of relations among the great powers. However, Fox has a bias to "maintain the existing power pattern in the world." While he recognizes the possibility of the emergence of fifteen to twenty atomic nations in the future, he urges policy development in the context of bipolarity. So his advocacy of "bargaining relations" and "balancing interests" is in the superpower relational context. He is sanguine that the atomic race will not lead to war and expects that when nations learn to produce bombs, the basis for "equal bargaining" will be laid.[20]

The international nuclear order that emerged after 1945 was based on attitudes and policies that deviated sharply from the advice of the pioneer American scholars in *The Absolute Weapon*. The nonproliferation drive was launched by President Kennedy with declarations about unstable and irresponsible leaders in the proliferating world, and this ethnocentricity is entrenched among the nonproliferation community in the Western world today. Several authors (Brodie, Wolfers, and Fox) believed that proliferation was inevitable, that loss of atomic monopoly ought to be the basis of international control of atomic energy, that there was value in multiple possession of atomic armament so as to relieve insecurity, and that one should create a setting for interstate bargaining. Fox urged a narrowing of the range of free choice. The NPT, suppliers' controls, the MTCR, and post-COCOM arrangements have been constructed on the premise that the line could be drawn after five nuclear powers. There is no appreciation of the point made by Dunn and Fox that limitation agreements and inspections are insufficient because the control issue is inseparable from the general problem of relations among the powers. Atomic energy concerns the vital security interests of a state, and there is a security dilemma: get rid of war and atomic warfare or acquire atomic deterrent capabilities. The old nuclear powers solved their security dilemma by acquiring nuclear deterrent capabilities, but the Western powers fail to recognize that the regional states also face a security dilemma. This observation supports Wolfers's discussion of three lines of defense. The old nuclear powers choose Wolfers's third line of defense, that is, take military steps to deter the enemy. Thereafter, the United States took the lead in developing international arrangements and improving bilateral relations with the Soviet Union (NPT and afterward). This was consistent with Fox's advice: balance interests and maintain the existing power pattern. The NPT and MTCR were developed on this basis. The advice that the great powers needed to limit their policy options was rejected in crafting the international nonproliferation arrangements, which were meant to restrict the new nuclear powers' options and to maintain or increase the advantages of the original nuclear states.

The International Nuclear Order (INO)

The INO reflects the realities of power struggles in modern international relations. It is quite sophisticated compared to the rigid expectations and technical procedures of the NPR. It responds to changing domestic-political, external-strategic, and nuclear circumstances in international and regional conflict. It is realistic because it recognizes the defects of the NPT/IAEA system. INO includes NPT/IAEA arrangements, but it has qualities that make it a system with definable units of behavior, patterns of frequent interactions, stabilizing capacity, and an awareness of changes in domestic, regional, and international contexts of proliferation and nonproliferation work.

Figure 2 predicts both cooperation and conflict between the old and the new nuclear states. Because the United States wants to reduce or eliminate the nuclear weapons capability of Israel, India, and Pakistan, a permanent line of tension exists in the bilateral relations between Washington and these countries. Yet Israel and Pakistan are American allies and India is a "friendly democracy." There are multiple channels of economic, diplomatic, and military cooperation. The balance sheet shows points of convergence and divergence in bilateral relationships between the United States and the new nuclear states.

The INO originated in embryonic form before the superpowers agreed to the provisions of the NPT (1968) and before the IAEA received a nonproliferation mandate (1970). The INO has several important features. First, the United States is determined to maintain its nuclear edge, and it officially rejected nuclear disarmament as a basis of its national security in 1952. American behavior reflects a classical principle of statecraft: a preponderance of power is the best way to preserve world order. America's nuclear strategy reflects this kind of thinking. This is a long-standing feature of U.S. diplomatic and military strategy that has endured changes of international structures—from bipolarity to multipolarity—and it is a permanent feature of the INO.

Second, the American nonproliferation policy recognizes the value of the principles of compromise and compensation as ways to accommodate national interests of other great (nuclear) powers. The accommodation has enabled the old nuclear states to be co-opted in the nonproliferation cause. The United States accommodated the four other declared nuclear powers when it became clear that they would not accept American hegemony in the nuclear sphere. Despite the asymmetries in the distribution of power among the five, and despite the diminished international roles of Britain and France after 1945, the United States recognized the status of the five nuclear powers in the NPT. Currently, agreements on nuclear technology cooperation exist between the United States, the United Kingdom, and France, and they foreshadow similar or more modest deals with China and the Russian Federation.[21] Thus American diplomatic behavior shifted from attempts at marginalization of the other older nuclear powers to accommodation of their strategic interests as the price to gain their support for the NPR.

Third, Israel, India, and Pakistan took the nuclear path in their quest for security, national development, and autonomy. India's civilian nuclear program came into being immediately after its independence, although the importance of atomic energy had entered Indian political consciousness during the 1930s and 1940s. Israel's nuclear program started in 1957 when the Israeli-French nuclear cooperation commenced. Pakistan's nuclear weapons program started in 1972 in the aftermath of the defeat in the Bangladesh War in 1971.

Three characteristics of the INO emerged before the NPR was created: the American faith in nuclear advantage, America's recognition of the importance of great power bargains as a basis for order, and the quest

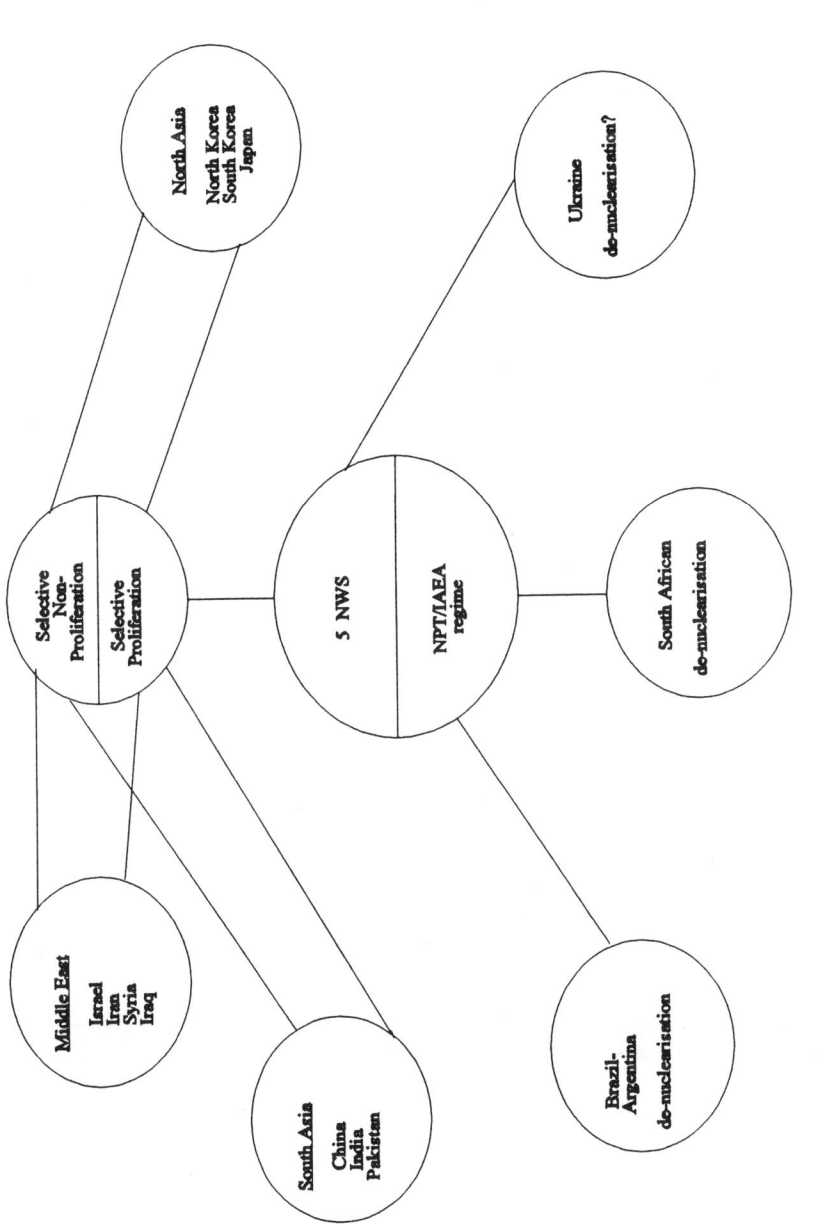

Fig. 2. The International Nuclear Order (INO). (Reprinted from A. Kapur, "Proliferation Dangers in the Third World," *Medicine and War* [Frank Cass] 10, no. 4 [October–December 1994]: 277.)

for autonomy and nuclear power in Israel and India, which occurred independently of the wishes of the great powers. While Israel was preoccupied with consideration of national security in a hostile environment, Indian concerns centered on international atomic energy arrangements, which were dominated by the great powers and which trivialized Indian defense and diplomatic aims and ambitions.

The NPT was an important turning point in Cold War history. It converted the danger of a bipolar confrontation into a bipolar partnership and then extended it into a multipolar (with the United Kingdom and France being the other poles) framework. These became the core powers in the international nuclear order. The NPT became a symbol of superpower cooperation on a vital issue. It also offered a legal and a strategic justification for a world of five nuclear powers. Cold War enemies became nonproliferation partners despite the Berlin Wall, opposing military pacts, proxy East-West confrontations, and other forms of enmity. The NPT showed the vitality of three strategic and diplomatic bargains: between the Americans and the Soviets, as the two became the NPT principals; between the United States and China, as the latter's nuclear and diplomatic status was assured even though it denounced the treaty initially; and between the USSR and China when the latter was given an equal position in the treaty despite the history of Sino-Soviet rivalry.

The fourth characteristic concerned the tension between nuclear disarmament as a basis of international security and the importance of nuclear weaponry as the foundation of international order. Nuclear disarmament was rejected as a basis of American national security in 1952, yet it finds a place in the NPT. The NPT message is confusing on this issue. Article VI speaks of nuclear disarmament as the eventual aim of the treaty. However, with five legitimate nuclear powers and without a time frame for nuclear disarmament, which at any rate requires the consent of the nuclear powers, the NPT handcuffed the disarmament process by making it dependent on the interests and policies of the older nuclear states. The Cold War has ended, but the multiple purposes of nuclear weaponry remain: to deter nuclear and general war; to protect allies; to maintain a global balance; and to guard against blackmail. In this context, the NPT fits into the realist view of power (rather than disarmament) as the basis of international order and international law. However, Article VI indicates that the international nuclear order has a utopian (false expectation) dimension, although the NPT's orientation fits primarily into the realist tradition. But this utopian element is weak and cosmetic. It lacks institutional strength, whereas the nuclear weapons constituencies are entrenched in world politics. With the enshrining of the nuclear status of the five nuclear powers in the NPT, the balance of power has shifted decisively in favor of the nuclear constituencies and against the disarmers. A Nobel prize for the Pugwash group is unlikely to change the balance.

The fifth characteristic of the INO shows the contradiction between the nonproliferation norm and the strategic interests of the major players. Virginia Foran's analysis is pertinent:

> The empirical evidence of the three cases of Israel, India and Pakistan unambiguously supports the claim that U.S. NP [nonproliferation] policy has been determined to a considerable extent by competing foreign policy goals, mostly arising out of the Cold War. . . . The United States' own declarations of support for the international nonproliferation regime have been undermined, as has its claim to leadership in that area.[22]

The tension between nonproliferation and other pressing interests is not confined to Cold War history. In 1995, the United States authorized military shipments to Pakistan (a friend and ally), despite the Pressler amendment, which required termination of aid. The scale of the aid or the nature of the equipment are not at issue. The central concern is not about the effect of the supply on the Indo-Pakistani military balance; American military supplies, like Chinese ones, add to the costs of Indian defense, although they are manageable from the Indian budgetary perspective. The issue concerns the American message: U.S. nonproliferation law is debatable and negotiable, and larger strategic issues at a given time determine whether nonproliferation goals are given priority. The strategy is pragmatic rather than a matter of conviction, principle, or law. In other words, taking America and China as examples of P-5 nonproliferation behavior, nonproliferation is a part of the hierarchy of strategic issues, but it is not always at the top of the hierarchy. A strategy of selective proliferation or selective nonproliferation is pursued. We should expect oscillation between the two, rather than dominance of the nonproliferation norm within P-5 governments.

The sixth and final characteristic shows three features in the nuclear behavior of the new nuclear states: there is an interaction between proliferation and nonproliferation activity in the external conduct and internal debates of the new nuclear states; there is policy development in both the proliferation and nonproliferation spheres of these states; finally, these states are developing their nuclear proliferation and nonproliferation policies in the context of a wider agenda, namely, to become regional centers of power and to acquire an autonomous position in the international system.[23]

The regional dimension has a life of its own: it is autonomous in relation to the norms and pressures of the global NPR. The new nuclear states participate in the global economy and in multilateral political diplomacy, and they interact with the major powers. With the end of the Cold War, their participation in the market economy and their exposure to so-called American unipolarity do not appear to have diminished their faith in self-help and autonomy. These observations suggest a need to inject realism into proliferation and nonproliferation studies by examining the scope and pattern of relationships between regional rivals and between the regional powers and the great powers. Two types of security interdependencies may be assessed: between regional pairs (Israel-Egypt, Israel-Iran, Israel-Syria, Israel-Iraq, India-Pakistan, India-China), where the interactions flow horizontally along channels of conflict, cooperation, or indifference; and between a regional power and an international power, where the interactions flow vertically along channels of conflict, cooperation, or indifference.

According to the "dominant-subordinate" states system paradigm, regional powers are dependent vis-à-vis an international power, whereas an international power is presumably independent and is able to dominate a weaker power. This paradigm is empirically false because the great international powers have limited freedom of choice in regional diplomatic and military affairs. The regional clusters in Figure 2 are the core players in that their politics and histories of conflict are local and parochial.

The vetoes against acceptance of nonproliferation policies are located in the domestic structures of the core regional powers. The policies to relieve stresses and strains among regional rivals also flow from these structures. To access these domestic forces, one must go outside the NPT and IAEA framework, suspend faith in a universal regime approach, and engage academic and government practitioners with the study of complex domestic and regional politics. This requires recalibration of arms controllers and regime builders who dismiss recent history when considering practical regional politics. The NPR is not equipped to examine regional dynamics except in terms of IAEA-supervised nuclear-weapon-free zones. To an extent, the U.S. government possesses the resources to integrate both regional and domestic forces into policy. But U.S. policy is handcuffed by its internal congressional and bureaucratic politics.

To recognize the regional dynamics in nuclear affairs other than in the NPT context is to undermine American NPT leadership. Yet the regional nuclear dimension is a vital part of the international nuclear order. India and Pakistan, and India and China, have moved toward a strategy of low-level nuclear deterrence by ambiguous means. Many view this as a move toward bilateral and regional stability and security. India and Pakistan have revealed their possession of nuclear weapons capability, and at the same time both have indicated a willingness to exercise restraint in their strategic behavior if they are not pushed to the wall. This approach also exists in Sino-Indian relations, since the mid-1960s. Both countries have developed confidence-building measures and limited transparency in their strategic relations. These policies indicate a shift away from a faith in security through disarmament. The regional philosophy is rather simple. Negotiated bilateral arms control measures that are formal and/or informal are preferable to unilateral measures or ones that give a foreign power a balancer and hence an intervenor role. India explicitly rejects such a role by Washington or Beijing because both are viewed as part of its strategic problem. Israel is more subtle in pointing a finger at the United States. It is noteworthy that both Israel and India favor bilateral deals in the regional context. India has a negative view of American brokerage in Indo-Pakistani affairs, whereas Israel accepts American brokerage because the Israeli leverage in U.S. politics provides an assurance of American support.

Conclusion

The nonproliferation regime provides a set of rules and regulations and commitments that are accepted by a group of states. A set of specific rights and obligations exists.[24] The NPR, especially its main component—the NPT, with 185 member states—fulfills the requirements of a regime, but it is not universal.[25] The MTCR is also a regime because a (smaller) group of states follow a set of rules with defined rights and obligations for its members.

This view of the NPR, however, raises a number of counterpoints. First, regime building and regime theorizing about nonproliferation fail to examine the hidden agendas of the regime and nonregime players. There is growing evidence that regime members may speak about the virtues of the regime but their actions are sometimes inconsistent with regime rules; the variations depend on the state of the political and strategic relationship with the suspect state and the interest of the parties. Susan Strange's critique about the neglect of nonregime behavior is relevant here.[26] If the most powerful members of a regime themselves are inconsistent in implementing the rules, or implement them on a politicized basis, should the regime theorists monitor the erosive behavior of the most powerful members of the regime?

Second, has multipolarity (or international systemic change from bipolarity to multipolarity during the Cold War and following its end) restricted the freedom of choice of the most powerful members of the NPT regime? *The Absolute Weapon* indicated that possession of nuclear weaponry did not increase diplomatic leverage. This point can be tested by assessing the impact of bipolarity and multipolarity on the nonproliferation policies of the great powers. The U.S. government tolerated Israeli proliferation because it was a valuable ally against Soviet expansion and Arab militancy in the Middle East. The Soviet government tolerated Indian proliferation because it was a valuable ally in Soviet relations with China, America, and the Third World. The U.S. and Chinese governments both tolerated Pakistani proliferation because of its value as an ally against Soviet and Indian expansion. *The Absolute Weapon* maintains that the issue of nuclear controls is inseparable from the problem of political relations among the great powers. Our assessment is that the range of choice of the nonproliferators depends on the level of unity or disunity among the great powers. Multipolarity minimizes the prospects of hegemonic stability in the NPR. That is, the security dilemmas of the great powers strain their ability to give nonproliferation the highest priority in the context of other pressing diplomatic and strategic priorities.

Third, it is easily argued that the new nuclear states acquired nuclear weapons because of their security dilemmas with regional rivals, because of their insecurity vis-à-vis unreliable and/or menacing great powers, and with a view to develop new bargains with the most powerful members of the international system. The presumption is that the regional states make rational choices in terms of their assessments of the nature and problem of systemic changes in international and regional affairs, and they pursue policies that are in their self-interest. Multipolarity in the regional and international sphere has created pressures as well as opportunities for the regional nuclear states to develop rational options to increase their freedom of action.

In these circumstances, the NPR builders have to carry a heavy burden to support the regime. Their ability to do so is constrained by international and regional power structures and circumstances; the costs for regime building and maintenance are not insignificant. To gain support for an indefinite extension of the NPT, the old nuclear powers had to promise a zero yield position on nuclear testing. This position requires domestic political bargaining with defense, scientific, bureaucratic, and congressional constituencies. As the debates about the SALT and ABM treaties show, the bargains are not easily arranged. The North Korean case shows that the United States had to negotiate with a pariah/enemy state to buy time for nonproliferation: the costs were tangible, in terms of oil and nuclear reactor supplies, and intangible, in terms of North Korea's ability to bring the United States to the bargaining table and the strain of U.S.-North Korean negotiations on U.S.-South Korean relations. Indo-American, Russo-American, and Sino-American interactions show that nonproliferation issues can poison relations, and the costs in terms of lost trust are intangible and enduring.

Fourth, controversies about the meaning of proliferation have placed a heavy burden on the regime builders. Is possession of nuclear weapons and missile delivery capability proliferation, or is proliferation revealed by overt weapons testing? The NPT takes the latter view, but the U.S. government in its attitude toward South Africa, Iran, India, and Pakistan takes the former view. Is there good or tolerable proliferation, or just bad and intolerable proliferation? U.S. policies differentiated between Israeli and South African proliferation and Libyan, North Korean, and Iranian proliferation. The NPT does not make such a distinction, but policymakers do. This means that treaty provisions are subject to political judgment.

History affords little support for the idea that great powers are more restrained and responsible than minor powers.[27] It suggests, rather, that they wish to monopolize the right to create international conflict.[28] Unless independent Western scholars and policy analysts grasp the messages of the new nuclear states and the wise thinking represented in *The Absolute Weapon*, the debate between the nonproliferation builders and the new proliferators is likely to remain a dialogue of the deaf, and the nonproliferation regime is likely to remain a game of smoke and mirrors.

NOTES

The author thanks the Social Sciences and Humanities Research Council of Canada for research support.

1. Bernard Brodie, ed., *The Absolute Weapon: Atomic Power and World Order* (New York: Harcourt, Brace, 1946).

2. William T. R. Fox, "International Control of Atomic Weapons," in Brodie, *The Absolute Weapon*, 192.

3. See George H. Quester, "Nuclear Pakistan and Nuclear India: Stable Deterrence or Proliferation Challenge?" *Strategic Studies Institute* (November 1992): 10, 21; Neil Joeck, "Tacit Bargaining and Stable Proliferation in South Asia," CISA Working Paper no. 66 (Los Angeles: Center for International and Strategic Affairs, University of California, April 1989); Peter R. Lavoy, "Civil-Military Relations, Strategic Conduct, and the Stability of Nuclear Deterrence in South Asia," in Scott D. Sagan, ed., *Civil-Military Relations and Nuclear Weapons* (Palo Alto, Calif.: Center for International Security and Arms Control, June 1994); and George Perkovich, "A Nuclear Third Way in South Asia," *Foreign Policy* 91 (Summer 1993): 86. For an alternate view, see Devin T. Hagerty, "Nuclear Deterrence in South Asia: The 1990 Indo-Pakistani Crisis," *International Security* 20 (Winter 1995–96): 79–114.

4. Interviews, New Delhi, December 1995 and August 1996. See also Ashok Kapur, "The CTBT and the Security of South Asia," *Disarmament Diplomacy* 4 (April 1996): 2–4.

5. See Ashok Kapur, *Pakistan's Nuclear Development* (London: Croom Helm, 1987), for a detailed assessment of Pakistani nuclear policies and motives.

6. On the Israeli nuclear weapons program, see Yair Evron, *Israel's Nuclear Dilemma* (Ithaca, N.Y.: Cornell University Press, 1994); and Seymour M. Hersh, *The Samson Option: Israel's Nuclear Arsenal and American Foreign Policy* (New York: Random House, 1991).

7. This section draws on confidential interviews with Israeli and Iranian officials and academic experts in Tel Aviv, New Delhi, Tehran, Toronto, and Waterloo, Ontario, during 1992–95.

8. For Indian views on the CTBT, see S. Pande, "N-test Ban and India," *Hindustan Times* (25 December 1995): 11; Vija K. Nair, "CTBT: Instrument for Eliminating Nuclear Weapons or Projection of US Policies?" *Agni* 1 (November 1995): 67–86; and statement by Ambassador A. Ghose at the Committee on Disarmament, United Nations, Geneva, 20 June 1996.

9. Martin Wight argues that powers of comparable strength compensate each other, while intervention governs the relations between stronger and weaker states; he also points out that such hegemony has never been accepted in international relations theory. See Martin Wight, *Power Politics,* ed. Hedley Bull and C. Holbraad (New York: Penguin Books, 1979), 186, 41.

10. Peter Pringle and James Spigelman, *Nuclear Barons* (London: Michael Joseph, 1982), 111.

11. See Ashok Kapur, "Rogue States and the International Nuclear Order," *International Journal* 51 (Summer 1996): 420–39.

12. An important manifestation of this change has been the Clinton administration's counterproliferation initiatives announced in 1993. On these initiatives, see Joseph F. Pilat and Walter L. Kirchner, "The Technological Promise of Counterproliferation," *Washington Quarterly* 18 (Winter 1995): 153–66.

13. "China Respects India's N-Policy: Ambassador," *The Times of India* (23 December 1995): 8.

14. "Foreign Minister to Move Russia Away from West," *The Globe and Mail* (13 January 1996): A1, A14.

15. The dictionary refers to "order" as methodical, tidy, and well regulated. This is hardly the case with world politics, past and present. "Order" could also mean "internationalism." However, Martin Wight points out that "[t]he most conspicuous theme in international history is not the growth of internationalism." Wight, *Power Politics,* 30.

16. "China Respects," 8.

17. Brodie, *The Absolute Weapon,* 11–13, 17, 67, 63, 87, 107.

18. Arnold Wolfers, "The Atomic Bomb in Soviet-American Relations," in Brodie, *The Absolute Weapon,* 113, 114–16, 118, 119–20, 124.

19. Wolfers, "Atomic Bomb in Soviet-American Relations," 132–34, 145–46.

20. Fox, "International Control of Atomic Weapons," 183–84, 191, 201, 182, 202.

21. "UK's Secret Deal on N-tests," *Guardian Weekly* (1 October 1995): 9; "That Nuclear Club Buzz," *Guardian Weekly,* editorial (1 October 1995): 12; "Anger at British Silence over New French N-test," *Guardian Weekly* (8 October 1995): 1.

The sharing of computer and explosion information by the United States with the other P-5 states was an inducement to bring them into the CTBT. See *International Security Digest* 3 (June 1996).

22. Virginia Foran, "Strategic Non-proliferation: Balancing Interests and Ideals," in Foran, ed., *The Making of U.S. Foreign Policy, 1945–1991* (London: Chadwick-Healey, 1992), 31.

23. Raimo Vayrynen, "Economic and Military Position of the Regional Power Centers," *Journal of Peace Research* 4, no. 17 (1979): 349–69, is among the few Western studies to take regional power centers seriously.

24. Cited in Robert O. Keohane, "Cooperation and International Regimes," in P. Williams et al., eds., *Classic Readings of International Relations* (Belmont, Calif.: Wadsworth Publishing, 1994), 241–42.

25. Keohane, "Cooperation and International Regimes," 245. For a general regime theory, see Stephen D. Krasner, ed., *International Regimes* (Ithaca, N.Y.: Cornell University Press, 1983); V. Rittberger, ed., *International Regimes in East-West Politics* (London: Pinter, 1990); A. L. George et al., eds., *US-Soviet Security Cooperation* (New York: Oxford University Press, 1988); T. V. Paul, "The NPT and Power Transitions in the International System," in Raju G. C. Thomas, ed., *The Nuclear Non-proliferation Regime, Prospects for the 21st Century* (Houndsmills, U.K.: Macmillan, forthcoming). Unfortunately, the North American scholarly literature does not offer a convincing thesis of nonproliferation as a security regime, nor does regime theory offer any case studies of security regimes that require sovereignty-sacrificing behavior by great powers.

26. Susan Strange, *"Cave! Hic Dragones:* A Critique of Regime Analysis," in Williams et al., *Classical Readings of International Relations,* 247.

27. Wight, *Power Politics,* 286–87.

28. Wight, *Power Politics,* 42–43.

Nonproliferation and Denuclearization

ROBERT A. MANNING AND ZACHARY S. DAVIS

For the first time since mushroom clouds illuminated the desert of New Mexico at the dawn of the nuclear age, the specter of global conflagration no longer looms over the human race. The Soviet threat, the organizing principle of U.S. security policy for the past fifty years, is gone. Long-held assumptions of arms control and nuclear strategy alike have been turned upside down. Not since the publication of *The Absolute Weapon* in 1946 has such an opportunity existed to rethink the relationship between nuclear weapons and world order.

The world is at a rare historic moment that offers a window of opportunity to control the atom as part of a broader reshaping of global institutions and patterns of interstate relations. Decisions made by the international community over the next decade will determine whether the spread of nuclear and other weapons of mass destruction will continue, or whether a defining feature of the emerging international order will be the delegitimization of such weapons. We argue that a new nuclear strategy is needed to guide the delegitimization process and reap maximum security benefits.

It does not require a presumption that civilization has evolved to new norms of conduct rendering war obsolete to envision a structure and ethic of global politics that ensures that future conflicts are not fought with nuclear weapons.[1] Prominent military leaders and former cold warriors have endorsed the idea that nuclear weapons should be devalued and marginalized, if not eventually removed from international politics.[2] The rate at which nuclear weapons can be withdrawn is, of course, contingent on a number of factors (as discussed in the chapters by James Wirtz and George Quester in this volume); we are not advocating universal disarmament. Nor do we have unrealistic expectations regarding the reliability of treaties and agreements for countries facing threats to their security. Indeed, the probability of nuclear use (either in a regional conflict or by terrorists) may be higher now than during the bipolar era. However, we believe that it is possible to craft a strategy that reduces the importance of nuclear weapons to national security. Such a strategy must be viewed as one element of a transformed international order built on a balance of interests and more comprehensive notions of security.

A strategic analysis of the influence of existing nuclear weapons on defense policies of nuclear weapon states and on future nonproliferation efforts is essential for continued U.S. leadership of the nonproliferation regime. We assume that U.S. leaders will guide international nonproliferation efforts in the post–Cold War era. This chapter seeks to define the elements of a comprehensive nuclear strategy: one that imposes obligations on the nuclear haves and have-nots; one that is designed to create an antiproliferation synergy. It outlines a conceptual framework in which nonproliferation policy, the U.S.-Russian build-down, regional security dynamics, and the future nuclear policies of the United States, Russia, and other nuclear powers are addressed as a single indivisible challenge.

Why a New Bargain?

Underlying this nonproliferation strategy is a hard-nosed vision of a postnuclear world, a return to the original intent of the Acheson-Lilienthal report and the Baruch Plan.[3] The danger of nuclear breakout and the limits of verification and enforcement are likely to prevent this from being achievable any time soon. But if the United States articulates such a vision and moves in this direction, it will open possibilities for leading the world toward a new nuclear bargain.

In an international order in which nuclear weapons are increasingly marginal to U.S. defense strategy, U.S. conventional superiority makes this approach a low-risk, high-payoff policy. Fostering a postnuclear ethic requires neither abandoning deterrence nor making the world safe for conventional war: Bosnia suggests that superpower nuclear weapons will have little bearing on post–Cold War regional/ethnic disputes. A minimum deterrence posture would be sufficient for any foreseeable challenges. Such a posture would help the United States to address the key security issue of the post–cold war era: the proliferation of weapons of mass destruction (WMD) in Asia, where rivalries abound among states with modern conventional weaponry, increasing ballistic missile capabilities, chemical weapons, and virtual, if undeclared, nuclear weapons capabilities. The challenge for this posture is evident from North Korea's flouting of the Nuclear Non-proliferation Treaty (NPT) to Iraq's clandestine efforts to acquire nuclear weapons.

The Gulf War highlighted the threat of regional conflicts, unfrozen by the end of the Cold War, being played out with weapons of mass destruction. Iraq dramatized the reality that small powers can now threaten U.S. forces and allies on distant battlefields with missiles and chemical, biological, or nuclear weapons. In the foreseeable future some such states may attain the capabilities to threaten the security of the United States. The ever-widening diffusion of technology, reflecting increasingly sophisticated industrial bases in non-Western countries, is an irreversible reality of the multipolar post–Cold War world.

In light of the reversal of the strategic logic of the previous era and the 1995 decision to extend indefinitely the NPT, the United States—indeed, the world—is now potentially better positioned to halt the spread of WMD than at any time since immediately after the Second World War. A series of momentous developments has reinforced the nuclear taboo: Arms reduction accords have eliminated entire categories of weapons (intermediate-range missiles), and after START II and III are implemented, U.S. and Russian nuclear arsenals will be reduced by some 90 percent from their Cold War peaks; Iraq's and North Korea's nuclear subterfuge sparked efforts to bolster nonproliferation norms; democratization has accompanied the rollback of proliferation in Argentina, Brazil, and South Africa; Ukraine, Kazakhstan, and Belarus gave up nuclear weapons and joined the NPT as non–weapons states; and a Comprehensive Test Ban Treaty (CTBT) has become a reality. Nuclear weapons are being devalued as the currency of power; the challenge is to direct and codify this trend.

For the United States, the logic of current realities—the end of a threat of global nuclear conflict, and new and emerging U.S. high-technology conventional military capabilities—point to a sharp de-emphasis of nuclear weapons in U.S. defense planning. It is increasingly persuasive to argue, as George Kennan did in 1949, that nuclear weapons should be viewed as "superfluous to our basic military posture—as something we are compelled to hold against the possibility that they might be used by our opponents."[4] In the future, the benefits for U.S. security of maintaining a robust, global nuclear triad will be surpassed by the advantages of the revolution in military affairs in a denuclearizing world.

With the eventual implementation of a CTBT, START II, and possibly START III, the next phase would include post-START reductions and a no-first-use policy. Adoption of such policies by nuclear weapons states could foster a new momentum for fully legitimizing nonproliferation norms. This would reduce the discriminatory and often hypocritical North-South features of nonproliferation policy. Making norms universal is an important tool for creating a credible strategy in which global supply-side restraints on the diffusion of technology and nuclear material are meshed with coherent policies addressing the source—regional, "demand-side" motivations.

The Clinton administration's post–Cold War nonproliferation policy review (PRD-8), building on the Bush administration policies in 1991–92, moved U.S. policy a few steps further in this direction.[5] In May 1995, the United States and the other nuclear weapons states made commitments to secure the extension of the NPT, which moved a bit further toward a new nuclear bargain. However, U.S. nuclear policies remain in a conceptual vacuum. The Clinton administration's 1994 Nuclear Posture Review produced a cautious hedge strategy that essentially reaffirmed the nuclear status quo and the logic of nuclear-dependent stability.[6] Reductions in U.S. and Russian nuclear weapons have been driven not by any new guiding strategic paradigm, but by the pragmatic goal of "locking in" cuts made possible by the demise of the Soviet Union. Even after START I and START II are implemented—still a daunting task—Washington and Moscow will each have some 3,500 nuclear weapons deployed. Even the proposed START III would leave each side with 2,000 to 2,500 deployed weapons. What strategic or political logic dictates this as an end point?

However admirable, traditional arms control has not engendered a new conceptual approach to the role of nuclear weapons in international security: How low can we go? What is the endgame? What is the relation of U.S. and Russian reductions to global efforts to curb the proliferation of nuclear and other WMD? So fundamental is the shift in the matrix of U.S. security concerns that former defense secretary Les Aspin once mused, "If we now had the opportunity to ban all nuclear weapons, we would."[7] A growing number of military commanders and defense officials have echoed this view in recent years.[8] Their perspective is not based on a moral judgment of nuclear weapons, but rather on an assessment of what best serves U.S. interests and defense requirements.

The dream of eliminating nuclear weapons is embodied in Article VI of the NPT, which commits parties to the treaty "to pursue negotiations in good faith on effective measures relating to cessation of the nuclear arms race at an early date and to nuclear disarmament." This was part of the tenuous global bargain by which non–weapon states accepted a two-tier system, agreeing to forgo the weapons option in exchange for access to the peaceful use of nuclear energy under safeguards. In the aftermath of the Cold War, approaching, if not realizing, NPT's Article VI obligation is now possible. If U.S. policy moves away from a two-tier, nuclear haves and have-nots regime, it will gain the moral and political high ground, making a new nuclear bargain possible. A new bargain, however, requires vision, sustained high-level engagement, and American leadership by example, not merely by admonition. The new logic of American security interests is not yet fully reflected in U.S. policies. Residual nuclear-force postures, doctrines, bureaucracies, and infrastructures accumulated over four decades of Cold War confrontation still exist. Bureaucratic inertia remains a potent obstacle to new thinking well after policies have lost their purpose.

The United States should adopt a three-pronged nonproliferation strategy that emphasizes

strengthened institutional restraints and norms on the acquisition of nuclear materials (and delivery systems) and the transfer of technology, with enhanced verification and enforcement as part of a new global bargain;
innovative diplomacy to address the regional conflicts that drive demand-side motivations for proliferation;
the development of counterproliferation capabilities ranging from improved intelligence and military capabilities to defensive systems.

Bottling the Genie: Rolling Back Proliferation

While it is difficult to quantify the nonproliferation impact of the American-Russian build-down, it endows both nuclear superpowers with a new political and moral authority on proliferation issues. The distinction between the vertical arms race and horizontal proliferation is eroding. The American-Russian arms reductions, along with post–Gulf War measures to strengthen non-nuclear norms, lay the basis for a new strategy toward nonproliferation. One effect of the build-down of U.S. and Russian nuclear weapons is that it reinforces the voluntary rollback of nuclear weapons programs by countries that view nuclear arsenals as more trouble than they are worth.

The cycle of arms reduction agreements and unilateral steps—the 1987 Intermediate Nuclear Force (INF) agreement, the 1990 Conventional Forces in Europe (CFE), Open Skies (1992), President Bush's 1991 tactical weapons initiative, the standing down from alert of some offensive forces, and START I and II—were watershed events with important ramifications for nonproliferation. Not only did they initiate a process of shrinking superpower arsenals from some 55,000 to 3,500 warheads, but they reversed the technological imperative, the relentless drive for more and better weapons. Moreover, these agreements fostered advances in verification that have expanded the possibilities for arms control and nonproliferation.[9]

While less revolutionary than the changes reversing the vertical arms race, substantial positive developments regarding horizontal proliferation have also occurred since the end of the Cold War. Iraq's ability to nearly complete a self-sufficient nuclear infrastructure highlighted the glaring deficiencies in the nonproliferation system and catalyzed a renewed sense of urgency—and established important precedents—to take corrective steps to fortify the regime. Consequently, the network of treaties—the keystone of which remains the NPT—export controls, safeguards, security commitments, and institutions that constitute the nonproliferation regime, though still inadequate, have been reinforced.[10]

In May 1995, 178 parties to the NPT decided to make the treaty permanent. Membership in the NPT is nearly universal—only a few countries have not joined. Efforts to put conditions on the extension of the NPT failed, not least of all because too many countries realized that the alternatives to a permanent NPT posed unacceptable risks of nuclear anarchy.[11] Nevertheless, most NPT members insisted on making explicit the link between vertical and horizontal proliferation.

The non–weapons states extracted important concessions from the nuclear weapons states to make progress toward satisfying the disarmament goals of Article VI. These included positive and negative security guarantees and commitments to negotiate a CTBT, which was concluded in September 1996. A strengthened review process for the treaty will oversee the expected progress and shape the response if the results are found wanting.[12] With the future of the NPT secured, the weapons states have an opportunity to consolidate the other key monitoring and enforcement components of the regime.

Prior to the Gulf War, the International Atomic Energy Agency (IAEA) had considered Iraq a model NPT adherent. Iraq's ability to pursue a secret parallel weapons program and its skill in evading export controls on dual-use items dealt a devastating blow to confidence in the IAEA's system of export controls. Without access for its inspectors, information to guide it, adequate resources, and the will to seek out problems, the IAEA could not be expected to verify that NPT commitments were being kept.

Learning from the lessons of Iraq (as well as lessons from North Korea and South Africa), the IAEA has undertaken significant reforms. These reforms were unveiled as a comprehensive package called "93 + 2" at the 1995 NPT extension conference.[13] In addition to a change of attitude toward inspections, the IAEA reaffirmed its dormant authority to conduct "special inspections" of undeclared sites. It has also asserted its right to receive intelligence reports from member states, many of which have shown increased willingness to share sensitive information with the agency. The 93 + 2 package also includes more intrusive inspection technology, such as environmental monitoring techniques to detect evidence of undeclared activity.[14] But no matter how effective the IAEA may be at detecting cheating, enforcement of the NPT is still the responsibility of the UN Security Council.

The defeat of Iraq in the Gulf War allowed the international community to discover the extent of Saddam Hussein's development of WMD and to eradicate them. As part of the terms of a ceasefire, UN Security Council Resolution 687 created the UN Special Commission, UNSCOM, with a mandate to conduct intrusive inspections of suspect sites anywhere in Iraq and to render harmless any facilities associated with WMD. The UN action to denuclearize Iraq set a precedent for the international enforcement of nonproliferation norms.

While the precedent of UNSCOM is important, however, its creation was a result of the exceptional circumstances surrounding Iraq's defeat. It is unlikely that such intrusive enforcement of prospective proliferators will be adopted elsewhere absent a major transgression; for example, North Korea's NPT violations were not enough to trigger Security Council sanctions. Nonetheless, the direct involvement of the UN Security Council in obtaining compliance with proliferation norms is an important by-product of the Iraq affair, as was the accession to the NPT of France and China, both permanent Security Council members, in 1992.

Another milestone in expanding UN Security Council engagement in countering proliferation is a benchmark statement issued on January 31, 1992. The council declared, "The proliferation of all weapons of mass destruction constitutes a threat to international peace and security." The UN statement said the council "will take appropriate measures in the case of any violation notified to them by the IAEA." This language creates a legal basis for the Security Council to authorize coercive action against proliferators under Chapter VII of the UN charter, a potentially important enforcement mechanism. Chapter VII coercive measures range from economic sanctions to the use of military force. Another political shock on the scale of breaking of the nonuse taboo may have to occur, however, before the international community acquires the political will to improve enforcement of nuclear norms.

A tightening of export controls both by individual countries (notably Germany) and by the Nuclear Suppliers Group (NSG) followed the embarrassing disclosures of Western suppliers to the Iraqi program. Members of the NSG, an informal grouping of twenty-seven exporting countries, have adopted guidelines for their export policies on nuclear materials in keeping with their NPT obligations "not in any way to assist" proliferation. In April 1992, the NSG expanded its export controls to include many dual-use technologies, and its members jointly declared a policy of requiring nations importing nuclear items to allow full-scope safeguards on all their nuclear activities. To promote transparency in civil nuclear operations, the IAEA has proposed tracking all nuclear exports as part of its 93 + 2 program. Locking in these improvements is essential to prevent a return to past practices.

Perhaps the most favorable developments have occurred on the demand side. No fewer than six countries have relinquished nuclear capabilities since the end of the Cold War. Throughout the 1980s, South Africa, Argentina, and Brazil were all pursuing nuclear weapons capabilities. The breakup of the Soviet Union left Ukraine, Kazakhstan, and Belarus with nuclear capabilities of their own. Yet each of these countries, like several others before them, decided to give up their nuclear weapons options.[15] A combination of domestic political developments, movement toward democracy, and international inducements persuaded these governments they would fare better without the bomb.

These nonproliferation successes are cause for optimism that the end of the Cold War is not destined to lead to nuclear anarchy, as some predicted.[16] Although many domestic and international factors contributed to these decisions, these states came to the conclusion that nuclear weapons were extraneous or detrimental to their security. The nonproliferation regime has grown stronger as nuclear weapons are gradually pushed to the margins of international politics. But the potential for a reversal of fortune should not be ignored. Adding new names to the list of countries that have abandoned nuclear weapons must be a primary objective of a new nonproliferation strategy.

Proliferation Challenges

It is easy to sketch hair-raising scenarios of nuclear catastrophes, from nuclear exchanges in yet another Indo-Pakistani conflict, or desperate North Korean assaults, to nuclear terrorism by an extremist group acquiring plutonium or a "loose nuke." Such scenarios are more than the stuff of post–Cold War political thrillers: they are genuine, if worst-case, concerns. Fortunately, these nightmares are more the exception—the troubling lacunae of the nonproliferation system—than the rule, and not necessarily the trend. Nevertheless, the ingredients for proliferation—insecurity, war, aggression, technology—have not disappeared.

It is too early in the post–Cold War era to predict whether there will be a new wave of proliferation or a withering of interest in nuclear options. The steady diffusion of technology has put nuclear, chemical, biological, missile, and cruise-missile technology within the reach of a growing list of nations and groups. The deceptive fact that no nation has overtly joined the nuclear club since China exploded a nuclear device in 1964 testifies to the potency of the nuclear taboo but overlooks the fact that "opaque" or "virtual" proliferation offers an intermediate status to countries wishing to keep their nuclear options open.

What would cause a new wave of proliferation? Ironically, the very success of U.S. forces in the Gulf, of their precision-guided munitions (PGMs) and electronic domination of the battlefield, may heighten the appeal of nuclear weapons to potential proliferators, who, lacking major power allies and faced with overwhelming conventional force, may see utility in the logic of the nuclear deterrence that guided the superpowers during the Cold War. When asked what he thought were the lessons of the Gulf War, the Indian military chief of staff reportedly replied, "Never fight the U.S. without nuclear weapons."[17] Other countries may try to follow in the footsteps of the nuclear superpowers, seeking to use nuclear threats to achieve political and military objectives. In more ways than one, North Korea may be a bellwether for things to come.

Shifts in regional balances of power could threaten the security of nations and rekindle widespread interest in nuclear weapons. In a world of confrontation and conflict, it might not take much to provoke a surge of proliferation in which worst-case planning, such as that which drove the American-Soviet arms race for fifty years, leads other countries to overestimate threats. Once the action-reaction pattern has begun, arms race spirals gain momentum that may take decades to slow. The American-Soviet arms race demonstrated that deterrence can be an open-ended objective that has no finite conclusion. Perceptions of missile gaps and "windows of vulnerability" could drive new nuclear states to duplicate the overkill arsenals of Washington and Moscow and to reproduce the costs and risks of the American-Soviet deterrence experience. South Asia may have already embarked on this path.

There is little reason to believe that other countries will do a better job than Washington and Moscow of discerning between an adversary's declared intentions and its technical capabilities. Moreover, the current system of IAEA safeguards has not provided adequate verification to overcome distrust, and recent improvements in safeguards do not go far enough to dispel suspicions. Official denials are not sufficient to eliminate anxiety, as has been illustrated by ongoing concerns about the nuclear intentions of Japan, Iran, and Algeria. Assurances of peaceful intent can be clouded by circumstantial evidence of bomb-related activities or technical capabilities. Whether or not such evidence provides conclusive proof of latent or "virtual" nuclear weapons programs, suspicious neighbors are likely to keep a watchful eye on developments.[18]

If the security situation in the former Soviet Union, South Asia, East Asia, or the Middle East were to degenerate into conflict, it is not hard to imagine a new wave of proliferation. In the Middle East, what would be the result of Iran, Iraq, Libya, or Algeria acquiring fissile materials? In Asia, what are the prospects for proliferation? North Korea possesses a secret cache of plutonium and the ability to make more. Japan plans to produce tons of plutonium—albeit under safeguards. China continues its across-the-board military buildup, including modernizing its nuclear forces. Two other countries in the region—South Korea and Taiwan—have in the past taken steps toward developing a nuclear option. Even if South Korea does not revive its interest in nuclear weapons or plutonium, it will inherit North Korea's nuclear legacy after reunification. How would the world respond to Vladimir Zhirinovsky's bellicose threats and territorial claims if he were to take power in Russia? If the risk of future proliferation is not high, it is also not negligible. The nonproliferation regime could not stem the tide of proliferation that could result from the disintegration of world order.

When the Soviet Union disintegrated, the chaos threatening to overrun Moscow's nuclear assets became a proliferation nightmare. Fortunately, the most urgent "loose nukes" dangers have not materialized. But weak controls over former Soviet nuclear assets remain a wild card in the proliferation deck. The United States and Russia have begun to address the immediate and long-term legacies of the Cold War. The immediate challenges are ensuring control over the arsenal and nuclear material of the former Soviet Union, preventing the diffusion of nuclear materials, technology, and know-how (via "brain drain"), and eliminating outdated Cold War doctrines, infrastructures, and operations. The longer-term challenges involve implementing START I, II, and III, verifying and safeguarding remaining stockpiles, and securing components and materials from retired warheads.

The United States and Russia have been moving from Cold War deterrence to mutual reassurance by reducing alert status, detargeting missiles, and exchanging data on warhead stockpiles. Yet this process of changing doctrines is largely declaratory, symbolic, and reversible. The symbolic role of nuclear doctrine in defining great power relationships did not end with the Cold War. The moves toward expansion of NATO, and US consideration of strategic defenses and scrapping the antiballistic missile (ABM) treaty underscore the lingering uncertainties of American-Russian relations and of the outcome of Russia's democratic experiment. Thus, the challenge remains for Washington and Moscow to adopt measures that facilitate a cooperative relationship while hedging against an uncertain outcome. One such measure would be to remove warheads from missiles as proposed by former Senator Sam Nunn.[19]

Foremost among these problems is safely storing and dismantling retired nuclear weapons and materials, particularly those that the United States and Russia must retire under current agreements and unilateral pledges. Under the Nunn-Lugar Cooperative Threat Reduction programs, the United States had appropriated $2 billion by 1997 to assist Russia and other former Soviet republics in this effort. These programs include assistance to enhance the safety and security of weapons and fissile material during transport to dismantlement and storage sites, START I implementation, fissile material accounting systems, and aid in the design of a storage facility for fissile material.[20] A related program is purchasing some 500 metric tons of highly enriched uranium (HEU) from dismantled Russian (and Ukrainian) weapons over a twenty-year period. Some of the profits from the sale will compensate Ukraine for giving up the weapons on its territory.[21]

Yet proposed congressional action to cut dismantlement aid to Russia could foreclose prospects for cooperative threat reduction programs. The proposed alternative strategy emphasizing maintenance of START I–level nuclear arsenals, NATO expansion, and abandonment of the ABM treaty in favor of early deployment of theater and national missile defenses would dim, if not end, prospects for establishing a new nuclear ethos.[22]

Competing Views of the Proliferation Problem

The proliferation threat transcends the end of the Cold War and may even increase as a multipolar distribution of power replaces the bipolar system. But not everyone agrees on the scope of the proliferation problem. In practice, not all proliferation is viewed equally by all governments—each has its own list of "rogue nations." But the nonproliferation regime is evidence of global consensus opposing any further spread of nuclear weapons. Advocates of a different approach have argued that the stability that marked the superpower deterrence relationship during the Cold War could be duplicated elsewhere by the spread of nuclear weapons. According to this view, proliferation should be embraced or tolerated, but not countered.[23]

The strategy we advocate rejects this positive view of proliferation for the following reasons. First, a complicated global network of deterrence relationships holds many opportunities for failure. While there is some validity to the argument that nuclear deterrence contributed to the absence of direct conflict between the United States and the Soviet Union throughout the "long peace" of the Cold War,[24] the history of American-Soviet nuclear deterrence includes a number of disturbing episodes in which the risk of nuclear war escalated. Recent research on the Cuban missile crisis suggests that officials in Washington and Moscow made decisions based on incorrect information and assumptions that could have had disastrous consequences.[25] Evolving deterrence dyads and triads might encounter similar crises.

The nuclear relationship between India and Pakistan is a case in point. Strategic analysts from India and Pakistan (and a few in the United

States) assert that the existence of undeclared, or "opaque," nuclear capabilities in South Asia creates a stable nuclear deterrent relationship. These analysts think that an overt nuclear arms race between the two countries can be avoided and that military conflicts such as those over the disputed territory of Kashmir do not pose unacceptable risks of nuclear escalation. To the contrary, in their view nuclear capabilities are believed to deter conventional as well as nuclear war. According to this view, nuclear deterrence in South Asia need not follow the American-Soviet model but can evolve to fit the unique circumstances of the region. Low-level, or supposedly "nonweaponized," nuclear deterrence between India and Pakistan is said to already exist without the need for nuclear testing, arms racing, or second-strike capabilities.

James Woolsey, the former Director of Central Intelligence, expressed a different view when he said "the arms race between India and Pakistan poses perhaps the most probable prospect for future use of weapons of mass destruction, including nuclear weapons."[26] This perspective was supported by reports that U.S. intelligence officials concluded during the Kashmir crisis of spring 1990 that India and Pakistan were on the brink of a war that threatened nuclear escalation. Military preparations in both countries supported this assessment. In late 1995 media reports described U.S. intelligence that India was preparing to conduct its first nuclear test since 1974, an event that would have provoked a reaction from Pakistan and elsewhere. In early 1996 India test-fired its nuclear-capable Prithvi missile.[27] Consequently, analysts argue that New Delhi and Islamabad are in the early stages of an arms race, which will eventually lead to new versions of the Cuban missile, Taiwan Straits, Korean, or Berlin crises. Sooner or later, however, leaders may fail to avert disaster.[28]

A second source of instability stems from inherent risks of human miscalculation and accidents associated with very complex technical systems such as nuclear weapons and their associated command and control systems. Here, too, the history of U.S. and Soviet nuclear weapons programs is replete with examples of nuclear accidents.[29] Political instability in nuclear weapon states adds another disturbing variable to the equation—creating the potential for rogue, criminal, or terrorist groups to acquire weapons.

A third reason for concern about nuclear anarchy is that leaders may not be satisfied with deterrence, but may be tempted to seek political leverage from their weapons through veiled threats and not-so-veiled blackmail. After the Second World War, some U.S. diplomats viewed the atomic bomb as a "winning weapon" that could enable them to dictate terms to Russia. Other nations may make similar miscalculations regarding the political-military utility of nuclear diplomacy. North Korea used nuclear blackmail to achieve many long-standing political and military objectives and extracted commitments for free nuclear reactors, free oil, food, and foreign investment to revive its moribund economy. Others may demand an even higher price. What would have been the effect on the UN-sanctioned Gulf War coalition if Saddam Hussein had announced that he possessed nuclear weapons?[30] Uncontrolled proliferation would reshape alliances, erode collective security, and, as Richard Harknett points out in his chapter of this book, limit power projection options.

Some people may acquire nuclear weapons not for prestige and not as a deterrent, but to use them. It is not unthinkable that governments would attempt to advance territorial claims or hegemonic ambitions by wielding and using nuclear weapons. How would the world react to a nuclear attack, especially if it were limited, it ended quickly, and casualties were comparable to other human tragedies? It is possible that one or more small nuclear wars would not represent a dire threat to humanity. Would the fifty-year-old consensus against the use of nuclear weapons endure? At the very least, any breach of the norm of nonuse would call into question the most important constraint on the use of force in international politics. An unacceptable risk of nuclear chaos would result from a combination of widespread conflict and the demise of the nonproliferation norm.

How should the world respond to successful proliferators? One school of thought advocates "managing proliferation" to reduce the risk of nuclear accidents in new nuclear weapons states. Conceptually, this is somewhat analogous to the controversy over providing contraceptives to teenagers: Does it encourage or legitimize undesirable behavior, or is it an appropriate precautionary measure to prevent consequences from unpreventable actions? Is stability enhanced by providing assistance to lessen the risk of accidental launches, breakdowns in command authority, or survivability to avoid a "use-it-or-lose-it" scenario?[31]

This is hardly a hypothetical issue. The 1990 Indian-Pakistani tensions over Kashmir and reports that Israel considered nuclear retaliation if Iraq had used chemical weapons during the Gulf War illustrate that these are real concerns. However, the risk of enhancing the effectiveness of emerging nuclear forces, legitimizing proliferation, and breaching of weapons states' NPT obligations militate against any attempt to manage proliferation. In particular, care must be taken to assure that negotiations for a fissile material cutoff convention do not embrace managed proliferation. Proliferators should not be excused from the consequences of their decisions to defy the nonproliferation norm. Little more than discussions of doctrine, or sharing published writings on the control of nuclear forces, would be advisable forms of assistance to opaque nuclear powers.

A Comprehensive Strategy: The Supply Side

Meeting the diverse proliferation challenges outlined above requires a synthesis of the elements in a three-tier framework: strengthened institutional restraints on the acquisition of nuclear materials and technology; innovative approaches to address demand-side motivations of real or potential proliferators in a proactive, anticipatory manner; and development of counterproliferation capabilities to deter and detect proliferation. For this to occur, nonproliferation issues must not be subordinated to other desired goals less vital to U.S. security.

From such a posture flows, among other things, the rationale for a comprehensive test ban, a ban on the production of fissile material, and post-START arms reductions. These are important policy instruments that can cap the existing nuclear weapons capabilities of declared and opaque weapons states and politically position the international community to reduce existing arsenals. These are also components of an approach that strengthens the nuclear taboo by moving away from discriminatory nonproliferation policies toward more universal norms with the United States leading by example.

Eliminating Cold War baggage is key to laying the basis for more universal norms delegitimizing nuclear weapons. The logic of START I, II, and III is to move the United States and Russia to a minimal deterrence, reassurance-focused nuclear posture, essentially maintaining a survivable deterrent to deter use or threat of use by adversaries.[32] This process is under way, opening the door to deeper reductions leading to negotiations among the five declared nuclear weapons states.

For U.S. defense planners, the so-called Revolution in Military Affairs (RMA)—the technology of microelectronics reconnaissance, surveillance, and pinpoint targeting, of electronic countermeasures, space-based sensors, and precision-guided "smart weapons"—is the future of warfare; nuclear weapons have taken on a secondary role in defense planning.[33] Much of what has been described as counterproliferation might be more accurately called military modernization. The RMA and the way it is projected to shape force modernization investments make a strategy of credible conventional deterrence possible. For example, innovative air- and sea-based missile firing platforms will make it possible to project devastating military force against WMD targets with precision and lower risk for U.S. soldiers and noncombatants.

Strengthening Norms and Institutions: The IAEA and the United Nations

Ideally, the 1995 NPT review conference should have provided a good occasion for a soul-searching examination of the new post–Cold War possibilities and of the shortcomings in the nonproliferation system. It is, nevertheless, not too late to strengthen the verification and enforcement mechanisms that give credibility to nonproliferation commitments. The IAEA's 93 + 2 program is a good start but will not achieve its potential if leading non-nuclear states such as Germany and Japan do not support it and it is not adequately funded. The decade-old freeze on the agency's budget and the chronic failure of members, including the United States, to pay their dues on time undermine efforts to strengthen the IAEA. Its annual budget of just over $200 million—only about $65 million of which supports safeguards—hardly compares with the cost of building and using military forces to combat proliferation.

More could be done to expand the IAEA's inspection capability. The combination of intelligence information to locate problems, technology to detect undeclared activity, and assertion of access rights will raise confidence that NPT commitments are being kept. If IAEA discovers problems—either refusal to allow inspections or evidence of undeclared activity—its only recourse is to report to the UN Security Council. Thus, enhancing the Security Council role in enforcing nonproliferation could give needed credibility to a new nonproliferation strategy.

The Security Council should devote resources and political support to promote nonproliferation norms. UNSCOM or a similar group should become a permanent arm of the Security Council. The Security Council also should assure there would be military retaliation against WMD use.[34] The Security Council should go beyond its January 1992 communiqué declaring proliferation a threat to international peace and security by issuing even stronger statements regarding international responses to WMD use. The security assurances issued in connection with NPT extension (which provide assurance of retaliation) lend credibility to the nonuse norm: if a proliferator successfully blackmails or uses nuclear weapons without decisive retaliation, then the entire regime could unravel. Finally, international financial institutions such as the World Bank and the International Monetary Fund should, at a minimum, factor in a country's nonproliferation credentials as part of the criteria in determining aid packages. The Security Council and its nonproliferation agency could be instrumental in determining nonproliferation bona fides.

Nuclear testing has been a long-standing grievance of non–weapons states and a symbol of the superpower arms race. The linkage to proliferation is mainly symbolic; countries such as India, Pakistan, Israel, North Korea, and Iraq did not develop nuclear weapons because the superpowers were testing; they did so based on their own security calculations or ambitions. Other determined proliferators might do so for the same reasons—with or without testing.

A CTBT will not end proliferation. Nevertheless, the symbolic value of a CTBT can be translated into strategic gains. With the reversal of the superpower arms race, and no need for exotic new warheads, the balance of arguments for and against a test ban shifted. While it is possible to develop nuclear weapons capability without testing, a CTBT will make it more difficult, particularly for the development of thermonuclear weapons.[35] A CTBT is a restraint viewed by many non–weapons states as a collateral NPT obligation of weapons states, which reduces the discriminatory character of the NPT. In 1995, the linkage between nonproliferation and a CTBT became unavoidable when many NPT members threatened to hold extension of the NPT hostage until a CTBT came into force. The nuclear weapons states agreed to complete a CTBT by 1996 with the understanding that failure to meet this goal could endanger the future of the NPT.[36] Not withstanding last-minute efforts by India to block the treaty, the text approved by the UN General Assembly in September 1996 fulfilled the NPT bargain.[37] For the nuclear weapons states, the CTBT will freeze certain technological advancements, but it will allow stewardship programs involving advanced simulation to assure the safety and reliability of enduring stockpiles.

A Real Fissile Material Cutoff

A cutoff of fissile material (highly enriched uranium and plutonium) production for weapons and the gradual establishment of an international antiplutonium regime could be another major component of a comprehensive strategy. President Clinton proposed a cutoff convention in 1993; negotiations on the first part—ending production for weapons—began in 1995. The second part—ending civil production of plutonium—remains controversial. Yet the distinction is artificial; both initiatives are needed to maximize a fissile material cutoff's contribution to a new nuclear strategy.

The United States stopped producing fissile material for weapons in 1988; Russia has pledged to do so by the year 2000 but will not achieve that goal without massive assistance. President Bush formally declared a unilateral cutoff in July 1992. President Clinton took the logical next step in his September 27, 1993, initiative: proposing a ban on the production of nuclear weapons material, a move aimed at the five weapons states plus

India, Israel, and Pakistan. The Clinton administration has also agreed to submit U.S. fissile material no longer needed for weapons purposes to IAEA inspection, something from which weapons states are exempt under the NPT.

To achieve a universal military fissile material cutoff, the United States should first negotiate with Russia to accelerate its timetable for a production cutoff, declare inventories of their respective stockpiles, negotiate reciprocal monitoring of warhead dismantling, and place a significant quantity of plutonium from dismantled U.S. and Russian warheads under IAEA control. Under its statute, the IAEA has the authority to take custody of excess, safeguarded fissile material.[38]

This U.S. and Russian precedent could lay the foundation for a multilateral convention prohibiting the production of fissile material for military uses that has been proposed by the Clinton administration. A willingness by the United States and Russia to yield surpluses from dismantled warheads to IAEA inspection and control would deprive threshold states of the argument that the regime is discriminatory.

Opaque capabilities, however, present a vexing problem for the cutoff proposal. On the one hand, a universal cutoff could cap production to prevent existing stockpiles (of weapons and/or materials) from growing. On the other hand, any treaty that legitimizes the possession of undeclared stockpiles would undermine the norm of nonproliferation by conferring a "junior weapons state" status on the threshold states. This may make it even more difficult to eliminate those programs and might even spur weapons development in neighboring states. Moreover, the problems associated with verifying undeclared stockpiles are daunting.[39] The extent to which these problems can be surmounted will determine the value of a fissile material cutoff.

Solving the second part of the cutoff problem—civil plutonium—also weighs heavily on its value for proliferation. The most difficult obstacle for a potential proliferator is how to acquire or produce sufficient weapons-grade HEU or plutonium. The assertion that reactor-grade plutonium cannot be used for weapons has been disproved.[40] Yet under the NPT, the possession and peaceful use of plutonium is permitted under safeguards—though it is highly doubtful that timely warning of a diversion can be guaranteed.[41] Thus, plutonium use (and the economics of reprocessing) inevitably leads to suspicions that non–weapons states are harboring nuclear options.

At the end of 1996, there were approximately 1,000 metric tons of plutonium globally. About 650 tons were produced by civilian reactors. Roughly 120 tons of that were separated from spent fuel and exist in weapons-usable form or in a form that can be used as fuel for nuclear reactors; the remainder is contained in unprocessed spent fuel. Some 260 tons of plutonium exist in deployed or surplus/dismantled nuclear weapons.[42] Plutonium in spent fuel might increase by some 300 percent by the end of this decade, to almost 1,400 metric tons. About 300 metric tons of plutonium in spent fuel produced in civilian reactors will have been separated by then too, if reprocessing plants in Europe and Japan are built and operated as planned.[43] The plutonium separated from spent fuel in civilian reactors could be enough to produce 47,000 bombs by 2003.[44]

A burgeoning surplus of civilian plutonium results from market realities that have overtaken plans and investments that were made in the energy-crisis-riven 1970s to develop plutonium-burning reactors, which create new plutonium as a result of the fission process. Plutonium "recycling" was viewed as a way for oil-dependent countries to create their own independent energy source. Breeder reactors would breed new plutonium, which would be extracted through reprocessing and made into new fuel. Plutonium also can be mixed with conventional reactor fuel as well to make a fuel known as mixed oxide, or MOX. But experimental breeder reactor programs have been plagued with problems. Utilities in Europe and Japan have balked at the price of a plutonium-based nuclear fuel cycle. German utilities have canceled contracts with British and French firms to recycle plutonium from German reactors. In the aftermath of the December 1995 accident and cover-up scandal at Japan's Monju breeder reactor, a fire at the Fugen experimental reactor, and the explosion and cover-up at the Tokai-Mura spent fuel facility in 1997, Japan's breeder program is under major reassessment and may be canceled.[45] Such a move would create a new situation in the global fuel cycle business, eroding the bureaucratic inertia impeding moves to end commercial use of plutonium.

Given the political and economic realities of the energy market, it is possible to vastly increase the nonproliferation benefits of a fissile material cutoff by including civil plutonium. A maximum fissile material cutoff could be achieved in a phased manner and could link the military and civil plutonium problems.

If the future of commercial plutonium use looks bleak, burning excess military plutonium in existing reactors is an option for disposing of excess plutonium from dismantled Russian and U.S. nuclear warheads.[46] While there is little support for a grand plutonium disposal scheme, a creative solution might link the problem of civilian plutonium with the need to dispose of excess military plutonium. One proposal under consideration is to alleviate the demand for civil plutonium production by substituting excess military plutonium, which could be burned as MOX in countries such as Japan that insist on using plutonium as an energy resource. The quid pro quo for supporting use of imported MOX containing excess weapons plutonium would be no further production of civil plutonium.

Under the best of circumstances, achieving an international regime to control plutonium would be a difficult and protracted process.[47] Achieving IAEA custodianship of excess stockpiles could start on a regional basis, accompanied by a formal cutoff of military production. Storage could be regionally based, with Britain, France, Russia, the United States, and China (for Asian states, this could be part of a Pacific Atomic Cooperation Association [PACATOM]) offering storage. Defining what is "excess" and establishing criteria for releasing plutonium to nations for R&D purposes would be a difficult challenge. One important positive incentive for adherence to a plutonium regime would be the globalization of the problem of ultimate disposal of excess plutonium.

Given the costs being borne by the United States to eliminate Cold War baggage, the goal of establishing international management of plutonium should be viewed as a form of burden sharing by Europe and Japan. The complexity and history of the issue suggests heavy-handed American diplomacy would be inappropriate and counterproductive. But giving priority to an active dialogue with U.S. allies about the problem of excess plutonium would be a good start toward ending commercial plutonium use.

Post-START Reductions: The Permanent Five's Role

If there is continued devolution of post–Cold War postures toward a minimum deterrence strategy, the 2,000–2,500 weapons each agreed to under START III become an arbitrary floor. At the same time, in a multipolar world of nuclear powers, let alone a turbulent one, fewer U.S. and Russian nuclear weapons do not necessarily enhance security or stability. The chapters in this volume by James Wirtz and George Quester illustrate the problems associated with multilateral and minimal nuclear deterrence. Nevertheless, changes in U.S. and Russian alert status, targeting, and operations, along with proper management of fissile material from dismantled weapons, are more important to stability in the short term than any further reductions. Moreover, the enormity of just implementing current agreements is pushing the bureaucratic, financial, and technical apparatus of both the United States and Russia to the limit. Nevertheless, U.S.-Russian statements of intent to pursue further reductions are a low-cost way to de-emphasize the role of nuclear weapons and to start linking future arms control to the actions of other declared and, eventually, opaque nuclear powers.[48]

Given the dramatic size of U.S. and Russian reductions and the reality that other declared (and opaque) nuclear powers have not reduced their arsenals comparably, the proper venue for future arms reduction efforts should be the Permanent Five (P-5) in the UN Security Council. The United States and Russia have taken the lead by declaring their willingness to make further cuts beyond START II. After START III, the next round of cuts could offer further reductions in U.S. and Russian arsenals, contingent on proportionate cuts by Britain, France, and China, each of whom has some 400 to 600 weapons. This could initiate a new arms reduction process to begin such cuts by 2010, which would also serve to reinforce the NPT bargain. Reductions in China's arsenal could have an enabling impact on the South Asian strategic equation and breathe life into the stillborn five-power (United States, Russia, China, India, Pakistan) talks proposed by the Bush and Clinton administrations. Conversely, regional proliferation scenarios could inhibit further reductions. India's posture or an East Asian arms race would affect Chinese, Russian, and American views of the nuclear balance. In addition, U.S. deployment of strategic missile defense systems beyond those permitted under the ABM treaty would likely end the possibility of reductions in the arsenals of declared nuclear powers. In such a case, missile defense could lead to vertical proliferation as China tried to avoid the neutralization of its deterrent.[49]

Nonetheless, this overview hints at the shape of a new nuclear bargain. One side of such a bargain would be the willingness of the declared nuclear powers to make significant reductions, perhaps even down to the level of 100 to 200 or fewer weapons, coupled with the retention of a substantial "virtual arsenal"—the capability to rebuild arsenals close to post-START levels within an anticipated warning time. The goal of a postnuclear world by no later than the end of the first nuclear century, in 2045, might be the declared objective.

New Doctrines: No First Use, Negative and Positive Security Assurances

Declaratory policy is a vital component of nuclear strategy. New U.S. doctrines are needed to guide the delegitimization strategy, which will shape nonproliferation diplomacy. Doctrinal change is most needed in three areas: the first-use posture, negative security assurances, and positive security assurances.

During the Cold War, many believed that extended deterrence required the threat of nuclear first use against a massive conventional Warsaw Pact attack. This threat no longer exists. President Bush's 1991 withdrawal of theater nuclear weapons worldwide further eroded the first-use rationale that might apply to South Korea. Before adopting a commitment to no first use, the United States would have to consult with NATO, South Korea, and Japan. Adopting a no-first-use pledge could be done jointly by the United States and Russia.[50] The two nuclear superpowers should then call for a uniform pledge from the P-5 of no first use against nations that adhere to the NPT. This would strengthen the norm of nonuse and reinforce negative security assurances issued in 1995 by the nuclear weapons states during the NPT conference. China has a longstanding, unqualified no-first-use pledge that could be reaffirmed in this context. Given the U.S. extended deterrence commitment to Japan and Korea, including China in an unqualified P-5 no-first-pledge has particular importance.

The positive and negative security assurances issued by the weapons states during the NPT extension conference illustrate the value of such symbolic measures.[51] As part of the nonproliferation bargain, when the NPT was to be opened for signature in 1968, the United States, the USSR, and Britain declared to the UN Security Council their intention "to provide assistance, in accord with the [UN] Charter, to any non-nuclear-weapon state party to the NPT that is a victim of an act of aggression or an object of a threat of aggression in which nuclear weapons are used." In Resolution 255, the Security Council endorsed this statement (also in 1968). The new assurances issued in 1995 are viewed by non–weapons states as good-faith efforts to recognize their concerns about the unfairness of the NPT.

The effectiveness of U.S. and multilateral security guarantees and enforcement efforts will be important factors in managing the demand side of regional proliferation and in reducing the likelihood of nuclear wars or threats. In East Asia, for example, credible U.S. treaty commitments with Japan and South Korea have contributed to regional stability and reduced ally incentives to acquire nuclear weapons. Washington's unique leverage over South Korea and Taiwan resulted in both nations' abandoning nuclear programs in the 1970s. In some cases, bilateral security guarantees remain the decisive factor in preventing or rolling back proliferation.

Export Control Regimes

In the quarter century since the NPT was negotiated, the industrial bases, and hence export capabilities, of a number of Third World nations have expanded. Many of these states also harbor resentment toward the discriminatory character of various international regimes. China, for example, is asked to adhere to MTCR guidelines, though it has no say in shaping the regime. Bringing emerging suppliers, particularly China and India, into the Nuclear Suppliers Group and the MTCR would help bridge North-South disputes over these mechanisms.

Despite the recent positive developments in strengthening multilateral regimes, a different trend in export controls threatens to undermine the post-Iraq efforts to strengthen barriers to proliferation. Economic pressures create tension between nonproliferation policy and export promotion activities. The tension is acute for dual-use high-technology such as computer and telecommunication equipment. Many governments, including the United States, increasingly view the global economic competitiveness of companies as a security issue. Thus, controls that hinder exports are viewed as detrimental to national economies. Many controls have been relaxed or eliminated. One international export control organization, COCOM, was disbanded in 1993 and was replaced by an informal group that possesses little or no authority. If the lessons of Iraq are ignored and the pressure to export prevails, then proliferators will find it easier to buy the materials they need to build WMD. In turn, this will exacerbate the proliferation threat and provide justification for military countermeasures.

Counterproliferation: The Military Dimension

Counterproliferation is a relatively new term in the nonproliferation lexicon. Early in the Clinton administration, it evoked considerable controversy and raised questions about the distinction between diplomatic and military responses to WMD development. Did counterproliferation include diplomacy, enhanced intelligence, managed proliferation, cooperative threat reduction, missile defense, exotic new weapons? And what was the role of nuclear weapons?

Many countries initially viewed counterproliferation as a unilateral U.S. threat to conduct preemptive strikes against potential WMD targets.[52] Initially inside American bureaucracies, turf wars broke out over control of counter- and nonproliferation policy and budgets, but the scope of counterproliferation is coming into focus. High on the list of priorities are advanced conventional weapons capable of defeating WMD on the battlefield, improved chemical and biological defenses, enhanced intelligence and detection capabilities, and development of theater ballistic missile defenses.[53] As mentioned earlier, these capabilities and advances in sensor technology, electronic countermeasures, and target penetration are all part of the RMA, which is occurring irrespective of counterproliferation policy.

Several pitfalls for counterproliferation have also come into focus. Iraq and North Korea both illustrate the many political and technical difficulties of using force against WMD targets. And there is the danger of a Catch-22: preemption as a norm legitimizes the very proliferation it seeks to eliminate. In addition, it is important that the energy and resources devoted to counterproliferation do not divert efforts from the rest of the nonproliferation agenda outlined herein. It is far less costly to prevent proliferation than to mount a military campaign to reverse it.

Missile Technology Control Regime

The spread of missiles underscores Bernard Brodie's predictions about WMD proliferation; the fear of a "bolt from the blue" is the primary driver of arms races around the world. While the dream of a defensive shield may someday come true, controlling missile proliferation still directly benefits U.S. and international security. Thus, the Missile Technology Control Regime, while flawed, remains a valuable contributor to a comprehensive strategy. Its twenty-seven members can slow the spread of missiles capable of carrying WMD payloads to the extent that they follow the regime's guidelines.

Despite the MTCR's contribution to nonproliferation, the most troubling missile developments often occur beyond the reach of the MTCR. The MTCR has not stopped indigenous missile development, such as North Korea's No-dong and Taepo-dong 1 and 2 missiles, and India's Prithvi and Agni missiles, nor has it prevented illicit transfers such as China's sales of the M-11 to Pakistan and cruise missiles to Iran. Nevertheless, the MTCR has established a beachhead for a global missile nonproliferation norm.

Missile technology is even more difficult to control than nuclear technology. This reality points to the limits of the MTCR's effectiveness and durability. There are, however, several ways to strengthen the missile control regime. Even within its current parameters, the MTCR could be made more effective. The MTCR could establish more formal export guidelines and a process for coordinating export licensing, perhaps adopting a "prenotification" rule that would require adherents to advise each other of pending export licenses to provide opportunities for consultation. In addition, requiring exporters to report sales of dual-use technologies legal under the MTCR within ninety days will help create a database. Such an initiative could be the part of a broader institutionalization centered on the formation of a permanent secretariat.[54]

If the West is serious about curbing missiles, the best hope for an effective and durable approach may lie in recasting the MTCR as an NPT-like bargain. One can envision broader adherence to a missile regime that called for nations to forgo missile capability in exchange for demand-side benefits. Such benefits would include security guarantees to those threatened by missiles, assured access to space launches at subsidized rates for smaller countries (or through creation of an international space-launch agency), or sharing benefits from commercial use of outer space, as envisioned in the 1967 Outer Space Treaty. While such a "missiles for peace" bargain would have some of the liabilities of the NPT's nuclear bargain, the net effect could weed out all but the most determined missile proliferators.

A Comprehensive Strategy: The Demand Side

Establishing global norms of behavior and curbing the diffusion of nuclear technology are important for setting standards, raising costs of proliferation, and buying time for further nonproliferation efforts. In particular, new global measures such as a test ban treaty, a cutoff of fissile material production, and bolstered security guarantees can have a significant impact on regional security dynamics. But the toughest proliferation problems are the result of regional conflicts that drive proliferants to acquire nuclear weapons to enhance their security or status. Thus, regional efforts tailored to meet the security concerns fueling conflict are ultimately the most effective bulwark against proliferation. Indeed, some global norms may be best achieved by building from the regional level up.

East Asia

In East Asia, where the interests of the United States, Japan, China, and Russia are joined, a regional security agenda can interact with the goal of global nonproliferation. Two major regional issues, North Korea's nuclear program and Japan's plans for commercial use of plutonium, are factors in regional proliferation motivations. How these issues are addressed will define international norms and shape East Asia's security environment.

Managing the transition to a reunified Korea is the most urgent security issue in Northeast Asia. No one wants a nuclear Korea, and everyone would like to see a gradual reunification process between South and North Korea. Implementing the October 21,1994, U.S.-North Korea agreement to replace Pyongyang's nuclear program with modern energy-producing reactors and other blandishments has become the leading edge of multilateral efforts to lure North Korea into the mainstream of international relations. The agreement could also work as a wedge to open North Korea. North Korea views foreign investment, aid, and trade as vital to regime survival but has proceeded only tentatively with economic reform and opening, fearful that an opening could undermine its political control. Common interest in facilitating such a process on the part of all surrounding powers may not persuade Pyongyang to make a full leap of faith. However, with such a confluence of interests, the Korean problem can serve as a catalyst for building a framework of political/security cooperation in East Asia.[55] If a denuclearized peninsula becomes a reality, the United States, Russia, and China could provide more specific security assurances.

Japan's plutonium reprocessing program, with its transporting and stockpiling of plutonium, has set off alarm bells across Asia, accentuating fears that a Korean bomb would beget a Japanese bomb. This reprocessing plan is of questionable economic rationale and increasingly faces criticism from Japan's electrical producers, politicians, and the public as well as from abroad.

South Korea is already dependent on nuclear power, and a reunified Korea might have an interest in reprocessing. Japan could alleviate regional anxieties and demonstrate global leadership on nonproliferation, which it claims as a top foreign policy priority, by pursuing a more economically rational course that sustains its energy security by building a fifty-year uranium stockpile in lieu of plutonium.[56]

Regional nuclear cooperation could be conducted under the auspices of an organization modeled after EURATOM, Europe's nuclear cooperation agency. An Asia-Pacific nuclear agency, or PACATOM, could oversee the nuclear fuel cycle to assure there are adequate safeguards over sensitive activities such as spent fuel storage, fuel fabrication, and enrichment. PACATOM might eventually develop a regional power grid that could help integrate North Korea and other developing countries into the Asian economy. Initially, it would involve China, Japan, Russia, the United States, and the two Koreas, though it would be inclusive and explicitly open to others in the region as they attain civil nuclear power. One possibility is for PACATOM to oversee a plan to burn excess plutonium (civil and military) in civilian reactors throughout the region.[57] Like EURATOM, PACATOM would augment, not replace, IAEA safeguards.

Any plan to substitute excess plutonium for new stocks would require Japan to renegotiate its British and French reprocessing contracts. Appropriate cancellation fees would help compensate for sunk costs. Reprocessing Japanese spent fuel constitutes roughly one-third of the business of British and French reprocessing facilities. However, such a change in Japanese plans would facilitate a rethinking of European commercial use of plutonium and could initiate progress toward eliminating commerce in weapons materials.

The acid test of U.S. nonproliferation policy is China. This is part of a much larger challenge: accepting China's emergence as a major global power and, conversely, China's acceptance of international norms. On virtually every aspect of the strategy outlined here—post-START reductions, a test ban treaty, fissile material cutoff, missile exports, Korea, South Asia, and Iran—China is the key factor. Without Chinese cooperation, realizing U.S. nonproliferation objectives is not possible. Yet this considerable strategic agenda is often treated as just another box to check on the laundry list of issues plaguing U.S.-China relations, from rhinoceros-horn imports and prison-labor exports to human rights in Tibet.

U.S. and Chinese interests may not necessarily diverge completely. But the volatility of the overall bilateral relationship has limited useful dialogue on strategic nuclear issues. Can U.S. trade and human rights concerns be tempered sufficiently to prevent a hothouse atmosphere from spilling over into the Sino-American strategic agenda? Such are the difficult trade-offs that may be involved in giving proliferation actual policy priority. China may prove to be an adversary of the United States and a revolutionary power rather than a quirky outlier moving, however erratically, toward global norms. But the consequences of such a determination are so grave that such a conclusion should be arrived at only after the exhaustion of patient diplomacy.

The Middle East

Nuclear weapons strongly influence the balance of power in the Middle East. The nuclear programs of Israel, Iran, Iraq, and Pakistan are defining features of the strategic landscape. Nuclear developments in Algeria, Libya and elsewhere also have the potential to spur further proliferation. Nevertheless, negotiations on the establishment of a WMD-free zone might eventually lead to a regional nonproliferation regime.

Israel remains an undeclared nuclear power with a substantial arsenal—perhaps 100 or more weapons—advanced fission or thermonuclear weapons, and growing missile capabilities. While Israeli nuclear logic is not difficult to comprehend in the context of Jewish history, Israel's nuclear weapons complicate the strategic calculus of the region. The security derived from such weapons might not endure if other countries in the region also acquired nuclear capabilities. The prospect of multiple nuclear deterrence relationships criss-crossing the Middle East holds little appeal for most strategic planners, particularly if such relationships depend on unstable or aggressive governments. Thus, Israel is faced with a choice: try to extend for as long as possible its position as the only nuclear-armed state in the region, or engage in arms control to stave off the emergence of new nuclear weapons states in the region.

Israel has, so far, managed to proceed on both tracks. As a major beneficiary of the global nonproliferation regime, Israel supports efforts to strengthen the NPT's norms and institutions. Unlike India, it did not oppose extension of the NPT and has expressed interest in joining eventually. Similarly, Israel also signed the CTBT in 1996. Moreover, it supports establishment of a verified Middle East Nuclear-Weapons-Free Zone Treaty—but only after it has implemented reliable peace settlements with its neighbors, and only if such a zone also banned chemical and biological weapons.

The prospects for nonproliferation in the Middle East are not hopeless. Israeli, U.S., and Arab officials have held detailed discussions on the requirements for establishing a WMD-free zone. As part of the Madrid peace process, an arms control working group studied a phased approach to ridding the region of WMD. The early stages of arms control could begin with symbolic and tentative confidence-building measures such as joint verification demonstration projects and reciprocal visits to sensitive facilities. Israel might make a virtue of a necessity by shutting down its aging Dimona reactor. These steps would dovetail with Israel's participation in a fissile materials cutoff convention.

Despite these promising developments, nuclear and other WMD capabilities in Iran, Iraq, Pakistan, and elsewhere constrain the prospects for arms control in the region and reinforce Israel's rationale for keeping counterproliferation options open. If Iraq's nuclear aspirations have been derailed, Iran has emerged as a major proliferation concern. Russian and Chinese nuclear sales to Tehran do not violate the NPT but undermine international efforts to prevent Iran from acquiring a nuclear infrastructure that would give it the technical basis for a nuclear option. Beyond laying the groundwork for a nuclear option, there are signs that Iran may try to exploit its nuclear relationship with Russia to acquire bomb materials not included in the contract.[58]

The Middle East calculus is also complicated by continuing, albeit low-level, interest in nuclear and other WMD capabilities by Libya, instability in Algeria, Pakistan's nuclear capabilities, questions about the intentions of Syria,[59] and chemical and biological programs throughout the region. For the near term, the fate of nonproliferation in the Middle East is tied to the peace process. The first steps toward a WMD-free zone will be tentative.

South Asia

There is little chance that U.S. policy can achieve a nonproliferation victory in South Asia, at least in the near future. Past efforts to jump-start arms control talks between India and Pakistan have failed. However, U.S. policy toward South Asia could still have consequences for nonproliferation norms and regimes. Should Washington accept and accommodate proliferation in South Asia, or continue to oppose it? South Asia presents the United States with a choice of whether to make nonproliferation a priority or to subordinate it to other interests.

Some have called for a new approach to the region. But ending nonproliferation sanctions to provide military and other assistance to New Delhi and Islamabad is not likely to lead to changes in either country's nuclear or missile programs. It is not clear that efforts to lift the Pressler amendment restrictions on aid to Pakistan or offering peaceful nuclear cooperation to assist India's unsafe reactors will produce benefits.[60] India's unrelenting opposition to the CTBT confirmed its mindset and raises questions about its reliability as a partner in a redefined nuclear order.

Conclusion: The "Pogo Factor"

"We have met the enemy and he is us," proclaimed the comic-strip sage Pogo. Clearly, there are limits to what any policy can achieve: there is no silver bullet that will resolve the complex set of issues under the rubric of nonproliferation. Just as it took the winding down of the Cold War to attain radical reductions in superpower nuclear arsenals, so long as fundamental regional security concerns are not addressed, so long as basic interests are not engaged, regimes and institutions will be imperfect instruments for halting the spread of weapons of mass destruction. While there is broad agreement that nonproliferation should now be at the top of the national security agenda, implementation of a new strategy may require organizational change.

The challenge to U.S. policy is to fashion a strategy to delegitimize nuclear weapons that follows the new logic of post–Cold War security dynamics and capitalizes on the possibilities opened by emerging strategic realities. Establishing new norms in concert with proactive diplomacy to resolve regional conflicts, meshing supply-side restraints and demand-side motivations, offer the best prospect of reversing proliferation. A fundamental question is: How important is nonproliferation, and what price is the United States prepared to pay to realize this objective? Is it prepared, for example, to put nonproliferation above other goals such as exports and human rights? And are key allies—the European Union and Japan—prepared to accord nonproliferation such priority?

In his September 27, 1993, UN General Assembly speech, President Clinton spoke of his intention "to weave non-proliferation more deeply into the fabric of all of our relationships with the world's nations and institutions." If nonproliferation is to actually receive this priority, it will require American leadership, a well-conceived strategy, and emphasis throughout U.S. foreign policy decisions. Nonproliferation goals must be reflected in the hierarchy of commercial trade, technology transfer, and country and regional policy choices and trade-offs.

The nonproliferation policy followed since the end of the Cold War takes small steps, generally in the right direction, but has lacked bold vision and consistent high-level attention. The disparate parts of a latent strategy are managed by numerous agencies and departments, overseen by too many congressional committees. In 1947, Congress passed the National Security Act to organize the government to cope with the challenges of the postwar world. Among other things, the law established the Central Intelligence Agency and the Air Force. If proliferation is the top threat to U.S. and world security, perhaps the time has come for an overhaul of the national security bureaucracy to focus American resources on the most urgent post–Cold War threats. Such a reorganization would greatly assist the implementation of the comprehensive nonproliferation strategy we advocate.

Bernard Brodie and his colleagues wrote *The Absolute Weapon* before the post–Second World War international order had taken shape. The book was nearly as speculative as it was timely. The fact that so much of the speculation has stood the test of time reflects favorably on the authors' understanding of international politics. We believe the fundamental assumptions that guided much of their thought hold true today. In that spirit, the strategy outlined here would concentrate diplomatic, military, and economic power to contain and eventually roll back proliferation. The strategy accepts the inherent limitations of international norms, treaties, and institutions where security may be at stake, but it is not dismissive of their utility—particularly where they reinforce the interests of the great powers. Such is the case with nonproliferation in the wake of the Cold War.

Forging an effective nonproliferation policy is emblematic of the need to build a post–Cold War international system that reflects the interests of a disparate group of states. Institutions are only as effective as the commitment of their participants; they do not function as self-sustaining mechanisms without leadership, nor do they eradicate ambitions or fears. In 1946, ambitions and fears severely limited the United Nations and doomed the Baruch Plan for international control of atomic energy. While the fundamental tenets of international security remain largely intact after the Cold War, we believe the new circumstances would not necessarily doom policies that internationalize certain aspects of the nonproliferation process. It may, unfortunately, be the case that only after the next use of weapons of mass destruction will the international community attain sufficient political will to pursue a nonproliferation agenda along the lines of that we have outlined.

Nonetheless, leadership—whether on regional security, human rights, or nonproliferation issues—depends on vision. The lowest common denominator of agreement among nations is an unreliable guide to peace and security. It is, therefore, necessary to offer a grand strategy for nuclear weapons as part of a broader vision of international security. Whether the political will exists to provide the leadership required remains to be seen.

NOTES

1. See Samuel P. Huntington, "The Clash of Civilizations," *Foreign Affairs* 72 (Summer 1993): 22–49, for the case for an emerging North-South confrontation as the post–Cold War paradigm.

2. General Andrew Goodpaster and General Lee Butler, *Joint Statement on Reduction of Nuclear Weapons Arsenals: Declining Utility, Continuing Risks* (Washington, D.C.: Stimson Center, December 1996). Other nuclear reduction proposals can be found at <http://www.stimson.org>

3. The Acheson-Lilienthal commission was appointed by President Truman to study and recommend how to deal with atomic fission, based on the realization that scientific knowledge would be diffused. The Baruch Plan was a U.S. initiative to place atomic energy under international control based on the Acheson-Lilienthal report's recommendations. The plan was vetoed by the USSR.

4. See "Memorandum by the Counselor," *Foreign Relations of the United States* 1 (1950): 22–44.

5. See "Fact Sheet: Clinton Policy on Arms Control and Non-proliferation," *The White House* (4 October 1996).

6. R. Jeffrey Smith, "Clinton Decides to Retain Bush Nuclear Arms Policy," *Washington Post* (22 September 1994): A1; William J. Perry, Secretary of Defense, "Nuclear Posture Review," in *Annual Report to the President and the Congress* (February 1995), 83.

7. Les Aspin, "From Deterrence to Denuking," in *Shaping Nuclear Policy in the 1990s: A Compendium of Views* (House Armed Services Committee, 1992). Aspin's paper is one of the most thoughtful government attempts to identify a post–Cold War logic and strategic agenda.

8. General Charles A. Horner, former head of the U.S. Space Command, said in July 1994, "The nuclear weapon is obsolete. I want to get rid of them all." *Boston Globe* (16 July 1994): 2. Others holding this view include Paul Nitze and Andrew Goodpaster, who both contributed to a report titled, *An Evolving US Nuclear Posture* (Washington, D.C.: Henry L. Stimson Center, December 1995).

9. On the status of verification, see Richard Davis et al., *Arms Control Verification: Looking Back and Looking Ahead,* report for the U.S. Department of

Energy by Science Applications International Corporation, June 1993; Patricia McFate, Sidney Graybeal, George Lindsey, and D. Marc Kilgour, *Constraining Proliferation: The Contribution of Verification Synergies*, report for the Canadian Department of External Affairs, Arms Control Division, March 1993.

10. On the debate over definitions of regimes for nonproliferation policy, see Zachary Davis, "The Realist Nuclear Regime," *Security Studies* 2 (Spring/Summer 1993): 79–100.

11. On the politics of NPT extension, see Lewis Dunn, "High Noon for the NPT," *Arms Control Today* 25 (July/August 1995): 3–9; and Mark Hibbs, "Outlook on the NPT, Special Report to the Readers of *Nucleonics Week, Inside NRC, and Nuclear Fuel*" (29 June 1995).

12. United Nations Security Council Resolution 984, Security Assurances, and unilateral security assurances issued by the five weapons states, reproduced in "Programme for Promoting Nuclear Non-proliferation," *Newsbrief* 30 (2d Quarter 1995).

13. Hans Blix, Director General, IAEA, *Statement to the Review and Extension Conference of the NPT* (17 April 1995).

14. Richard Hooper, "Strengthening IAEA Safeguards in an Era of Nuclear Cooperation," *Arms Control Today* 25 (November 1995): 14–18; Christopher Wren, "Making It Easier to Uncover Nuclear Arms," *New York Times* (16 June 1995): 6.

15. On why countries give up nuclear options, see Mitchell Reiss, *Bridled Ambition: Why Countries Constrain Their Nuclear Capabilities* (Washington, D.C.: Woodrow Wilson Center/Johns Hopkins University Press, 1995).

16. Examples of worst-case predictions for future world order include Benjamin Frankel, "The Brooding Shadow: Systemic Incentives and Nuclear Weapons Proliferation," in Zachary S. Davis and Benjamin Frankel, *The Proliferation Puzzle: Why Nuclear Weapons Spread and What Results* (London: Frank Cass, 1994): 37–79; and John Mearsheimer, "Back to the Future: Instability in Europe after the Cold War," *International Security* 15 (Summer 1990): 5–56.

17. Cited in Aspin, "From Deterrence to Denuking."

18. The concept of virtual proliferation is developed by Roger Molander and Peter Wilson in *The Nuclear Asymptote: On Containing Nuclear Proliferation* (Santa Monica, Calif.: RAND, 1993). Virtual proliferation creates the technical means to produce nuclear weapons following a political decision to do so, enabling countries to keep nuclear options open without violating nonproliferation commitments. Sweden and Japan are often cited as having such virtual capabilities.

19. Sam Nunn and Bruce Blair, "From Nuclear Deterrence to Nuclear Safety," *Washington Post* (22 June 1997).

20. *Cooperative Threat Reduction* (Department of Defense, Office of Assistant Secretary of Defense for Policy, May 1995).

21. Under the Tripartite Statement of 1993, proceeds from Russian HEU sales to the United States will be used to compensate Ukraine for the value of HEU contained in warheads removed from its territory. Most of the compensation will be in the form of fuel rods for Ukrainian reactors.

22. John Isaacs, "Right Says Arms Control Wrong," *Bulletin of the Atomic Sci-*

entists 51 (September/October 1995): 18–19. The components of an alternative strategy restricting aid to the former Soviet Union and emphasizing missile defenses were contained in the House and Senate defense authorization bills for FY 1996. On Congress and nuclear assistance to Russia, see Jason Ellis, "Nunn-Lugar's Mid-life Crisis," *Survival* 39 (Spring 1997): 84–111.

23. See chapters by Waltz in Scott Sagan and Kenneth Waltz, *The Spread of Nuclear Weapons: A Debate* (New York: W. W. Norton, 1995). The classic example is Kenneth Waltz, *The Spread of Nuclear Weapons: More May Be Better*, Adelphi Paper no. 171 (London: International Institute for Strategic Studies, 1981).

24. John Lewis Gaddis, *The Long Peace: Inquiries into the History of the Cold War* (New York: Oxford University Press, 1987).

25. On the thirtieth anniversary of the Cuban missile crisis in 1993, newly declassified documents confirmed that mutual misperceptions brought John F. Kennedy and Nikita Khrushchev close to nuclear war. Documents and testimony of participants confirm that the missiles in Cuba were operational and were not equipped with permissive action links to prevent unauthorized launch by field commanders. Furthermore, Kennedy did not know that in addition to the medium-range missiles, the Soviets had placed tactical nuclear weapons in Cuba that were to be used to protect the island in the event of a U.S. invasion. Unlike the missiles, which were to be launched only by a direct order from Moscow, tactical weapons were under the control of Soviet field commanders in Cuba. Against this backdrop, Fidel Castro apparently proposed to Khrushchev "the immediate launching of a nuclear strike on the United States." See Mary S. McAuliffe, ed., *CIA Documents on the Cuban Missile Crisis, 1962* (Washington, D.C.: Central Intelligence Agency, 1992); Fedor Burlatsky, "Castro Wanted a Nuclear Strike," *New York Times* (23 October 1992): 33; and Tad Szulc, "Cuba 62: A Brush with Armageddon," review of books on the Cuban missile crisis, *Washington Post Book World* (15 November 1992): 1.

26. R. James Woolsey, testimony before the Senate Governmental Affairs Committee, 24 February 1993, and before the House Foreign Affairs Committee, Subcommittee on International Security, International Organizations, and Human Rights, 28 July 1993.

27. R. Jeffrey Smith, "Possible Nuclear Arms Test by India Concerns U.S.," *Washington Post* (16 December 1995): 17; Barry Schweid, "U.S. Expresses Concern over Possible Nuclear Test, Missile Deployment," Associated Press (17 January 1996).

28. Debate continues over how close India and Pakistan were to nuclear war in 1990. Some analysts, particularly those from South Asia, remain skeptical about the interpretation that New Delhi and Islamabad were on the brink of such a war. See Seymour Hersh, "On the Nuclear Edge," *The New Yorker* (29 March 1993): 56; William Burrows and Robert Windrem, *Critical Mass: The Dangerous Race for Superweapons in a Fragmenting World* (New York: Simon and Schuster, 1994); and Reiss, *Bridled Ambition.*

29. Scott Sagan, *The Limits of Safety* (Princeton, N.J.: Princeton University Press, 1993); and Sagan, "The Perils of Proliferation: Organization Theory, Deterrence Theory, and the Spread of Nuclear Weapons," *International Security* 18 (Spring 1994): 66–107.

30. This scenario is developed in Robert Blackwill and Albert Carnesale, eds., *The New Nuclear Nations* (New York: Council on Foreign Relations, 1993).
31. See Lewis A. Dunn *Containing Nuclear Proliferation,* Adelphi Paper no. 263 (London: International Institute for Strategic Studies, 1991), 46–50. Also see Gregory F. Giles, "Safeguarding the Undeclared Nuclear Arsenals," *Washington Quarterly* 16 (Spring 1993): 173–86.
32. Bruce Blair, *Global Zero Alert for Nuclear Forces,* (Center for International and Security Studies, University of Maryland, Project on Rethinking Arms Control, paper no. 13, 1994).
33. On the revolution in military affairs, see Peter Wilson, Robert Manning, and Col. Richard Klass, *Defense in the Information Age: A New Blueprint* (Progressive Policy Institute, December 1995); Andrew Krepinevich, "Cavalry to Computer: The Pattern of Military Revolutions," *The National Interest* (Fall 1994); Ted Galdi, *Revolution in Military Affairs? Competing Concepts, Organizational Responses, Outstanding Issues,* CRS Report 95-1170 (11 December 1995); Molander and Wilson, *The Nuclear Asymptote,* appendix A; Dan Gouré, "The Military Technical Revolution," *Washington Quarterly* 16 (Autumn 1993); and Richard J. Harknett, "Information Warfare and Deterrence," *Parameters* 26 (Autumn 1996): 93–107.
34. United Nations Association, *Confronting the Proliferation Danger: The Role of the U.N. Security Council,* Report of the UNA-USA Project on the Security Council and Non-proliferation (July 1995). William T. R. Fox addressed the issue of Security Council action in "International Control of Atomic Weapons," in Bernard Brodie, ed., *The Absolute Weapon: Atomic Power and World Order* (New York: Harcourt, Brace, 1946), 195.
35. Christopher Paine and Thomas Cochran, *The Role of Hydronuclear Tests and Other Low-Yield Nuclear Explosions and Their Status Under a Comprehensive Test Ban* (Nuclear Resources Defense Council, March 1995).
36. Principles and Objectives for Nuclear Non-proliferation and Disarmament, NPT/CONF. 1995/L.5, 10 May 1995. The pledge by the weapons states to exercise "utmost restraint" prior to completion of a CTBT appears in 4(a). Paragraphs 5, 6, and 7 support nuclear-weapon-free zones (NWFZs).
37. See Barbara Crossette, "U.N. Endorses a Treaty to Halt All Nuclear Testing," *New York Times* (11 September 1996): 3.
38. Statute of the International Atomic Energy Agency, Article IX, "Supplying of Materials."
39. Kathleen Bailey, "A Critique of the Fissile Material Cutoff Proposal," Lawrence Livermore National Laboratory, Directors Series on Proliferation, no. 8 (1 June 1995); Brian Chow, Richard Speier, and Gregory Jones, *The Proposed Fissile Material Cutoff: Next Steps* (Rand Corporation, 1995).
40. J. Carson Mark, *Reactor Grade Plutonium's Explosive Properties* (Nuclear Control Institute, August 1990); Thomas Cochran and Christopher Paine, *The Amount of Plutonium and Highly Enriched Uranium Needed for Pure Fission Nuclear Weapons* (Natural Resources Defense Council, April 1994).
41. Marvin Miller, *Are IAEA Safeguards on Plutonium Bulk-Handling Facilities Effective?* (Nuclear Control Institute, August 1990). On timely warning, see

Leonard Weiss, "The Concept of Timely Warning," *Congressional Record* (21 March 1988), reproduced in *The Nuclear Non-proliferation Factbook* (Senate Committee on Governmental Affairs, December 1994).

42. Plutonium data figures are from David Albright, Frans Berkhout, and William Walker, *Plutonium and Highly Enriched Uranium 1996* (New York: Oxford University Press, 1997).

43. Cited in Paul Leventhal, "Weapons-Usable Nuclear Materials: Eliminate Them?" in Kathleen Bailey, ed., *Director's Series on Proliferation* (Livermore National Laboratory, June 1993).

44. Brian G. Chow and Kenneth A. Solomon, *Limiting the Spread of Weapon-Usable Fissile Materials* (Rand Corporation, November 1993).

45. Sheryl WuDunn, "Accident at A-Plant Leads Japan to Debate," *New York Times* (17 December 1995): 4; *The Economist* (20 January 1996): 36; Andrew Pollack, "After Accident, Japan Rethinks Its Nuclear Hopes," *New York Times* (21 March 1997): A8.

46. On plutonium security and options for burning excess plutonium, see National Academy of Sciences, *Management and Disposition of Excess Weapons Plutonium: Reactor Related Options* (Washington, D.C.: National Academy Press, 1995); Eugene Skolinoff, Tatsujiro Suzuki, and Kenneth Oye, *International Responses to Japanese Plutonium Programs* (Center for International Studies, Massachusetts Institute of Technology, August 1995); and American Nuclear Society, *Protection and Management of Plutonium*, Special Panel Report (August 1995).

47. See George Perkovich, "The Plutonium Genie," *Foreign Affairs* 72 (Summer 1993): 153–65, for an outline of the problems and a political road map to achieve such a regime.

48. The White House, "Joint Statement on Parameters on Future Reductions in Nuclear Forces," Office of the Press Secretary, Helsinki, Finland, 21 March 1997.

49. Banning Garrett and Bonnie Glaser, "Chinese Perspectives on Nuclear Arms Control," *International Security* 20 (Winter 1995–96): 43–78.

50. Russia's November 1993 abandonment of its no-first-use pledge and adoption of a policy modeled on that of the United States was mainly aimed at Ukraine and thus may be reversible.

51. UN Resolution 984 and security assurances by weapons states, *Newsbrief* 30 (2nd Quarter 1995).

52. Mitchell Reiss and Harald Muller, eds., *International Perspectives on Counterproliferation*, Working Paper No. 99 (Washington, D.C.: Woodrow Wilson Center, January 1995).

53. "Report on Activities and Programs for Countering Proliferation," Report to Congress by the Counterproliferation Program Review Committee, Department of Defense, May 1995; *Washington Quarterly* 18 (Winter 1995), articles by Paul Gebbard, Joseph Pilat, Senator Domenici, Harald Muller, and Mitchell Reiss; Barry Schnieder, *Radical Responses to Radical Regimes, Evaluating Preemptive Counter-proliferation*, McNair Paper 41 (National Defense University, May 1995); William H. Lewis and Stuart E. Johnson, eds., *Weapons of Mass Destruction: New Perspectives on Counterproliferation*, Institute for National Strategic

Studies (Washington, D.C.: National Defense University Press, 1995); Zachary Davis and Mitchell Reiss, *Counterproliferation Doctrine: Issues for Congress,* CRS Report 94–734 (September 1994).

54. See Janne Nolan, testimony before the House Subcommittee on Arms Control, International Security, and Science, hearing on "Proliferation and Arms Control in the 1990's," 3 March 1992. Her testimony includes a number of recommendations that contributed to those listed here.

55. For a discussion of the logic and agenda of such a Northeast Asian political entity, see Robert A. Manning, "The Asian Paradox: Toward a New Architecture," *World Policy Journal* 10 (Fall 1993): 55–64.

56. See Paul Leventhal and Steven Dolley, *A Japanese Strategic Uranium Reserve: A Safe and Economic Alternative to Plutonium* (Washington, D.C.: Nuclear Control Institute, 12 April 1993).

57. Such a plan would involve the fabrication of mixed oxide, or MOX, fuel for use in light water reactors. See Robert Manning, "PACATOM: Nuclear Cooperation in Asia," *Washington Quarterly* 20 (Spring 1997): 217–32.

58. See James Woolsey, House testimony. Also see Zachary Davis and Warren Donnelly, *Iran's Nuclear Activities and the Congressional Response,* CRS Issue Brief 92076 (30 June 1993); Stuart Goldman, Kenneth Katzman, and Zachary Davis, *Russian Nuclear Reactor and Conventional Arms Transfers to Iran,* CRS Report 95–641 (23 May 1995); and David A. Schwarzbach, *Iran's Nuclear Program: Energy or Weapons?* (Natural Resources Defense Council, 7 September 1995).

59. Syria bought nuclear equipment from China in the early 1990s and attempted to purchase a reactor from Argentina in 1995. Michael Wise, "UN Agency Blocks Sale of Reactor to Syria," *Washington Post* (7 December 1991): 26; "Syria Visit to Argentina over Nuclear Reactor," Reuters (14 August 1995).

60. Legislation in the 104th Congress lifted some nuclear sanctions on Pakistan. On the congressional debate over lifting the ban, see *Congressional Record* (20 September 1995): S13941–71. The Clinton administration also proposed expanding nuclear safety cooperation with India. Moses Manoharan, "India, US to Cooperate on N-Power Safety," Reuters (14 July 1995); "NRC Cooperation with India," *Inside NRC* (14 November 1994).

Contributors

Zachary S. Davis is an analyst of international nuclear affairs at the Congressional Research Service in Washington, D.C.

Colin S. Gray is Professor of Politics and Director of the Centre for Security Studies at the University of Hull, England.

Richard J. Harknett is Associate Professor of Political Science at the University of Cincinnati, Ohio.

Ashok Kapur is Professor of Political Science at the University of Waterloo, Ontario.

Robert A. Manning is a Senior Fellow at the Council on Foreign Relations.

William C. Martel is Associate Professor of International Relations and Russian Studies at the U.S. Air War College, Montgomery, Alabama.

Eric Mlyn is Assistant Professor of Political Science at the University of North Carolina, Chapel Hill.

John Mueller is Professor of Political Science at the University of Rochester.

T. V. Paul is Associate Professor of Political Science at McGill University, Montreal.

George H. Quester is Professor of Government and Politics at the University of Maryland.

James J. Wirtz is Associate Professor of National Security Affairs at the U.S. Naval Post-graduate School, Monterey, California.

Index

Abshire, David M., 130n
Absolute Weapon, The, 2, 4, 5, 8, 10, 12, 28, 39n, 48, 73, 168, 171, 180, 189, 213, 237, 239, 245, 249, 250, 257–59 passim, 263, 291
Acheson-Lilienthal Report, 11, 264
Adler, Emanuel, 161n
African Nuclear-Weapon-Free Zone Treaty, 202
Albright, David, 296n
Alliances, nuclear, 152, 155–56
Allison, Graham T., 209n
Ambrose, Stephen E., 92n
Amrine, Michael, 187n
Andrain, Charles, 229n
Antiballistic missile systems. *See* Strategic defense
Antiballistic Missile Treaty, 258, 272–73, 282
Antisubmarine warfare (ASW), 173
Arkin, William M., 45n, 211n, 212n
Arms control, 5, 9–12, 34, 102, 107, 140–42, 168, 246, 267
  history, 3
  verification regimes, 10
Arms race, 3, 8, 107, 179, 267, 271, 274
  negative arms race, 73
  stability, 138, 141, 143, 149–51, 153, 155–56
Arquilla, John, 100–101, 124n, 125n, 126n, 128n, 129n, 130n, 132n, 134n
Aron, Raymond, 218, 232n
Art, Robert J., 40n, 68n, 89, 90, 97n, 98n
Asmus, Ronald D., 127n

Aspin, Les, 292n, 293n
Assured destruction, 12
Atomic Energy Commission, 178
Aum Shinrikyo cult, 221–22, 227
Axelrod, Robert, 68n, 161n
Ayton, Andrew, 129n

B-2 Stealth bomber, 200
Bacevich, A. J., 134n
Bailey, Kathleen C., 131n, 134n, 295n
Balance of terror, 103
Baldwin, David, 15n, 27, 32, 41n, 43n, 68n
Ball, Desmond, 199, 209n, 210n
Ballistic missile defense. *See* Strategic defense
Bartlett, C. J., 13 n.1
Baruch Plan, 11, 179, 264, 291
Battle of Berlin, 52
Bendix, Reinhard, 230n
Bentham van dem Bergh, Godfried van, 91n
Beres, Louis Rene, 160n
Berger, Thomas U., 94n
Berkhout, Frans, 296n
Berlin Blockade, 180
Betts, Richard K., 41n, 42n, 127n, 131n, 157n, 159n
Binder, David, 93n
Bing, George, 187n
Bipolarity, 2, 4, 6, 21, 39, 49, 138–40, 149–50, 156, 216–17, 252, 254, 257, 263
Blackaby, Frank, 42n
Blackwill, Robert, 295n
Blainey, Geoffrey, 67n

301

Blair, Bruce G., 126n, 163n, 187n, 188n, 295n
Blair, Clay, 188n
Blight, James, 86, 96n, 157n
Bluhm, William T., 231n
Bobbitt, Philip, 71n
Boer War, 112
Boldrick, Michael R., 125n, 133n
Bomber gap, 171
"Bombs in the basement," 176, 184
Bond, Brian, 130–31n
Boulding, Kenneth, 25, 41n
Boyde cycle, 108, 128n
Boyle, Francis Anthony, 98n
Bracken, Paul, 163n
Brecher, Michael, 40n
Brecht, Arnold, 230n, 231n, 232n
Brodie, Bernard, 2–5, 7, 8, 10, 11, 14n, 15n, 22, 39n, 40n, 41n, 43n, 47–48, 54, 66n, 73, 95n, 101, 126n, 129n, 147, 167, 168, 171, 174, 178, 180, 186n, 187n, 188n, 189–90, 191, 207, 208n, 213, 214, 217, 229n, 232n, 234n, 237, 249, 250, 259n, 260n, 285, 291
Brown, Frederick J., 95n
Brown, R. Allen, 129n
Brzezinski, Zbigniew, 146, 161n
Buchan, Glenn C., 71n
Builder, Carl H., 132n
Bull, Hedley, 14n
Bundy, McGeorge, 14n, 29, 34, 42n, 43n, 44n, 93n, 158n
Bunn, George, 211n
Burin, Frederick S., 92n
Burns, John, 72n
Burns, William P., 186n
Burrows, William, 294n
Bush, George, 93n
Butler, General Lee, 292n
Butow, Robert J. C., 93n
Buzan, Barry, 68–69n

Caldwell, Captain Warren, Jr., 101, 126n
Callwell, Charles E., 112, 130n

Cambone, Stephen A., 208n, 209n, 212n
Carnesale, Albert, 295n
Carter, Ashton, 119, 163n
Cashman, Greg, 13n
Caporaso, James A., 40n, 42n, 163n
Checkel, Jeff, 162n
Chow, Brian, 295n, 296n
Christenson, Thomas, 152, 164n
Churchill, Winston, 134n
Cimbala, Stephen J., 125n
City-avoidance, 194–95
Clausewitz, Carl von, 66n, 67n, 100, 110, 115–16, 128n, 132n
"Clash of civilizations," 88
Clemens, Walter, 161n
Clinton, William J., 13n
CNN effect, 88
Cochran, Thomas, 295n
Cohen, Eliot A., 128n, 132n
Cohen, Peter, 161n
Cold War, end of, 1–2, 11, 30
  role of nuclear weapons in, 78–79
  United States nuclear policy, 199–208
Collateral damage, 175
Communist ideology
  abandonment by Soviet Union, 78–79
  as risk averse, 76–77
Comprehensive Test Ban Treaty (CTBT), 35, 63, 65, 193, 201, 241, 243, 247–48, 265, 268, 278, 289–90
Contestable vs. incontestable costs of war, 50–53, 61, 62, 117, 153–54
Contestability, defined, 53
Conventional Forces in Europe (CFE) Treaty, 267
Conventional paradigm, 48–49, 65
Conventional war/deterrence
  contrasted to nuclear war/deterrence, 48–50, 53, 59, 61–62, 74, 153–54
  threat of nuclear escalation, 77, 184
Cooperation under anarchy, 53–58
Coordinating Committee on Export

Controls (COCOM), 247, 251, 284
Corbett, Percy, 2, 15n
Costigliola, Frank, 44n
Cottam, Richard, 233n
Counterforce, 4
Counterproliferation, 63, 284
Cousins, Norman, 15n
Crane, Conrad C., 187n
Crawford, Neta C., 95n
Crevald, Martin van, 67n, 127n, 128n, 130n, 133n
Crisis stability, 9, 138, 143–46, 149, 152–53, 155–56, 171–72
   defined, 143, 172
   and nuclear alliances, 152
Cuban Missile Crisis, 23, 82, 86, 273–74
Cyberwar, 99–100, 111

Daalder, Ivo H., 125n, 186n, 187n, 209n, 210n
David, Stephen, 163n
Davis, Lynn Etheridge, 196, 209n
Davis, Paul K., 132n
Davis, Richard, 292–93n
Davis, Zachary, 5, 11, 14n, 293n, 297n
Dean, Jonathan, 209n, 211n
Delicate balance of terror, 168, 180
Department of Defense (DoD) FY 1981 Annual Report, 198
Deterrence, 5, 20, 38, 54, 59, 102, 104, 141, 148, 171, 184, 205, 272
   Brodie image of, 215, 218, 220, 216–23 passim, 224–25, 227
   commitments, 3
   conventional, 59, 154, 276
   credibility of threats, 61, 82, 121, 193
   enduring rivalry, 23–24, 26, 37
   and epistemic communities, 146
   extended, 4, 11, 21, 24, 121, 169, 185, 199, 240, 244, 283
   finite, 167
   millenarian image of, 8, 213, 219–25, 228
   minimal, 9, 137, 144, 167–74, 176–77, 179–80, 182, 185, 264, 281
   defined, 167
   arguments against, 172–75
   nonweaponized, 185, 240, 274
   nuclear, 7, 20, 23, 54, 40n, 104, 118, 138, 140, 143, 156, 171, 174, 184–85, 193, 214–19, 228, 249
   particularistic vs. universal constructs, 213–18, 220, 223–25, 227–28, 249
   and rationality, 145, 214–15, 217–18, 220
   retaliation in kind 4, 7, 138–39
   role in ending Cold War, 103
   and utilitarianism, 215–16
Deutch, John, 159n
Deutsch, Karl, 229n, 233n
Diehl, Paul F., 40n
Diesing, Paul, 40n
Diplomacy of violence, 154
Disarmament, 10–11, 65, 73, 89, 172, 177, 181–82, 243, 246, 254, 266
   substantial disarmament, 170
Doctrine for Joint Nuclear Operations, 202
Dolley, Steven, 187n, 297n
Domenici, Senator, 296n
Domke, William, 13n, 41n
Donnelly, Warren, 297n
Doughty, Robert Allan, 131n
Dowler, Thomas W., 211n
Downs, Anthony, 230n
Dr. Strangelove, 87
Duffy, Michael, 129n
Dunn, Frederick, 2, 5, 7–8, 12, 14n, 15n, 249, 251
Dunn, Lewis A., 133n, 293n, 295n
Dupuy, R. Ernest, 67n
Dupuy, Trevor, 67n

Eayrs, James, 186n
Einstein, Albert, 74, 91n
Elam, Miriam Fendius, 72n
Ellis, Jason, 294n
Eltis, David, 129n

Ember, Carol R., 158n
Epistemic community, 146–48
Escalation, 225, 274
   effectiveness as source of deterrence, 77, 169
EURATOM, 287
Evangelista, Matthew, 233n
Evron, Yair, 188n, 260n
Ewing, Humphrey Crum, 127n

Fail Safe, 87
Fate of the Earth, The, 87
Falkland Islands, 34, 81–82
Feaver, Peter Douglas, 163n
Feiveson, Harold, 186–87n
First strike. *See* Splendid first-strike
Fissile material cutoff, 278–81, 288
FitzSimmonds, James R., 128n
Flexible response, 169, 181, 193
Flew, Antony, 231n
Foran, Virginia, 261n
Force de frappe, 33, 181
Foreign policy and the irrelevance of nuclear weapons, 83–89
Forsberg, Randall, 209n
Foucault, Michel, 161n
Fox, William, 2, 10, 13, 15n, 63, 67n, 68n, 71n, 250–51, 259n, 260n, 295n
Frankel, Benjamin, 14n, 293n
Freedman, Lawrence, 41n, 209n
Frye, Alton, 209n
Fukuyama, Francis, 78, 93n, 158n
Fuller, J. F. C., 112–13, 130n

Gaddis, John, 21, 40n, 42n, 71n, 74, 75, 91n, 93n, 94n, 156, 157n, 158n, 165n, 294n
Galdi, Ted, 295n
Gallagher, Matthew, 161n
Gardner, Gary T., 131n
Garrett, Banning N., 232n, 296n
Garrity, Patrick, 38, 40n, 43n, 45n, 125n, 133n, 208n, 209n, 212n
Garthoff, Raymond L., 93n, 162n
Gaulle, Charles de, 94n

Gaylor, Noel, 43n
Gebbard, Paul, 296n
George, Alexander L., 229n, 261n
Gjelstad, Jorn, 134n
Giles, Gregory F., 295n
Gilpin, Robert, 13n, 21, 40n, 55, 69n, 70n, 94n
Glaser, Bonnie S., 232n, 296n
Glaser, Charles, 90, 97n, 145, 160n, 164n, 208n
Goertz, Gary, 40n
Goldblat, Jozef, 42n
Goldgeier, James, 163n
Goldman, Stuart, 297n
Gooch, John, 131n
Goodpaster, Andrew, 292n
Gompert, David C., 40n, 43n, 125n, 210n
Gordon, Ellen, 96n
Gottfried, Kurt, 187n
Gowing, Margaret, 43n
Graham, Thomas W., 94n
Gray, Colin, 5, 6, 7, 14n, 70n, 125n, 126n, 128n, 131n, 133n, 138–39, 145–46, 157n, 157–58n, 159n, 160n, 208n, 234n
Graybeal, Sidney, 293n
Great power status
   defined, 64
   and nuclear weapons, 33–35, 65
   traits, 34–35
Green, Philip, 229n
Grieco, Joseph, 55, 58, 59, 68n, 69n, 70n
Griffith, John, 43n
Gulf War, 24, 52, 60, 81–82, 120, 123, 154, 264, 267, 271
Gulf War Air Power Survey, 108

Hagerty, Devin T., 259n
Haggard, Stephen, 42n
Hall, John, 41n
Hallin, Daniel C., 97n
Hallion, Richard P., 132n
Halperin, Morton, 14n, 168, 170, 186n, 187n, 217, 229n, 231n

Harknett, Richard, 5, 6, 14n, 15n, 40n, 69n, 71n, 72n, 117, 132n, 154, 164n, 230–31n, 275, 295n
Harries, Owen, 93n
Hart, Basil Liddell, 67n
Haas, Ernst, 161–62n
Haas, Peter, 146, 161n
Hauser, Richard D., Jr., 128n
Hayden, H. T., 125n
Healey, Denis, 94n
Hermann, Richard, 160n
Herring, Eric, 42n
Hersh, Seymour M., 260n, 294n
Herwig, Holger H., 134n
Herz, John H., 14–15n, 158n
Hipple, Frank von, 186–87n
Hiroshima, 1, 3, 9, 49, 74, 175–80
Hoopes, Townsend, 159n
Hooper, Richard, 293n
Hopf, Ted, 157n
Hopkins, John, 188n
Hosmer, Stephen T., 92n
Howard, Joseph S., II, 211n
Howard, Michael, 102–3, 126n
Hughes, Wayne P., Jr., 128n
Huntington, Samuel, 68n, 88, 90, 96n, 97n, 98n, 126n, 146, 161n, 221, 233n, 292n
Huth, Paul, 15n
Hypernationalism, 86

Iklé, Fred, 125n, 126n, 127n
Inadvertent nuclear war, 149
Information age, 99–100, 102, 116
  advantages of nuclear weapons in, 116–19
  and demise of Soviet Union, 106
  disadvantages of nuclear weapons in, 114–16
  as latest fashion, 107
Information dominance, 114, 116
Information war, 99, 108–9, 111, 114, 118, 119, 124
  as center of gravity in battle, 115
  as permanent dimension of war, 108, 114
  as revolution in military affairs, 114–16
Integrative power
  and China, 37
  and international leadership, 20, 25
Intercontinental ballistic missiles (ICBMs), 25, 194–96, 198, 200–201, 206
  Minuteman III missile, 204
  MX missile, 198, 201, 205
Intermediate Nuclear Force Agreement (INF) 1987, 267
International Atomic Energy Agency (IAEA), 10, 237, 242–43, 245, 271, 279, 281
  "93+2" package, 268–69, 277
  safeguards, 246, 251–52, 256, 287
International Monetary Fund (IMF), 277
International Nuclear Order (INO), 251–52, 254–55
Isaacs, John, 293–94n

Jablonsky, David, 159–60n
Jackman, Robert, 41n
Janis, Irving, 67n
Jervis, Robert, 15n, 58, 66n, 67n, 69n, 74, 82, 91n, 95n, 129n, 157n, 158n, 159n, 160n, 161n, 163n, 164n, 186n, 191, 208n, 229n
Joeck, Neil, 259n
Johnson, Stuart E., 296–97n
Johnston, Alastair Iain, 127n, 232n
Joint Strategic Target Planning Staff, 202
Jomini, Antoine Henri de, 130n
Jones, Charles, 68–69n
Jones, Gregory, 295n
Jones, Rodney W., 211n

Kahan, Jerome H., 159n, 160n
Kahn, Herman, 14n, 67n, 143, 159n, 160n, 185n, 229n
Kahneman, Daniel, 70n
Kaiser, Karl, 14n
Kaplan, Fred, 13n, 209n

Kaplan, Morton, 70n, 156, 165n
Kaplan, Robert D., 126n
Kapur, Ashok, 5, 11, 259n, 260n
Karsh, Efraim, 233n
Katzenstein, Peter J., 94n
Katzman, Kenneth, 297n
Kaufman, Robert, 158–59n
Kaufmann, William W., 14n, 70n
Kaysen, Carl, 74–75, 91n, 94n, 187n
Keaney, Thomas A., 128n
Keegan, John, 127n
Keeny, Spurgeon, 15n
Kegley, Charles, 68n
Kennan, George, 265
Kennedy, Paul, 94n
Keohane, Robert, 68n, 69n, 261n
Kier, Elizabeth, 233n
Kilgour, D. Marc, 293n
Kimball, Warren, 13n
Kirchner, Walter L., 260n
Kissinger, Henry, 13n, 14n, 72n, 159n, 185n, 229n, 232n, 233n, 234n
Klass, Colonel Richard, 295n
Klyza, Christopher McGrory, 212n
Knock, Thomas, 13n
Knorr, Klaus, 29, 39n, 42n, 43n
Kohl, Wilfrid, 44n
Kolkowicz, Roman, 161n
Korean War, 30, 36
Krasner, Stephen D., 68n, 261n
Kraus, Sidney, 94n
Krepinevich, Andrew, 110, 125n, 128n, 128–29n, 295n
Kugler, Richard L., 127n
Kuhn, Thomas, 66n
Kull, Stephen, 160–61n
Kurth, James, 96n, 233n

Lachow, Irving, 125n
Lackey, Douglas, 31, 42n
Lake, David, 158n
Lambakis, Steven, 132n
Lambeth, Benjamin, 161n
Larrabee, F. Stephen, 127n
Larssen, Christer, 187n
Larus, Joel, 188n

Lavoy, Peter, 66n, 259n
Layne, Christopher, 90, 94n, 98n, 159n, 164n, 187n
Law of the instrument and nuclear weapons, 147
Lebow, Richard Ned, 15n, 67n, 68n, 126n, 127n, 160n, 163n, 176, 187n, 216, 217, 229n, 231n, 232n
Lebovic, James H., 157n
Leonhard, Robert, 128n
Leventhal, Paul, 187n, 296n, 297n
Lewis, John Wilson, 45n
Lewis, William H., 296–97n
Libicki, Martin, 109, 120, 124–25n, 128n, 129n, 133n
Lieber, Richard, 90, 97n
Limited nuclear options, 196–97
Limited war, 102
Lind, William S., 128n
Lindsey, George, 293n
Little, Richard, 68–69n
Lockwood, Dunbar, 186n, 212n
Lodgaard, Sverre, 42n
Lomperis, Timothy J., 234n
Luard, Evan, 91n
Luke, Timothy, 161n, 162n
Lupton, David E., 131–32n
Luttwak, Edward, 67n, 70n
Lynn-Jones, Sean, 69n

Mahan, Alfred Thayer, 41n, 112, 130n
Mandelbaum, Michael, 91–92n, 97n, 131n, 160n, 162n
Maneuverable Reentry Vehicles (MARVs), 190
Manhattan Project, 177, 179
Mann, Leon, 67n
Manning, Robert, 5, 11, 295n, 297n
Mark, J. Carson, 295n
Marshall, Andrew W., 114, 128n, 129n
Martel, William C., 5, 8, 9, 142, 230n, 231n
Martin, Lisa, 68n, 69n
Maxwell, Stephen, 230n
May, Michael, 187n